D1796386
9781107440753

CAMBRIDGE ENGLISH CLASSICS

Grace Abounding and The Pilgrim's Progress

by

John Bunyan

JOHN BUNYAN

Baptized at Elstow Church, November 30th 1628
Died in London, August 31st 1688

He is buried in the Nonconformist Burial-place
Bunhill Fields

JOHN BUNYAN

GRACE ABOUNDING

AND

THE PILGRIM'S PROGRESS

THE TEXT EDITED BY

JOHN BROWN, D.D.

CAMBRIDGE:
at the University Press
1907

CAMBRIDGE UNIVERSITY PRESS WAREHOUSE,
C. F. CLAY, MANAGER.
London: FETTER LANE, E.C.
Glasgow: 50, WELLINGTON STREET.

Leipzig: F. A. BROCKHAUS.
New York: G. P. PUTNAM'S SONS.
Bombay and Calcutta: MACMILLAN AND CO., LTD.

NOTE.

THE text of *Grace Abounding to the Chief of Sinners* here adopted is that of the sixth edition published in 1688, the year of Bunyan's death. Till 1883 this was the earliest we possessed but in that year a copy of the first edition of 1666 was acquired for the Library of the British Museum. On comparison it was seen at once that by the time of the sixth edition the work had been greatly enlarged by its author, receiving additions of no fewer than fifty or sixty paragraphs. Of the second edition no copy is known; and all the knowledge we possess of the third edition of 1679 is derived from an item in the Trinity Term Catalogue of Stationers' Hall of that year, recently published by Mr Arber. It would appear that the additions referred to had by this time been made, as this further issue is described as "The Third Edition corrected and much enlarged." Probably in consequence of the expiration of the censorship of the Press in 1679 two other editions followed in quick succession, for that of 1680 is described as the fifth. Of the fourth edition no existing copy is known. A unique copy of the fifth edition was included in the Collection of the late W. G. Thorpe, Esq., of the Middle Temple, but in 1904 it was sold and cannot now be traced. The title-page of the first edition is reproduced on p. viii:

The supplement to *Grace Abounding*, entitled *A Relation of the Imprisonment* was not published during Bunyan's lifetime, nor indeed, as the title indicates, till 1765, remaining till that year in the possession of his family. It was ultimately sold to James Buckland, the publisher in Paternoster Row, for five guineas, by Hannah Bunyan, Bunyan's great granddaughter, who died at Bedford February 15th, 1770, aged seventy-six. It is an eminently characteristic production of Bunyan's pen.

The text of *The Pilgrim's Progress* adopted for Part I is that of the eleventh edition of 1688, the one which received Bunyan's latest emendations. Only two copies of this edition are known: the one in the British Museum, which is defective to the extent of having no fewer than nineteen leaves missing; and the other, a perfect copy, and therefore unique, which has furnished the text of the present edition. It has been kindly lent by its owner, an American gentleman, who not only possesses an unrivalled collection of Bunyan first editions, but also the original warrant for Bunyan's committal to the town gaol on Bedford Bridge in 1676, during which second imprisonment of six months he wrote his Pilgrim Dream.

NOTE

The text selected for Part II, the story of Christiana and her children, is that of the second edition, published in 1687, the one which received the author's latest additions and emendations. Some of Bunyan's most characteristic touches are to be found in the marginal notes he appended to the text. In Part II there are no fewer than 384 of these, in addition to Scripture references, and of these 384 as many as 148 were added for the first time to this second edition of 1687. The present work has been printed from a perfect and rare copy of this edition kindly lent for the purpose by Eliot Pye-Smith Reed, Esq., of Earlsmead, Hampstead Heath, son of the late Sir Charles Reed, a well-known expert in everything relating to Bunyan.

J. B.

15 *June*, 1907.

GRACE ABOUNDING

TO THE

CHIEF OF SINNERS:

OR,

A Brief and Faithful Relation of the exceeding Mercy of God in Christ to His poor Servant,

JOHN BUNYAN;

Wherein is particularly showed the manner of his conversion, his sight and trouble for sin, his dreadful temptations, also how he despaired of God's mercy, and how the Lord at length through Christ did deliver him from all the guilt and terror that lay upon him.

Whereunto is added a brief relation of his call to the work of the ministry, of his temptations therein, as also what he hath met with in prison. All which was written by his own hand there, and now published for the support of the weak and tempted people of God.

'*Come* and *hear, all ye that fear God, and I will declare what he hath done for my soul.*'—Psal. lxvi. 16.

London: Printed by George Larkin, 1666.

Grace Abounding
TO THE
CHIEF
OF
SINNERS:

OR,

A Brief and Faithful Relation of the exceeding Mercy of God in Christ, to His poor Servant

JOHN BUNYAN.

NAMELY,

In his Taking of him out of the Dunghil, and Converting of him to the Faith of his Blessed Son, Jesus Christ.

HERE

Is also particularly shewed, what Sight of, and what Trouble he had for Sin; and also, what various Temptations he hath met with, and how God hath carried him through them.

Corrected, and much Enlarged now by the Author, for the Benefit of the Tempted and Dejected Christian.

The Sixth Edition, Corrected.

Come and hear, all ye that fear God, and I will declare what he hath done for my soul, Psal. 66. 16.

LONDON, Printed for *Nath. Ponder,* at the *Pea-cock* in the *Poultry,* over against the *Stocks-Market,* 1688.

A

PREFACE:

OR,

Brief Account

OF THE

PUBLISHING this WORK.

WRITTEN

By the Author thereof, and dedicated to those whom God hath counted him worthy to beget to Faith, by his Ministry in the Word.

C*Hildren, Grace be with you*, Amen. *I being taken from you in presence, and so tied up, that I cannot perform that duty, that from God doth lie upon me, to you-ward, for your further edifying and building up in Faith and Holiness*, &c. *yet that you may see my Soul hath fatherly care and desire after your spiritual and everlasting welfare, I now once again, as before from the top of* Shenir *and* Hermon, *so now from* the Lions Dens, and from the Mountains of the Leopards *(Song* 4. 8.*) do look yet after you all, greatly longing to see your safe Arrival into* THE *desired Haven.*

I thank God upon every Remembrance of you, and rejoice even while I stick between the Teeth of the Lions in the Wilderness, at the Grace, and Mercy, and Knowledge of Christ our Saviour, which God hath bestowed upon you, with abundance of Faith and Love. Your Hungrings and Thirstings also after further Acquaintance with the Father, in his Son; your Tenderness of Heart, your Trembling at Sin, your sober and holy Deportment also before both God and Men, is great Refreshment to me; for you are my Glory and Joy, 1 *Thes*. 2. 20.

I have sent you here inclosed, a drop of that Honey that I have taken out of the Carcase of a Lion, Judg. 14. 5, 6, 7, 8. *I have eaten thereof my self also, and am much refreshed thereby. (Temptations, when we meet them at first, are as the Lion that roared upon* Sampson; *but if we overcome them, the next time we see them, we shall find a Nest of Honey within them.) The* Philistines *understand me not. It is something a Relation of the Work of God upon my Soul, even from the very first, till now; wherein you may perceive my Castings down, and Risings up; for he woundeth, and his hands make whole. It is written in the Scripture,* Isa. 38, 19. The father to the children shall make known the truth of God. *Yea, it was for this Reason I lay so long at* Sinai, (Lev. 4. 10, 11.) *to see the Fire, and the Cloud, and the Darkness,* that I might fear the Lord all the days of my Life upon Earth, and tell of his wondrous Works to my Children, *Psal*. 78. 3, 4, 5.

Moses, Numb. 33. 1, 2. *writ of the Journeyings of the Children of* Israel, *from* Egypt, *to the Land of* Canaan; *and commanded also, that they did remember their forty Years Travel in the Wilderness:* Thou shalt remember all the way which the Lord thy God led thee these forty years in the Wilderness, to humble thee, and to prove thee, and to know what was in thine heart, whether thou wouldest keep his commandments, or no, *Deut*. 8. 2, 3. *Wherefore this I have endeavoured to do; and not only so, but to publish it also; that, if God will, others may be put in remembrance of what he hath done for their Souls, by reading his Work upon me.*

It is profitable for Christians to be often calling to mind the very Beginnings of Grace with their Souls. It is a night to be much observed to the Lord, for bringing them out from the Land of *Egypt*. This is that Night of the Lord, to be observed of all the Children of *Israel*, in their Generations, *Exod*. 12. 42. My God, *saith* David, *Psal*. 42. 6. My Soul is cast down within me; but I will remember thee from the Land of

Jordan, and of the *Hermonites*, from the Hill *Mizar. He remembred also the Lion and the Bear, when he went to fight with the Giant of* Gath, 1 Sam. 17. 36, 37.

It was Paul's *accustomed manner*, Act. 22. *and that, when tried for his Life*, Act. 24. *even to open before his Judges the manner of his Conversion : He would think of that Day, and that Hour, in which he first did meet with Grace ; for he found it supported him. When God had brought the Children of* Israel *out of the* Red-Sea, *far into the Wilderness ; yet they must turn quite about thither again, to remember the drowning of their Enemies there*, Numb. 14. 25. *for though they sang his Praise before, yet they soon forgat his Works*, Psal. 106. 11, 12.

In this Discourse of mine, you may see much ; much, I say, of the Grace of God towards me : I thank God, I can count it much ; for it was above my Sins, and Satan's Temptations too. I can remember my Fears, and Doubts, and sad Months with comfort ; they are as the head of Goliah *in my Hand : There was nothing to* David *like* Goliah's *Sword, even that Sword that should have been sheathed in his Bowels ; for the very sight and remembrance of that did preach forth God's Deliverance to him. Oh, the Remembrance of my great Sins, of my great Temptations, and of my great Fears of perishing for ever ! They bring fresh into my Mind the Remembrance of my great Help, my great Support from Heaven, and the great Grace that God extended to such a Wretch as I.*

My dear Children, call to mind the former Days, and Years of ancient Times : Remember also your Songs in the Night, and commune with your own Hearts, Psal. 73. 5, 6, 7, 8, 9, 10, 11, 12. *Yea, look diligently, and leave no Corner therein unsearched ; for that is Treasure hid, even the Treasure of your first and second Experience of the Grace of God toward you. Remember, I say, the Word that first laid hold upon you : Remember your Terrors of Conscience, and Fear of Death and Hell : Remember also your Tears and Prayers to God ; yea, how you sighed under every Hedge of Mercy. Have you never an Hill* Mizar *to remember ? Have you forgot the Close, the Milk-house, the Stable, the Barn, and the like, where God did visit your Souls ? Remember also the Word ; the Word, I say, upon which the Lord hath caused you to hope : If you have sinned against Light, if you are tempted to blaspheme, if you are down in Despair, if you think God fights against you, or if Heaven is hid from your Eyes ; remember, it was thus with your Father* ; but out of them all the Lord delivered me.

I could have enlarged much in this my Discourse of my Temptations and Troubles for Sin ; as also, of the merciful Kindness, and Working of God with my Soul : I could also have stepped into a Stile much higher than this, in which I have here discoursed, and could have adorned all things more than here I have seemed to do ; but I dare not : God did not play in tempting of me ; neither did I play, when I sunk as into a bottomless Pit, when the Pangs of Hell caught hold upon me ; *wherefore I may not play in relating of them, but be plain and simple, and lay down the thing as it was : He that liketh it, let him receive it ; and he that does not, let him produce a better.* Farewel.

My dear Children,

The Milk and Honey is beyond this Wilderness: God be merciful to you, and grant you be not slothful to go in to possess the Land.

John Bunyan.

Grace Abounding
TO THE
CHIEF
OF
SINNERS:
OR,
A brief Relation of the exceeding Mercy of God in Christ, to his poor Servant, *John Bunyan*.

IN this my relation of the merciful working of God upon my Soul, it will not be amiss, if in the first place, I do, in a few words, give you an hint of my Pedigree, and manner of bringing up; that thereby the goodness and bounty of God towards me, may be the more advanced and magnified before the sons of men.

2. For my Descent then, it was, as is well known by many, of a low and inconsiderable generation; my father's house being of that rank that is meanest, and most despised of all the families in the Land. Wherefore I have not here, as others, to boast of Noble Blood, or of an high-born state according to the flesh; though, all things considered, I magnifie the heavenly Majesty, for that by this door he brought me into this World, to partake of the Grace and Life that is in Christ by the Gospel.

3. But yet, notwithstanding the meanness and inconsiderableness of my Parents, it pleased God to put it into their hearts, to put me to School, to learn both to read and write; the which I also attained, according to the rate of other poor men's children; though to my shame, I confess, I did soon lose that little I learnt, even almost utterly, and that long before the Lord did work his gracious work of Conversion upon my Soul.

4. As for my own natural life, for the time that I was without God in the world, it was, indeed, *according to the course of this world, and the spirit that now worketh in the children of disobedience*, Eph. 2. 2, 3. It was my delight, to be taken captive by the Devil, *at his will*, 2 Tim. 2. 26. being filled with all unrighteousness: The which did also so strongly work, and put forth it self, both in my heart and life, and that from a child, that I had but few Equals (especially considering my years, which were tender, being few) both for cursing, swearing, lying and blaspheming the holy Name of God.

5. Yea, so setled and rooted was I in these things, that they became as a second Nature to me; the which, as I also have with soberness considered since, did so offend the Lord, that even in my childhood he did scare and affright me with fearful dreams, and did terrifie me with dreadful visions: For often, after I had spent this and the other day in sin, I have in my bed been greatly afflicted, while asleep, with the apprehensions of Devils, and wicked Spirits, who still, as I then thought, laboured to draw [m]e away with them; of which I could never be rid.

6. Also I should, at these years, be greatly afflicted and troubled with the thoughts of the fearful torments of Hell-fire; still fearing that it would be my lot to be found, at last, among those Devils, and hellish Fiends, who are there bound down with the chains and bonds of darkness, unto the judgment of the great Day.

7. These things, I say, when I was but a child, about nine or ten years old, did so distress my Soul, that then, in the midst of my many sports, and childish vanities, amidst my vain companions, I was often much cast down and afflicted in my mind therewith; yet could I not let go my sins: Yea, I was also then so overcome with despair of Life and Heaven, that I

should often wish, either that there had been no Hell, *or that I had been a Devil*; supposing they were only tormentors, that if it must needs be, that I indeed went thither, I might be rather a tormentor, than be tormented my self.

8. A while after, these terrible dreams did leave me, which I also soon forgot; for my pleasures did quickly cut off the remembrance of them, as if they had never been: Wherefore with more greediness, according to the strength of nature, I did still let loose the reins to my lust, and delighted in all transgression against the Law of God: So that until I came to the state of Marriage, I was the very ringleader of all the Youth that kept me company, in all manner of vice and ungodliness.

9. Yea, such prevalency had the lusts and fruits of the flesh, in this poor Soul of mine, that had not a miracle of precious Grace prevented, I had not only perished by the stroak of Eternal Justice, but had also laid my self open, even to the stroak of those Laws, which bring some to disgrace, and open shame, before the face of the world.

10. In these days the thoughts of Religion were very grievous to me; I could neither endure it my self, nor that any other should: So that when I have seen some read in those books that concerned Christian Piety, it would be as it were a prison to me. *Then I said unto God, Depart from me, for I desire not the knowledge of thy ways*, Job 21. 14, 15. I was now void of all good consideration; Heaven and Hell were both out of sight and mind; and as for Saving and Damning, they were least in my thoughts. *O Lord, thou knowest my life; and my ways were not hid from thee.*

11. But this I well remember, That though I could my self sin with the greatest delight and ease, and also take pleasure in the vileness of my companions; yet even then, if I have at any time seen wicked things by those who professed goodness, it would make my spirit tremble. As once, above all the rest, when I was in my heighth of vanity, yet hearing one to swear, that was reckoned for a religious man, it had so great a stroak upon my spirit, that it made my heart ake.

12. But God did not utterly leave me, but followed me still; not now with convictions, but judgments; yet such as were mixed with mercy. For once I fell into a crick of the

Sea, and hardly escaped drowning: Another time I fell out of a Boat, into *Bedford*-River, but Mercy yet preserved me alive: Besides, another time, being in the field with one of my companions, it chanced that an Adder passed over the highway; so I having a stick in mine hand, struck her over the back; and having stunned her, I forced open her mouth with my stick, and plucked her sting out with my fingers; by which act, had not God been merciful to me, I might, by my desperateness, have brought my self to mine end.

13. This also I have taken notice of, with thanksgiving; When I was a Soldier, I, with others, were drawn out to go to such a place to besiege it; but when I was just ready to go, one of the Company desired to go in my room; to which, when I had consented, he took my place; and coming to the Siege, as he stood Sentinel, he was shot into the head with a Musket-bullet, and died.

14. Here, as I said, were Judgments and Mercy, but neither of them did awaken my Soul to Righteousness; wherefore I sinned still, and grew more and more rebellious against God, and careless of mine own Salvation.

15. Presently after this, I changed my condition into a married state; and my mercy was, to light upon a wife, whose father was counted godly: This woman and I, though we came together as poor as poor might be, (not having so much house-hold-stuff as a dish or spoon betwixt us both) yet this she had for her part, *The Plain Man's Path-way to Heaven*, and *The Practice of Piety*, which her father had left her, when he died. In these two books I should sometimes read with her, wherein I also found some things that were somewhat pleasing to me; (but all this while I met with no conviction.) She also would be often telling of me, *what a godly man her father was, and how he would reprove and correct vice, both in his house, and amongst his neighbours*; *what a strict and holy life he lived in his day, both in word and deed.*

16. Wherefore these books, with this relation, though they did not reach my heart, to awaken it about my sad and sinful state, yet they did beget within me some desires to Religion: So that, because I knew no better, I fell in very eagerly with the Religion of the times; to wit, to go to Church twice a day, and that too with the foremost; and there should very devoutly,

both say and sing as others did, yet retaining my wicked life: But withal, I was so over-run with the spirit of Superstition, that I adored, and that with great devotion, even all things (both the High-place, Priest, Clerk, Vestments, Service, and what else) belonging to the Church; counting all things holy, that were therein contained; and especially, the Priest and Clerk most happy, and without doubt, greatly blessed, because they were the Servants, as I then thought, of God; and were principal in the holy Temple, to do his work therein.

17. This conceit grew so strong, in little time, upon my spirit, that had I but seen a Priest (though never so sordid and debauched in his life) I should find my spirit fall under him, reverence him, and knit unto him; yea, I thought, for the love I did bear unto them (supposing they were the Ministers of God) I could have lain down at their feet, and have been trampled upon by them; their Name, their Garb, and Work did so intoxicate and bewitch me.

18. After I had been thus for some considerable time, another thought came in my mind; and that was, Whether *we* were of the *Israelites*, or no? For finding in the Scriptures, that they were once the peculiar people of God, thought I, If I were once of this race, my Soul must needs be happy. Now again I found within me a great longing to be resolved about this Question, but could not tell how I should: At last, I asked my father of it; who told me, *No, we were not.* Wherefore then I fell in my spirit, as to the hopes of that, and so remained.

19. But all this while, I was not sensible of the danger and evil of sin; I was kept from considering that sin would damn me, what Religion soever I followed, unless I was found in Christ: Nay, I never thought of him, nor whether there was such an one, or no. *Thus Man, while blind, doth wander, but wearieth himself with vanity: for he knoweth not the way to the City of God*, Eccles. 10. 15.

20. But one day (amongst all the Sermons our Parson made) his Subject was, to treat of the Sabbath-day, and of the evil of breaking that, either with labour, sports, or otherwise: (Now I was, notwithstanding my Religion, one that took much delight in all manner of vice; and especially, *that* was the day that I did solace my self therewith.) Wherefore I fell in my

Conscience under his Sermon, thinking and believing that he made that Sermon on purpose to shew me my evil-doing: And at that time I felt what guilt was, though never before, that I can remember; but then I was, for the present, greatly loaden therewith, and so went home when the Sermon was ended, with a great burthen on my spirit.

21. This, for that instant, did benumb the sinews of my best delights, and did imbitter my former pleasures to me: But behold, it lasted not; for before I had well dined, the trouble began to go off my mind, and my heart returned to its old course: But Oh! how glad was I, that this trouble was gone from me, and that the fire was put out, that I might sin again without control! Wherefore, when I had satisfied Nature with my food, I shook the Sermon out of my mind, and to my old custom of sports and gaming I returned with great delight.

22. But the same day, as I was in the midst of a game at Cat, and having struck it one blow from the hole, just as I was about to strike it the second time, a voice did suddainly dart from Heaven, into my Soul, which said, *Wilt thou leave thy sins, and go to Heaven*; *or have thy sins, and go to Hell?* At this I was put to an exceeding maze; wherefore, leaving my Cat upon the ground, I looked up to Heaven, and was as if I had, with the eyes of my understanding, seen the Lord Jesus looking down upon me, as being very hotly displeased with me, and as if he did severely threaten me with some grievous punishment for these, and other my ungodly practices.

23. I had no sooner thus conceived in my mind, but suddainly this conclusion was fastned on my spirit (for the former hint did set my sins again before my face:) *That I had been a great and grievous sinner, and that it was now too late for me to look after Heaven*; *for Christ would not forgive me, nor pardon my transgressions.* Then I fell to musing upon this also; and while I was thinking of it, and fearing lest it should be so, I felt my heart sink in despair, concluding it was too late; and therefore I resolved in my mind, I would go on in sin: For, thought I, if the case be thus, my state is surely miserable; miserable if I leave my sins, and but miserable if I follow them: I can but be damned; and if it must be so, I had as good be damned for many sins, as be damned for few.

24. Thus I stood in the midst of my play, before all that

then were present; but yet I told them nothing: But, I say, I having made this conclusion, I returned desperately to my sport again; and I well remember, that presently this kind of despair did so possess my Soul, that I was perswaded, I could never attain to other comfort than what I should get in sin; for Heaven was gone already, so that on that I must not think: Wherefore I found within me a great desire to take my fill of sin, still studying what sin was yet to be committed, that I might taste the sweetness of it; and I made as much haste as I could to fill my belly with its delicates, lest I should die before I had my desire; for that I feared greatly. In these things, *I protest before God, I lye not*, neither do I feign this form of speech; these were really, strongly, and with all my heart, my desires: *The good Lord whose mercy is unsearchable, forgive me my transgressions.*

25. (And I am very confident, that this temptation of the Devil is more usual amongst poor creatures than many are aware of, even to over-run the spirits with a scurfy and seared frame of heart, and benumbing of conscience; which frame he stilly and slily supplieth with such despair, that though not much guilt attendeth Souls, yet they continually have a secret conclusion within them, that there is no hopes for them; *for they have loved sins, therefore after them they will go*, Jer. 2. 25. and 18. 12.)

26. Now therefore I went on in sin with great greediness of mind, still grudging that I could not be so satisfied with it as I would. This did continue with me about a month, or more: But one day, as I was standing at a neighbour's shop-window, and there cursing and swearing, and playing the mad-man, after my wonted manner, there sate within the woman of the house, and heard me; who, though she also was a very loose and ungodly wretch, yet protested that I swore and cursed at that most fearful rate, that she was made to tremble to hear me; and told me further, *That I was the ungodliest fellow, for swearing, that ever she heard in all her life; and that I, by thus doing, was able to spoil all the Youth in the whole Town, if they came but in my company.*

27. At this reproof I was silenced, and put to secret shame; and that too, as I thought, before the God of Heaven: Wherefore while I stood there, and hanging down my head, I

wished with all my heart that I might be a little child again, that my father might learn me to speak without this wicked way of swearing; for, thought I, I am so accustomed to it, that it is but in vain for me to think of a reformation, for I thought it could never be.

28. But how it came to pass, I know not; I did, from this time forward, so leave my swearing, that it was a great wonder to my self to observe it; and whereas before I knew not how to speak, unless I put an Oath before, and another behind, to make my words have authority; now I could, without it, speak better, and with more pleasantness, than ever I could before. All this while I knew not Jesus Christ, neither did I leave my sports and play.

29. But quickly after this, I fell in company with one poor man, that made profession of Religion; who, as I then thought, did talk pleasantly of the Scriptures, and of the matters of Religion: Wherefore falling into some love and liking to what he said, I betook me to my Bible, and began to take great pleasure in reading, but especially with the Historical part thereof; for as for *Paul*'s Epistles, and such like Scriptures, I could not away with them; being as yet ignorant, either of the corruptions of my nature, or of the want and worth of Jesus Christ to save me.

30. Wherefore I fell to some outward Reformation, both in my words and life, *and did set the Commandments before me for my way to Heaven*; which Commandments I also did strive to keep, and, as I thought, did keep them pretty well sometimes, and then I should have comfort; yet now and then should break one, and so afflict my Conscience; but then I should repent, and say, I was sorry for it, and promise God to do better next time, and there get help again, for then I thought I pleased God as well as any man in *England*.

31. Thus I continued about a year; all which time our Neighbours did take me to be a very godly man, a new and religious man, and did marvel much to see such a great and famous alteration in my life and manners; and indeed, so it was, though yet I knew not Christ, nor Grace, nor Faith, nor Hope; for, as I have well seen since, had I then died, my state had been most fearful.

32. But, I say, my Neighbours were amazed at this my

great Conversion; from prodigious prophaneness, to something like a moral life; and truly, so they well might; for this my Conversion was as great, as for *Tom* of *Bethlem* to become a sober man. Now therefore they began to praise, to commend, and speak well of me, both to my face, and behind my back. Now I was, as they said, become godly; now I was become a right honest man. But, Oh! when I understood that these were their words and opinions of me, it pleased me mighty well: For though as yet I was nothing but a poor painted Hypocrite, yet I loved to be talked of, as one that was truly Godly. I was proud of my Godliness; and indeed, I did all I did, either to be seen of, or to be well spoken of by men: And thus I continued for about a twelve-month, or more.

33. Now you must know, that before this, I had taken much delight in ringing; but my Conscience beginning to be tender, I thought such practice was but vain, and therefore forced my self to leave it, yet my mind hanckered; wherefore I should go to the Steeple-house, and look on, though I durst not ring: But I thought this did not become Religion neither, yet I forced my self, and would look on still: But quickly after, I began to think, *How if one of the Bells should fall?* Then I chose to stand under a main Beam, that lay overthwart the Steeple, from side to side, thinking there I might stand sure. But then I should think again, Should the Bell fall with a swing, it might first hit the wall, and then re-bounding upon me, might kill me, for all this Beam: This made me stand in the Steeple door; and now, thought I, I am safe enough; for if a Bell should then fall, I can slip out behind these thick walls, and so be preserved notwithstanding.

34. So after this, I would yet go to see them ring, but would not go further than the Steeple-door; but then it came into my head, How if the Steeple it self should fall? and this thought (it may fall for ought I know) when I stood and looked on, did continually so shake my mind, that I durst not stand at the Steeple-door any longer, but was forced to flee, for fear the Steeple should fall upon my head.

35. Another thing was, my dancing; I was a full year, before I could quite leave that; but all this while, when I thought I kept this or that Commandment, or did, by word or deed, any thing that I thought were good, I had great peace

in my Conscience; and should think with my self, God cannot chuse but be now pleased with me; yea, to relate it in my own way, I thought no man in *England* could please God better than I.

36. But, poor wretch as I was, I was all this while ignorant of Jesus Christ, and going about to establish my own Righteousness; and had perished therein, had not God, in mercy, shewed me more of my state by nature.

37. But upon a day, the good Providence of God did cast me to *Bedford*, to work on my Calling; and in one of the streets of that Town, I came where there were three or four poor women sitting at a door, in the Sun, talking about the things of God; and being now willing to hear them discourse, I drew near to hear what they said, for I was now a brisk Talker also my self, in the matters of Religion: But I may say, *I heard, but I understood not*; for they were far above, out of my reach: Their talk was about a new birth, the work of God on their hearts, also how they were convinced of their miserable state by nature; they talked how God had visited their Souls with his love in the Lord Jesus, and with what words and promises they had been refreshed, comforted and supported against the temptations of the Devil: Moreover, they reasoned of the suggestions and temptations of Satan in particular; and told to each other, by which they had been afflicted, and how they were born up under his assaults: They also discoursed of their own wretchedness of heart, of their unbelief; and did contemn, slight and abhor their own Righteousness, as filthy and insufficient to do them any good.

38. And me-thought they spake, as if joy did make them speak; they spake with such pleasantness of Scripture-language, and with such appearance of Grace in all they said, that they were to me, as if they had found a new world, as if they were *people that dwelt alone, and were not to be reckoned amongst their Neighbours*, Numb. 23. 9.

39. At this I felt my own heart began to shake, and mistrust my condition to be naught; for I saw, that in all my thoughts about Religion and Salvation, the new Birth did never enter into my mind, neither knew I the comfort of the Word and Promise, nor the deceitfulness and treachery of my own wicked heart. As for secret thoughts, I took no notice of

them; neither did I understand what Satan's temptations were, nor how they were to be withstood and resisted, *&c.*

40. Thus therefore, when I had heard and considered what they said, I left them, and went about my employment again, but their talk and discourse went with me; also my heart would tarry with them, for I was greatly affected with their words, both because by them I was convinced, that I wanted the true tokens of a truly godly man, and also because by them I was convinced of the happy and blessed condition of him that was such an one.

41. Therefore I should often make it my business to be going again and again into the company of these poor people, for I could not stay away; and the more I went amongst them, the more I did question my condition; and, as I still do remember, presently I found two things within me, at which I did sometimes marvel; (especially considering what a blind, ignorant, sordid and ungodly wretch but just before I was:) The one was a very great softness and tenderness of heart, which caused me to fall under the conviction of what by Scripture they asserted; and the other was, a great bending in my mind to a continual meditating on them, and on all other good things which at any time I heard or read of.

42. By these things my mind was now so turned, that it lay like an Horse-leach at the Vein, still crying out, *Give, give*, *Prov.* 30. 15. Yea, it was so fixed on Eternity, and on the things about the Kingdom of Heaven (that is so far as I knew, though as yet, God knows, I knew but little) that neither pleasures, nor profits, nor perswasions, nor threats could loose it, or make it let go its hold; and though I may speak it with shame, yet it is, in very deed, a certain truth, it would then have been as difficult for me to have taken my mind from Heaven to Earth, as I have found it often since to get again from Earth to Heaven.

43. One thing I may not omit: There was a young man in our Town, to whom my heart before was knit more than to any other; but he being a most wicked creature for cursing and swearing, and whoring, I now shook him off, and forsook his company; but about a quarter of a year after I had left him, I met him in a certain Lane, and asked him how he did; he, after his old swearing and mad way, answered, He was well.

But, Harry, said I, *why do you swear and curse thus? What will become of you, if you die in this condition?* He answered me in a great chafe, *What would the Devil do for company, if it were not for such as I am?*

44. About this time I met with some *Ranters* Books, that were put forth by some of our Country-men; which Books were also highly in esteem by several old Professors; some of these I read, but was not able to make a judgment about them; wherefore, as I read in them, and thought upon them (feeling my self unable to judge) I should betake my self to hearty prayer, in this manner; *O Lord, I am a fool, and not able to know the Truth from Error: Lord, leave me not to my own Blindness, either to approve of, or condemn this Doctrine: If it be of God, let me not despise it; if it be of the Devil, let me not embrace it. Lord, I lay my Soul, in this matter, only at thy foot; let me not be deceived, I humbly beseech thee.* I had one religious intimate Companion all this while, and that was the poor man that I spoke of before; but about this time, he also turned a most devilish *Ranter*, and gave himself up to all manner of filthiness, especially Uncleanness: He would also deny that there was a God, Angel, or Spirit; and would laugh at all exhortations to sobriety: When I laboured to rebuke his wickedness, he would laugh the more, and pretend that he had gone through all Religions, and could never light on the right, till now: He told me also, that in little time, I should see all Professors turn to the ways of the *Ranters*. Wherefore, abominating those cursed principles, I left his company forthwith, and became to him as great a stranger, as I had been before a familiar.

45. Neither was this man only a temptation to me, but my Calling lying in the Country, I happened to light into several peoples company; who, though strict in Religion formerly, yet were also swept away by these *Ranters*. These would also talk with me of their ways, and condemn me as legal and dark; pretending that they only had attained to perfection, that could do what they would, and not sin. Oh! These temptations were suitable to my flesh, I being but a young man, and my nature in its prime; but God, who had, as I hope, designed me for better things, kept me in the fear of his Name, and did not suffer me to accept of such cursed principles.

And blessed be God, who put it into my heart to cry to him to be kept and directed, still distrusting mine own wisdom; for I have since seen even the effect of that prayer, in his preserving me, not only from *Ranting* Errors, but from those also that have sprung up since. The Bible was precious to me in those days.

46. And now, me-thought, I began to look into the Bible with new eyes, and read as I never did before; and especially the Epistles of the Apostle St. *Paul* were sweet and pleasant to me; and indeed, I was then never out of the Bible, either by reading, or meditation; still crying out to God, that I might know the truth, and way to Heaven and Glory.

47. And as I went on and read I lighted on that passage, *To one is given by the Spirit, the word of wisdom*; *to another, the word of knowledge by the same Spirit*; *and to another, faith*, &c. 1 *Cor.* 12. And though, as I have since seen, that by this Scripture the Holy Ghost intends, in special, things extraordinary, yet on me it then did fasten with conviction, that I did want things ordinary, even that understanding and wisdom that other Christians had. On this word I mused, and could not tell what to do; especially, this word [*Faith*] put me to it; for I could not help it, but sometimes must question whether I had *any* Faith, or no; but I was loath to conclude, I had *no* Faith; for if *I do so*, thought I, then I shall count my self a very Cast-away indeed.

48. No, said I with my self, though I am convinced that I am an ignorant Sot, and that I want those blessed Gifts of Knowledge and Understanding that other good people have; yet at a venture I will conclude, I am not altogether faithless, though I know not what Faith is: For it was shewed me, and that too (as I have seen since) by Satan, that those who conclude themselves in a faithless state, have neither rest nor quiet in their souls; and I was loth to fall quite into despair.

49. Wherefore by this suggestion, I was, for a while, made afraid to see my want of Faith; but God would not suffer me thus to undo and destroy my Soul, but did continually, against this my blind and sad conclusion, create still within me such suppositions, insomuch that I could not rest content, until I did now come to some certain knowledge, whether I had Faith, or no; this always running in my mind, *But how if you want Faith*

indeed? But how can you tell you have Faith? And besides, I saw for certain, if I had it not, I was sure to perish for ever.

50. So that though I endeavoured at the first to look over the business of Faith, yet in a little time, I better considering the matter, was willing to put my self upon the trial, whether I had Faith, or no. But alas, poor wretch! so ignorant and brutish was I, that I knew, to this day, no more how to do it, than I know how to begin and accomplish that rare and curious piece of Art, which I never yet saw or considered.

51. Wherefore while I was thus considering, and being put to my plunge about it (for you must know, that as yet I had, in this matter, broken my mind to no man, only did hear and consider) the Tempter came in with his delusion, *That there was no way for me to know I had Faith, but by trying to work some Miracle*; urging those *Scriptures* that seem to look that way, for the inforcing and strengthning his temptation. Nay, one day, as I was betwixt *Elstow* and *Bedford* the temptation was hot upon me, to try if I had Faith, by doing some Miracle; which Miracle, at that time, was this; I must say to the *Puddles* that were in the Horse-pads, *Be dry*; and to the *dry places*, *Be you the puddles:* And truly, one time I was going to say so indeed; but just as I was about to speak, this thought came into my mind; *But go under yonder Hedge, and pray first, that God would make you able:* But when I had concluded to pray, this came hot upon me; That if I prayed, and came again, and tried to do it, and yet did nothing notwithstanding, then be sure I had no Faith, but was a Cast-away, and lost. Nay, thought I, if it be so, I will not try yet, but will stay a little longer.

52. So I continued at a great loss; for I thought, if they only had Faith, which could do so wonderful things, then I concluded, that for the present I neither had it, nor yet for time to come were ever like to have it. Thus I was tossed betwixt the Devil and my own ignorance, and so perplexed, especially at some times, that I could not tell what to do.

53. About this time, the state and happiness of these poor people at *Bedford* was thus, *in a kind of Vision*, presented to me: I saw, as if they were set on the Sunny-side of some high Mountain, there refreshing themselves with the pleasant beams of the Sun, while I was shivering and shrinking in the Cold, afflicted with Frost, Snow and dark Clouds: Me-thought also,

betwixt me and them, I saw a Wall that did compass about this Mountain; now through this Wall my Soul did greatly desire to pass; concluding, that if I could, I would go even into the very midst of them, and there also comfort my self with the heat of their Sun.

54. About this Wall I thought my self to go again and again, still prying as I went, to see if I could find some way or passage, by which I might enter therein; but none could I find for some time: At the last, I saw, as it were, a narrow gap, like a little door-way, in the Wall, thorough which I attempted to pass: Now the passage being very strait and narrow, I made many offers to get in, but all in vain, even until I was well nigh quite beat out by striving to get in; at last with great striving, me-thought I at first did get in my head, and after that, by a sideling striving, my shoulders, and my whole body: Then was I exceeding glad, and went and sate down in the midst of them, and so was comforted with the light and heat of their Sun.

55. Now this Mountain and Wall, *&c.* was thus made out to me; the Mountain signified the Church of the Living God; the Sun that shone thereon, the comfortable shining of his merciful Face on them that were therein; the Wall I thought was the Word, that did make separation between the Christians and the World; and the Gap which was in this Wall, I thought, was Jesus Christ, who is the Way to God the Father, *Joh.* 14. 6. *Mat.* 7. 14. But forasmuch as the Passage was wonderful narrow, even so narrow, that I could not but with great difficulty enter in thereat, it shewed me, that none could enter into Life, but those that were in down-right earnest, and unless also they left this wicked World behind them; for here was only room for Body and Soul, but not for Body and Soul, and Sin.

56. This resemblance abode upon my Spirit many days; all which time I saw my self in a forlorn and sad condition, but yet was provoked to a vehement hunger and desire to be one of that number that did sit in the Sun-shine: Now also I should pray, where-ever I was; whether at home, or abroad; in house, or field; and should also often, with lifting up of heart, sing that of the fifty first *Psalm*, *O Lord*, *consider my distress*; for as yet I knew not where I was.

57. Neither as yet could I attain to any comfortable

perswasion that I had Faith in Christ; but instead of having satisfaction, here I began to find my Soul to be assaulted with fresh doubts about my future happiness; especially with such as these, *Whether I was elected: But how if the Day of Grace should now be past and gone?*

58. By these two temptations I was very much afflicted and disquieted; sometimes by one, and sometimes by the other of them. And first, to speak of that about my questioning my Election; I found at this time, that though I was in a flame to find the way to Heaven and Glory, and though nothing could beat me off from this, yet this question did so offend and discourage me, that I was, especially at some times, as if the very strength of my body also had been taken away by the force and power thereof. This Scripture also did seem to me, to trample upon all my desires; *It is neither in him that willeth, nor in him that runneth; but in God that sheweth mercy*, Rom. 9.

59. With this Scripture I could not tell what to do, for I evidently saw, unless that the great God, of his infinite Grace and Bounty, had voluntarily chosen me to be a Vessel of Mercy, though I should desire, and long, and labour until my heart did break, no good could come of it. Therefore this would still stick with me, *How can you tell you are elected? And what if you should not? How then?*

60. O Lord, thought I, what if I should not indeed? It may be, you are not, said the Tempter: It may be so indeed, thought I. Why then, said Satan, you had as good leave off, and strive no further; for if, indeed, you should not be elected and chosen of God, there is no talk of your being saved; *For it is neither in him that willeth, nor in him that runneth; but in God that sheweth mercy.*

61. By these things I was driven to my wits end, not knowing what to say, or how to answer these temptations; (indeed, I little thought that Satan had thus assaulted me, but that rather it was my own prudence, thus to start the question;) for that the Elect only attained Eternal Life, that I, without scruple, did heartily close withal; but that my self was one of them, there lay the question.

62. Thus therefore, for several days, I was greatly assaulted and perplexed; and was often, when I have been walking, ready to sink where I went, with faintness in my mind: But one day,

after I had been so many weeks oppressed and cast down therewith, as I was now quite giving up the Ghost of all my hopes of ever attaining life, that sentence fell with weight upon my spirit, *Look at the generations of old, and see: Did ever any trust in God, and were confounded?*

63. At which I was greatly lightned, and encouraged in my Soul; for thus at that very instant, it was expounded to me: *Begin at the beginning of* Genesis, *and read to the end of the* Revelations, *and see if you can find that there was any that ever trusted in the Lord, and was confounded.* So coming home, I presently went to my Bible, to see if I could find that saying, not doubting but to find it presently; for it was so fresh, and with such strength and comfort on my spirit, that I was as if it talked with me.

64. Well, I looked, but I found it not; only it abode upon me: Then I did ask first this good man, and then another, if they knew where it was; but they knew no such place. At this I wonder'd, that such a sentence should so suddainly, and with such comfort and strength, sieze and abide upon my heart, and yet that none could find it (for I doubted not, but it was in holy Scripture.)

65. Thus I continued above a year, and could not find the place; but at last, casting my eye into the *Apocrypha*-books, I found it in *Ecclesiasticus*, *Ecclus.* 2. 10. This, at the first, did somewhat daunt me; but because by this time I had got more experience of the love and kindness of God, it troubled me the less; especially when I considered, that though it was not in those Texts that we call Holy and Canonical, yet forasmuch as this sentence was the sum and substance of many of the Promises, it was my duty to take the comfort of it; and I bless God for that word, for it was of God to me: That word doth still, at times, shine before my face.

66. After this, that other doubt did come with strength upon me, *But how if the Day of Grace should be past and gone?* How if you have over-stood the time of Mercy? Now I remember, that one day, as I was walking into the Country, I was much in the thoughts of this, *But how if the Day of Grace be past?* And to aggravate my trouble, the Tempter presented to my mind those good people of *Bedford*, and suggested thus unto me; That these being converted already,

they were all that God would save in those parts; and that I came too late, for these had got the Blessing before I came.

67. Now was I in great distress, thinking in very deed, that this might well be so; wherefore I went up and down bemoaning my sad condition; counting my self far worse than a thousand fools for standing off thus long, and spending so many years in sin as I have done; still crying out, Oh, that I had turned sooner! Oh, that I had turned seven years ago! It made me also angry with my self, to think that I should have no more wit, but to trifle away my time, till my Soul and Heaven were lost.

68. But when I had been long vexed with this fear, and was scarce able to take one step more, just about the same place where I received my other encouragement, these words broke in upon my mind, *Compel them to come in, that my house may be filled; and yet there is room*, Luk. 14. 22, 23. These words, but especially them, *And yet there is room*, were sweet words to me; for truly, I thought that by them I saw that there was place enough in Heaven for me; and moreover, that when the Lord Jesus did speak these words, he then did think of me; and that he knowing the time would come, that I should be afflicted with fear that there was no place left for me in his bosom, did before speak this word, and leave it upon record, that I might find help thereby against this vile temptation. This I then verily believed.

69. In the light and encouragement of this Word, I went a pretty while; and the comfort was the more, when I thought that the Lord Jesus should think on me so long ago, and that he should speak them words on purpose for my sake; for I did think verily, that he did on purpose speak them, to encourage me withal.

70. But I was not without my temptations to go back again; temptations, I say, both from Satan, mine own heart, and carnal acquaintance; but, I thank God, these were outweighed by that sound sense of Death, and of the Day of Judgment, which abode, as it were, continually in my view. I should often also think on *Nebuchadnezzar*; of whom it is said, *He had given him all the kingdoms of the earth*, Dan. 5. 18, 19. Yet, thought I, if this great man had all his portion

in this World, one hour in Hell-fire would make him forget all. Which Consideration was a great help to me.

71. I was also made, about this time, to see something concerning the Beasts that *Moses* counted clean, and unclean: I thought those Beasts were types of men; the *clean*, types of them that were the people of God; but the *unclean*, types of such as were the children of the wicked One. Now I read, that the clean Beasts *chewed the Cud*; that is, thought I, they shew us, we must feed upon the Word of God: They also *parted the Hoof*; I thought that signified, we must part, if we would be saved, with the ways of ungodly men. And also, in further reading about them, I found, that though we did chew the Cud, as the *Hare*; yet if we walked with claws, like a Dog; or if we did part the Hoof, like the *Swine*; yet if we did not chew the Cud, as the Sheep, we were still, for all that, but unclean: for I thought the *Hare* to be a type of those that talk of the Word, yet walk in ways of sin; and that the *Swine* was like him that parteth with his outward pollutions, but still wanteth the word of Faith, without which, there could be no way of Salvation, let a man be never so devout, *Deut.* 14. After this, I found by reading the Word, that those that must be glorified with Christ in another World, *must be called by him here*; called to the partaking of a share in his Word and Righteousness, and to the comforts and first fruits of his Spirit, and to a peculiar interest in all those heavenly things, which do indeed, fore fit the Soul for that Rest, and House of Glory, which is in Heaven above.

72. Here again I was at a very great stand; not knowing what to do, fearing I was not called; for, thought I, if I be not called, what then can do me good? None but those who are effectually called, inherit the Kingdom of Heaven. But oh, how I now loved those words that spake of a *Christian's Calling!* as when the Lord said to one, *Follow me*; and to another, *Come after me:* And, oh, thought I, that he would say so to me too! How gladly would I run after him!

74. I cannot now express with what longings and breathings in my Soul, I cried to Christ to call me. Thus I continued for a time, all on a flame to be converted to Jesus Christ; and did also see at that day, such glory in a converted state, that I could not be contented without a share therein. Gold! Could

it have been gotten for Gold, what could I have given for it! Had I had a whole World, it had all gone ten thousand times over for this, that my Soul might have been in a converted state.

75. How lovely now was every one in my eyes, that I thought to be converted men and women! They shone, they walked like a people that carried the Broad Seal of Heaven about them. Oh! I saw the lot was fallen to them in pleasant places, and they had a goodly Heritage, *Psal.* 16. But that which made me sick, was that of Christ, in *Mark*; *He went up into a Mountain, and called to him whom he would, and they came unto him*, Mar. 3. 13.

76. This Scripture made me faint and fear, yet it kindled fire in my Soul. That which made me fear, was this; lest Christ should have no liking to me, for he called *whom he would.* But, Oh! the glory that I saw in that condition did still so engage my heart, that I could seldom read of any that Christ did call, but I presently wished, *Would I had been in their Cloaths, Would I had been born* Peter, *Would I had been born* John; *Or would I had been by, and had heard him when he called them; how would I have cried, O Lord, call me also? But, Oh! I feared he would not call me.*

77. And truly, the Lord let me go thus many months together, and shewed me nothing; either that I was already, or should be called hereafter: But at last, after much time spent, and many groans to God, that I might be made partaker of the holy and heavenly Calling, that word came in upon me, *I will cleanse their blood that I have not cleansed, for the Lord dwelleth in Zion*, Joel 3. 21. These words I thought were sent, to encourage me to wait still upon God; and signified unto me, that if I were not already, yet time might come, I might be in truth converted unto Christ.

78. About this time I began to break my mind to those poor people in *Bedford*, and to tell them my condition; which when they had heard, they told Mr. *Gifford* of me; who himself also took occasion to talk with me, and was willing to be well perswaded of me, though I think but from little grounds: But he invited me to his house, where I should hear him confer with others, about the dealings of God with their Souls; from all which I still received more conviction, and from that time

began to see something of the vanity, and inward wretchedness of my wicked heart, for as yet I knew no great matter therein; but now it began to be discovered unto me, and also to work at that rate as it never did before. Now I evidently found, that lusts and corruptions put forth themselves within me, in wicked thoughts and desires, which I did not regard before; my desires also for Heaven and Life began to fail; I found also, that whereas before my Soul was full of longings after God, now it began to hanker after every foolish vanity; yea, my heart would not be moved to mind that that was good; it began to be careless, both of my Soul, and Heaven; it would now continually hang back, both to, and in every duty; and was as a clog on the leg of a Bird, to hinder me from flying.

79. Nay, thought I, now I grow worse and worse; now I am farther from conversion than ever I was before: Wherefore I began to sink greatly in my Soul, and began to entertain such discouragement in my heart, as laid me as low as Hell. If now I should have burned at the Stake, I could not believe that Christ had love for me: Alas! I could neither hear him, nor see him, nor feel him, nor favour any of his things: I was driven as with a Tempest, my heart would be unclean, the *Canaanites* would dwell in the Land.

80. Sometimes I would tell my condition to the people of God; which, when they heard, they would pity me, and would tell me of the Promises; but they had as good have told me, that I must reach the Sun with my finger, as have bidden me receive, or relie upon the Promise; and as soon as I should have done it, all my sense and feeling was against me; and I saw I had an heart that would sin, and that lay under a Law that would condemn.

81. These things have often made me think of the Child which the Father brought to Christ; *who, while he was yet a coming to him, was thrown down by the Devil*; *and also so rent and torn by him, that he lay and wallowed, foaming*, Luk. 9. 42. Mar. 9. 20.

82. Further, in these days, I should find my heart to shut it self up against the Lord, and against his holy Word: I have found my Unbelief to set, as it were, the shoulder to the door, to keep him out; and that too even then, when I have, with many a bitter sigh, cried, Good Lord, break it open: *Lord*,

break these Gates of Brass, and cut the Bars of iron asunder, Psal. 107. 16. Yet that word would sometimes create in my heart a peaceable pause, *I girded thee, tho thou hast not known me*, Isa. 45. 5.

83. But all this while, as to the act of sinning, I never was more tender than now; my hinder parts were inward; I durst not take a pin, or stick, though but so big as a straw; for my Conscience now was sore, and would smart at every touch: I could not now tell how to speak my words, for fear I should misplace them. Oh, how gingerly did I then go, in all I did or said! I found my self as on a miry Bog, that shook if I did but stir, and was, as there left both of God, and Christ, and the Spirit, and all good things.

84. But I observe, though I was such a great sinner before conversion, yet God never much charged the guilt of the sins of my Ignorance upon me; only he shewed me, I was lost if I had not Christ, because I had been a sinner. I saw that I wanted a perfect Righteousness, to present me without fault before God; and this Righteousness was no where to be found, but in the Person of Jesus Christ.

85. But my original and inward pollution, that, that was my plague and my affliction; that I saw, at a dreadful rate, always putting forth it self within me; that I had the guilt of, to amazement; by reason of that, I was more loathsome in mine own eyes, than was a toad, and I thought I was so in God's eyes too: Sin and corruption, I said, would as naturally bubble out of my heart, as water would bubble out of a fountain: I thought now, that every one had a better heart than I had; I could have changed heart with any body; I thought, none but the Devil himself could equalize me for inward wickedness, and pollution of mind. I fell therefore at the sight of my own vileness, deeply into despair; for I concluded, that this condition that I was in, could not stand with a state of Grace: Sure, thought I, I am forsaken of God; sure I am given up to the Devil, and to a reprobate mind: and thus I continued a long while, even for some years together.

86. While I was thus afflicted with the fears of my own damnation, there were two things would make me wonder; the one was, when I saw old people hunting after the things of this life, as if they should live here always: The other was,

when I found Professors much distressed, and cast down, when they met with outward losses; as of Husband, Wife, Child, &c. Lord! thought I, what a-do is here about such little things as these! What seeking after carnal things by some, and what grief in others for the loss of them! If they so much labour after, and spend so many tears for the things of this present life, how am I to be bemoaned, pitied, and prayed for! My Soul is dying, my soul is damning. Were my Soul but in a good condition, and were I but sure of it; ah, how rich should I esteem my self, though blest but with Bread and Water! I should count those but small afflictions, and should bear them as little burthens. *A wounded Spirit, who can bear?*

87. And though I was thus troubled, and tossed, and afflicted with the sight, and sense, and terrour of my own wickedness, yet I was afraid to let this sense and sight go quite off my mind; for I found, that unless guilt of Conscience was taken off the right way, that is, by the Blood of Christ, a man grew rather worse for the loss of his trouble of mind, than better. Wherefore, if my guilt lay hard upon me, then I should cry that the Blood of Christ might take it off: And if it was going off without it (for the sense of sin would be sometimes as if it would die, and go quite away) then I would also strive to fetch it upon my heart again by bringing the punishment for sin in Hell-fire upon my spirit; and should cry, *Lord, let it not go off my heart, but the right way, but by the Blood of Christ, and by the application of thy mercy, through him, to my Soul*; for that Scripture lay much upon me, *Without shedding of blood, there is no remission*, Heb. 9. 22. And that which made me the more afraid of this, was, because I had seen some, who, though when they were under wounds of Conscience, would cry and pray; yet seeking rather present ease from their trouble, than pardon for their sin, cared not how they lost their guilt, so they got it out of their mind: Now having got it off the wrong way, it was not sanctified unto them; but they grew harder, and blinder, and more wicked after their trouble. This made me afraid, and made me cry to God the more, that it might not be so with me.

88. And now I was sorry that God had made me a man, for I feared I was a Reprobate: I counted Man, as unconverted, the most doleful of all the Creatures. Thus being afflicted and

tossed about my sad condition, I counted my self alone, and above the most of men, unblessed.

89. Yea I thought it impossible that ever I should attain to so much goodness of heart, as to thank God that he had made me a man. Man, indeed, is the most noble, by creation, of all creatures in the visible World; but by sin, he had made himself the most ignoble. The beasts, birds, fishes, *&c.* I blessed their condition; for they had not a sinful nature, they were not obnoxious to the wrath of God, they were not to go to Hell-fire after death; I could therefore have rejoiced, had my condition been as any of theirs.

[9]0. In this condition I went a great while; but when comforting time was come, I heard one preach a Sermon upon these words in the *Song*, (*Song* 4. 1.) *Behold, thou art fair, my Love*; *behold, thou art fair:* But at that time he made these two words, *My Love*, his chief and subject-matter; from which, after he had a little opened the Text, he observed these several Conclusions: 1. *That the Church, and so every saved Soul, is Christ's Love, when loveless.* 2. *Christ's Love without a cause.* 3. *Christ's Love, when hated of the World.* 4. *Christ's Love, when under temptation, and under desertion.* 5. *Christ's Love, from first to last.*

91. But I got nothing by what he said at present; only when he came to the Application of the fourth Particular, this was the word he said; *If it be so, that the saved Soul is Christ's Love, when under temptation and desertion*; *then, poor tempted Soul, when thou art assaulted and afflicted with temptations, and the hidings of God's Face, yet think on these two words,* MY LOVE, *still.*

92. So as I was going home, these words came again into my thoughts; and I well remember, as they came in, I said thus in my heart, *What shall I get by thinking on these two words?* This thought had no sooner passed through my heart, but these words began thus to kindle in my spirit, *Thou art my Love, thou art my Dove*, twenty times together; and still as they ran thus in my mind, they waxed stronger and warmer, and began to make me look up; but being as yet between hope and fear, I still replied in my heart, *But is it true? But is it true?* At which, that sentence fell in upon me, *He wist not that It was true, which was done unto him of the Angel*, Act. 12. 9.

93. Then I began to give place to the Word, which, with power, did over and over make this joyful sound within my Soul, *Thou art my Love*, *thou art my Love*; *and nothing shall separate thee from my Love:* And with that, *Rom.* 8. 39 came into my mind. Now was my heart filled full of comfort and hope, and now I could believe that my sins should be forgiven me; yea, I was now so taken with the love and mercy of God, that, I remember, I could not tell how to contain till I got home: I thought I could have spoken of his Love, and have told of his mercy to me, even to the very Crows that sate upon the plowed lands before me, had they been capable to have understood me: Wherefore I said in my soul, with much gladness, *Well*, *I would I had a Pen and Ink here*, *I would write this down before I go any further*; *for surely*, *I will not forget this forty years hence:* But, alas! within less than forty days, I began to question all again; and by times, fell to my old courses again; which made me begin to question all still.

94. Yet still at times, I was helped to believe, that it was a true manifestation of Grace unto my Soul, though I had lost much of the life and savour of it. Now, about a week or fortnight after this, I was much followed by this Scripture; *Simon*, *Simon*, *behold*, *Satan hath desired to have you*, Luk. 22. 31. and sometimes it would sound so loud within me, yea, and, as it were, call so strongly after me, that once, above all the rest, I turned my head over my shoulder, thinking verily that some man had, behind me, called me; being at a great distance, methought, he called so *loud:* It came, as I have thought since, to have stirred me up to prayer, and to watchfulness: It came to acquaint me, that a cloud and storm was coming down upon me; but I understood it not.

95. Also, as I remember, *that* time that it called to me so loud, was the *last* time that it sounded in mine ears; but methinks I hear still with what a loud voice these words, *Simon*, *Simon*, sounded in my ears: I thought verily, as I have told you, that some body had called after me, that was half a mile behind me: And although that was not my name, yet it made me suddainly look behind me; believing that he that called so loud, meant me.

96. But so foolish was I, and ignorant, that I knew not the reason of this sound (which, as I did both see and feel soon

after, was sent from Heaven, as an Alarm, to awaken me to provide for what was coming;) only I should muse, and wonder in my mind, to think what should be the reason that this Scripture, and that at this rate, so often, and so loud, should still be sounding and ratling in mine ears: But, as I said before, I soon after perceived the end of God therein.

97. For about the space of a month after, a very great storm came down upon me, which handled me twenty times worse than all I had met with before: it came stealing upon me, now by one piece, then by another; first, all my comfort was taken from me, then darkness siezed upon me; after which, whole floods of blasphemies, both against God, Christ and the Scriptures, was poured upon my spirit, to my great confusion and astonishment. These blasphemous thoughts were such as stirred up questions in me against the very *Being* of God, and of his only beloved Son: As, whether there were in truth, a God, or Christ? And whether the holy Scriptures were not rather a fable, and cunning story, than the holy and pure Word of God?

98. The Tempter also would much assault me with this: *How can you tell but that the* Turks *had as good Scriptures to prove their* Mahomet *the Saviour, as we have to prove our* Jesus *is? And could I think that so many ten thousands, in so many Countries and Kingdoms, should be without the knowledge of the right way to Heaven (if there were indeed an Heaven;) and that we only, who live in a corner of the Earth, should alone be blessed therewith? Every one doth think his own Religion rightest; both* Jews, *and* Moors, *and Pagans; and how if all our Faith, and Christ, and Scriptures should be but a Think so too?*

99. Sometimes I have endeavoured to argue against these suggestions, and to set some of the Sentences of blessed *Paul* against them; but, alas! I quickly felt, when I thus did, such arguings as these would return again upon me; *Though we made so great a matter of* Paul, *and of his words, yet how could I tell but that, in very deed, he being a subtile and cunning man, might give himself up to deceive with strong delusions; and also take the pains and travel, to undo and destroy his Fellows.*

100. These suggestions (with many other, which at this time I may not, nor dare not utter, neither by word or pen) did make such a siezure upon my spirit, and did so overweigh my

heart, both with their number, continuance, and fiery force, that I felt as if there were nothing else but these from morning to night within me, and as though indeed there could be room for nothing else ; and also concluded, that God had, in very wrath to my Soul, given me up to them, to be carried away with them, as with a mighty whirl-wind.

101. Only by the distaste that they gave unto my spirit, *I felt there was something in me that refused to embrace them.* But this consideration I then only had, when God gave me leave to swallow my spittle ; otherwise, the noise, and strength, and force of these temptations would drown and over-flow, and, as it were, bury all such thoughts, or the remembrance of any such thing. While I was in this temptation, I should find often my mind suddainly put upon it, to curse and swear, or to speak some grievous thing of God, or Christ his Son, and of the Scriptures.

102. Now I thought, *surely I am possessed of the Devil:* At other times again, I thought I should be bereft of my wits ; for instead of lauding and magnifying of God the Lord with others, if I have but heard him spoken of, presently some most horrible blasphemous thought or other would bolt out of my heart against him : So that whether I did think that God was, or again did think there were no such thing; no love, nor peace, nor gracious disposition could I feel within me.

103. These things did sink me into very deep despair; for I concluded, that such things could not possibly be found amongst them that loved God. I often, when these tempta tions have been with force upon me, did compare my self to the case of such a child, whom some Gypsie hath by force took up in her arms, and is carrying from friend and Country: Kick sometimes I did, and also shriek and cry; but yet I was as bound in the wings of the temptation, and the wind would carry me away. I thought also of *Saul*, and of the evil Spirit that did possess him; and did greatly fear, that my condition was the same with that of his, 1 *Sam.* 16. 14.

104. In these days, when I have heard others talk of what was the sin against the Holy Ghost, then would the Tempter so provoke me to desire to sin that sin, that I was as if I could not, must not, neither should be quiet until I had committed it;

now no sin would serve but that: if it were to be committed by speaking of such a word, then I have been as if my mouth would have spoken that word, whether I would or no. And in so strong a measure was this temptation upon me, that often I have been ready to clap my hand under my chin, to hold my mouth from opening; and to that end also I have had thoughts at other times, to leap with my head downward, into some Muck-hill-hole or other, to keep my mouth from speaking.

105. Now again I beheld the condition of the Dog and Toad, and counted the estate of every thing that God had made, far better than this dreadful state of mine, and such as my Companions was: Yea, gladly would I have been in the condition of Dog or Horse, for I knew they had no Soul to perish under the everlasting weight of Hell, or sin, as mine was like to do. Nay, and though I saw this, felt this, and was broken to pieces with it; yet that which added to my sorrow, was, that I could not find, that with all my Soul I did desire deliverance. That Scripture also did tear and rend my Soul, in the midst of these distractions, *The wicked are like the troubled sea, which cannot rest; whose waters cast up mire and dirt: There is no peace to the wicked, saith my God*, Isa. 57. 20, 21.

106. And now my heart was, at times, exceeding hard; if I would have given a thousand pound for a tear, I could not shed one; no, nor sometimes scarce desire to shed one. I was much dejected, to think that this would be my lot. I saw, some could mourn and lament their sin; and others, again, could rejoice, and bless God for Christ; and others, again, could quietly talk of, and with gladness remember the Word of God; while I only was in the storm, or tempest. This much sunk me, I thought my condition was alone, I should therefore much bewail my hard hap; but get out of, or get rid of these things, I could not.

107. While this temptation lasted, which was about a year, I could attend upon none of the Ordinances of God, but with sore and great affliction; yea, then was I most distressed with blasphemies: If I have been hearing the Word, then uncleanness, blasphemies and despair would hold me a Captive there; if I have been reading, then sometimes I had suddain thoughts to question all I read; sometimes again, my mind would be so

strangely snatched away, and possessed with other things, that I have neither known, nor regarded, nor remembred so much as the Sentence that but now I have read.

108. In prayer also I have been greatly troubled at this time; sometimes I have thought I have felt him, behind me, pull my cloaths: He would be also continually at me in time of prayer, to have done; break off, make haste, you have prayed enough, and stay no longer; still drawing my mind away. Sometimes also he would cast in such wicked thoughts as these; that I must pray to him, or for him: I have thought sometimes of that, *Fall down*, or *If thou wilt fall down and worship me*, Mat. 4. 9.

109. Also when because I have had wandering thoughts in the time of this duty, I have laboured to compose my mind, and fix it upon God; then with great force hath the Tempter laboured to distract me, and confound me, and to turn away my mind, by presenting to my heart and fancy, the form of a Bush, a Bull, a besom, or the like, as if I should pray to those: To these also he would (at some times especially) so hold my mind, that I was as if I could think of nothing else, or pray to nothing else but to these, or such as they.

110. Yet at times I should have some strong and heart-affecting apprehensions of God, and the reality of the truth of his Gospel: But, Oh! how would my heart, at such times, put forth it self with unexpressible groanings! My whole Soul was then in every word; I should cry with pangs after God, that he would be merciful unto me: But then I should be daunted again with such conceits as these; I should think that God did mock at these my prayers; saying, and that in the audience of the holy Angels, *This poor simple wretch doth hanker after me, as if I had nothing to do with my mercy, but to bestow it on such as he. Alas, poor Soul! How art thou deceived! It is not for such as thee, to have favour with the Highest.*

111. Then hath the Tempter come upon me also with such discouragements as these: *You are very hot for mercy, but I will cool you; this frame shall not last always: Many have been as hot as you, for a spurt; but I have quenched their Zeal.* (And with this, such and such, who were fallen off, would be set before mine eyes:) Then I should be afraid that I should do so too. But, thought I, I am glad this comes into my mind:

Well, I will watch, and take what heed I can. *Though you do*, said Satan, *I shall be too hard for you*; *I will cool you insensibly*, *by degrees*, *by little and little. What care I*, saith he, *though I be seven years in chilling your heart*, *if I can do it at last? Continual rocking will lull a crying child asleep: I will ply it close*, *but I will have my end accomplished. Though you be burning hot at present*, *yet if I can pull you from this fire*, *I shall have you cold before it be long.*

112. These things brought me into great straits; for as I at present could not find my self fit for present death, so I thought, to live long, would make me yet more unfit; for time would make me forget all, and wear even the remembrance of the evil of sin, the worth of Heaven, and the need I had of the blood of Christ to wash me, both out of mind and thought: But I thank Christ Jesus, these things did not at present make me slack my crying, but rather did put me more upon it (*like her who met with the Adulterer*, *Deut.* 22. 26.) in which days, that was a good word to me, after I had suffered these things a while; *I am perswaded*, *that neither heighth*, *nor depth*, *nor death*, *nor life*, &c. *shall separate us from the love of God which is in Christ Jesus*, Rom. 8. 38. And now I hoped, long life should not destroy me, nor make me miss of Heaven.

113. Yet I had some supports in this temptation, though they were then all questioned by me. That in *Jer.* 3. at the first, was something to me; and so was the consideration of *ver.* 5. of that Chapter; that though we have spoken and done as evil things as we could, yet we should cry unto God, *My Father*, *thou art the Guide of my Youth*; and should return unto him.

114. I had also once a sweet glance from that in 2 *Cor.* 5. 12. *For he hath made him to be sin for us*, *who knew no sin*, *that we might be made the righteousness of God in him.* I remember that one day, as I was sitting in a Neighbour's house, and there very sad at the consideration of my many blasphemies; and as I was saying in my mind, *What ground have I to think*, *that I*, *who have been so vile and abominable*, *should ever inherit eternal life*? That word came suddainly upon me, *What shall we say to these things? If God be for us*, *who can be against us?* Rom. 8. 31. That also was an help unto me, *Because I live*, *you shall live also*, Joh. 14. 19. But these words were but

hints, touches, and short visits, though very sweet when present; only they lasted not; *but, like to* Peter's *sheet, of a suddain were caught up from me, to Heaven again,* Act. 10. 16.

115. But afterwards the Lord did more fully and graciously discover himself unto me; and indeed, did quite, not only deliver me from the guilt that, by these things, was laid upon my Conscience, but also from the very filth thereof; for the temptation was removed, and I was put into my right mind again, as other Christians were.

116. I remember that one day, as I was travelling into the Country, and musing on the wickedness and blasphemy of my heart, and considering of the enmity that was in me to God, that Scripture came in my mind, *He hath made peace by the blood of his cross,* Col. 1. 20. By which I was made to see, both again and again, that day, that God and my Soul were friends by this Blood; yea, I saw that the Justice of God, and my sinful Soul, could embrace and kiss each other through this Blood. This was a good day to me; I hope I shall not forget it.

117. At another time, as I was set by the fire, in my house, and musing on my wretchedness, the Lord made that also a precious word unto me; *Forasmuch then as the children are partakers of flesh and blood, he also himself likewise took part of the same, that through death, he might destroy him that had the power of death; that is, the Devil; and deliver those who, through the fear of death, were all their life subject to bondage,* Heb. 2. 14, 15. I thought that the glory of those words was then so weighty on me, that I was both once and twice ready to swoon as I sate; yet not with grief and trouble, but with solid joy and peace.

118. At this time also I sate under the Ministery of holy Mr. *Gifford,* whose Doctrine, by God's Grace, was much for my stability. This man made it much his business to deliver the people of God from all those false and unsound tests, that by nature we are prone to. He would bid us take special heed, that we took not up any truth upon trust; as from this, or that, or any other man or men; but to cry mightily to God, that he would convince us of the reality thereof, and set us down therein by his own Spirit, in the holy Word: *For,* said he, *if you do otherwise, when temptations come, if strongly, you not having*

received them with evidence from Heaven, will find, you want that help and strength, now to resist, that once you thought you had.

119. This was as seasonable to my Soul, as the former and latter Rain in their season; for I had found, and that by sad experience, the truth of these his words; (for I had felt, *no man can say*, especially when tempted of the Devil, *that Jesus Christ is Lord, but by the Holy Ghost.*) Wherefore I found my Soul, through Grace, very apt to drink in this Doctrine, and to incline to pray to God, that in nothing that pertained to God's Glory, and my own eternal happiness, he would suffer me to be without the confirmation thereof from Heaven; for now I saw clearly, there was an exceeding difference betwixt the notion of flesh and blood, and the Revelations of God in Heaven; also a great difference between that Faith that is feigned, and according to Man's wisdom, and of that which comes by a man's being born thereto of God, *Mat.* 16. 15. 1 *Joh.* 5. 1.

120. But, Oh! now, how was my Soul led from truth to truth by God! Even from the Birth and Cradle of the Son of God, to his Ascention, and second coming from Heaven, to judge the World!

121. Truly, I then found, upon this account, the great God was very good unto me; for, to my remembrance, there was not any thing that then I cried to God, to make known, and reveal unto me, but he was pleased to do it for me: I mean, not one part of the Gospel of the Lord Jesus, but I was orderly led into it: Me thought I saw with great evidence, from the relation of the four Evangelists, the wonderful work of God, in giving Jesus Christ to save us, from his conception and Birth, even to his second coming to Judgment: Me-thought I was as if I had seen him born, as if I had seen him grow up, as if I had seen him walk through this World, from the Cradle, to the Cross; to which also, when he came, I saw how gently he gave himself to be hanged, and nailed on it, for my sins, and wicked doings. Also as I was musing on this his progress, that dropped on my spirit, *He was ordained for the slaughter*, 1 Pet. 1. 12, 20.

122. When I have considered also the truth of his Resurrection, and have remembred that word, *Touch me not*, *Mary*, &c. I have seen, as if he had leaped out of the Grave's mouth,

for joy that he was risen again, and had got the conquest over our dreadful foes, *Joh.* 20. 17. I have also, in the Spirit, seen him a Man on the Right-Hand of God the Father, for me; and have seen the manner of his coming from Heaven, to judge the World with Glory, and have been confirmed in these things by these Scriptures following, *Act.* 1. 9, 10. & 7. 56. & 10. 42. *Heb.* 7. 24. & 8. 38. *Rev.* 1. 18. 1 *Thes.* 4. 17, 18.

123. Once I was troubled to know whether the Lord Jesus was Man as well as God, and God as well as Man; and truly, in those days, let men say what they would, unless I had it with evidence from Heaven, all was nothing to me, I counted not my self set down in any truth of God. Well, I was much troubled about this Point, and could not tell how to be resolved; at last, that in *Rev.* 5. came into my mind: *And I beheld, and lo, in the midst of the throne, and of the four beasts, and in the midst of the elders, stood a Lamb.* In the midst of the Throne, thought I, there is his Godhead; in the midst of the Elders, there is his Manhood: But Oh! me-thought this did glister! it was a goodly touch, and gave me sweet satisfaction. That other Scripture also did help me much in this, *To us a Child is born, to us a Son is given, and the Government shall be upon his shoulder, and his Name shall be called Wonderful Counsellor, the mighty God, the Everlasting Father, the Prince of Peace,* &c. Isa. 9. 6.

124. Also besides these teachings of God, in his Word, the Lord made use of two things to confirm me in this truth; the one was, the Errors of the *Quakers*; and the other was, the Guilt of Sin; for as the *Quakers* did oppose this Truth, so God did the more confirm me in it, by leading me into the Scriptures that did wonderfully maintain it.

125. The Errors that this people then maintained were,

1. That the holy Scriptures were not the Word of God.

2. That every man in the World had the Spirit of Christ, Grace, Faith, *&c.*

3. That Christ Jesus, as crucified, and dying sixteen hundred years ago, did not satisfie Divine Justice for the sins of his people.

4. That Christ's Flesh and Blood was within the Saints.

5. That the Bodies of the Good and Bad that are buried in the Church-yard, shall not arise again.

6. That the Resurrection is past with good men already.

7. That that Man Jesus, that was crucified between two thieves, on Mount *Calvary*, in the Land of *Canaan*, by *Jerusalem*, was not ascended up above the starry Heavens.

8. That he should not, even the same Jesus that died by the hand of the *Jews*, come again at the last day; and, as Man, judge all Nations, *&c.*

126. Many more vile and abominable things were in those days fomented by them, by which I was driven to a more narrow search of the Scripture, and was, through their light and testimony, not only enlightned, but greatly confirmed and comforted in the truth; and, as I said, the guilt of sin did help me much; for still as that would come upon me, the Blood of Christ did take it off again, and again, and again; and that too sweetly, according to the Scriptures. *O friends! cry to God to reveal Jesus Christ unto you; there is none teacheth like him.*

127. It would be too long here to stay, to tell you in particular how God did set me down in all the things of Christ, and how he did, that he might so do, lead me into his words; yea, and also how he did open them unto me, and make them shine before me, and cause them to dwell with me, talk with me, and comfort me over and over, both of his own Being, and the Being of his Son, and Spirit, and Word, and Gospel.

128. Only this, as I said before, I will say unto you again, that in general, he was pleased to take this course with me: first to suffer me to be afflicted with temptation concerning them, and then reveal them to me: As sometimes I should lie under great guilt for sin, even crushed to the ground therewith; and then the Lord would shew me the death of Christ; yea, and so sprinkle my Conscience with his Blood, that I should find, and that before I was aware, that in that Conscience, where but just now did reign and rage the Law, even there would rest and abide the peace and love of God, through Christ.

129. Now I had an evidence, as I thought, of my Salvation from Heaven, with many golden Seals thereon, all hanging in my sight: Now could I remember this manifestation, and the other discovery of Grace, with comfort; and should often long

and desire that the last day were come, that I might be for ever inflamed with the sight, and joy, and communion of him, whose head was crowned with thorns, whose Face was spit on, and Body broken, and Soul made an Offering for my sins: For whereas before I lay continually trembling at the mouth of Hell, now me-thought I was got so far there-from, that I could not, when I looked back scarce discern it: And, Oh! thought I, that I were fourscore Years old now, that I might die quickly, that my Soul might be gone to rest.

130. But before I had got thus far out of these my Temptations, I did greatly long to see some ancient godly man's experience, who had writ some hundreds of years before I was born; for those who had writ in our days, I thought, (but I desire them now to pardon me,) that they had writ only that which others felt, or else had, through the strength of their Wits and Parts, studied to answer such Objections as they perceived others were perplexed with, without going down themselves into the deep. Well, after many such longings in my mind, the God in whose hands are all our days and ways, did cast into my hand (one day) a Book of *Martin Luther*; it was his Comment on the *Galatians*; it also was so old, that it was ready to fall piece from piece if I did but turn it over. Now I was pleased much that such an old Book had fallen into my hand; the which, when I had but a little way perused, I found my condition, in his experience, so largely and profoundly handled, as if his Book had been written out of my heart. This made me marvel; for thus thought I, *This Man could not know anything of the state of Christians now, but must needs write and speak the experience of former days.*

131. Besides he doth most gravely also in that Book, debate of the rise of these temptations, namely, Blasphemy, Desperation, and the like; showing that the Law of *Moses* as well as the Devil, Death, and Hell hath a very great hand therein: The which, at first, was very strange to me; but considering and watching, I found it so indeed. But of particulars here I intend nothing; only this methinks I must let fall before all men, I do prefer this book of *Martin Luther* upon the *Galatians*, (excepting the holy Bible,) before all the Books that ever I have seen, as most fit for a wounded Conscience.

132. And now I found, as I thought, that I loved Christ dearly: Oh! me-thought my Soul cleaved unto him, my affections cleaved unto him: I felt love to him as hot as fire; and now, as *Job* said, I thought I should die in my nest; but I did quickly find that my great love was but little, and that I, who had, as I thought, such burning love to Jesus Christ, could let him go again for a very trifle. God can tell how to abase us, and can hide pride from Man. Quickly after this my love was tried to purpose.

133. For after the Lord had, in this manner, thus graciously delivered me from this great and sore temptation, and had set me down so sweetly in the Faith of his holy Gospel, and had given me such strong consolation and blessed evidence from Heaven, touching my interest in his love through Christ; the tempter came upon me again, and that with a more grievous and dreadful temptation than before.

134. And that was, *to sell and part with this most blessed Christ, to exchange him for the things of this life, for any thing.* The temptation lay upon me for the space of a year, and did follow me so continually, that I was not rid of it one day in a month; no, not sometimes one hour in many days together, unless when I was asleep.

135. And though in my judgment I was perswaded, that those who were once effectually in Christ (as I hoped, through his Grace, I had seen my self) could never lose him for ever; (*For the land shall not be sold for ever, for the land is mine*, saith God, *Lev.* 25. 23.) yet it was a continual vexation to me, to think that I should have so much as one such thought within me against a Christ, a Jesus, that had done for me as he had done; and yet then I had almost none others, but such blasphemous ones.

136. But it was neither my dis-like of the thought, nor yet any desire and endeavour to resist it, that in the least did shake or abate the continuation, or force and strength thereof; for it did always, in almost whatever I thought, inter-mix it self therewith, in such sort, that I could neither eat my food, stoop for a pin, chop a stick, or cast mine eye to look on this or that, but still the temptation would come, *Sell Christ for this, or sell Christ for that; sell him, sell him.*

137. Sometimes it would run in my thoughts, not so little

as an hundred times together; *Sell him, sell him, sell him:* against which, I may say, for whole hours together, I have been forced to stand as continually leaning and forcing my spirit against it, lest haply, before I were aware, some wicked thought might arise in my heart, that might consent thereto; and sometimes also the Tempter would make me believe I had consented to it, but then should I be as tortured upon a Rack for whole days together.

138. This temptation did put me to such scares, lest I should at some times, I say, consent thereto, and be overcome therewith, that by the very force of my mind, in labouring to gain-say and resist this wickedness, my very body would be put into action, or motion, by way of pushing or thrusting with my hands, or elbows; still answering, as fast as the destroyer said, *sell him; I will not, I will not, I will not, I will not; no, not for thousands, thousands, thousands of Worlds:* Thus reckoning, lest I should, in the midst of these assaults, set too low a value of him, even until I scarce well knew where I was, or how to be composed again.

139. At these seasons he would not let me eat my food at quiet; but, forsooth, when I was set at the table, at my meat, I must go hence to pray; I must leave my food now, just now; so counterfeit holy also would this Devil be. When I was thus tempted, I should say in my self, *Now I am at meat, let me make an end. No,* said he, *you must do it now, or you will displease God, and despise Christ.* Wherefore I was much afflicted with these things; and because of the sinfulness of my nature (imagining that these things were impulses from God) I should deny to do it, as if I denied God; and then should I be as guilty because I did not obey a temptation of the Devil, as if I had broken the Law of God indeed.

140. But to be brief, one morning as I did lie in my bed, I was, as at other times, most fiercely assaulted with this temptation, *to sell, and part with Christ*; the wicked suggestion still running in my mind, *Sell him, sell him, sell him, sell him, sell him,* as fast as a man could speak: Against which also, in my mind, as at other times, I answered, *No, no, not for thousands thousands, thousands,* at least twenty times together: But at last, after much striving, even until I was almost out of breath, I felt this thought pass through my heart, *Let him go, if he will*; and I

thought also that I felt my heart freely consent thereto. Oh, the diligence of Satan! Oh, the desperateness of Man's heart!

141. Now was the battle won, and down fell I, as a Bird that is shot from the top of a tree, into great guilt, and fearful despair. Thus getting out of my bed, I went mopeing into the field; but, God knows, with as heavy an heart as mortal man, I think, could bear; where for the space of two hours, I was like a man bereft of life, and as now past all recovery, and bound over to eternal punishment.

142. And withal, that Scripture did sieze upon my Soul, *Or prophane person, as* Esau, *who for one morsel of meat, sold his birth-right: for ye know, how that afterwards, when he would have inherited the blessing, he was rejected; for he found no place of repentance, though he sought it carefully, with tears,* Heb. 12. 16, 17.

143. Now was I as one bound, I felt my self shut up unto the Judgment to come; nothing now, for two years together, would abide with me, but damnation, and an expectation of damnation: I say, nothing now would abide with me but this, save some few moments for relief, as in the sequel you will see.

144. These words were to my Soul, like fetters of Brass to my legs; in the continual sound of which, I went for several months together. But about ten or eleven a-clock on that day, as I was walking under an hedge (full of sorrow and guilt, God knows) and bemoaning my self for this hard hap, that such a thought should arise within me, suddainly this sentence bolted in on me, *The blood of Christ remits all guilt.* At this, I made a stand in my spirit: With that, this word took hold upon me, *The blood of Jesus Christ his Son, cleanseth us from all sin,* 1 Joh. 1. 7.

145. Now I began to conceive peace in my Soul, and methought I saw as if the Tempter did lear and steal away from me, as being ashamed of what he had done. At the same time also I had my sin and the Blood of Christ thus represented to me, that my sin, when compared to the Blood of Christ, was no more to it, than this little clot or stone before me, is to this vast and wide field that here I see. This gave me good encouragement for the space of two or three hours; in which

time also, me-thought I saw, by faith, the Son of God, as suffering for my sins: But because it tarried not, I therefore sunk in my spirit under exceeding guilt again.

146. But chiefly by the afore-mentioned Scripture, concerning *Esau*'s selling of his Birth-right; for that Scripture would lie all day long, all the week long; yea, all the year long in my mind, and hold me down, so that I could by no means lift up my self; for when I would strive to turn me to this Scripture, or that, for relief, still that Sentence would be sounding in me, *For ye know how that afterwards, when he would have inherited the blessing, he found no place of repentance, though he sought it carefully with tears.*

147. Sometimes, indeed, I should have a touch from that in *Luk.* 22. 31. *I have prayed for thee, that thy faith fail not*; but it would not abide upon me; neither could I indeed, when I considered my state, find ground to conceive in the least, that there should be the root of that Grace within me, having sinned as I had done. Now was I tore and rent in an heavy case, for many days together.

148. Then began I with sad and careful heart, to consider of the nature and largeness of my sin, and to search in the Word of God, if I could in any place espy a word of promise, or any encouraging sentence, by which I might take relief. Wherefore I began to consider that of *Mar.* 3. *All manner of sins and blasphemies shall be forgiven unto the sons of men, where-with-soever they shall blaspheme.* Which place, methought, at a blush, did contain a large and glorious Promise for the pardon of high offences; but considering the place more fully, I thought it was rather to be understood, as relating more chiefly to those who had, while in a natural estate, committed such things as there are mentioned; but not to me, who had not only received light and mercy, but that had both after, and also contrary to that, so slighted Christ as I had done.

149. I feared therefore that this wicked sin of mine might be that sin unpardonable, of which he there thus speaketh, *But he that shall blaspheme against the Holy Ghost, hath never forgiveness, but is in danger of eternal damnation*, Mar. 3. And I did the rather give credit to this, because of that sentence in the *Hebrews*, *For you know how that afterwards, when he would have inherited the blessing, he was rejected; for he found no place of*

repentance, though he sought it carefully with tears. And this stuck always with me.

150. And *now* was I both a burthen and a terror to my self; nor did I ever so know, as *now*, what it was to be weary of my life, and yet afraid to die. Oh, how gladly now would I have been any body but my self! Any thing but a man! and in any condition but mine own! For there was nothing did pass more frequently over my mind, than that it was impossible for me to be forgiven my transgression, and to be saved from wrath to come.

151. And now began I to labour to call again time that was past; wishing a thousand times twice told, that the day was yet to come, when I should be tempted to such a sin; concluding with great indignation, both against my heart, and all assaults, how I would rather have been torn in pieces, than found a consenter thereto. But, alas! these thoughts, and wishings, and resolvings were now too late to help me; the thought had passed my heart, God hath let me go, and I am fallen. *O!* thought I, *that it was with me as in months past, as in the days when God preserved me!* Job 29. 2.

152. Then again, being loth and unwilling to perish, I began to compare my sin with others, to see if I could find that any of those that are saved, had done as I had done. So I considered *David*'s Adultery and Murther, and found them most heinous crimes; and those too committed after Light and Grace received: But yet, by considering, I perceived that his transgressions were only such as were against the Law of *Moses*; from which the Lord Christ could, with the consent of his Word, deliver him: But mine was against Gospel; yea, against the Mediator thereof; I had sold my Saviour.

153. Now again should I be as if racked upon the wheel, when I considered that, besides the guilt that possessed me, I should be so void of Grace, so bewitched. What, thought I, must it be no sin but this? Must it needs be the *great transgression?* Psal. 19. 13. Must *that* wicked one touch my Soul? 1 *Joh.* 5. 18. Oh, what stings did I find in all these sentences!

154. What, thought I, is there but *one* sin that is unpardonable? But *one* sin that layeth the Soul without the reach of Gods Mercy? And must I be guilty of *that?* Must

it needs be that? is there but *one* sin, amongst *so many* millions of sins, for which there is no forgiveness; and must I commit *this?* Oh, unhappy *sin!* Oh, unhappy *Man!* These things would so break and confound my Spirit, that I could not tell what to do; I thought, at times, they would have broke my wits; and still, to aggravate my misery, that would run in my mind, *You know how that afterwards, when he would have inherited the blessing, he was rejected. Oh! none knows the terrors of these days but my self.*

155. After this, I came to consider of *Peter*'s sin, which he committed in denying his Master: And, indeed, this came nighest to mine, of any that I could find; for he had denied his Saviour, as I, after light and mercy received; yea, and that too, after warning given him. I also considered, that he did it both once and twice; and that, after time to consider betwixt. But though I put all these circumstances together, that, if possible, I might find help, yet I considered again, that his was but *a denial of his Master*, but mine was *a selling of my Saviour*. Wherefore I thought with my self, that I came nearer to *Judas*, than either to *David* or *Peter*.

156. Here again my torment would flame out and afflict me; yea, it would grind me, as it were, to powder, to consider the preservation of God towards others, while I fell into the snare; for in my thus considering of other men's sins, and comparing of them with mine own, I could evidently see, God preserved them, notwithstanding their wickedness, and would not let them, as he had let me, become a Son of Perdition.

157. But Oh, how did my Soul at this time prize the preservation that God did set about his people! Ah, how safely did I see them walk, whom God had hedged in! They were within his care, protection and special providence: Though they were full as bad as I, by nature; yet, because he loved them, he would not suffer them to fall without the range of mercy: But as for me, I was gone, I had done it; he would not preserve me, nor keep me; but suffered me, because I was a Reprobate, to fall as I had done. Now did those blessed places that speak of God's keeping his people, shine like the Sun before me, tho not to comfort me, yet to shew me the blessed state and heritage of those whom the Lord had blessed.

158. Now I saw, that as God had his hand in all provi-

dences and dispensations that overtook his Elect, so he had his hand in all the temptations that they had to sin against him; not to animate them unto wickedness, but to chuse their temptations and troubles for them; and also to leave them, for a time, to such sins only, as might not destroy, but humble them; as might not put them beyond, but lay them in the way of the renewing of his mercy. But Oh, what love, what care, what kindness and mercy did I now see, mixing it self with the most severe and dreadful of all God's ways to his people! He would let *David*, *Hezekiah*, *Solomon*, *Peter*, and others fall, but he would not let them fall into sin unpardonable, nor into Hell for sin. Oh! thought I, these be the men that God hath loved; these be the men that God, though he chastiseth them, keeps them in safety by him; and them whom he makes to abide under the shadow of the Almighty. But all these thoughts added sorrow, grief and horrour to me, as whatever I now thought on, it was killing to me. If I thought how God kept his own, that was killing to me; if I thought of how I was fallen my self, that was killing to me. As all things wrought together for the best, and to do good to them that were the called, according to his purpose; so I thought that all things wrought for my damage, and for my eternal overthrow.

159. Then again I began to compare my sin with the sin of *Judas*, that, if possible, I might find if mine differed from that which, in truth is unpardonable: And, Oh! thought I, if it should differ from it, though but the breadth of an hair, what an happy condition is my Soul in! And by considering, I found that *Judas* did his intentionally, but mine was against my prayer and strivings; besides, his was committed with much deliberation, but mine in a fearful hurry, on a suddain; all this while I was tossed to and fro, like the Locusts, and driven from trouble to sorrow; hearing always the sound of *Esau*'s fall in mine ears, and of the dreadful consequences thereof.

160. Yet this consideration about *Judas* his sin, was, for a while, some little relief unto me; for I saw I had not, as to the circumstances, transgressed so foully as he: But this was quickly gone again; for I thought with my self, there might be more ways than one to commit the unpardonable sin; also I thought that there might be degrees of that, as well as of

other transgressions; wherefore, for ought I yet could perceive, this iniquity of mine might be such as might never be passed by.

161. I was often now ashamed that I should be like such an ugly man as *Judas*: I thought also how loathsome I should be unto all the Saints at the Day of Judgment: Insomuch that now I could scarce see a good man, that I believed had a good Conscience, but I should feel my heart tremble at him, while I was in his presence. Oh! now I saw a glory in walking with God, and what a mercy it was to have a good Conscience before him.

162. I was much about this time tempted to content my self, by receiving some false Opinion; as that there should be no such thing as a Day of Judgment, that we should not rise again, and that sin was no such grievous thing; the Tempter suggesting thus, *For if these things should indeed be true, yet to believe otherwise, would yield you ease for the present. If you must perish, never torment your self so much before hand; drive the thoughts of damning out of your mind, by possessing your mind with some such conclusions, that* Atheists *and* Ranters *use to help themselves withal.*

163. But, Oh! when such thoughts have led through my heart, how, as it were, within a step, hath Death and Judgement been in my view! Me-thought the Judge stood at the door, I was as if it was come already; so that such things could have no entertainment. But methinks I see by this, that Satan will use any means, to keep the Soul from Christ; he loveth not an awakened frame of spirit; security, blindness, darkness and error, is the very kingdom and habitation of the wicked One.

164. I found it hard work now to pray to God, because despair was swallowing me up; I thought I was, as with a tempest, driven away from God; for always when I cried to God for mercy, this would come in, *'Tis too late; I am lost, God hath let me fall; not to my correction, but condemnation: My sin is unpardonable; and I know, concerning* Esau, *how that after he had sold his Birth-right, he would have received the Blessing, but was rejected.* About this time I did light on that dreadful story of that miserable mortal, *Francis Spira:* A book that was to my troubled spirit, as salt, when rubbed into a fresh wound; every sentence in that book, every groan of that man, with all the rest

of his actions in his dolours, as his tears, his prayers, his gnashing of teeth, his wringing of hands, his twining, and twisting, and languishing, and pining away under that mighty hand of God that was upon him, was as knives and daggers in my Soul; especially, that sentence of his was frightful to me, *Man knows the beginnings of sin, but who bounds the issues thereof?* Then would the former sentence, as the conclusion of all, fall like an hot thunder-bolt again upon my Conscience; *for you know how that afterwards, when he would have inherited the blessing, he was rejected; for he found no place of repentance, though he sought it carefully with tears.*

165. Then should I be struck into a very great trembling, insomuch that at some times I could, for whole days together, feel my very body, as well as my mind, to shake and totter under the sense of the dreadful judgment of God, that should fall on those that have sinned that most fearful and unpardonable sin. I felt also such a clogging and heat at my stomach, by reason of this my terror, that I was, especially at some times, as if my breast-bone would have split asunder; then I thought of that concerning *Judas, who by his falling head long, burst asunder, and all his bowels gushed out*, Act. 1.

166. I feared also that this was the mark that the Lord did set on *Cain*, even continual fear and trembling under the heavy load of guilt that he had charged on him for the blood of his brother *Abel.* Thus did I wind, and twine, and shrink under the burthen that was upon me; which burthen also did so oppress me, that I could neither stand, nor go, nor lie either at rest or quiet.

167. Yet that saying would sometimes come to mind, *He hath received gifts for the rebellious*, Psal. 68. 18. *The rebellious*, thought I; Why, surely they are such as once were under subjection to their Prince; even those who, after they have sworn subjection to his Government, have taken up Arms against him; and this, thought I, is my very condition; I once loved him, feared him, served him; but now I am a rebel, I have sold him, I have said, *Let him go, if he will*; but yet he has gifts for rebels, and then why not for me?

168. This sometimes I thought on, and should labour to take hold thereof, that some, though small refreshment might have been conceived by me; but in this also I missed of my

desire, I was driven with force beyond it, I was like a man going to execution, even by *that* place where he would fain creep in, and hide himself, but may not.

169. Again, after I had thus considered the sins of the *Saints* in particular, and found *mine* went beyond them, then I began to think thus with my self; Set case I should put *all theirs* together, and *mine alone* against them, might I not then find some encouragement? For if mine, though bigger than any one, yet should be but equal to all, then there is hopes; for that Blood that hath virtue enough in it to wash away all theirs, hath virtue enough in it to do away mine, though this one be full as big, if not bigger than all theirs. Here again, I should consider the sin of *David*, of *Solomon*, of *Manasseh*, of *Peter*, and the rest of the great offenders; and should also labour what I might, with fairness, to aggravate and heighten their sins by several circumstances.

170. I should think with my self, that *David* shed blood to cover his Adultery, and that by the Sword of the Children of *Ammon*; a work that could not be done, but by continuance, deliberate contrivance, which was a great aggravation to his sin. But then this would turn upon me; Ah! but these were but sins against the Law, from which there was a Jesus sent to save them; but yours is a sin against the Saviour, and who shall save you from that?

171. Then I thought on *Solomon*, and how he sinned in loving strange women, in falling away to their Idols, in building them Temples, in doing this after light, in his old age, after great mercy received: But the same Conclusion that cut me off in the former consideration, cut me off as to this; namely, that all those were but sins against the Law, for which God had provided a remedy; *but I had sold my Saviour*, and there now remained no more Sacrifice for sin.

172. I would then add to these men's sins, the sins of *Manasseh*; how that he built Altars for Idols in the House of the Lord; he also observed times, used inchantments, had to do with Wizzards, was a Wizzard, had his familiar Spirits, burnt his Children in the fire in Sacrifice to Devils, and made the Streets of *Jerusalem* run down with the blood of Innocents. These, thought I, are great sins, sins of a bloody colour; but yet it would turn again upon me, *They are none of them of the*

nature of yours; *you have parted with Jesus, you have sold your Saviour.*

173. This one consideration would always kill my heart, *My sin was point-blank against my Saviour*; and that too, at that heighth, that I had in my heart said of him, *Let him go if he will.* Oh! me-thoughts this sin was bigger than the sins of a Country, of a Kingdom, or of the whole World; *no* one pardonable, nor *all* of them together, was able to equal mine; mine out-went them every one.

174. Now I should feel my mind to flee from God, as from the face of a dreadful Judge; yet this was my torment, I could not escape his hand: (*It is a fearful thing to fall into the hands of the living God*, Heb. 10). But, blessed be his Grace, that Scripture, in these flying fits, would call, as running after me, *I have blotted out*, *as a thick cloud*, *thy transgressions*; *and as a cloud*, *thy sins: return unto me*, *for I have redeemed thee*, Isa. 44. 22. This, I say, would come in upon my mind, when I was fleeing from the face of God; for I did flee from his face, that is, my mind and spirit fled before him; by reason of his highness, I could not endure: Then would the text cry, *Return unto me*; it would cry aloud, with a very great voice, *Return unto me*, *for I have redeemed thee.* Indeed, this would make me make a little stop, and as it were look over my shoulder, behind me, to see if I could discern that the God of Grace did follow me with a pardon in his hand; but I could no sooner do that, but all would be clouded and darkned again by that sentence, *For you know how that afterwards*, *when he would have inherited the blessing*, *he found no place of repentance*, *though he sought it carefully with tears.* Wherefore I could not return, but fled, though at some times it cried, *Return*, *return*, as if it did hollow after me: But I feared to close in therewith, lest it should not come from God; for that other, as I said, was still sounding in my Conscience, *For you know how that afterwards*, *when he would have inherited the blessing*, *he was rejected*, &c.

175. Once, as I was walking to and fro in a good man's shop, bemoaning of my self in my sad and doleful state, afflicting my self with self-abhorrence for this wicked and ungodly thought; lamenting also this hard hap of mine, for that I should commit so great a sin, greatly fearing I should not be pardoned; praying also in my heart, that if this sin of mine did

differ from that against the Holy Ghost, the Lord would shew it me: And being now ready to sink with fear, suddainly there was as if there had rushed in at the window, the noise of wind upon me, but very pleasant, and as if I had heard a voice speaking, *Didst ever refuse to be justified by the Blood of Christ?* And withal, my whole life of profession past, was in a moment opened to me, wherein I was made to see, that designedly I had not: So my heart answered groaningly, *No.* Then fell with power that Word of God upon me, *See that ye refuse not him that speaketh*, Heb. 12. 25. This made a strange seisure upon my spirit, it brought light with it, and commanded a silence in my heart of all those tumultuous thoughts that before did use, like masterless hell-hounds, to roar and bellow, and make an hideous noise within me. It shewed me also, that Jesus Christ had yet a word of Grace and Mercy for me, that he had not, as I had feared, quite forsaken and cast off my Soul; yea, this was a kind of a chide for my proneness to desparation; a kind of threatning of me, if I did not, notwithstanding my sins, and the heinousness of them, venture my Salvation upon the Son of God. But as to my determining about this strange dispensation, what it was, I know not; or from whence it came, I know not; I have not yet, in twenty years time, been able to make a judgment of it: *I thought then what here I should be loth to speak.* But verily, that suddain rushing wind was as if an Angel had come upon me, but both it and the Salutation I will leave until the Day of Judgment; only this I say, it commanded a great calm in my Soul; it persuaded me there might be hope; it showed me, as I thought, what the sin unpardonable was, and that my Soul had yet the blessed privilege to flee to Jesus Christ for Mercy. But, I say, concerning this dispensation, I know not what yet to say unto it; which was, also, in truth, the cause that, at first, I did not speak of it in the Book. I do now, also, leave it to be thought on by men of sound Judgment. I lay not the stress of my Salvation thereupon, but upon the Lord Jesus, in the Promise; yet, seeing I am here unfolding of my secret things, I thought it might not be altogether in-expedient to let this also show it self, though I cannot *now* relate the matter as there I did experience it. This lasted, in the savour of it, for about three or four days, and then I began to mistrust and to despair again.

176. Wherefore, still my life hung in doubt before me, *not knowing which way I should tip*; only this I found my Soul's desire, even to cast itself at the foot of Grace, by prayer and supplication. But, oh! 'twas hard for me now to bear the face to pray to this Christ for mercy, against whom I had thus most vilely sinned: 'Twas hard work, I say, to offer to look him in the face against whom I had so vilely sinned; and indeed, I have found it as difficult to come to God by prayer, after backsliding from him, as to do any other thing. Oh, the shame that did *now* attend me! especially when I thought I am *now* a-going to pray to him for mercy that I had so lightly esteemed but a while before! I was ashamed; yea, even confounded, because this villainy had been committed by me; but I saw there was but one way with me, I must go to him and humble my self unto him, and beg that he, of his wonderful mercy, would show pity to me, and have mercy upon my wretched sinful Soul.

177. Which, when the Tempter perceived, he strongly suggested to me, *That I ought not to pray to God*; *for prayer was not for any in my case, neither could it do me good, because I had rejected the Mediator, by whom all prayers came with acceptance to God the Father*; *and without whom no prayer could come into his presence: Wherefore, now to pray is but to add sin to sin*; *yea, now to pray, seeing God has cast you off, is the next way to anger and offend him more than you ever did before.*

178. *For God*, saith he, *hath been weary of you for these several years already, because you are none of his*; *your bawlings in his ears hath been no pleasant voice to him, and, therefore, he let you sin this sin, that you might be quite cut off, and will you pray still?* This the Devil urged, and set forth that, in *Numbers*, when *Moses* said to the children of *Israel*, *That because they would not go up to possess the land when God would have them, therefore, for ever after he did bar them out from thence, though they prayed they might with tears*, Num. 14. 36, 37, &c.

179. As 'tis said in another place, Ex. 21. 14: *The man that sins presumptuously shall be taken from God's Altar that he may die:* Even as *Joab* was by King *Solomon*, when he thought to find shelter there, 1 *Kings* 2. 28, &c. These places did pinch me very sore; yet, my case being desperate, I thought

with myself I can but die; and if it must be so, it shall once be said, *That such an one died at the foot of Christ in prayer.* This I did, but with great difficulty, God doth know; and that because, together with this, still that saying about *Esau* would be set at my heart, even like a flaming Sword to keep the way of the Tree of Life, lest I should take thereof, and live. Oh! Who knows how hard a thing I found it, to come to God in prayer?

180. I did also desire the prayers of the people of God for me, but I feared that God would give them no heart to do it; yea, I trembled in my soul to think that some or other of them would shortly tell me, that God had said those words to them that he once did say to the Prophet concerning the Children of Israel, *Pray not thou for this people, for I have rejected them,* Jer. 11. 14. So, *pray not for him, for I have rejected him.* Yea, I thought that he had whispered this to some of them already, only they durst not tell me so, neither durst I ask them of it, for fear, if it should be so, it would make me quite besides myself: *Man knows the beginning of sin,* (said Spira,) *but who bounds the issues thereof?*

181. About this time I took an opportunity to break my mind to an ancient Christian, and told him all my case: I told him also, that I was afraid that I had sinned the sin against the Holy Ghost; and he told me, *He thought so too.* Here, therefore, I had but cold comfort; but, talking a little more with him, I found him, though a good man, a stranger to much combat with the Devil. Wherefore, I went to God again, as well as I could, for mercy still.

182. Now also did the Tempter begin to mock me in my misery, saying, *That seeing I had thus parted with the Lord Jesus, and provoked him to displeasure, who would have stood between my Soul and the flame of devouring fire, there was now but one way; and that was,* To pray that God the Father would be the Mediator betwixt his Son and me, *that we might be reconciled again, and that I might have that blessed benefit in him, that his blessed Saints enjoyed.*

183. Then did that Scripture sieze upon my soul, *He is of one mind, and who can turn him?* Oh! I saw 'twas as easie to perswade him to make a new World, a new Covenant, or new Bible, besides that we have already, as to pray for such a thing.

This was to persuade him that what he had done already was meer folly, and to perswade with him to alter; yea, to disannul the whole way of Salvation: And then would that saying rent my soul asunder, *Neither is there salvation in any other; for there is none other name under heaven, given amongst men, whereby we must be saved*, Acts 4. 12.

184. Now, the most free, and full, and gracious words of the Gospel were the greatest torment to me; yea, nothing so afflicted me as the thoughts of Jesus Christ. The remembrance of a Saviour, because I had cast him off, brought forth the villany of my sin, and my loss by it, to mind; nothing did twinge my Conscience like this: Every time that I thought of the Lord Jesus, of his Grace, Love, Goodness, Kindness, Gentleness, Meekness, Death, Blood, Promises and blessed Exhortations, Comforts and Consolations, it went to my Soul like a Sword; for still, unto these my considerations of the Lord Jesus, these thoughts would make place for themselves in my heart: *Ay, this is the Jesus, the loving Saviour, the Son of God, whom you have parted with, whom you have slighted, despised, and abused. This is the* only *Saviour, the* only *Redeemer, the* only *one that could so love sinners as to wash them from their sins in his own most precious Blood: But you have no part nor lot in this Jesus, you have put him from you, you have said in your heart,* Let him go if he will. *Now therefore, you are severed from him; you have severed your self from him. Behold, then, his Goodness, but your self to be no partaker of it.* Oh, thought I, what have I lost! What have I parted with! What have dis-inherited my poor Soul of! Oh! 'tis sad to be destroyed by the Grace and Mercy of God; to have the Lamb, the Saviour, turn Lion and Destroyer, *Rev.* 6. I also trembled, as I have said, at the sight of the Saints of God; especially at those that greatly loved him, and that made it their business to walk continually with him in this World; for they did, both in their words, their carriages, and all their expressions of tenderness and fear to sin against their precious Saviour, condemn, lay guilt upon, and also add continual affliction and shame unto my soul, *The dread of them was upon me, and I trembled at God's* Samuels, 1 *Sam.* 16. 4.

185. Now also the Tempter began a-fresh to mock my Soul another way, saying *That Christ, indeed, did pity my case,*

and was sorry for my loss; but forasmuch as I had sinned and transgressed, as I had done, he could by no means help me, nor save me from what I feared; for my sin was not of the nature of theirs, for whom he bled and died; neither was it counted with those that were laid to his charge, when he hanged on the Tree: Therefore, unless he should come down from Heaven, and die a-new for this sin, though indeed he did greatly pity me, yet I could have no benefit of him. These things may seem ridiculous to others, even as ridiculous as they were in themselves, but to me they were most tormenting cogitations; every of them augmented my misery, that Jesus Christ should have so much love as to pity me, when yet he could not help me; nor did I think that the reason why he could not help me, was, because his Merits were weak, or his Grace and Salvation spent on others already, but because his faithfulness to his threatning would not let him extend his mercy to me. Besides, I thought, as I have already hinted, that my sin was not within the bounds of that pardon, that was wrapped up in a promise; and if not, then I knew assuredly, that it was more easie for Heaven and Earth to pass away, than for me to have Eternal Life. So that the ground of all these fears of mine did arise from a stedfast belief that I had of the stability of the holy Word of God, and also from my being misinformed of the nature of my sin.

186. But, Oh, how this would add to my affliction, to conceit that I should be guilty of such a sin, for which he did not die. These thoughts would so confound me, and imprison me, and tie me up from faith, that I knew not what to do: But, Oh, thought I, that he would come down again! Oh, that the work of Man's Redemption was yet to be done by Christ! How would I pray him, and intreat him to count and reckon this sin amongst the rest for which he died? But this Scripture would strike me down, as dead; *Christ being raised from the dead, dieth no more: death hath no more dominion over him*, Rom. 6. 9.

187. Thus, by the strange and unusual assaults of the Tempter, was my Soul like a broken Vessel, driven as with the Winds, and tossed sometimes head-long into despair; sometimes upon the Covenant of Works, and sometimes to wish that the new Covenant, and the conditions thereof, might, so far forth as I thought my self concerned, be turned another way, and

changed. *But in all these, I was but as those that jostle against the Rocks; more broken, scattered and rent.* Oh, the unthought of imaginations, frights, fears and terrors, that are affected by a thorough application of guilt, yielding to desperation! *This is the man that hath his dwelling among the tombs, with the dead; that is always crying out, and cutting himself with stones*, Mar. 5. 1, 2, 3. But, I say, all in vain; Desparation will not comfort him, the old Covenant will not save him: Nay, Heaven and Earth shall pass away, before one jot or tittle of the Word and Law of Grace shall fail, or be removed. This I saw, this I felt, and under this I groaned; yet this advantage I got thereby, namely, a further confirmation of the certainty of the way of Salvation, and that the Scriptures were the Word of God. Oh! I cannot now express what then I saw and felt of the steadiness of Jesus Christ, the Rock of Man's Salvation: What was done, could not be undone, added to, nor altered. I saw, indeed, that sin might drive the Soul beyond Christ, even the sin which is unpardonable; but woe to him that was so driven, for the Word would shut him out.

188. Thus was I always sinking, whatever I did think, or do. So one day I walked to a neighbouring Town, and sate down upon a Settle in the Street, and fell into a very deep pause about the most fearful state my sin had brought me to; and after long musing, I lifted up my head, but me thought I saw, as if the Sun that shineth in the Heavens did grudge to give light; and as if the very stones in the Street, and tiles upon the houses, did bend themselves against me; me-thought that they all combined together, to banish me out of the World; I was abhorred of them, and unfit to dwell among them, or be partaker of their benefits, because I had sinned against the Saviour. Oh, how happy now was every creature, over I was! For they stood fast, and kept their station, but I was gone and lost.

189. Then breaking out in the bitterness of my Soul, I said to my self, with a grievous sigh, *How can God comfort such a wretch as I?* I had no sooner said it, but this returned upon me, as an echo doth answer a voice, *This sin is not unto death.* At which I was as if I had been raised out of a Grave, and cried out again, *Lord, how couldst thou find out such a word as this?* For I was filled with admiration at the fitness, and also at the

unexpectedness of the sentence. The fitness of the word, the rightness of the timing of it, the power, and sweetness, and light, and glory that came with it also, was marvellous to me to find. I was now, for the time, out of doubt, as to that about which I so much was in doubt before: My fears before *were*, that my sin was not pardonable, and so that I had no right to pray, to repent, *&c.* or that if I did, it would be of no advantage, or profit to me. But now, thought I, if *this sin* is not unto death, then it is pardonable; therefore from this I have encouragement to come to God by Christ for mercy; to consider the promise of forgiveness, as that which stands with open arms to receive me, as well as others. This therefore was a great easement to my mind; to wit, that my sin was pardonable, that it was not the sin unto death, (1 *Joh.* 5. 16, 17.) None but those that know what my trouble (by their own experience) was, can tell what relief came to my Soul by this consideration: It was a release to me from my former bonds, and a shelter from the former storm: I seemed now to stand upon the same ground with other sinners, and to have as good right to the Word and Prayer as any of they.

190. Now, I say, I was in hopes that my sin was not unpardonable, but that there might be hopes for me to obtain forgiveness. But, Oh, how Satan now did lay about him, for to bring me down again! But he could by no means do it, neither this day, nor the most part of the next; for this good sentence stood like a mill-post at my back: Yet towards the evening of the next day, I felt this word begin to leave me, and to withdraw its supportation from me; and so I returned to my old fears again, but with a great deal of grudging and peevishness, for I feared the sorrow of despair; nor could my faith now longer retain this word.

191. But the next day at evening, being under many fears, I went to seek the Lord; and as I prayed, I cried, and my Soul cried to him in these words, with strong cries; *O Lord, I beseech thee, shew me, that thou hast loved me with an everlasting love*, Jer. 31. 3. I had no sooner said it, but with sweetness this returned upon me, as an echo, or sounding again, *I have loved thee with an everlasting love.* Now I went to bed in quiet; also when I awaked the next morning, it was fresh upon my Soul; and I believed it.

192. But yet the Tempter left me not, for it could not be so little as an hundred times, that he, that day, did labour to break my peace. Oh, the combats and conflicts that I did then meet with, as I strove to hold by this word! That of *Esau* would fly in my face like Lightning: I should be sometimes up and down twenty times in an hour; yet God did bear me up, and keep my heart upon this word; from which I had also, for several days together, very much sweetness, and comfortable hopes of pardon: For thus it was made out unto me, *I loved thee whilst thou wast committing this sin, I loved thee before, I love thee still, and I will love thee for ever.*

193. Yet I saw my sin most barbarous, and a filthy crime, and could not but conclude, and that with great shame and astonishment, that I had horridly abused the holy Son of God; wherefore I felt my soul greatly to love and pity him, and my bowels to yearn towards him; for I saw he was still my friend, and did reward me good for evil; yea, the love and affection that then did burn within, to my Lord and Saviour Jesus Christ, did work, at this time, such a strong and hot desire of revengement upon my self, for the abuse I had done unto him, that, to speak as I then thought, had I had a thousand gallons of blood within my veins, I could freely then have spilt it all at the command and feet of this my Lord and Saviour.

194. And as I was thus in musing, and in my studies, considering how to love the Lord, and to express my love to him, that saying came in upon me, *If thou, Lord, shouldst mark iniquity, O Lord, who should stand? but there is forgiveness with thee, that thou mayest be feared*, Psal. 130. 4. These were good words to me, especially the latter part thereof; to wit, that there is forgiveness with the Lord, that he might be feared; that is, as then I understood it, that he might be loved, and had in reverence; for it was thus made out to me, *That the great God did set so high an esteem upon the love of his poor Creatures, that rather than he would go without their love, he would pardon their transgressions.*

195. And now was that word fulfilled on me, and I was also refreshed by it; *Then shall they be ashamed and confounded, and never open their mouth any more because of their shame, when I am pacified towards them for all that they have done, saith the Lord God*, Ezek. 16. 36. Thus was my Soul at this time (and,

as I then did think, for ever) set at liberty from being afflicted with my former guilt and amazement.

196. But before many weeks were over, I began to despond again, fearing lest, notwithstanding all that I had enjoyed, yet I might be deceived, and destroyed at the last; for this consideration came strong into my mind, *That whatever comfort and peace I thought I might have from the word of the promise of Life, yet unless there could be found in my refreshment a concurrence and agreement in the Scriptures, let me think what I will thereof, and hold it never so fast, I should find no such thing at the end*; *for the Scriptures cannot be broken*, Joh. 10. 35.

197. Now began my heart again to ake, and fear I might meet with disappointment at the last. Wherefore I began with all seriousness to examine my former comfort, and to consider whether one that had sinned as I had done, might with confidence trust upon the faithfulness of God, laid down in those words by which I had been comforted, and on which I had leaned my self: But now were brought those sayings to my mind, *For it is impossible for those who were once enlightned, and have tasted the heavenly Gift, and were made partakers of the Holy Ghost, and have tasted the good Word of God, and the Powers of the World to come, if they shall fall away, to renew them again unto Repentance*, Heb. 6. *For if we sin wilfully, after we have received the knowledge of the truth, there remains no more sacrifice for sin, but a certain fearful looking for of Judgment and fiery indignation, which shall devour the adversaries*, Heb. 10. *Even as* Esau, *who for one morsel of meat, sold his Birth-right: For you know how that afterwards, when he would have inherited the blessing, he was rejected*; *for he found no place of repentance, though he sought it carefully with tears*, Heb. 12.

198. Now was the Word of the Gospel forced from my Soul; so that no promise or encouragement was to be found in the Bible for me: And now would that saying work upon my spirit, to afflict me, *Rejoice not, O Israel, for joy, as other people*, Hos. 9. 1. For I saw indeed, there was cause of rejoicing for those that held to Jesus; but as for me, I had cut my self off by my transgressions, and left my self neither foot-hold, nor hand-hold, amongst all the stays and props in the precious Word of Life.

199. And truly, I did now feel my self to sink into a gulf,

as an house whose foundation is destroyed. I did liken my self, in this condition, unto the case of some child that was fallen into a Mill-pit; who, though it could make some shift to scrabble and sprawl in the water, yet because it could find neither hold for hand nor foot, therefore at last it must die in that condition. So soon as this fresh assault had fastned on my Soul, that Scripture came into my heart, *This for many days*, Dan. 10. 14. And, indeed, I found it was so; for I could not be delivered, nor brought to peace again, until well-nigh two years and an half were compleatly finished. Wherefore these words, though in themselves, they tended to discouragement, yet to me, who feared this condition would be eternal, they were at some times as an help and refreshment to me.

200. For, thought I, *many days* are not for ever, *many days* will have an end; therefore seeing I was to be afflicted, not a few, but *many days*, yet I was glad it was but *for many days.* Thus, I say, I could re-call my self sometimes, and give my self an help; for as soon as ever the words came into my mind, at first, I knew my trouble would be long; yet this would be but sometimes, for I could not always think on this, nor ever be helped by it, though I did.

201. Now while these Scriptures lay before me, and laid sin anew at my door, that saying in *Luk.* 18. 1. with others, did encourage me to prayer: Then the Tempter again laid at me very sore; suggesting, *That neither the Mercy of God, nor yet the Blood of Christ, did at all concern me, nor could they help me for my sin; therefore it was but in vain to pray.* Yet, thought I, *I will pray: But*, said the Tempter, *your sin is unpardonable. Well*, said I, *I will pray. 'Tis to no boot*, said he. *Yet*, said I, *I will pray.* So I went to prayer to God; and while I was at prayer, I uttered words to this effect, *Lord, Satan tells me, that neither thy Mercy, nor Christ's Blood is sufficient to save my Soul: Lord, shall I honour thee most, by believing thou wilt and canst; or him, by believing thou neither wilt nor canst? Lord, I would fain honour thee, by believing thou wilt and canst.*

202. And as I was thus before the Lord, that Scripture fastned on my heart, [*O man, great is thy faith*,] Mat. 15. 28. even as if one had clapped me on the back, as I was on my knees before God: Yet I was not able to believe this, that this was a prayer of faith, till almost six months after; for I could

not think that I had faith, or that there should be a word for me to act faith on; therefore I should still be, as sticking in the jaws of desperation, and went mourning up and down, in a sad condition.

203. There was nothing now that I longed for more, than to be put out of doubt, as to this thing in question, and as I was vehemently desiring to know if there was indeed hopes for me, these words came rolling into my mind; *Will the Lord cast off for ever? and will he be favourable no more? Is his mercy clean gone for ever? doth his promise fail for evermore? Hath God forgotten to be gracious? hath he in anger shut up his tender mercies?* Psal. 77. 7, 8, 9. And all the while they run in my mind, me-thought, I had this still as the answer, *'Tis a question whether he hath, or no; it may be, he hath not.* Yea, the interrogatory seemed to me, to carry in it a sure affirmation, that indeed he had not, nor would so cast off, but would be favourable; that his promise doth not fail, and that he had not forgotten to be gracious, nor would in anger shut up tender mercy: Something also there was upon my heart at the same time, which I cannot now call to mind; which, with this Text, did sweeten my heart, and make me conclude, that his mercy might not be quite gone, nor clean gone for ever.

204. At another time, I remembred, I was again much under this Question, *Whether the Blood of Christ was sufficient to save my Soul?* In which doubt I continued, from morning, till about seven or eight at night; and at last, when I was, as it were, quite worn out with fear, lest it should not lay hold on me, these words did sound suddainly within my heart, *He is able:* But me-thought, this word *Able*, was spoke loud unto me; it shewed a *great* word, it seemed to be writ in *great* letters, and gave such a justle to my fear and doubt (I mean, for the time it tarried with me, which was about a day) as I never had from that, all my life, either before or after, *Heb.* 7. 25.

205. But one morning when I was again at prayer, and trembling under the fear of this, *That no Word of God could help me*, that piece of a sentence darted in upon me, *My Grace is sufficient.* At this, me-thought, I felt some stay, as if there might be hopes. But, oh, how good a thing it is, for God to send his Word! for, about a fortnight before, I was looking on

this very place, and then I thought it could not come near my Soul with comfort, therefore I threw down my Book in a pet: Then I thought it was not large enough for me; no, not large enough; but now it was as if it had Arms of Grace so wide, that it could not only inclose me, but many more such as I besides.

206. By these words I was sustained, yet not without exceeding conflicts, for the space of seven or eight weeks; for my peace would be in it, and out, sometimes twenty times a day; comfort now, and trouble presently; peace now, and before I could go a furlong, as full of fear and guilt as ever heart could hold: And this was not only now and then, but my whole seven weeks experience; for this about *the sufficiency of Grace*, and *that* of *Esau*'s parting with his Birth-right, would be like a pair of Scales within my mind; sometimes one end would be uppermost, and sometimes again the other; according to which, would be my peace or trouble.

207. Therefore I still did pray to God, that he would come in with this Scripture more fully on my heart; to wit, that he would help me to apply the whole sentence, for as yet I could not: That he gave, that I gathered; but further I could not go, for as yet it only helped me to hope there might be mercy for me; *My Grace is sufficient:* And though it came no further, it answered my former question; to wit, that there was hope; yet, because *for thee*, was left out, I was not contented, but prayed to God for that also. Wherefore, one day, as I was in a Meeting of God's People, full of sadness and terrour, for my fears again were strong upon me; and, as I was now thinking, my Soul was never the better, but my case most sad and fearful, these words did with great power suddainly break in upon me; *My Grace is sufficient for thee, my Grace is sufficient for thee, my Grace is sufficient for thee*, three times together: And, Oh! me-thought that every word was a mighty word unto me; as *my*, and *Grace*, and *sufficient*, and *for thee*; they were then, and sometimes are still far bigger than others be.

208. At which time my understanding was so enlightned, that I was as though I had seen the Lord Jesus look down from Heaven, through the Tiles, upon me, and direct these words unto me. This sent me mourning home, it broke my heart,

and filled me full of joy, and laid me low as the dust; only it stayed not long with me, I mean, in this glory, and refreshing comfort; yet it continued with me for several weeks, and did encourage me to hope: But so soon as that powerful operation of it was taken off my heart, that other, about *Esau*, returned upon me as before; so my Soul did hang as in a pair of Scales again; sometimes up, and sometimes down; now in peace, and anon again in terrour.

209. Thus I went on for many weeks, sometimes comforted, and sometimes tormented; and especially at some times my torment would be very sore, for all those Scriptures forenamed, in the *Hebrews*, would be set before me, as the only Sentences that would keep me out of Heaven. Then again I should begin to repent that ever that thought went thorough me; I should also think thus with my self, *Why, how many Scriptures are there against me? There are but three or four: And cannot God miss them, and save me for all them?* Sometimes again I should think, *Oh, if it were not for these three or four words, now how might I be comforted!* And I could hardly forbear, at some times, but to wish them out of the Book.

210. Then me-thought I should see as if both *Peter*, and *Paul*, and *John*, and all the Writers, did look with scorn upon me, and hold me in derision; and as if they said unto me, *All our words are truth, one of as much force as another: It is not we that have cut you off, but you have cast away your self: There is none of our sentences that you must take hold upon, but these, and such as these: It is impossible; there remains no more sacrifice for sin*, Heb. 6. *And it had been better for them, not to have known the Will of God, than after they have known it, to turn from the holy commandment delivered unto them*, Heb. 10. *For the Scriptures cannot be broken*, 2 Pet. 2. 21.

211. These, as the Elders of the City of Refuge, I saw, were to be the Judges both of my case and me, while I stood, with the Avenger of blood at my heels, trembling at their Gate for deliverance; also with a thousand fears and mistrusts, I doubted that they would shut me out for ever, *Josh.* 20. 3, 4.

212. Thus I was confounded, not knowing what to do, nor how to be satisfied in this question, *Whether the Scriptures could agree in the salvation of my Soul?* I quaked at the

Apostles; I knew their words were true, and that they must stand for ever.

213. And I remember one day, as I was in divers frames of spirit, and considering that these frames were still according to the nature of the several Scriptures that came in upon my mind; if this of Grace, then was I quiet; but if that of *Esau*, then tormented; *Lord*, thought I, *if both these Scriptures would meet in my heart at once, I wonder which of them would get the better of me.* So methought I had a longing mind that they might come both together upon me; yea, I desired of God they might.

214. Well, about two or three days after, so they did indeed; they bolted both upon me at a time, and did work and struggle strangely in me for a while; at last, that about *Esau's* birthright began to wax weak, and withdraw, and vanish; and this about the sufficiency of Grace prevailed with peace and joy. And as I was in a muse about this thing, that Scripture came home upon me, *Mercy rejoiceth against judgment*, James 2. 13.

215. This was a wonderment to me; yet truly I am apt to think it was of God; for the Word of the Law and wrath must give place to the Word of Life and Grace; because, though the Word of Condemnation be glorious, yet the Word of Life and Salvation doth far exceed in glory, 2 *Cor.* 3. 8, 9, 10, 11, *Mar.* 9. 5, 6, 7, *John* 6. 37. Also, that *Moses* and *Elias* must both vanish, and leave Christ and his Saints alone.

216. This Scripture did also most sweetly visit my soul; *And him that cometh to me I will in no wise cast out*, John 6. 37. Oh the comfort that I have had from this word, *in no wise!* As who should say, *by no means, for no thing, whatever he hath done.* But Satan would greatly labour to pull this promise from me, telling of me *That Christ did not mean me, and such as I; but sinners of a lower rank, that had not done as I had done.* But I should answer him again, *Satan, here is in these words no such exception; but, him that comes; him, any him; him that cometh to me I will in no wise cast out.* And this I well remember still, that of all the slights that Satan used to take this scripture from me, yet he never did so much as put this Question, *But do you come aright?* And I have thought, the reason was, because he thought I knew full well what coming a-right was; for I saw

that to come a-right was to come as I was, a vile and ungodly sinner, and to cast my self at the feet of Mercy, condemning my self for sin. If ever Satan and I did strive for any word of God in all my life, it was for this good word of Christ; he at one end and I at the other. Oh, what work did we make! It was for this in John, I say, that we did so tug and strive: He pulled and I pulled; but, God be praised, I got the better of him, I got some sweetness from it.

217. But, notwithstanding all these helps, and blessed words of Grace, yet that of *Esau's* selling of his Birth-right would still at times distress my Conscience; for though I had been most sweetly comforted, and that but just before, yet when that came into my mind, 'twould make me fear again, I could not be quite rid thereof, 'twould every day be with me: wherefore now I went another way to work, even to consider the nature of this blasphemous thought; I mean, if I should take the words at the largest, and give them their own natural force and scope, even every word therein. So when I had thus considered, I found that if they were fairly taken, they would amount to this, *That I had freely left the Lord Jesus Christ to his choice, whether he would be my Saviour or no*; for the wicked words were these, *Let him go if he will.* Then that Scripture gave me hope, *I will never leave thee nor forsake thee*, Heb. 13. 5. *O Lord*, said I, *but I have left thee.* Then it answered again, *But I will not leave thee.* For this I thank God also.

218. Yet I was grievous afraid he should, and found it exceeding hard to trust him, seeing I had so offended him. I could have been exceeding glad that this thought had never befallen, for then I thought I could, with more ease and freedom abundance, have lean'd on his Grace. I see it was with me, as it was with *Joseph's* Brethren; the guilt of their own wickedness did often fill them with fears that their Brother would at last despise them, *Gen.* 50. 15, 16 *&c.*

219. Yet above all the Scriptures that I yet did meet with, that in *Josh.* 20 was the greatest comfort to me, which speaks of the slayer that was to flee for refuge: *And if the avenger of blood pursue the slayer, then*, saith *Moses*, *they that are the elders of the city of refuge shall not deliver him into his hand, because he smote his neighbour unwittingly, and hated him not afore-time.* Oh, blessed be God for this word: I was

convinced that I was the Slayer; and that the Avenger of Blood pursued me, that I felt with great terrour; only now it remained that I inquire whether I have right to enter the City of Refuge: So I found, that he must not, *who lay in wait to shed blood:* It was not the wilful *Murtherer*, but he who *unwittingly* did it, he who did it unawares shed blood; not out of spight, or grudge, or malice, he that shed it unwittingly; even he who did not *hate his Neighbour before.* Wherefore,

220. I thought verily I was the man that must enter, because I had smitten my Neighbour *unwittingly, and hated him not afore-time:* I hated him not afore-time; no, I prayed unto him, was tender of sinning against him; yea, and against this wicked temptation I had strove for a twelvemonth before; yea, and also when it did pass through my heart, it did in spight of my Teeth: wherefore I thought I had right to enter this City, and the Elders, which are the Apostles, were not to deliver me up. This therefore was great Comfort to me, and did give me much ground of hope.

221. Yet being very critical, for my smart had made me that I knew not what ground was sure enough to bear me, I had one question that my Soul did much desire to be resolved about; and that was, *Whether it be possible for any Soul that hath indeed sinned the unpardonable sin, yet after that to receive, though but the least true spiritual comfort from God through Christ?* The which after I had much considered, I found the answer was, No, they could not; and that for these Reasons:

222. First, Because those that have sinned that sin, they are debarred a share in the Blood of Christ, and being shut out of that, they must needs be void of the least ground of hope, and so of spiritual comfort, *for to such there remains no more sacrifice for sin*, Heb. 10. 26, 27. Secondly, Because they are denyed a share in the Promise of Life: they shall never be forgiven, neither in this World, nor in that which is to come, *Mat.* 12. 31. Thirdly, The Son of God excludes them also from a share in his blessed Intercession, being for ever ashamed to own them both before his holy Father, and the blessed Angels in Heaven, *Mark* 8.

223. When I had with much deliberation considered of this matter, and could not but conclude that the Lord had comforted me, and that too after this my wicked sin; then methought

I durst venture to come nigh unto those most fearful and terrible Scriptures, with which all this while I had been so greatly affrighted, and on which indeed before I durst scarce cast mine Eye, (yea, had much ado an hundred times to forbear wishing of them out of the Bible, for I thought they would destroy me) but now, I say, I began to take some measure of incouragement, to come close to them, to read them, and consider them, and to weigh their scope and tendency.

224. The which when I began to do, I found their visage changed; for they looked not so grimly as before I thought they did: And first I came to the sixth of the *Hebrews*, yet trembling for fear it should strike me; which when I had considered, I found that the falling there intended, was a falling *quite away*; That is, as I conceived, a falling from, and an absolute denying of the Gospel of remission of sins by Christ; for, from them the Apostle begins his Argument, *vers.* 1, 2, 3. Secondly, I found that this falling away, must be openly, even in the view of the World, even so as *to put Christ to an open shame.* Thirdly, I found that those he there intended, were for ever shut up of God both in blindness, hardness, and impenitency: *It is impossible they should be renewed again unto Repentance.* By all these particulars, I found, to Gods everlasting Praise, my sin was not the sin in this place intended.

First, I confessed I was fallen, but not fallen away, that is from the profession of Faith in Jesus unto eternal Life.

Secondly, I confessed that I had put Jesus Christ to *shame* by my sin, but not to open *shame.* I did not deny him before men, nor condemn him as a fruitless one before the World.

Thirdly, Nor did I find that God had shut me up, or denyed me to come (though I found it hard work indeed to come) to him by sorrow and repentance: blessed be God for unsearchable Grace.

225. Then I considered that in the tenth of the *Hebrews*; and found that the *wilful sin* there mentioned, is not every wilful sin, but that sin which doth throw off Christ, and then his Commandments too. Secondly, That must also be done openly, before two or three Witnesses, to answer that of the Law, *vers.* 28. Thirdly, This sin cannot be committed but with great despite done to the Spirit of Grace; despising both

the disswasions from that sin, and the perswasions to the contrary. But the Lord knows, though this my sin was devilish, yet it did not amount to these.

226. And as touching that in the twelfth of the *Hebrews*, about *Esau's* selling his Birth-right, though this was that which killed me, and stood like a spear against me; yet now I did consider, First, That his was not a hasty thought against the continual labour of his Mind; but a thought consented to, and put in practice likewise, and that too after some deliberation: *Gen.* 25. Secondly, It was a publick and open action, even before his Brother, if not before many more; this made his sin of a far more heinous nature then otherwise it would have been. Thirdly, He continued to slight his Birth-right: *He did eat and drink, and went his way; thus* Esau *despised his Birth-right*: yea, twenty years after he was found to despise it still. And Esau *said, I have enough, my Brother, keep that thou hast to thy self*, Gen. 33. 9.

227. Now as touching this, *That* Esau *sought a place of Repentance*: thus I thought, First, This was not for the *Birth-right*, but *the blessing*; this is clear from the Apostle, and is distinguished by *Esau* himself, *he hath taken away my Birth-right*, (that is, formerly) *and now he hath taken away my blessing also*, Gen. 27. 36. Secondly, Now this being thus considered, I came again to the Apostle, to see what might be the mind of God, in a New-Testament stile and sense concerning *Esau*'s sin; and so far as I could conceive, this was the mind of God, *That the Birth-right* signified *Regeneration*, and the *Blessing* the *Eternal Inheritance*; for so the Apostle seems to hint, *Lest there be any prophane Person, as* Esau, *who for one morsel of meat sold his Birth-right*; as if he should say, Lest there be any Person amongst you that shall cast off all those blessed beginnings of God that at present are upon him, in order to a new Birth, lest they become as *Esau*, even be rejected *afterwards*, when they would inherit the Blessing.

228. For many there are, who in the day of Grace and Mercy, despise those things which are indeed the Birth-right to Heaven, who yet when the deciding day appears, will cry as loud as *Esau*, *Lord, Lord, open to us*, but then, *as Isaac* would not repent, no more will God the Father, but will say, *I have blessed these, yea, and they shall be blessed*; but as for you,

Depart, you are workers of Iniquity, Gen. 27. 32. Luke 13. 25, 26, 27.

229. When I had thus considered these Scriptures, and found that thus to understand them, was not against, but according to other Scriptures; this still added further to my encouragement and comfort, and also gave a great blow to that Objection, to wit, *That the Scriptures could not agree in the Salvation of my Soul.* And now remained only the hinder part of the Tempest, for the thunder was gone beyond me, only some drops did still remain, that now and then would fall upon me; but because my former frights and anguish were very sore and deep, therefore it did oft befall me still, as it befalleth those that have been scared with Fire, I thought every voice was *fire, fire*; every little touch would hurt my tender Conscience.

230. But one day, as I was passing in the field, and that too with some dashes on my Conscience, fearing lest yet all was not right, suddenly this sentence fell upon my Soul, *Thy Righteousness is in Heaven*; and me-thought withal, I saw with the Eyes of my Soul, Jesus Christ at Gods right hand, there, I say, was my righteousness; so that where ever I was, or whatever I was a doing, God could not say of me, *He wants my Righteousness*, for that was just before him. I also saw moreover, that it was not my good frame of Heart that made my Righteousness better, nor yet my bad frame that made my Righteousness worse; for my Righteousness was Jesus Christ himself, *the same yesterday, to day, and for ever*; Heb. 13. 8.

231. Now did my Chains fall off my Legs indeed, I was loosed from my Afflictions and Irons, my Temptations also fled away; so that from that time those dreadful Scriptures of God left off to trouble me; now went I also home rejoycing, for the Grace and Love of God; So when I came home, I looked to see if I could find that Sentence, *Thy Righteousness is in Heaven*; but could not find such a saying, wherefore my Heart began to sink again, only that was brought to my remembrance, 1 *Cor.* 1. 33. *He is made unto us of God, Wisdom, Righteousness, Sanctification, and Redemption*; by this word I saw the other Sentence true.

232. For by this Scripture, I saw that the Man Christ

Jesus, as he is distinct from us, as touching his bodily presence, so he is our Righteousness and Sanctification before God, here therefore I lived, for some time, very sweetly at peace with God through Christ; O me thought Christ! Christ! there was nothing but Christ that was before my Eyes, I was not now (only) for looking upon this and the other benefits of Christ apart, as of his Blood, Burial, or Resurrection, but considered him as whole Christ; as he in whom all these, and all his other Vertues, Relations, Offices and Operations met together, and that as he sat on the right hand of God in Heaven.

233. 'Twas glorious to me to see his exaltation, and the worth and prevalency of all his benefits, and that because now I could look from my self to him, and should reckon, that all those Graces of God that now were green on me, were yet but like those crackt-groats and four pence-half-pennies that rich men carry in their Purses, when their Gold is in their Trunks at home; O, I saw my Gold was in my Trunk at home! in Christ my Lord and Saviour! Now Christ was all; all my Wisdom, all my Righteousness, all my Sanctification, and all my Redemption.

234. Further, The Lord did also lead me into the Mystery of Union with the Son of God, that I was joyned to him, that I was flesh of his flesh, and bone of his bone, and now was that a sweet word to me, in *Ephes.* 5. 30. By this also was my Faith in him, as my Righteousness, the more confirmed in me; for if he and I were one, then his Righteousness was mine, his Merits mine, his Victory also mine. Now could I see my self in Heaven and Earth at once; in Heaven by my Christ, by my Head, by my Righteousness and Life, though on Earth by my Body or Person.

235. Now I saw Christ Jesus was looked on of God, and should also be looked upon by us as that common or publick Person, in whom all the whole body of his Elect are always to be considered and reckoned; that we fulfilled the Law by him, died by him, rose from the dead by him, got the Victory over Sin, Death, the Devil, and Hell, by him; when he died, we died, and so of his Resurrection. *Thy dead men shall live, together with my dead body shall they arise*, saith he, Isa. 26. And again, *After two days he will revive* us, *and the third day* we *shall live in his sight*, Hosea 6. 2. Which is now fulfilled

by the sitting down of the Son of Man on the right hand of the Majesty in the Heavens; according to that to the *Ephesians*, *He hath raised us up together*, *and made us sit together in heavenly Places in Christ Jesus*, Ephes. 2. 6.

236. Ah these blessed considerations and Scriptures, with many other of like nature, were in those days made to spangle in mine Eyes, so that I have cause to say; *Praise ye the Lord God in his Sanctuary*, *Praise him in the Firmament of his Power*, *Praise him for his mighty Acts*, *Praise him according to his excellent Greatness*, Psal. 150. 1, 2.

237. Having thus in few words given you a taste of the sorrow and affliction that my Soul went under, by the guilt and terror that this my wicked thought did lay me under; and having given you also a touch of my deliverance therefrom, and of the sweet and blessed comfort that I met with afterwards, (which comfort dwelt about a twelve month with my Heart, to my unspeakable admiration) I will now (God willing) before I proceed any further, give you in a word or two, What, as I conceive, was the cause of this temptation; and also after that, what advantage at the last it became unto my Soul.

238. For the causes, I conceived they were principally two; of which two also I was deeply convinced all the time this trouble lay upon me. The first was, for that I did not, when I was delivered from the temptation that went before, *still pray to God to keep me from temptations that were to come*; for though, as I can say in truth, my Soul was much in Prayer before this tryal seized me. Yet then I prayed only, or at the most, principally, for the removal of present troubles, and for fresh discoveries of his love in Christ; which I saw afterwards was not enough to do; I also should have prayed, that the great God would keep me from the evil that was to come.

239. Of this I was made deeply sensible by the Prayer of Holy *David*, who when he was under present Mercy, yet prayed that God would hold him back from sin, and temptation to come: *For then*, saith he, *shall I be upright*, *and I shall be innocent from the Great Transgression*, Psal. 16. 13. By this very word was I gauled and condemned quite through this long temptation.

240. That also was another word that did much condemn me for my folly, in the neglect of this Duty, *Heb.* 4. 16. *Let us therefore come boldly to the throne of Grace, that we may obtain mercy, and find Grace to help in time of need*: This I had not done, and therefore was thus suffered to sin and fall, according to what is written, *Pray that you enter not into temptation*: and truly this very thing is to this day of such weight and awe upon me, that I dare not, when I come before the Lord, go off my knees until I intreat him for help and mercy against the temptations that are to come; and I do beseech thee, Reader, that thou learn to beware of my negligence by the afflictions that for this thing I did for days, and months, and years, with sorrow undergo.

241. Another cause of this temptation was, That I had tempted God; and on this manner did I do it: Upon a time my Wife was great with Child, and before her full time was come, her pangs as of a Woman in Travel, were fierce and strong upon her, even as if she would immediately have fallen in labour, and been delivered of an untimely Birth: Now at this very time it was, that I had been so strongly tempted to question the Being of God; wherefore, as my Wife lay crying by me, I said, but with all secresie imaginable, even thinking in my heart, *Lord, if thou wilt now remove this sad affliction from my Wife, and cause that she be troubled no more therewith this Night*, (and now were her pangs just upon her) *then I shall know that thou canst discern the most secret thoughts of the Heart.*

242. I had no sooner said it in my heart, but her pangs were taken from her, and she was cast into a deep sleep, and so continued till Morning; at this I greatly marvelled, not knowing what to think; but after I had been awake a good while, and heard her cry no more, I fell to sleep also; So when I waked in the Morning, it came upon me again, even what I had said in my heart the last Night, and how the Lord had shewed me that he knew my secret Thoughts, which was a great astonishment unto me for several weeks after.

243. Well, about a year and a half afterwards that wicked sinful thought, of which I have spoken before, went thorow my wicked heart, even this thought, *Let Christ go if he will*; so when I was fallen under guilt for this, the remembrance of my other thought, and of the effect thereof, would also come upon

me with this retort, which also carried rebuke along with it, *Now you may see that God doth know the most secret thoughts of the Heart.*

244. And with this, that of the passages that were betwixt the Lord, and his Servant *Gideon*, fell upon my Spirit; how because that *Gideon* tempted God with his Fleece both wet and dry, when he should have believed and ventured upon his word, therefore the Lord did afterwards so try him, as to send him against an innumerable company of Enemies. And that too as to outward appearance, without any strength or help, *Judg.* 6. 7. Thus he served me, and that justly, for I should have believed his Word, and not have put an *If* upon the All-seeingness of God.

245. And now to shew you something of the advantages that I also have gained by this temptation; and first, by this I was made continually to possess in my Soul a very wonderful sense both of the Being and Glory of God, and of his beloved Son; in the temptation that went before, my Soul was perplexed with unbelief, blasphemy, hardness of Heart, questions about the Being of God, Christ, the Truth of the Word, and certainty of the World to come; I say, then I was greatly assaulted, and tormented with Atheism, but now the case was otherwise, now was God and Christ continually before my Face, though not in a way of comfort, but in a way of exceeding dread and terror. The Glory of the Holiness of God did at this time break me to pieces, and the Bowels and Compassion of Christ did break me as on the Wheel; for I could not consider him but as a lost and rejected Christ, the remembrance of which, was as the continual breaking of my Bones.

246. The Scriptures also were wonderful things unto me; I saw that the truth and verity of them, were the Keys of the Kingdom of Heaven; *those* that the Scriptures favour, *they* must inherit bliss; but *those* that they oppose and condemn, *must* perish for evermore: O this word, *For the Scriptures cannot be broken*, would rend the Caul of my Heart? and so would that other, *Whose sins ye remit, they are remitted; but whose sins ye retain, they are retained*: Now I saw the Apostles to be the Elders of the City of Refuge, *Josh.* 20. 4. those that they were to receive in, were received to Life; but those that they shut out, were to be slain by the avenger of Blood.

247. Oh! One Sentence of the Scripture did more afflict and terrifie my mind, I mean those Sentences that stood against me (as sometimes I thought they every one did) more, I say than an Army of forty thousand men that might have come against me. Wo be to him against whom the Scriptures bend themselves.

248. By this temptation I was made to see more into the Nature of the Promises, than ever I was before; for I lying now trembling under the mighty hand of God, continually torn and rent by the thundering of his Justice; this made me with careful Heart, and watchful Eye, with great fearfulness, to turn over every leaf, and with much diligence mixt with trembling, to consider every Sentence, together with its natural force and latitude.

249. By this temptation also, I was greatly holden off my former foolish practice, of putting by the word of promise when it came into my mind; for now, though I could not suck that comfort and sweetness from the Promise, as I had done at other times, yet, like to a man a sinking, I should catch at all I saw; formerly I thought I might not meddle with the promise, unless I felt its comfort, but now 'twas no time thus to do, the avenger of Blood too hardly did pursue me.

250. Now therefore I was glad to catch at *that* word, which yet I feared, I had no ground nor right to own; and even to leap into the bosom of that promise, that yet I fear'd did shut its Heart against me. Now also I should labour to take the Word as God hath laid it down, without restraining the natural force of one syllable thereof; O what did I now see in that blessed sixth of *John*, *And him that comes to me*, *I will in no wise cast out! John*. 6. 30. Now I began to consider with my self, that God had a bigger mouth to speak with, than I had a heart to conceive with; I thought also with my self, that he spake not his words in haste, or in an unadvised heat, but with infinite Wisdom and Judgment, and in very truth and faithfulness, 2 *Sam*. 3. 28.

251. I should in these days, often in my greatest Agonies, even flounce towards the Promise, (as the Horses do towards sound Ground, that yet stick in the mire) concluding, (though as one almost bereft of his wits through fear) on this I will rest and stay, and leave the fulfilling of it to the God of Heaven

that made it. O! many a pull hath my heart had with Sathan, for that blessed sixth of *John*; I did not now, as at other times, look principally for comfort, (though, O how welcome would it have been unto me!) But now a word, a word to lean a weary Soul upon, that I might not sink for ever! 'twas that I hunted for.

252. Yea, often when I have been making to the Promise, I have seen as if the Lord would refuse my Soul for ever; I was often as if I had run upon the Pikes, and as if the Lord had thrust at me, to keep me from him, as with a flaming Sword. Then I should think of *Esther*, who went to petition the King contrary to the Law, *Esth*. 4. 16. I thought also of *Benhadad*'s Servants, who went with Ropes upon their Heads to their Enemies for mercy, 1 *King*. 20. 31. *&c.* The Woman of *Canaan* also, that would not be daunted, though called Dog by Christ, *Mat*. 15. 22. *&c.* and the man that went to borrow bread at Midnight, *Luke* 1. 5, 6, 7, 8, *&c.* were great encouragements unto me.

253. I never saw those heights and depths in Grace and Love, and Mercy, as I saw after this temptation! Great Sins do draw out great Grace; and where guilt is most terrible and fierce, there the mercy of God in Christ, when shewed to the Soul, appears most high and mighty; when *Job* had passed through his Captivity, *he had twice as much as he had before*, Job. 42. 10. Blessed be God for Jesus Christ our Lord. Many other things I might here make observation of, but I would be brief, and therefore shall at this time omit them, and do pray God that my harms may make others fear to offend, lest they also be made to bear the Iron Yoke as I did.

I had two or three times, at or about my deliverance from this temptation, such strange apprehensions of the Grace of God, that I could hardly bear up under it, it was so out of measure amazing, when I thought it could reach me, that I do think, if that sense of it had abode long upon me, it would have made me uncapable for business.

254. Now I shall go forward to give you a relation of other of the Lords dealings with me, at sundry other seasons, and of the temptations I then did meet withal. I shall begin with what I met with when I first did joyn in fellowship with the People of God in *Bedford*. After I had propounded to the Church,

that my desire was to walk in the Order and Ordinances of Christ with them, and was also admitted by them: while I thought of that blessed Ordinance of Christ, which was his last Supper with his Disciples before his death, that Scripture, *Do this in remembrance of me*, Luke 22. 19. was made a very precious word unto me: for by it the Lord did come down upon my Conscience with the discovery of his death for my sins, and as I then felt, did as if he plunged me in the vertue of the same. But, behold, I had not been long a partaker at that Ordinance, but such fierce and sad temptations did attend me at all times therein, both to blaspheme the Ordinance, and to wish some deadly thing to those that then did eat thereof: that lest I should at any time be guilty of consenting to these wicked and fearful thoughts, I was forced to bend my self, all the while to pray to God to keep me from such Blasphemies: and also to cry to God to bless the Bread and Cup to them, as it went from mouth to mouth. The reason of this temptation I have thought since, was, because I did not with that reverence as became me at first, approach to partake thereof.

255. Thus I continued for three quarters of a Year, and could never have rest nor ease: but at the last the Lord came in upon my Soul with that same Scripture, by which my Soul was visited before: and after that, I have been usually very well and comfortable in the partaking of that blessed Ordinance, and have, I trust, therein discerned the *Lords Body* as broken for my sins, and that his precious blood hath been shed for my Transgressions.

256. Upon a time I was somewhat inclining to a Consumption, wherewith about the Spring I was suddenly and violently seized, with much weakness in my outward man: insomuch that I thought I could not live. Now began I afresh to give my self up to a serious examination after my state and condition for the future, and of my evidences for that blessed World to come; For it hath, I bless the name of God, been my usual course, as always, so especially in the day of affliction, to endeavour to keep my interest in Life to come, clear before mine Eye.

257. But I had no sooner began to recall to mind my former experience, of the goodness of God to my Soul, but there came flocking into my mind, an innumerable company of

my Sins and Transgressions, amongst which these were at this time most to my Affliction, namely my deadness, dulness, and coldness in holy Duties; my wandrings of heart, of my wearisomness in all good things, my want of love to God, his ways and People, with this at the end of all, *Are these the fruits of Christianity? Are these the tokens of a blessed man?*

258. At the apprehensions of these things, my sickness was doubled upon me, for now was I sick in my inward man, my Soul was clog'd with guilt; now also was all my former experience of God's goodness to me, quite taken out of my mind, and hid as if they had never been, nor seen: Now was my Soul greatly pinched between these two considerations, *Live I must not*, *Die I dare not*; Now I sunk and fell in my spirit, and was giving up all for lost; but as I was walking up and down in the house as a man in a most woful state, that Word of God took hold of my heart. *Ye are justified freely by his Grace, through the Redemption that is in Christ Jesus*, Rom. 3. 24. But oh what a turn it made upon me!

259. Now was I as one awaked out of some troublesome sleep and dream, and listning to this Heavenly Sentence, I was as if I heard it thus expounded to me; *Sinner, thou thinkest that because of thy Sins and Infirmities, I cannot save thy Soul; but behold, my Son is by me, and upon him I look, and not on thee, and deal with thee according as I am pleased with him.* At this I was greatly lightned in my Mind, and made to understand that God could justifie a sinner at any time, it was but his looking upon Christ, and imputing of his benefits to us, and the work was forthwith done.

260. And as I was thus in a muse, that Scripture also came with great power upon my Spirit, *Not by works of Righteousness that we have done, but according to his Mercy he hath saved us*, &c. 2 *Tim.* 1. 9. *Tit.* 3. 5. Now was I got on high, I saw my self within the Arms of Grace and mercy, and though I was before afraid to think of a dying hour, yet now I cryed, *Let me die*: now Death was lovely and beautiful in my sight, for I saw *we shall never live indeed till we be gone to the other World.* O, methought this Life is but a slumber, in comparison of that above; at this time also I saw more in those words, *Heirs of God*, (*Rom.* 8. 17.) then ever I shall be able to express while I live in this World; *Heirs of God!* God himself

is the portion of the Saints. This I saw and wondered at, but cannot tell you what I saw.

261. Again, as I was at another time very ill and weak, all that time also the Tempter did beset me strongly, (for I find he is much for assaulting the Soul, when it begins to approach towards the Grave, then is his Opportunity) labouring to hide from me my former experience of Gods goodness; Also setting before me the terrors of Death, and the Judgment of God, insomuch, that at this time, through my fear of miscarrying for ever (should I now die) I was as one dead before Death came, and was as if I had felt my self already descending into the Pit; methought, I said there were no way but to Hell I must; but behold, just as I was in the midst of those fears, these words of the Angels carrying *Lazarus* into *Abrahams* bosom, darted in upon me, as who should say, *So it shall be with thee, when thou dost leave this World.* This did sweetly revive my Spirit, and help me to hope in God; which when I had with comfort mused on a while, that word fell with great weight upon my mind, *O Death, where is thy sting, O Grave, where is thy victory?* 1 Cor. 15. 55. At this I became both well in body and mind at once, for my sickness did presently vanish, and I walked comfortably in my Work for God again.

262. At another time, though, just before, I was pretty well and savoury in my Spirit, yet suddenly there fell upon me a great cloud of darkness, which did so hide from me the things of God and Christ, that I was as if I had never seen or known them in my life: I was also so over-run in my Soul with a sensless, heartless frame-of-spirit, that I could not feel my Soul to move or stir after Grace and Life by Christ; I was as if my loyns were broken, or as if my hands and feet had been tied or bound with Chains. At this time also I felt some weakness to seize upon my outward man, which made still the other affliction the more heavy and uncomfortable to me.

263. After I had been in this condition some three or four days, as I was sitting by the fire, I suddenly felt this Word to sound in my Heart, *I must go to Jesus*; at this my former darkness and Atheism fled away, and the blessed things of Heaven were set within my view. While I was on this sudden thus overtaken with surprize; Wife, said I, is there ever such a Scripture, *I must go to Jesus*? she said she could not tell;

therefore I sat musing still to see if I could remember such a place; I had not sat above two or three minutes, but that came bolting in upon me, *And to an innumerable Company of Angels*; and withal, *Hebrews* the twelfth, about the Mount *Sion* was set before mine Eyes, *Heb.* 12. 22, 23, 24.

264. Then with Joy I told my Wife, *O now I know, I know!* but that night was a good night to me, I never had but few better; I longed for the company of some of God's People, that I might have imparted unto them what God had shewed me; Christ was a precious Christ to my Soul that Night, I could scarce lie in my Bed for Joy, and Peace, and Triumph, through Christ; this great Glory did not continue upon me until Morning, yet the twelfth of the Author to the *Hebrews*, Heb. 12. 22, 23. was a blessed Scripture to me for many days together after this.

265. The Words are these, *You are come to Mount* Sion, *to the City of the living God, to the Heavenly* Jerusalem, *and to an innumerable company of Angels, to the general Assembly and Church of the first-born which are written in Heaven, to God the Judge of all, and to the Spirits of just men made perfect, and to Jesus the Mediator of the New Testament, and to the blood of sprinkling, that speaketh better things than that of* Abel. Thorow this blessed Sentence, the Lord led me over and over, first to this Word, and then to that, and shewed me wonderful glory in every one of them. These words also have oft since this time been great refreshment to my Spirit. Blessed be God for having mercy on me.

A brief Account of the Authors Call to the Work of the Ministry.

266. AND now I am speaking my Experience, I will in this place thrust in a word or two concerning my Preaching the Word, and of God's dealing with me in that particular also: For after I had been about five or six years awakened, and helped my self to see both the want and worth

of Jesus Christ our Lord, and also inabled to venture my Soul upon him: some of the most able among the Saints with us, I say, the most able for Judgment, and Holiness of Life, as they conceived, did perceive that God had counted me worthy to understand something of his Will in his holy and blessed Word, and had given me utterance in some measure to express what I saw, to others for edification; therefore they desired me, and that with much earnestness, that I would be willing at some times to take in hand, in one of the Meetings, to speak a word of Exhortation unto them.

267. The which, though at the first it did much dash and abash my Spirit, yet being still by them desired and intreated, I consented to their request, and did twice at two several Assemblies, (but in private) though with much weakness and infirmity, discover my Gift amongst them; at which they not only seemed to be, but did solemnly protest, as in the sight of the great God, they were both affected and comforted, and gave thanks to the Father of Mercies for the grace bestowed on me.

268. After this, sometimes when some of them did go into the Country to teach, they would also that I should go with them; where, though as yet I did not, nor durst not, make use of my Gift in an open way, yet more privately still, as I came amongst the good People in those places, I did sometimes speak a word of Admonition unto them also; the which they as the other, received with rejoycing at the mercy of God to me-ward, professing their Souls were edified thereby.

269. Wherefore, to be brief, at last, being still desired by the Church, after some solemn Prayer to the Lord, with fasting, I was more particularly called forth, and appointed to a more ordinary and publick Preaching the Word, not only to and amongst them that believed, but also to offer the Gospel to those that had not yet received the Faith thereof: About which time I did evidently find in my Mind a secret pricking forward thereto; though, I bless God, not for desire of vain Glory, for at that time I was most sorely afflicted with the fiery darts of the Devil, concerning my Eternal State.

270. But yet could not be content, unless I was found in the Exercise of my Gift, unto which also I was greatly animated, not only by the continual desires of the Godly, but also by that

saying of *Paul* to the *Corinthians*, *I beseech you*, *Brethren*, (*ye know the houshold of* Stephanus, *that it is the first fruits of* Achaia, *and that they have addicted themselves to the Ministry of the Saints*) *that you submit your selves unto such*, *and to every one that helpeth with us*, *and laboureth*, 1 Cor. 16. 15, 16.

271. By this Text I was made to see that the Holy Ghost never intended that men who have Gifts and Abilities, should bury them in the earth, but rather did command and stir up such to the Exercise of their Gift, and also did commend those that were apt and ready so to do, *They have addicted themselves to the Ministry of the Saints*: This Scripture in these days did continually run in my mind to incourage me, and strengthen me in this my work for God; I have been also incouraged from several other Scriptures and Examples of the Godly, both specified in the Word and other ancient Histories, *Acts* 8. 4. and 18. 24, 25. *&c.* 1 *Pet.* 4. 10. *Rom.* 12. 6. Fox *Acts* and *Mon.*

272. Wherefore, though of my self, of all the Saints the most unworthy, yet I, but with great fear and trembling at the sight of my own weakness, did set upon the work, and did according to my Gift, and the proportion of my Faith, Preach that blessed Gospel that God had shewed me in the Holy Word of Truth: Which when the Country understood, they came in to hear the Word by hundreds, and that from all parts, though upon sundry and divers accounts.

273. And I thank God, he gave unto me some measure of bowels and pity for their Souls, which also did put me forward to labour with great diligence and earnestness to find out such a word as might, if God would bless, lay hold of, and awaken the Conscience, in which also the good Lord had respect to the desire of his Servant; for I had not preached long, before some began to be touched, and to be greatly afflicted in their Minds at the apprehension of the greatness of their Sin, and of their need of Jesus Christ.

274. But I at first could not believe that God should speak by me to the heart of any man, still counting my self unworthy, yet those who thus were touched would love me and have a peculiar respect for me; and though I did put it from me, that they should be awakened by me, still they would confess it, and affirm it before the Saints of God; they would

also bless God for me (unworthy Wretch that I am!) and count me God's Instrument that shewed to them the way of Salvation.

275. Wherefore seeing them in both their words and deeds to be so constant, and also in their Hearts so earnestly pressing after the knowledge of Jesus Christ, rejoycing that ever God did send me where they were; then I began to conclude it might be so, that God had owned in his Work such a foolish one as I; and then came that Word of God to my heart with much sweet refreshment, *The blessing of them that were ready to perish is come upon me*; *yea*, *I caused the Widdows heart to sing for joy*, Job. 29. 13.

276. At this therefore I rejoyced, yea, the tears of those whom God did awaken by my Preaching, would be both solace and encouragement to me; for I thought on those Sayings, *Who is he that maketh me glad*, *but the same that is made sorry by me?* 2 Cor. 2. 2. And again, *Though I be not an Apostle to others*, *yet doubtless I am unto you*, *for the Seal of my Apostleship are ye in the Lord*, 1 Cor. 6. 2. These things therefore were as another Argument unto me that God had called me to, and stood by me in this Work.

277. In my Preaching of the Word, I took special notice of this one thing, namely, That the Lord did lead me to begin where his Word begins with Sinners, that is, to condemn all flesh, and to open and alledge, that the curse of God by the Law doth belong to, and lay hold on all men as they come into the World, because of Sin. Now this part of my Work I fulfilled with great sense, for the terrors of the Law, and guilt for my Transgressions, lay heavy on my Conscience, I preached what I felt, what I smartingly did feel, even that under which my poor Soul did groan and tremble to astonishment.

278. Indeed I have been as one sent to them from the dead; I went my self in Chains to preach to them in Chains, and carried that fire in my own Conscience, that I perswaded them to beware of. I can truly say, and that without dissembling, that when I have been to preach, I have gone full of guilt and terror even to the Pulpit-door, and there it hath been taken off, and I have been at liberty in my mind until I have done my work; and then immediately, even before I could get down the Pulpit-stairs, I have been as bad as I was before.

Yet God carried me on, but surely with a strong hand; for neither Guilt nor Hell could take me off my Work.

279. Thus I went for the space of two years, crying out against mens sins, and their fearful state because of them. After which, the Lord came in upon my own Soul with some staid peace and comfort through Christ; for he did give me many sweet discoveries of his Blessed Grace thorow him; Wherefore now I altered in my preaching, (for still I preached what I saw and felt) now therefore I did much labour to hold forth Jesus Christ in all his Offices, Relations, and Benefits unto the World, and did strive also to discover, to condemn, and remove those false supports and props on which the World doth both lean, and by them fall and perish. On these things also I staid as long as on the other.

280. After this, God led me into something of the Mystery of the Union of Christ; wherefore that I discovered and shewed to them also. And when I had travelled through these three chief points of the Word of God, about the space of five years or more, I was caught in my present practice, and cast into Prison, where I have lain above as long again to confirm the Truth by way of suffering, as I was before in testifying of it, according to the Scriptures, in a way of Preaching.

281. When I have been in Preaching, I thank God, my heart hath often, all the time of this and the other exercise, with great earnestness cryed to God that he would make the Word effectual to the Salvation of the Soul; still being grieved lest the Enemy should take the Word away from the Conscience, and so it should become unfruitful; Wherefore I should labour so to speak the Word, as that thereby (if it were possible) the sin and Person guilty might be particularized by it.

282. Also when I have done the Exercise, it hath gone to my heart to think the Word should now fall as Rain on stony places; still wishing from my heart, O that they who have heard me speak this day, did but see as I do, what Sin, Death, Hell, and the Curse of God, is; and also what the Grace, and Love, and Mercy of God is, thorow Christ, to men in such a case as they are, who are yet estranged from him. And indeed, I did often say in my heart before the Lord, *That if to*

be hanged up presently before their Eyes, would be a means to awaken them, and confirm them in the Truth, I gladly should be contented.

283. For I have been in my Preaching, especially when I have been engaged in the Doctrine of Life by Christ, without Works, as if an Angel of God had stood by at my back to encourage me; O, it hath been with such Power and heavenly Evidence upon my own Soul, while I have been labouring to unfold it, to demonstrate it, and to fasten it upon the Conscience of others, that I could not be contented with saying, *I believe and am sure*; *methought I was more than sure* (if it be lawful to express my self) that those things which then I asserted, were true.

284. When I went first to Preach the Word abroad, the Doctors and Priests of the Country did open wide against me; but I was perswaded of this, not to render rayling for rayling, but to see how many of their carnal Professors I could convince of their miserable state by the Law, and of the want and worth of Christ; for, thought I, *This shall answer for me in time to come, when they shall be for my hire before their face*, Gen. 30. 33.

285. I never cared to meddle with things that were controverted, and in dispute amongst the Saints, especially things of the lowest Nature; yet it pleased me much to contend with great earnestness for the Word of Faith, and the Remission of Sins by the Death and Sufferings of Jesus; but I say, as to other things, I should let them alone, because I saw they engendred strife, and because that they neither in doing, nor in leaving undone, did commend us to God to be his: Besides, I saw my Work before me did run in another Channel, even to carry an awakening word; to that therefore did I stick and adhere.

286. I never endeavoured to, nor durst make use of other mens lines, *Rom.* 15. 18. (though I condemn not all that do) for I verily thought, and found by experience, that what was taught me by the Word and Spirit of Christ, could be spoken, maintained and stood to, by the soundest and best established Conscience; and though I will not now speak all that I know in this matter; yet my experience hath more interest in that Text of Scripture, *Gal.* 1. 11, 12. than many amongst men are aware.

287. If any of those who were awakened by my Ministry, did after that fall back, (as sometimes too many did) I can truly say their loss hath been more to me, then if one of my own Children, begotten of my body, had been going to its Grave; I think verily I may speak it without any offence to the Lord, nothing hath gone so near me as that, unless it was the fear of the loss of the Salvation of my own Soul: I have counted as if I had goodly Buildings and Lordships in those places where my Children were born: my heart hath been so wrapt up in the glory of this excellent Work, that I counted my self more blessed and honoured of God by this, than if he had made me the Emperour of the Christian World, or the Lord of all the glory of the Earth without it! O these words! *He that converteth a Sinner from the error of his way, doth save a Soul from death*, Jam. 5. 20. *The fruit of the Righteous, is a Tree of Life; and he that winneth Souls, is wise*, Prov. 11. 30. *They that be wise, shall shine as the brightness of the Firmament, and they that turn many to righteousness, as the Stars for ever and ever*, Dan. 12. 3. *For what is our hope, or joy, or crown of rejoycing? are not even ye in the presence of our Lord Jesus Christ at his coming? for, ye are our glory and joy*, 1 Thes. 2. 19, 20. These, I say, with many others of a like nature, have been great refreshments to me.

288. I have observed, That where I have had a Work to do for God, I have had first as it were the going of God upon my Spirit to desire I might preach there: I have also observed, that such and such Souls in particular have been strongly set upon my heart, and I stirred up to wish for their Salvation; and that these very Souls have, after this, been given in as the fruits of my Ministry. I have observed, that a Word cast in by the by, hath done more execution in a Sermon, than all that was spoken besides: sometimes also when I have thought I did no good, then I did most of all; and at other times when I thought I should catcht them, I have fished for nothing.

289. I have also observed, that where there hath been a Work to do upon Sinners, there the Devil hath begun to roar in the hearts, and by the mouths of his Servants. Yea, oftentimes when the wicked World hath raged most, there hath been Souls awakened by the Word: I could instance particulars, but I forbear.

290. My great desire in my fulfilling my Ministry, was, to get into the darkest places of the Country, even amongst those People that were furthest off of profession; yet not because I could not endure the Light, (for I feared not to shew my Gospel to any) but because I found my Spirit did lean most after awakening and converting-Work, and the Word that I carried did lean it self most that way also; *Yea, so have I strived to preach the Gospel, not where Christ was named, lest I should build upon another man's Foundation*, Rom. 15. 20.

291. In my preaching, I have really been in pain, and have, as it were, travelled to bring forth Children to God, neither could I be satisfied, unless some fruits did appear in my Work: if I were fruitless, it mattered not who commended me; but if I were fruitful, I cared not who did condemn. I have thought of that, *Lo, Children are an Heritage of the Lord; and the fruit of the Womb is his reward. As Arrows in the hand of a mighty man, so are Children of the Youth. Happy is the man that hath filled his Quiver full of them; they shall not be ashamed, but they shall speak with the Enemies in the Gate*, Psal. 127. 3, 4, 5.

292. It pleased me nothing to see People drink in Opinions, if they seemed ignorant of Jesus Christ, and the worth of their own Salvation, sound conviction for Sin, especially for Unbelief, and an heart set on fire to be saved by Christ, with strong breathings after a truly sanctified Soul: that it was that delighted me; those were the Souls I counted blessed.

293. But in this Work, as in all other, I had my temptations attending me, and that of divers kinds, as sometimes I should be assaulted with great discouragement therein, fearing that I should not be able to speak a word at all to edification; nay, that I should not be able to speak sense unto the people; at which times I should have such a strange faintness and strengthlesness seize upon my body, that my legs have scarce been able to carry me to the place of Exercise.

294. Sometimes again, when I have been preaching, I have been violently assaulted with thoughts of blasphemy, and strongly tempted to speak the words with my mouth before the Congregation. I have also at some time, even when I have

begun to speak the Word with much clearness, evidence, and liberty of speech, yet been before the ending of that Opportunity, so blinded, and so estranged from the things I have been speaking, and have also been so straitned in my speech, as to utterance before the People, that I have been as if I had not known or remembred what I have been about, or, as if my head had been in a bag all the time of the Exercise.

295. Again, When at sometimes I have been about to Preach upon some smart and searching portion of the Word, I have found the Tempter suggest, *What! will you preach this? this condemns your self, of this your own Soul is guilty*; *wherefore preach not of it at all, or if you do, yet so mince it, as to make way for your own escape*; *lest instead of awakening others, you lay that guilt upon your own Soul, as you will never get from under.*

296. But, I thank the Lord, I have been kept from consenting to these so horrid suggestions, and have rather, as *Sampson*, bowed my self with all my might to condemn Sin and Transgression where ever I found it, yea though therein also I did bring guilt upon my own Conscience; *Let me dye*, thought I, *with the Philistines*, *Judg*. 16. 29, 30. rather than deal corruptly with the blessed Word of God; *Thou that teachest another, teachest thou not thy self?* it is far better that thou do judge thy self, even by preaching plainly unto others, then that thou, to save thy self, imprison the Truth in Unrighteousness: Blessed be God for his help also in this.

297. I have also, while found in this blessed Work of Christ, been often tempted to pride and liftings up of Heart; and though I dare not say, I have not been affected with this, yet truly the Lord of his precious mercy hath so carried it towards me, that for the most part I have had but small joy to give way to such a thing: for it hath been my every days portion to be let into the evil of my own heart, and still made to see such a multitude of Corruptions and Infirmities therein, that it hath caused hanging down of the head under all my Gifts and Attainments; I have felt this Thorn in the Flesh (2 *Cor*. 12. 8, 9,) the very Mercy of God to me.

298. I have had also together with this some notable place or other of the Word presented before me, which word hath

contained in it some sharp and piercing Sentence concerning the perishing of the Soul, notwithstanding gifts and parts; as for instance, that hath been of great use unto me, *Though I speak with the Tongue of Men and Angels, and have not Charity, I am become as sounding brass, and a tinkling Cymbal*, 1 Cor. 13. 1, 2.

299. A tinkling Cymbal, is an Instrument of Musick with which a skilful Player can make such melodious and heart-inflaming Musick, that all who hear him play, can scarcely hold from dancing; and yet behold, the Cymbal hath not Life, neither comes the Musick from it, but because of the Art of him that plays therewith, so then the Instrument at last may come to naught and perish, though in times past such Musick hath been made upon it.

300. Just thus, I saw, it was and will be with them who have Gifts, but want saving-Grace; they are in the hand of Christ, as the Cymbal in the hand of *David*; and as *David* could with the Cymbal make that Mirth in the Service of God, as to elevate the hearts of the Worshippers, so Christ can use these gifted men, as with them to affect the Souls of his People in his Church; yet when he hath done all, hang them by, as lifeless, though sounding Cymbals.

301. This consideration therefore, together with some others, were, for the most part, as a Maul on the head of Pride, and desire of vain-glory: What, thought I, shall I be proud because I am a sounding Brass? Is it so much to be *a Fiddle? Hath not the least Creature that hath* life, more of God in it than these? Besides, I knew *'twas Love should never die*, but these must cease and vanish: So I concluded, a little Grace, a little Love, a little of the true Fear of God is better than all these Gifts: Yea, and I am fully convinced of it, that it is possible for Souls that can scarce give a man an answer, but with great confusion as to method, I say, it is possible for them to have a thousand times more Grace, and so to be more in the love and favour of the Lord, than some who by vertue of the Gift of Knowledge, can deliver themselves like Angels.

302. Thus therefore I came to perceive, that though gifts in themselves were good to the thing for which they are designed, to wit, the Edification of others, yet empty and

without power to save the Soul of him that hath them, if they be *alone*: Neither are they, as so, any sign of a mans state to be happy, being only a dispensation of God to some, of whose improvement or non-improvement they must when a little love more is over, give an account to him that is ready to judge the quick and the dead.

303. This shewed me too, that gifts being alone, were dangerous, not in themselves, but because of those evils that attend them that have them, to wit, pride, desire of vain glory, self-conceit, *&c.* all which were easily blown up at the applause, and commendation of every unadvised Christian, to the endangering of a poor Creature to fall into the condemnation of the Devil.

304. I saw therefore that he that hath Gifts, had need be let into a sight of the nature of them, to wit, that they come short of making of him to be in a truly saved condition, lest he rest in them, and so fall short of the grace of God.

305. He hath also cause to walk humbly with God, and be little in his own Eyes, and to remember withall, that his Gifts are not his own, but the Churches, and that by them he is made a Servant to the Church, and he must also give at last an account of his Stewardship unto the Lord Jesus, and to give a good account, will be a blessed thing!

306. Let all men therefore prize a little with the fear of the Lord, (Gifts indeed are desirable) but yet great Grace and small Gifts are better then great Gifts and no Grace. It doth not say, the Lord gives Gifts and Glory, but the Lord gives Grace and Glory! and blessed is such an one; to whom the Lord gives Grace, true Grace, for that is a certain forerunner of Glory.

307. But when Satan perceived that his thus tempting and assaulting of me would not answer his design; to wit, to overthrow my Ministry, and make it ineffectual as to the ends thereof: then he tryed another way, which was, to stir up the minds of the ignorant, and malicious, to load me with slanders and reproaches; now therefore I may say, That what the Devil could devise, and his instruments invent, was whirled up and down the Country against me, thinking, as I said, that by that means they should make my Ministry to be abandoned.

308. It began therefore to be rumored up and down among the People, that I was a Witch, a Jesuit, a High-way-man, and the like.

309. To all which, I shall only say, God knows that I am innocent. But as for mine accusers, let them provide themselves to meet me before the Tribunal of the Son of God, there to answer for all these things (with all the rest of their Iniquities) unless God shall give them Repentance for them, for the which I pray with all my heart.

310. But that which was reported with the boldest confidence, was, that I had my *Misses*, my *Whores*, my *Bastards*, yea, *two Wives at once*, and the like. Now these slanders (with the other) I glory in, because but slanders, foolish, or knavish lies, and falshoods cast upon me by the Devil and his Seed, and should I not be dealt with thus wickedly by the World, I should want one sign of a Saint and Child of God. Blessed are you (said the Lord Jesus) *when man shall revile you and persecute you, and shall say all manner of evil of you falsly for my sake, rejoyce and be exceeding glad, for great is your Reward in Heaven; for so persecuted they the Prophets which were before you*, Mat. 5. 11.

311. These things therefore upon mine own account trouble me not, no, though they were twenty times more than they are. I have a good Conscience, and whereas they speak evil of me, as an evil doer, they shall be shamed that falsly accuse my good Conversation in Christ.

312. So then, what shall I say to those that have thus bespattered me? Shall I threaten them? Shall I chide them? Shall I flatter them? Shall I entreat them to hold their Tongues? no, not I, were it not for that these things make them ripe for damnation that are the Authors and Abettors, I would say unto them; *Report it!* because 'twill increase my Glory.

313. Therefore I bind these lies and slanders to me as an ornament, it belongs to my Christian Profession, to be vilified, slandered, reproached, and reviled; and since all this is nothing else, as my God and my Conscience do bear me witness: I rejoyce in reproaches for Christs sake.

314. I also calling all these fools, or knaves that have thus made it any thing of their business to affirm any of the things

aforenamed of me, namely, that I have been naught with other Women, or the like. When they have used to the utmost of their endeavours, and made the fullest enquiry that they can to prove against me truly, that there is any Woman in Heaven, or Earth, or Hell, that can say, that I have at any time, in any place, by day or night, so much as attempted to be naught with them, and speak I thus, to beg mine Enemies into a good esteem of me: No, not I: I will in this beg belief of no man: believe, or disbelieve me in this, all is a case to me.

315. My Foes have mist their mark in this their shooting at me. I am not the man, I wish that they themselves be guiltless, if all the Fornicators and Adulterers in *England* were hang'd by the Neck till they be dead, *John Bunyan*, the object of their Envy, would be still alive and well. I know not whether there be such a thing as a Woman breathing under the Copes of the whole Heaven, but by their Apparel, their Children, or by common Fame, except my Wife.

316. And in this I admire the Wisdom of God, that he made me shie of Women from my first Conversion until now. Those know, and can also bear me witness, with whom I have been most intimately concerned; that it is a rare thing to see me carry it pleasant towards a Woman; the common Salutation of Women I abhor, 'tis odious to me in whomsoever I see it. Their Company alone I cannot away with. I seldom so much as touch a Womans Hand, for I think these things are not so becoming me. When I have seen good men Salute those Women that they have visited, or that have visited them, I have at times made my objection against it, and when they have answered that it was but a piece of Civility, I have told them it is not a comely sight: some indeed have urged the holy kiss, but then I have asked why they made baulks, why they did salute the most handsom, and let the ill favoured go? thus how laudable so ever such things have been in the Eyes of others, they have been unseemly in my sight.

317. And now for a wind up in this matter, I calling not only Men, but Angels to prove me guilty of having carnally to do with any Woman save my Wife, nor am I afraid to do it a second time, knowing that it cannot offend the Lord in such a case, to call God for a Record upon my Soul that in these things I am innocent. Not that I have been thus kept because

of any goodness in me, more than in any other, but God has been merciful to me and has kept me, to whom I pray that he will keep me still, not only from this but from every evil way and work, and preserve me to his Heavenly Kingdom. *Amen.*

318. Now as Sathan laboured by reproaches and slanders to make me vile among my Country-men, that, if possible, my Preaching might be made of none effect, so there was added hereto a long and tedious Imprisonment, that thereby I might be frighted from my Service for Christ, and the World terrified, and made afraid to hear me Preach, of which I shall in the next place give you a brief account.

A brief Account of the Authors Imprisonment.

319. HAving made Profession of the Glorious Gospel of Christ a long time, and Preached the same about five years; I was apprehended at a Meeting of good People in the Countrey, (among whom, had they let me alone, I should have preached that day, but they took me away from amongst them) and had me before a Justice; who, after I had offered security for my appearing at the next Sessions, yet committed me, because my Sureties would not consent to be bound that I should Preach no more to the People.

320. At the Sessions after, I was indicted for an Upholder and Maintainer of Unlawful Assemblies and Conventicles, and for not Conforming to the National Worship of the Church of *England*; and after some Conference *there* with the Justices, they taking my plain dealing with them for a Confession, as they termed it, *of the Indictment, did Sentence me to perpetual banishment, because I refused to Conform.* So being again delivered up to the Goalers hands, I was had home to Prison, and there have lain now compleat twelve years, waiting to see what God will suffer these men to do with me.

321. In which condition I have continued with much content through Grace, but have met with many turnings and

goings upon my Heart, both from the Lord, Satan, and my own Corruptions; by all which (glory be to Jesus Christ) I have also received, among many things, much Conviction, Instruction, and Understanding, of which at large I shall not here discourse; onely, give you in a hint or two, a word that may stir up the Godly to bless God, and to pray for me; and also to take encouragement, should the case be their own, *Not to fear what man can do unto them.*

322. I never had in all my life so great an in-let into the Word of God as now: them Scriptures that I saw nothing in before, are made in this place and state to shine upon me; Jesus Christ also was never more real and apparent than now; here I have seen him and felt him indeed: O that word, *We have not preached unto you cunningly devised Fables*, 2 Pet. 1. 16. and that, *God raised Christ from the Dead*; *and gave him Glory, that your Faith and Hope might be in God*, 1 Pet. 1. 2. were blessed words unto me in this my imprisoned Condition.

323. These three or four Scriptures also have been great refreshment, in this condition, to me! *John* 14. 1, 2, 3, 4. *John* 16. 33. *Col.* 3. 3, 4. *Heb.* 12. 22, 23, 24. So that sometimes, when I have been in the savour of them, I have been able to laugh at destruction, *and to fear neither the Horse nor his Rider.* I have had sweet sights of the forgiveness of my Sins in this place, and of my being with Jesus in another World: *O the Mount Sion, the heavenly Jerusalem, the innumerable Company of Angels, and God the Judge of all, and the Spirits of Just men made perfect, and Jesus*, have been sweet unto me in this place: I have seen *that* here, that I am perswaded I shall never, while in this World be able to express; I have seen a truth in that Scripture, *Whom having not seen, ye love*; *in whom, though now you see him not yet believing, ye rejoyce with joy unspeakable, and full of Glory.* 1 Pet. 1. 8.

324. I never knew what it was for God to stand by me at all turns, and at every offer of Satan to afflict me, *&c.* as I have found him since I came in hither; for look how fears have presented themselves, so have supports and encouragements; yea, when I have started, even as it were, at nothing else but my shadow, yet God, as being very tender of me, hath not suffered me to be molested, but would with one Scripture or another strengthen me against all; insomuch that I have often

said, *Were it lawful, I could pray for greater trouble, for the greater comforts sake*, Eccl. 7. 14. 2 Cor. 1. 5.

325. Before I came to Prison, I saw what was a coming, and had especially two Considerations warm upon my heart; the first was, How to be able to encounter Death, should that be here my portion, For the first of these, that Scripture, *Col.* 1. 11. was great information to me, namely, to pray to God *to be strengthned with all might, according to his glorious power, unto all patience and long-suffering with joyfulness*; I could seldom go to prayer before I was imprisoned, but for not so little as a year together, this Sentence or sweet Petition, would, as it were, thrust it self into my mind, and perswade me, that if ever I would go thorow long suffering, I must have all patience, especially if I would endure it joyfully.

326. As to the second Consideration, that Saying, (2 *Cor.* 1. 9.) was of great use unto me, *But we had the sentence of death in our selves, that we might not trust in our selves, but in God that raiseth the dead*: By this Scripture I was made to see that if ever I would suffer rightly, I must first pass a sentence of death upon every thing that can properly be called a thing of this life, even to reckon my self, my Wife, my Children, my Health, my Enjoyments and all, as dead to me, and my self as dead to them.

327. The second was, to live upon God that is invisible; as *Paul* said in another place, The way not to faint, is *to look not at the things that are seen, but at the things that are not seen; for the things that are seen, are temporal, but the things that are not seen, they are eternal*: And thus I reasoned with my self; if I provide only for a Prison, then the Whip comes at unawares, and so doth also the Pillory: Again, if I provide only for these, then I am not fit for banishment; further, if I conclude that banishment is the worst, then if Death come, I am surprized; so that I see the best way to go thorow sufferings is to trust in God through Christ, as touching the World to come; and as touching this World, to *count the Grave my House, to make my Bed in Darkness, to say to Corruption, Thou art my Father, and to the Worm, Thou art my Mother and Sister*; that is, to familiarize these things to me.

328. But notwithstanding these helps, I found my self a man, and compassed with Infirmities; the parting with my

Wife and poor Children hath often been to me in this place, as the pulling the Flesh from my Bones; and that not only because I am somewhat too too fond of these great Mercies, but also because I should have often brought to my mind the many hardships, miseries and wants that my poor Family was like to meet with, should I be taken from them, *especially my poor blind Child*, who lay nearer my heart then all I had besides; O the thoughts of the hardship I thought my blind one might go under, would break my heart to pieces.

329. Poor Child! thought I, what sorrow art thou like to have for thy Portion in this World? Thou must be beaten, must beg, suffer hunger, cold, nakedness, and a thousand Calamities, though I cannot now endure the Wind should blow upon thee: But yet recalling my self, thought I, I must venture you all with God, though it goeth to the quick to leave you; O, I saw in this condition, I was as a man who was pulling down his House upon the head of his Wife and Children; yet thought I, I must do it, I must do it: And now I thought of those *two Milch-Kine that were to carry the Ark of God into another Country, and to leave their Calves behind them*, 1 Sam. 6. 10, 11, 12.

330. But that which helped me in this temptation, was divers considerations, of which three in special here I will name; the first was, the consideration of those two Scriptures, *Leave thy Fatherless Children, I will preserve them alive, and let thy Widows trust in me:* and again, *The Lord said, Verily it shall go well with thy Remnant, verily, I will cause the Enemy to entreat thee well in the time of evil*, &c. Jer. 49. 11. Chap. 15. 11.

331. I had also this Consideration, that if I should now venture all for God, I engaged God to take care of my concernments; but if I forsook him and his ways, for fear of any trouble that should come to me or mine; then I should not only falsifie my profession, but should count also that my Concernments were not so sure, if left at Gods feet, whilst I stood to and for his Name, as they would be if they were under my own care, though with the denial of the way of God. This was a smarting consideration, and was as spurs unto my Flesh: That Scripture also greatly helped it to fasten the more upon me, where Christ prays against *Judas*, that God would dis-

appoint him in all his selfish thoughts, which moved him to sell his Master. Pray read it soberly, *Psal.* 109. 6, 7, 8, *&c.*

332. I had also another Consideration, and that was, The dread of the Torments of Hell, which I was sure they must partake of, that for fear of the Cross do shrink from their Profession of Christ, his Word and Laws, before the Sons of men: I thought also of the Glory that he had prepared for those that in Faith, and Love, and Patience stood to his ways before them, These things, I say, have helped me, when the thoughts of the misery that both my self and mine, might, for the sake of my Profession, be exposed to, hath lain pinching on my Mind.

333. When I have indeed conceited that I might be banished for my Profession, then I have thought of that Scripture, *They were stoned, they were sawn asunder, were tempted, were slain with the Sword; they wandered about in Sheep-Skins, and Goat-Skins, being destitute, afflicted, tormented, of whom the World was not worthy*, for all they thought they were too bad to dwell and abide amongst them. I have also thought of that saying; *The Holy Ghost witnesseth in every City, that Bonds and Afflictions abide me*; I have verily thought that *my* Soul and *it*, have sometimes reasoned about the sore and sad estate of a banished and exiled condition, how they are exposed to Hunger, to Cold, to Perils, to Nakedness, to Enemies, and a thousand Calamities; and at last it may be to die in a Ditch, like a poor forlorn and desolate Sheep. But I thank God hitherto I have not been moved by these most *delicate* reasonings, but have rather by them more approved my Heart to God.

334. *I will tell you of a pretty business; I was once above all the rest, in a very sad and low Condition for many Weeks, at which time also I being but a young Prisoner, and not acquainted with the Laws, had this lay much upon my Spirit, That my Imprisonment might end at the Gallows for ought that I could tell; now therefore Satan laid hard at me to beat me out of heart, by suggesting thus unto me; But how if when you come indeed to die you should be in this Condition; that is, as not to savour the things of God, nor to have any evidence upon your Soul for a better state hereafter? (for indeed at that time all the things of God were hid from my Soul.)*

335. *Wherefore when I at first began to think of this, it was a great trouble to me: for I thought with my self, that in the Condition I now was in, I was not fit to die, neither indeed did think I could if I should be called to it: Besides, I thought with my self, if I should make a scrambling shift to clamber up the Ladder, yet I should either with quaking or other symptoms of fainting, give occasion to the Enemy to reproach the Way of God and his People, for their Timorousness. This therefore lay with great trouble upon me, for methought I was ashamed to die with a pale Face, and tottering Knees, for such a Cause as this.*

336. *Wherefore I pray'd to God that he would comfort me, and give me strength to do and suffer what he should call me to; yet no comfort appear'd, but all continued hid: I was also at this time so really possessed with the thought of death, that oft I was as if I was on the Ladder with the Rope about my Neck; only this was some Encouragement to me, I thought I might now have an opportunity to speak my last words to a Multitude which I thought would come to see me die; and thought I, if it must be so, if God will but convert one Soul by my very last words, I shall not count my Life thrown away, nor lost.*

337. But yet all the things of God were kept out of my sight, and still the Tempter followed me with, *But whither must you go when you die? What will become of you? Where will you be found in another World? What evidence have you for Heaven and Glory, and an Inheritance among them that are sanctified?* Thus was I tossed for many Weeks, and knew not what to do; at last this Consideration fell with weight upon me, *That it was for the Word and way of God that I was in this Condition, wherefore I was engaged not to flinch an hairs breadth from it.*

338. I thought also, that God might chuse whether he would give me comfort now, or at the hour of Death; but I might not therefore chuse whether I would hold my Profession or no: I was bound, but he was free, yea, 'twas my Duty to stand to his Word, whether he would ever look upon me or save me at the last: Wherefore, thought I, save the point being thus, I am for going on, and venturing my eternal State with Christ, whether I have comfort here or no; if God doth not come in, thought I, *I will leap off the Ladder even blindfold into Eternity, sink or swim, come Heaven, come Hell;*

Lord Jesus, if thou wilt catch me, do; if not, I will venture for thy Name.

339. I was no sooner fixed upon this Resolution, but that word dropt upon me, *Doth Job serve God for nought?* As if the Accuser had said, Lord, *Job* is no upright Man, he serves thee for by-Respects; *Hast thou not made an Hedge about him,* &c. *but put forth now thine Hand, and touch all that he hath, and he will curse thee to thy Face.* How now, thought I, is this the sign of an upright Soul, to desire to serve God when all is taken from him; Is he a godly Man that will serve God for nothing rather than give out? Blessed be God; Then I hope I have an upright Heart, for I am resolved (God giving me strength) never to deny my Profession, though I have nothing at all for my Pains; and as I was thus considering, that Scripture was set before me, *Psal.* 44. 12. *&c.*

340. Now was my Heart full of Comfort, for I hoped it was sincere; I would not have been without this Tryal, for much; I am comforted every time I think of it, and I hope I shall bless God for ever for the teaching I have had by it. Many more of the dealings of God towards me, I might relate. *But these out of the spoils won in Battel have I dedicated to maintain the House of God,* 1 Chron. 26. 27.

THE CONCLUSION.

1. OF all the Temptations that ever I met with in my Life, to question the Being of God and Truth of his Gospel, is the worst, and worst to be borne; when this Temptation comes, it takes away my Girdle from me, and removeth the Foundation from under me: O, I have often thought of that word, *Have your Loyns girt about with Truth*; and of that, *When the Foundations are destroyed, what can the Righteous do?*

2. Sometimes, when after sin committed, I have looked for sore Chastizement from the Hand of God, the very next that I have had from him hath been the discovery of his Grace. Sometimes, when I have been comforted, I have called my self a Fool for my so sinking under trouble. And then again when I have been cast down, I thought I was not wise to give such way to comfort. With such strength and weight have both these been upon me.

3. I have wondred much at this one thing, that though God doth visit my Soul with never so blessed a discovery of himself, yet I have found again, that such hours have attended me afterwards, that I have been in my Spirit so filled with darkness, that I could not so much as once conceive, what that God and that Comfort was with which I have been refreshed.

4. I have sometimes seen more in a line of the Bible, then I could well tell how to stand under, and yet at another time the whole Bible hath been to me as dry as a stick; or rather my Heart hath been so dead and dry unto it, that I could not conceive the least dram of Refreshment, tho' I have look't it all over.

5. Of all tears, they are best that are made by the Blood of Christ; and of all Joy, that is the sweetest that is mixt with mourning over Christ: Oh! 'tis a goodly thing to be on our knees with Christ in our Arms, before God. I hope I know something of these things.

6. I find to this day seven Abominations in my Heart; 1. Inclinings to Unbelief. 2. Suddenly to forget the Love and Mercy that Christ manifesteth. 3. A leaning to the Works of the Law. 4. Wandrings and coldness in Prayer. 5. To forget to watch for that I pray for. 6. Apt to murmur because I have no more, and yet ready to abuse what I have. 7. I can do none of those things which God commands me, but my Corruptions will thrust in themselves. When I would do good, evil is present with me.

7. These things I continually see and feel, and am afflicted and oppressed with, yet the Wisdom of God doth order them for my good. 1. They make me abhor my self. 2. They keep me from trusting my Heart. 3. They convince me of the Insufficiency of all inherent Righteousness. 4. They shew me the Necessity of fleeing to Jesus. 5. They press me to pray unto God. 6. They shew me the need I have to watch and be sober. 7. And provoke me to pray unto God through Christ to help me, and carry me through this World.

FINIS.

A

RELATION

OF THE

IMPRISONMENT

OF

Mr. JOHN BUNYAN,

Minister of the Gospel at BEDFORD,

In NOVEMBER, 1660.

His Examination before the Justices, his Conference with the Clerk of the Peace, what passed between the Judges and his Wife, when she presented a Petition for his Deliverance, &c.

Written by himself, and never before published.

Blessed are ye which are persecuted for righteousness sake, for theirs is the kingdom of Heaven.
Blessed are ye when men shall revile you and persecute you, and shall say all manner of evil against you falsly for my name's sake.
Rejoice and be exceeding glad, for great is your reward in Heaven, for so persecuted they the Prophets which were before you.

MAT. V. 10, 11, 12.

LONDON:

Printed for JAMES BUCKLAND, at the Buck, in Paternoster-Row.

MDCCLXV.

The Relation of my Imprisonment in the month of November, 1660, *when*, *by the good hand of my God*, *I had for five or six years together*, *without any great interruption*, *freely preached the blessed Gospel of our Lord Jesus Christ*; *and had also*, *through his blessed Grace*, *some encouragement by his blessing thereupon : The Devil*, *that old enemy of mans salvation*, *took his opportunity to inflame the hearts of his vassals against me*, *insomuch that at the last*, *I was laid out for by the warrant of a justice*, *and was taken and committed to prison. The relation thereof is as followeth :*

UPON the 12th of this instant November, 1660, I was desired by some of the friends in the country to come to teach at *Samsell*, by *Harlington*, in *Bedfordshire*. To whom I made a promise, if the Lord permitted, to be with them on the time aforesaid. The justice hearing thereof, (whose name is Mr. *Francis Wingate*) forthwith issued out his warrant to take me, and bring me before him, and in the mean time to keep a very strong watch about the house where the meeting should be kept, as if we that was to meet together in that place did intend to do some fearful business, to the destruction of the country; when alas, the constable, when he came in, found us only with our Bibles in our hands, ready to speak and hear the word of God; for we was just about to begin our exercise. Nay, we had begun in prayer for the blessing of God upon our opportunity, intending to have preached the Word of the Lord unto them there present: But the constable coming in prevented us. So that I was taken and forced to depart the room. But had I been minded to have played the coward, I could have escaped, and kept out of his hands. For when I was come to my friend's house, there was whispering that that day I should be taken, for there was a warrant out to take me; which when my friend heard, he being somewhat timorous, questioned whether we had best have our meeting or not: And whether it might not be better for me to depart, lest they should take me and have me before the Justice, and after that send me to prison, (for he knew better than I what spirit they were of, living by them) to whom I said, no: By no means, I will not stir, neither will I have the meeting dismissed for this. Come, be of good chear, let us not be daunted, our cause is good, we need not be ashamed of it, to preach Gods word, it is so good a work, that we shall be well rewarded, if we suffer for that; or to this purpose—(But as for my friend, I think he was more afraid of me, than of himself.) After this I walked into the close, where I somewhat seriously considering the matter, this came into my mind: That I had shewed myself hearty and couragious in my preaching, and had, blessed be Grace, made it my business to encourage others; therefore thought I, if I should now run, and make an escape, it will be of a very ill savour in the country. For what will my weak and newly converted brethren think of it? But that I was not so strong in deed, as I was in word. Also I feared that if I should run now there was a warrant out for me, I might by so doing make them afraid to stand, when great words only should be spoken to them. Besides I thought, that seeing God of his mercy should chuse me to go upon the forlorn hope in this country; that is, to be the first, that should be opposed, for the Gospel; if I should fly, it might be a discouragement to the whole body that might follow after. And further, I thought the world thereby would take occasion at my cowardliness, to have blasphemed the Gospel, and to have had some ground to suspect worse of me and my profession, than I deserved. These things, with others considered by me, I came in again to the house, with a full resolution to keep the meeting, and not to go away, though I could have been gone about an hour before the officer apprehended me; but I would not; for I was resolved to see the utmost of what they could say or do unto me: For blessed be the Lord, I knew of no evil that I had said or done. And so, as aforesaid, I begun the meeting: But being prevented by the constable's coming in with his warrant to take me, I could not proceed: But before I went away, I spake some few words of counsel and encouragement to the people, declaring to them, that they see we was prevented of our opportunity to speak and hear the word of God, and was like to suffer for the same: desiring them that they should not be discouraged: For it was a mercy to suffer upon so good account: For we might have been apprehended as thieves or murderers, or for other wickedness; but blessed be God it was not so, but we suffer as christians for well doing: And we had better be the persecuted, than the persecutors, &c. But the constable and the justice's man waiting on us, would not be at quiet till they had me away, and that we departed the house: But because the justice was not at home that day, there was a friend of mine engaged for me to bring me to the constable on the morrow morning. Otherwise the constable must have charged a watch with me, or have secured me some other ways, my crime was so great. So on the next morning we went to the constable, and so to the justice. He asked the constable what we did where we was met together, and what we had with us. I trow, he meant whether we had armour or not; but when the constable told him that there was only met a few of us together to preach and hear the word, and no sign of any thing else, he could not well tell what to say: Yet because he had sent for me, he did adventure to put out a few proposals to me, which was to this effect. Namely, What I did there? and why I did not content myself with following my calling: For it was against the law, that such as I should be admitted to do as I did.

John Bunyan. To which I answered, that the intent of my coming thither, and to other places, was to instruct, and counsel people to forsake their sins, and close in with Christ, lest they did miserably perish; and that I could do both these without confusion, (to wit) follow my calling, and preach the word also.

At which words, he was in a chafe, as it appeared; for he said that he would break the neck of our meetings.

Bun. I said, it may be so. Then he wished me to get me sureties to be bound for me, or else he would send me to the jail.

My sureties being ready, I call'd them in, and when the bond for my appearance was made, he told them, that they was bound to keep me from preaching; and that if I did preach, their bonds would be forfeited. To which I answered, that then I should break them; for I should not leave speaking the word of God: Even to counsel, comfort, exhort, and teach the people among whom I came; and I thought this to be a work that had no hurt in it: But was rather worthy of commendation, than blame.

Wing. Whereat he told me, that if they would not be so bound, my mittimus must be made, and I sent to the jail, there to lie to the quarter-sessions.

Now while my mittimus was a making, the justice was withdrawn; and in comes an old enemy to the truth, Dr. *Lindale*, who, when he was come in, fell to taunting at me with many reviling terms.

Bun. To whom I answered, that I did not come thither to talk with him, but with the justice. Whereat he supposed that I had nothing to say for myself, triumphed as if he had got the victory. Charging and condemning me for medling with that for which I could shew no warrant. And asked me if I had taken the oaths? and if I had not, 'twas pity but that I should be sent to prison, &c.

I told him, that if I was minded, I could answer to any sober question that he should put to me. He then urged me again, how I could prove it lawful for me to preach, with a great deal of confidence of the victory.

But at last, because he should see that I could answer him if I listed, I cited him to that in Peter, which saith, *As every man hath received the gift, even so let him minister the same, &c.*

Lind. I, saith he, to whom is that spoken?

Bun. To whom, said I, why to every man that hath received a gift from God. Mark, saith the Apostle, *As every man that hath received a gift from God, &c.* And again, *You may all prophesy one by one.* Whereat the man was a little stopt, and went a softlier pace: But not being willing to lose the day, he began again, and said:

Lind. Indeed I do remember that I have read of one Alexander a Coppersmith, who did much oppose, and disturb the Apostles. (Aiming 'tis like at me, because I was a Tinker.)

Bun. To which I answered, that I also had read of very many priests and pharisees, that had their hands in the blood of our Lord Jesus Christ.

Lind. I, saith he, and you are one of those scribes and pharisees: for you, with a pretence, make long prayers to devour widows houses.

Bun. I answered, that if he had got no more by preaching

and praying than I had done, he would not be so rich as now he was. But that Scripture coming into my mind, *Answer not a fool according to his folly*, I was as sparing of my speech as I could, without prejudice to truth.

Now by this time my mittimus was made, and I committed to the constable to be sent to the jail in Bedford, &c.

But as I was going, two of my brethren met with me by the way, and desired the constable to stay, supposing that they should prevail with the justice, through the favour of a pretended friend, to let me go at liberty. So we did stay, while they went to the justice, and after much discourse with him, it came to this; that if I would come to him again, and say some certain words to him, I should be released. Which when they told me, I said if the words was such that might be said with a good conscience, I should, or else I should not. So through their importunity I went back again, but not believing that I should be delivered: For I feared their spirit was too full of opposition to the truth, to let me go, unless I should in something or other, dishonour my God, and wound my conscience. Wherefore as I went, I lift up my heart to God, for light, and strength, to be kept, that I might not do any thing that might either dishonour him, or wrong my own soul, or be a grief or discouragement to any that was inclining after the Lord Jesus Christ.

Well, when I came to the justice again, there was Mr. *Foster* of Bedford, who coming out of another room, and seeing of me by the light of the candle (for it was dark night when I went thither) he said unto me, who is there, *John Bunyan?* with such seeming affection, as if he would have leaped in my neck and kissed me, which made me somewhat wonder, that such a man as he, with whom I had so little acquaintance, and besides, that had ever been a close opposer of the ways of God, should carry himself so full of love to me: But afterwards, when I saw what he did, it caused me to remember those sayings, *Their tongues are smoother than oil, but their words are drawn swords.* And again, *Beware of men, &c.* When I had answered him, that blessed be God I was well, he said, What is the occasion of your being here? or to that purpose. To whom I answered, that I was at a meeting of people a little way off, intending to speak a word of exhortation to them; the justice hearing thereof (said I) was pleased to send his warrant, to fetch me before him, &c.

Fost. So (said he) I understand: But well, if you will promise to call the people no more together, you shall have your liberty to go home; for my brother is very loath to send you to prison, if you will be but ruled.

Bun. Sir (said I) pray what do you mean by calling the people together? my business is not any thing among them when they are come together, but to exhort them to look after the salvation of their souls, that they may be saved, &c.

Fost. Saith he, we must not enter into explication, or dispute now; but if you will say you will call the people no more together, you may have your liberty; if not, you must be sent away to prison.

Bun. Sir, said I, I shall not force or compel any man to hear me, but yet if I come into any place where there is a people met together, I should, according to the best of my skill and wisdom, exhort and counsel them to seek out after the Lord Jesus Christ, for the salvation of their souls.

Fost. He said, that was none of my work; I must follow my calling, and if I would but leave off preaching, and follow my calling, I should have the justice's favour, and be acquitted presently.

Bun. To whom I said, that I could follow my calling and that too, namely, preaching the word: And I did look upon it as my duty to do them both, as I had an opportunity.

Fost. He said, to have any such meetings was against the law; and therefore he would have me leave off, and say, I would call the people no more together.

Bun. To whom I said, that I durst not make any further promise: For my conscience would not suffer me to do it. And again, I did look upon it as my duty to do as much good as I could, not only in my trade, but also in communicating to all people wheresoever I came, the best knowledge I had in the word.

Fost. He told me, that I was the nearest the Papists of any, and that he would convince me of immediately.

Bun. I asked him wherein?

Fost. He said, in that we understood the Scriptures literally.

Bun. I told him, that those that was to be understood literally we understood them so; but for those that was to be understood otherwise, we endeavoured so to understand them.

Fost. He said, which of the Scriptures do you understand literally?

Bun. I said, this, *He that believes shall be saved.* This was to be understood, just as it is spoken; that whosoever believeth in Christ, shall, according to the plain and simple words of the text, be saved.

Fost. He said, that I was ignorant, and did not understand the Scriptures; for how (said he) can you understand them, when you know not the original Greek? &c.

Bun. To whom I said, that if that was his opinion, that none could understand the Scriptures, but those that had the original Greek, &c. then but a very few of the poorest sort should be saved, (this is harsh) yet the Scripture saith, *That God hides his things from the wise and prudent*, (that is from the learned of the world) *and reveals them to babes and sucklings.*

Fost. He said there was none that heard me, but a company of foolish people.

Bun. I told him that there was the wise as well as the foolish that do hear me; and again, those that are most commonly counted foolish by the world, are the wisest before God. Also, that God had rejected the wise, and mighty, and noble, and chosen the foolish, and the base.

Fost. He told me, that I made people neglect their calling; and that God had commanded people to work six days, and serve him on the seventh.

Bun. I told him, that it was the duty of people, (both rich and poor) to look out for their souls on them days, as well as for their bodies: And that God would have his people exhort one another daily, while it is called to day.

Fost. He said again, that there was none but a company of poor simple ignorant people that come to hear me.

Bun. I told him, that the foolish and the ignorant had most need of teaching and information; and therefore it would be profitable for me to go on in that work.

Fost. Well, said he, to conclude, but will you promise that you will not call the people together any more? and then you may be released, and go home.

Bun. I told him, that I durst say no more than I had said. For I durst not leave off that work which God had called me to.

So he withdrew from me, and then came several of the justices servants to me, and told me, that I stood so much upon a niceity. Their master, they said, was willing to let me go; and if I would but say I would call the people no more together, I might have my liberty, &c.

Bun. I told them, there was more ways than one, in which a man might be said to call the people together. As for instance, if a man get upon the market-place, and there read a book, or the like, though he do not say to the people, Sirs, come hither and hear; yet if they come to him because he reads, he, by his very reading, may be said to call them together; because they would not have been there to hear, if he had not been there to read. And seeing this might be termed a calling the people together, I durst not say, I would not call them together; for then, by the same argument, my preaching might be said to call them together.

Wing. and Fost. Then came the Justice and Mr. Foster to me again (we had a little more discourse about preaching, but because the method of it is out of my mind, I pass it) and when they saw that I was at a point, and would not be moved nor perswaded,

Mr. Foster told the justice, that then he must send me away to prison. And that he would do well also, if he would present all them that was the cause of my coming among them to meetings. Thus we parted.

And verily as I was going forth of the doors, I had much ado to forbear saying to them, that I carried the peace of God along with me: But I held my peace, and blessed be the Lord, went away to prison with God's comfort in my poor soul.

After I had lain in the jail five or six days, the brethren sought means again to get me out by bondsmen, (for so run my mittimus, that I should lie there till I could find sureties) they went to a justice at Elstow, one Mr. Crumpton, to desire him to take bond for my appearing at the quarter-sessions. At the first he told them he would, but afterwards he made a demur at the business, and desired first to see my mittimus, which run to this purpose; That I went about to several conventicles in this county, to the great disparagement of the government of the church of England, &c. When he had seen it, he said that there might be something more against me, than was expressed in my mittimus: And that he was but a young man, therefore he durst not do it. This my jailor told me. Whereat I was not at all daunted, but rather glad, and saw evidently that the Lord had heard me, for before I went down to the justice, I begged of God, that if I might do more good by being at liberty than in prison, that then I might be set at liberty: But if not, his will be done; for I was not altogether without hopes, but that my imprisonment might be an awakening to the Saints in the country, therefore I could not tell well which to chuse. Only I in that manner did commit the thing to God. And verily at my return, I did meet my God sweetly in the prison again, comforting of me and satisfying of me that it was his will and mind that I should be there.

When I came back again to prison, as I was musing at the slender answer of the Justice, this word dropt in upon my heart with some life, *For he knew that for envy they had delivered him.*

Thus have I in short, declared the manner, and occasion of my being in prison; where I lie waiting the good will of God, to do with me, as he pleaseth; knowing that not one hair of my head can fall to the ground without the will of my Father which is in Heaven. Let the rage and malice of men be never so great, they can do no more, nor go no farther than God permits them: But when they have done their worst, we know all things shall work together for good to them that love God.

Farewell.

RELATION OF IMPRISONMENT

Here is the Sum of my Examination, before Justice Keelin, Justice Chester, Justice Blundale, Justice Beecher, and Justice Snagg, &c.

AFTER I had lain in prison above seven weeks, the quarter-sessions was to be kept in Bedford, for the county thereof; unto which I was to be brought; and when my jailor had set me before those Justices, there was a bill of indictment preferred against me. The extent thereof was as followeth; That John Bunyan of the town of Bedford, labourer, being a person of such and such conditions, he hath (since such a time) devilishly and perniciously abstained from coming to church to hear divine service, and is a common upholder of several unlawful meetings and conventicles, to the great disturbance and distraction of the good subjects of this kingdom, contrary to the laws of our sovereign lord the king, &c.

The Clerk. When this was read, the clerk of the sessions said unto me; What say you to this?

Bun. I said, that as to the first part of it, I was a common frequenter of the church of God. And was also, by grace, a member with them people, over whom Christ is the Head.

Keelin. But saith Justice *Keelin* (who was the judge in that court) Do you come to church (you know what I mean) to the parish church, to hear divine service?

Bun. I answered, no, I did not.

Keel. He asked me why?

Bun. I said, because I did not find it commanded in the word of God.

Keel. He said we were commanded to pray.

Bun. I said, but not by the Common Prayer-book.

Keel. He said how then?

Bun. I said with the spirit. As the Apostle saith, *I will pray with the spirit with understanding.* 1 Cor. xiv. 15.

Keel. He said, we might pray with the spirit with understanding, and with the Common Prayer-book also.

Bun. I said that those prayers in the Common Prayer-book, was such as was made by other men, and not by the motions of the Holy Ghost, within our Hearts; and as I said the Apostle saith, he will pray with the spirit and with understanding; not with the spirit and the Common Prayer-book.

Another Justice. What do you count prayer? Do you think it is to say a few words over before, or among a people?

Bun. I said, no, not so; for men might have many elegant, or excellent words, and yet not pray at all: But when a man prayeth, he doth through a sense of those things which he wants (which sense is begotten by the spirit) pour out his heart before God through Christ; though his words be not so many, and so excellent as others are.

Justices. They said, that was true.

Bun. I said, this might be done without the Common Prayer-book.

Another. One of them said, (I think it was Justice *Blundale*, or Justice *Snagg*) How should we know, that you do not write out your prayers first, and then read them afterwards to the people? This he spake in a laughing way.

Bun. I said, it is not our use, to take a pen and paper and write a few words thereon, and then go and read it over to a company of people.

But how should we know it, said he?

Bun. Sir, it is none of our custom, said I.

Keel. But said Justice *Keelin*, it is lawful to use Common Prayer, and such like forms: For Christ taught his disciples to pray, as John also taught his disciples. And further, said he, cannot one man teach another to pray? Faith comes by hearing: And one man may convince another of sin, and therefore prayers made by men, and read over, are good to teach, and help men to pray.

While he was speaking these words, God brought that word into my mind, in the eighth of the Romans, at the 26th verse: I say God brought it, for I thought not on it before: but as he was speaking, it came so fresh into my mind, and was set so evidently before me, as if the Scripture had said, Take me, take me; so when he had done speaking,

Bun. I said, Sir, the Scripture saith, that *it is the spirit as helpeth our infirmities*; for we know not what we should pray for as we ought: But the spirit itself maketh intercession for us, with sighs and groanings which cannot be uttered. Mark, said I, it doth not say the Common Prayer-book teacheth us how to pray, but the spirit. *And it is the spirit that helpeth our infirmities*, saith the Apostle; he doth not say it is the Common Prayer-book.

And as to the Lord's Prayer, although it be an easy thing to say *Our Father, &c.* with the mouth; yet there is very few that can, in the spirit, say the two first words of that Prayer; that is, that can call God their Father, as knowing what it is to be born again, and as having experience, that they are begotten of the spirit of God: Which if they do not, all is but babbling, &c.

Keel. Justice *Keelin* said, that that was a truth.

Bun. And I say further, as to your saying that one man may convince another of sin, and that faith comes by hearing, and that one man may tell another how he should pray, &c. I say men may tell each other of their sins, but it is the spirit that must convince them.

And though it be said that *faith comes by hearing:* Yet it is the spirit that worketh faith in the heart through hearing, or else *they are not profited by hearing.*

And that though one Man may tell another how he should pray: Yet, as I said before, he cannot pray, nor make his condition known to God, except the spirit help. It is not the Common Prayer-book that can do this. It is the *spirit that sheweth us our sins*, and the *spirit that sheweth us a Saviour*: And the spirit that stireth up in our hearts desires to come to God, for such things as we stand in need of, even sighing out our souls unto him for them with *groans which cannot be uttered.* With other words to the same purpose. At this they were set.

Keel. But says Justice *Keelin*, what have you against the Common Prayer-book?

Bun. I said, Sir, if you will hear me, I shall lay down my reasons against it.

Keel. He said I should have liberty; but first, said he, let me give you one caution; take heed of speaking irreverently of the Common Prayer-book: For if you do so, you will bring great damage upon yourself.

Bun. So I proceeded, and said, my first reason was; because it was not commanded in the word of God, and therefore I could not do it.

Another. One of them said, where do you find it commanded in the Scripture, that you should go to *Elstow*, or *Bedford*, and yet it is lawful to go to either of them, is it not?

Bun. I said, to go to *Elstow* or *Bedford*, was a civil thing, and not material, though not commanded, and yet God's word allowed me to go about my calling, and therefore if it lay there, then to go thither, *&c.* But to pray, was a great part of the divine worship of God, and therefore it ought to be done according to the rule of God's word.

Another. One of them said, he will do harm; let him speak no further.

Just. Keel. Justice *Keelin* said, No, no, never fear him, we are better established than so; he can do no harm, we know the Common Prayer-book hath been ever since the Apostles time, and is lawful to be used in the church.

Bun. I said, shew me the place in the epistles, where the Common Prayer-book is written, or one text of Scripture, that commands me to read it, and I will use it. But yet, notwithstanding, said I, they that have a mind to use it, they have their liberty; that is, I would not keep them from it, but for our parts, we can pray to God without it. Blessed be his name.

With that one of them said, who is your God, Beelzebub? Moreover, they often said, that I was possessed with the spirit of delusion, and of the Devil. All which sayings, I passed over, the Lord forgive them! And further, I said, blessed be the Lord for it, we are encouraged to meet together, and to pray, and exhort one another; for we have had the comfortable presence of God among us, for ever blessed be his holy name.

Keel. Justice *Keeling* called this pedlers French, saying that I must leave off my canting. The Lord open his eyes!

Bun. I said, that we ought to exhort one another daily, while it is called to-day, &c.

Keel. Justice *Keeling* said, that I ought not to preach. And asked me where I had my authority? with many other such like words.

Bun. I said, that I would prove that it was lawful for me, and such as I am, to preach the word of God.

Keel. He said unto me, by what Scripture?

I said, by that in the first epistle of *Peter*, the ivth chap. the 11th ver. and *Acts* the xviiith, with other Scriptures, which he would not suffer me to mention. But said, hold; not so many, which is the first?

Bun. I said, this. *As every man hath received the gift, even so let him minister the same unto another, as good stewards of the manifold grace of God: If any man speak, let him speak as the oracles of God*, &c.

Keel. He said, let me a little open that Scripture to you. *As every man hath received the gift*; that is, said he, as every man hath received a trade, so let him follow it. If any man have received a gift of tinkering, as thou hast done, let him follow his tinkering. And so other men their trades. And the divine his calling, *&c.*

Bun. Nay, Sir, said I, but it is most clear, that the Apostle speaks here of preaching the word; if you do but compare both the verses together, the next verse explains this gift what it is; saying, *If any man speak, let him speak as the oracles of God:* So that it is plain, that the Holy Ghost doth not so much in this place exhort to civil callings, as to the exercising of those gifts that we have received from God. I would have gone on, but he would not give me leave.

Keel. He said, we might do it in our families, but not otherways.

Bun. I said, if it was lawful to do good to some, it was lawful to do good to more. If it was a good duty to exhort our families, it is good to exhort others: But if they held it a sin to meet together to seek the face of God, and exhort one another to follow Christ, I should sin still: For so we should do.

Keel. He said he was not so well versed in Scripture as to dispute, or words to that purpose. And said, moreover, that they could not wait upon me any longer; but said to me, then you confess the indictment, do you not? Now, and not till now, I saw I was indicted.

Bun. I said, this I confess, we have had many meetings together, both to pray to God, and to exhort one another, and that we had the sweet comforting presence of the Lord among us for our encouragement, blessed be his name therefore. I confessed myself guilty no otherwise.

Keel. Then said he, hear your judgment. You must be had back again to prison, and there lie for three months following; and at three months end, if you do not submit to go to church to hear divine service, and leave your preaching, you must be banished the realm: And if, after such a day as shall be appointed you to be gone, you shall be found in this realm, *&c.* or be found to come over again without special licence from the King, *&c.* you must stretch by the neck for it, I tell you plainly; and so he bid my jailor have me away.

Bun. I told him, as to this matter, I was at a point with him: For if I was out of prison to day, I would preach the Gospel again to-morrow, by the help of God.

Another. To which one made me some answer: But my jailor pulling me away to be gone, I could not tell what he said.

Thus I departed from them; and I can truly say, I bless the Lord *Jesus Christ* for it, that my heart was sweetly refreshed in the time of my examination, and also afterwards, at my returning to the prison: So that I found *Christ*'s words more than bare trifles, where he saith, he *will give a mouth and wisdom, even such as all the adversaries shall not resist, or gainsay.* And that his peace no man can take from us.

Thus have I given you the substance of my examination. The Lord make these profitable to all that shall read or hear them. Farewell.

RELATION OF IMPRISONMENT

The Substance of some Discourse had between the Clerk of the Peace and myself; when he came to admonish me, according to the tenor of that Law, by which I was in Prison.

WHEN I had lain in prison other twelve weeks, and now not knowing what they intended to do with me, upon the third of *April*, comes Mr. *Cobb* unto me, (as he told me) being sent by the Justices to admonish me, and demand of me submittance to the church of *England*, *&c.* The extent of our discourse was as followeth.

Cobb. When he was come into the house he sent for me out of my chamber; who, when I was come unto him, he said, Neighbour *Bunyan*, how do you do?

Bun. I thank you Sir, said I, very well, blessed be the Lord.

Cobb. Saith he, I come to tell you, that it is desired, you would submit yourself to the laws of the land, or else at the next sessions it will go worse with you, even to be sent away out of the nation, or else worse than that.

Bun. I said, that I did desire to demean myself in the world, both as becometh a man and a christian.

Cobb. But, saith he, you must submit to the laws of the land, and leave off those meetings which you was wont to have: For the statute law is directly against it; and I am sent to you by the Justices to tell you, that they do intend to prosecute the law against you, if you submit not.

Bun. I said, Sir, I conceive that that law by which I am in prison at this time, doth not reach or condemn, either me, or the meetings which I do frequent: That law was made against those, that being designed to do evil in their meetings, make the exercise of religion their pretence to cover their wickedness. It doth not forbid the private meetings of those that plainly and simply make it their only end to worship the Lord, and to exhort one another to edification. My end in meeting with others is simply to do as much good as I can, by exhortation and counsel, according to that small measure of light which God hath given me, and not to disturb the peace of the nation.

Cobb. Every one will say the same, said he; you see the late insurrection at *London*, under what glorious pretences they went, and yet indeed they intended no less than the ruin of the kingdom and commonwealth.

Bun. That practice of theirs, I abhor, said I; yet it doth not follow, that because they did so, therefore all others will do so. I look upon it as my duty to behave myself under the King's government, both as becomes a man and a christian; and if an occasion was offered me, I should willingly manifest my loyalty to my Prince, both by word and deed.

Cobb. Well, said he, I do not profess myself to be a man that can dispute; but this I say, truly neighbour *Bunyan*, I would have you consider this matter seriously, and submit yourself; you may have your liberty to exhort your neighbour in private discourse, so be you do not call together an assembly of people; and truly you may do much good to the church of Christ, if you would go this way; and this you may do, and the law not abridge you of it. It is your private meetings that the law is against.

Bun. Sir, said I, if I may do good to one by my discourse, why may I not do good to two? And if to two, why not to four, and so to eight, *&c.*

Cobb. I, saith he, and to a hundred, I warrant you.

Bun. Yes, Sir, said I, I think I should not be forbid to do as much good as I can.

Cobb. But, saith he, you may but pretend to do good, and indeed, notwithstanding, do harm, by seducing the people; you are therefore denied your meeting so many together, lest you should do harm.

Bun. And yet, said I, you say the law tolerates me to discourse with my neighbour; surely there is no law tolerates me to seduce any one; therefore if I may by the law discourse with one, surely it is to do him good; and if I by discoursing may do good to one, surely, by the same law, I may do good to many.

Cobb. The law, saith he, doth expresly forbid your private meetings, therefore they are not to be tolerated.

Bun. I told him, that I would not entertain so much

uncharitableness of that parliament in the 35th of *Elizabeth*, or of the Queen herself, as to think they did by that law intend the oppressing of any of God's ordinances, or the interrupting any in the way of God; but men may, in the wresting of it, turn it against the way of God; but take the law in itself, and it only fighteth against those that drive at mischief in their hearts and meetings, making religion only their cloak, colour, or pretence; for so are the words of the statute. *If any meetings, under colour or pretence of religion*, &c.

Cobb. Very good; therefore the King seeing that pretences are usually in, and among people, as to make religion their pretence only; therefore he, and the law before him, doth forbid such private meetings, and tolerates only public; you may meet in public.

Bun. Sir, said I, let me answer you in a similitude; set the case that, at such a wood corner, there did usually come forth thieves to do mischief, must there therefore a law be made, that every one that cometh out there shall be killed? May not there come out true men as well as thieves, out from thence? Just thus is it in this case; I do think there may be many, that may design the destruction of the commonwealth: But it doth not follow therefore that all private meetings are unlawful; those that transgress, let them be punished: And if at any time I myself, should do any act in my conversation as doth not become a man and christian, let me bear the punishment. And as for your saying I may meet in public, if I may be suffered, I would gladly do it: Let me have but meeting enough in public, and I shall care the less to have them in private. I do not meet in private because I am afraid to have meetings in public. I bless the Lord that my heart is at that point, that if any man can lay any thing to my charge, either in doctrine or practice, in this particular, that can be proved error or heresy, I am willing to disown it, even in the very market-place. But if it be truth, then to stand to it to the last drop of my blood. And Sir, said I, you ought to commend me for so doing. To err, and to be a heretic, are two things; I am no heretic, because I will not stand refractorily to defend any one thing that is contrary to the word; prove any thing which I hold to be an error, and I will recant it.

Cobb. But goodman *Bunyan*, said he, methinks you need

not stand so strictly upon this one thing, as to have meetings of such public assemblies. Cannot you submit, and, notwithstanding do as much good as you can, in a neighbourly way, without having such meetings?

Bun. Truly Sir, said I, I do not desire to commend myself, but to think meanly of myself; yet when I do most despise myself, taking notice of that small measure of light which God hath given me, also that the people of the Lord (by their own saying) are edified thereby: Besides, when I see that the Lord, through grace, hath in some measure blessed my labour, I dare not but exercise that gift which God hath given me, for the good of the people. And I said further, that I would willingly speak in public if I might.

Cobb. He said, that I might come to the public assemblies and hear. What though you do not preach? you may hear: Do not think yourself so well enlightened, and that you have received a gift so far above others; but that you may hear other men preach. Or to that purpose.

Bun. I told him, I was as willing to be taught as to give instruction, and I looked upon it as my duty to do both; for, said I, a man that is a teacher, he himself may learn also from another that teacheth; as the Apostle saith: *We may all prophecy one by one, that all may learn.* That is, every man that hath received a gift from God, he may dispense it, that others may be comforted; and when he hath done, he may hear, and learn, and be comforted himself of others.

Cobb. But, said he, what if you should forbear awhile; and sit still, till you see further, how things will go?

Bun. Sir, said I, *Wickliffe* saith, that he which leaveth off preaching and hearing of the word of God for fear of excommunication of men, he is already excommunicated of God, and shall in the day of judgment be counted a traitor to Christ.

Cobb. I, saith he, they that do not hear shall be so counted indeed; do you therefore hear.

Bun. But Sir, said I, he saith, he that shall leave off either preaching or hearing, *&c.* That is, if he hath received a gift for edification, it is his sin, if he doth not lay it out in a way of exhortation and counsel, according to the proportion of his gift; as well as to spend his time altogether in hearing others preach.

Cobb. But, said he, how shall we know that you have received a gift?

Bun. Said I, let any man hear and search, and prove the doctrine by the Bible.

Cobb. But will you be willing, said he, that two indifferent persons shall determine the case, and will you stand by their judgment.

Bun. I said, are they infallible?

Cobb. He said, no.

Bun. Then, said I, it is possible my judgment may be as good as theirs: But yet I will pass by either, and in this matter be judged by the Scriptures; I am sure that is infallible, and cannot err.

Cobb. But, said he, who shall be judge between you, for you take the Scriptures one way, and they another.

Bun. I said, the Scripture should, and that by comparing one Scripture with another; for that will open itself, if it be rightly compared. As for instance, if under the different apprehensions of the word *Mediator*, you would know the truth of it, the Scriptures open it, and tell us, that he that is a mediator, must take up the business between two, and a mediator is not a mediator of one, *but God is one, and there is one mediator between God and man, even the man Christ Jesus.* So likewise the Scripture calleth Christ a *compleat*, or perfect, or able *high-priest*. That is opened in that he is called man, and also God. His blood also is discovered to be effectually efficacious by the same things. So the Scripture, as touching the matter of meeting together, *&c.* doth likewise sufficiently open itself and discover its meaning.

Cobb. But are you willing, said he, to stand to the judgment of the Church?

Bun. Yes Sir, said I, to the approbation of the church of God, (the church's judgment is best expressed in Scripture.) We had much other discourse, which I cannot well remember, about the laws of the nation, submission to governments; to which I did tell him, that I did look upon myself as bound in conscience to walk according to all righteous laws, and that whether there was a King or no; and if I did any thing that was contrary, I did hold it my duty to bear patiently the penalty of the law, that was provided against such offenders; with many more words to the like effect. And said, moreover, that to cut off all occasions of suspicion from any, as touching the harmlessness of my doctrine in private, I would willingly take the pains to give any one the notes of all my sermons: For I do sincerely desire to live quietly in my country, and to submit to the present authority.

Cobb. Well, neighbour *Bunyan*, said he, but indeed I would wish you seriously to consider of these things, between this and the quarter-sessions, and to submit yourself. You may do much good if you continue still in the land: But alas, what benefit will it be to your friends, or what good can you do to them, if you should be sent away beyond the seas into *Spain*, or *Constantinople*, or some other remote part of the world? Pray be ruled.

Jaylor. Indeed, Sir, I hope he will be ruled.

Bun. I shall desire, said I, in all godliness and honesty to behave myself in the nation whilst I am in it. And if I must be so dealt withal, as you say, I hope God will help me to bear what they shall lay upon me. I know no evil that I have done in this matter, to be so used. I speak as in the presence of God.

Cobb. You know, saith he, that the Scripture saith, *the powers that are, are ordained of God.*

Bun. I said, yes, and that I was to submit to the King as supreme, also to the governors, as to them that are sent by him.

Cobb. Well then, said he, the King then commands you, that you should not have any private meetings; because it is against his law, and he is ordained of God, therefore you should not have any.

Bun. I told him, that *Paul* did own the powers that were in his day, as to be of God; and yet he was often in prison under them for all that. And also, though *Jesus Christ* told *Pilate*, that he had no power against him, but of God, yet he died under the same *Pilate*; and yet, said I, I hope you will not say, that either *Paul*, or Christ, was such as did deny magistracy, and so sinned against God in slighting the ordinance. Sir, said I, the law hath provided two ways of obeying: The one to do that which I in my conscience do believe that I am bound to do, actively; and where I cannot obey actively, there

I am willing to lie down, and to suffer what they shall do unto me. At this he sate still and said no more; which when he had done, I did thank him for his civil and meek discoursing with me; and so we parted.

O! that we might meet in Heaven!

Farewell. *J. B.*

Here followeth a Discourse between my Wife and the Judges, with others, touching my Deliverance at the Assises following; the which I took from her own Mouth.

AFTER that I had received this sentence of banishing, or hanging, from them, and after the former admonition, touching the determination of Justices, if I did not recant; just when the time drew nigh, in which I should have abjured, or have done worse (as Mr. *Cobb* told me) came the time in which the King was to be crowned. Now at the coronation of Kings, there is usually a releasement of divers prisoners, by virtue of his coronation; in which privilege also I should have had my share; but that they took me for a convicted person, and therefore, unless I sued out a pardon, (as they called it) I could have no benefit thereby, notwithstanding, yet forasmuch as the coronation proclamation did give liberty from the day the King was crowned, to that day twelvemonth to sue them out: Therefore, though they would not let me out of prison, as they let out thousands, yet they could not meddle with me, as touching the execution of their sentence; because of the liberty offered for the suing out of pardons. Whereupon I continued in prison till the next assizes, which are called *Midsummer* assizes, being then kept in *August*, 1661.

Now at that assizes, because I would not leave any possible means unattempted that might be lawful; I did, by my wife, present a petition to the Judges three times, that I might be heard, and that they would impartially take my case into consideration.

The first time my wife went, she presented it to Judge *Hales*, who very mildly received it at her hand, telling her that he would do her and me the best good he could; but he feared, he said, he could do none. The next day again, least they should, through the multitude of business forget me, we did throw another petition into the coach to Judge *Twisdon*; who, when he had seen it, snapt her up, and angrily told her that I was a convicted person, and could not be released, unless I would promise to preach no more, *&c.*

Well, after this, she yet again presented another to Judge *Hales* as he sate on the bench, who, as it seemed, was willing to give her audience. Only Justice *Chester* being present, stept up and said, that I was convicted in the court, and that I was a hot spirited fellow (or words to that purpose) whereat he waved it, and did not meddle therewith. But yet, my wife being encouraged by the High Sheriff, did venture once more into their presence (as the poor widow did to the unjust Judge) to try what she could do with them for my liberty, before they went forth of the town. The place where she went to them, was to the *Swan Chamber*, where the two Judges, and many Justices and Gentry of the country, was in company together. She then coming into the chamber with a bashed face, and a trembling heart, began her errand to them in this manner.

Woman. My Lord, (directing herself to Judge *Hales*) I make bold to come once again to your Lordship to know what may be done with my husband.

Judge Hales. To whom he said, Woman, I told thee before I could do thee no good; because they have taken that for a conviction which thy husband spoke at the sessions: And unless there be something done to undo that, I can do thee no good.

Woman. My Lord, said she, he is kept unlawfully in prison, they clap'd him up before there were any proclamation against the meetings; the indictment also is false: Besides, they never asked him whether he was guilty or no; neither did he confess the indictment.

One of the Justices. Then one of the Justices that stood by, whom she knew not, said, My Lord, he was lawfully convicted.

Wom. It is false, said she; for when they said to him, do

you confess the indictment? He said only this, that he had been at several meetings, both where there was preaching the word, and prayer, and that they had God's presence among them.

Judge Twisdon. Whereat Judge *Twisdon* answered very angrily, saying, what you think we can do what we list; your husband is a breaker of the peace, and is convicted by the law, *&c.* Whereupon Judge *Hales* called for the Statute Book.

Wom. But said she, my Lord, he was not lawfully convicted.

Chester. Then Justice *Chester* said, my Lord, he was lawfully convicted.

Wom. It is false, said she; it was but a word of discourse that they took for a conviction (as you heard before.)

Chest. But it is recorded, woman, it is recorded, said Justice *Chester.* As if it must be of necessity true because it was recorded. With which words he often endeavoured to stop her mouth, having no other argument to convince her, but it is recorded, it is recorded.

Wom. My Lord, said she, I was a-while since at *London*, to see if I could get my husband's liberty, and there I spoke with my Lord *Barkwood*, one of the house of Lords, to whom I delivered a petition, who took it of me and presented to some of the rest of the house of Lords, for my husband's releasement; who, when they had seen it, they said, that they could not release him, but had committed his releasement to the Judges, at the next assises. This he told me; and now I come to you to see if any thing may be done in this business, and you give neither releasement nor relief. To which they gave her no answer, but made as if they heard her not.

Chest. Only Justice *Chester* was often up with this, He is convicted, and it is recorded.

Wom. If it be, it is false, said she.

Chest. My Lord, said Justice *Chester*, he is a pestilent fellow, there is not such a fellow in the country again.

Twis. What, will your husband leave preaching? If he will do so, then send for him.

Wom. My Lord, said she, he dares not leave preaching, as long as he can speak.

Twis. See here, what should we talk any more about such a fellow? Must he do what he lists? He is a breaker of the peace.

Wom. She told him again, that he desired to live peaceably, and to follow his calling, that his family might be maintained; and moreover said, my Lord, I have four small children, that cannot help themselves, of which one is blind, and have nothing to live upon, but the charity of good people.

Hales. Hast thou four children? said Judge *Hales*; thou art but a young woman to have four children.

Wom. My Lord, said she, I am but mother-in-law to them, having not been married to him yet full two years. Indeed I was with child when my husband was first apprehended: But being young and unaccustomed to such things, said she, I being smayed at the news, fell into labour, and so continued for eight days, and then was delivered, but my child died.

Hales. Whereat, he looking very soberly on the matter, said, Alas poor woman!

Twis. But Judge *Twisdon* told her, that she made poverty her cloak; and said, moreover, that he understood, I was maintained better by running up and down a preaching, than by following my calling.

Hales. What is his calling? said Judge *Hales*.

Answer. Then some of the company that stood by, said, A Tinker, my Lord.

Wom. Yes, said she, and because he is a Tinker, and a poor man; therefore he is despised, and cannot have justice.

Hales. Then Judge *Hales* answered, very mildly, saying, I tell thee, woman, seeing it is so, that they have taken what thy husband spake, for a conviction; thou must either apply thyself to the King, or sue out his pardon, or get a writ of error.

Chest. But when Justice *Chester* heard him give her this counsel; and especially (as she supposed) because he spoke of a writ of error, he chaffed, and seemed to be very much offended; saying, my Lord, he will preach and do what he lists.

Wom. He preacheth nothing but the word of God, said she.

Twis. He preach the word of God! said *Twisdon* (and withal, she thought he would have struck her) he runneth up and down, and doth harm.

Wom. No, my Lord, said she, it's not so, God hath owned him, and done much good by him.

Twis. God! said he, his doctrine is the doctrine of the Devil.

Wom. My Lord, said she, when the righteous judge shall appear, it will be known, that his doctrine is not the doctrine of the Devil.

Twis. My Lord, said he, to Judge *Hales*, do not mind her, but send her away.

Hales. Then said Judge *Hales*, I am sorry, woman, that I can do thee no good; thou must do one of those three things aforesaid, namely; either to apply thyself to the King, or sue out his pardon, or get a writ of error; but a writ of error will be cheapest.

Wom. At which *Chester* again seemed to be in a chaffe, and put off his hat, and as she thought, scratched his head for anger: But when I saw, said she, that there was no prevailing to have my husband sent for, though I often desired them that they would send for him, that he might speak for himself, telling them, that he could give them better satisfaction than I could, in what they demanded of him; with several other things, which now I forget; only this I remember, that though I was somewhat timerous at my first entrance into the chamber, yet before I went out, I could not but break forth into tears, not so much because they were so hard-hearted against me, and my husband, but to think what a sad account such poor creatures will have to give at the coming of the Lord, when they shall there answer for all things whatsoever they have done in the body, whether it be good, or whether it be bad.

So, when I departed from them, the book of Statute was brought, but what they said of it, I know nothing at all, neither did I hear any more from them.

RELATION OF IMPRISONMENT

Some Carriages of the Adversaries of God's Truth with me at the next Assises, which was on the nineteenth of the first Month, 1662.

I Shall pass by what befel between these two assizes, how I had, by my Jailor, some liberty granted me, more than at the first, and how I followed my wonted course of preaching, taking all occasions that was put into my hand to visit the people of God, exhorting them to be stedfast in the faith of Jesus Christ, and to take heed that they touched not the Common Prayer, *&c.* but to mind the word of God, which giveth direction to Christians in every point, being able to make the man of God perfect in all things through faith in Jesus Christ, and thoroughly to furnish him up to all good works. Also how I having, I say, somewhat more liberty, did go to see Christians at *London*, which my enemies hearing of, was so angry, that they had almost cast my Jailor out of his place, threatning to indite him, and to do what they could against him. They charged me also, that I went thither to plot and raise division, and make insurrection, which, God knows, was a slander; whereupon my liberty was more straightened than it was before; so that I must not look out of the door. Well, when the next sessions came, which was about the 10th of the 11th month, I did expect to have been very roundly dealt withal; but they passed me by, and would not call me, so that I rested till the assises, which was the 19th of the first month following; and when they came, because I had a desire to come before the judge, I desired my Jailor to put my name into the kalender among the felons, and made friends to the Judge and High Sheriff, who promised that I should be called; so that I thought what I had done might have been effectual for the obtaining of my desire: But all was in vain; for when the assises came, though my name was in the kalender, and also though both the Judge and Sheriff had promised that I should appear before them, yet the Justices and the Clerk of the peace, did so work it about, that I, notwithstanding, was defered, and might not appear: And though I say, I do not know of all their carriages towards me, yet this I know, that the Clerk of the peace did discover himself to be one of my greatest opposers: For, first he came to my Jailor, and told him that I must not go down before the Judge, and therefore must not be put into the kalender; to whom my Jailor said, that my name was in already. He bid him put me out again; my Jailor told him that he could not: For he had given the Judge a kalender with my name in it, and also the Sheriff another. At which he was very much displeased, and desired to see that kalender that was yet in my Jailor's hand, who, when he had gave it him, he looked on it, and said it was a false kalender; he also took the kalender and blotted out my accusation, as my Jailor had writ it. (Which accusation I cannot tell what it was, because it was so blotted out) and he himself put in words to this purpose: That *John Bunyan* was committed in prison; being lawfully convicted for upholding of unlawful meetings and conventicles, *&c.* But yet for all this, fearing that what he had done, unless he added thereto, it would not do, he first run to the Clerk of the assises; then to the Justices, and afterwards, because he would not leave any means unattempted to hinder me, he comes again to my Jailor, and tells him, that if I did go down before the Judge, and was released, he would make him pay my fees, which he said was due to him; and further, told him, that he would complain of him at the next quarter sessions for making of false kalenders, though my Jailor himself, as I afterwards learned, had put in my accusation worse than in itself it was by far. And thus was I hindred and prevented at that time also from appearing before the Judge: And left in prison. Farewell.

JOHN BUNYAN.

THE
Pilgrim's Progress
FROM
THIS WORLD
TO
That which is to Come:
Delivered under the Similitude of a
DREAM,
Wherein is Discovered
The Manner of his setting out,
His Dangerous JOURNEY,
AND
Safe Arrival at the Desired Country.

By *JOHN BUNYAN.*

The Eleventh Edition with Additions, and the Cuts.

I have used Similitudes, Hosea 12. 10.

Licensed and entred according to Order.

LONDON,
Printed for *Nathanael Ponder,* at the *Peacock* in the *Poultry* near the Church, 1688.

Advertisement.

THE

SECOND PART

OF THE

Pilgrims Progress.

THE Pilgrims Progress, from this World to that which is to come; The Second Part: delivered under the Similitude of a *Dream*, wherein is set forth the Manner of the setting out of *Christians* Wife and Children, their dangerous Journey, and safe Arrival at the desired Country, by *John Bunyan.* *I have used Similitudes*, Hos. 12. 10. Price One Shilling.

The Authors Apology for his BOOK.

When at the first I took my Pen in hand
Thus for to write; I did not understand,
That I at all should make a little Book
In such a Mode: Nay, I had undertook
To make another; which when almost done,
Before I was aware, I this begun;
And thus it was: I writing of the way
And race of Saints in this our Gospel day,
Fell suddenly into an Allegory
About their Journey, and the way to Glory,
In more than Twenty things, which I set down:
This done, I Twenty more had in my Crown;
And they again began to multiply,
Like sparks that from the coals of fire do fly:
Nay then, thought I, if that you breed so fast,
I'll put you by your selves, lest you at last
Should prove ad infinitum, *and eat out*
The Book that I already am about.
Well, so I did; but yet I did not think
To shew to all the World my Pen and Ink
In such a mode, I only thought to make
I knew not what: Nor did I undertake
Thereby to please my Neighbour; no not I,
I did it mine own self to Gratifie.
Neither did I but vacant seasons spend
In this my Scribble; Nor did I intend
But to divert my self in doing this,
From worser thoughts, which make me do amiss.

Thus I set Pen to Paper with delight,
And quickly had my thoughts in black and white.
For having now my Method by the end,
Still as I pull'd, it came; and so I pen'd
It down; until it came at last to be
For length and breadth the bigness which you see.
Well, when I had thus put my ends together,
I shew'd them others, that I might see whether
They would condemn them, or them justifie:
And some said, let them live; some let them die:
Some said, John, *Print it; others said, not so:*
Some said it might do good; others said, no.
Now was I in a straight; and did not see
Which was the best thing to be done by me:
At last I thought, since you are thus divided,
I print it will, and so the case decided.
For, Thought I, some I see would have it done,
Though others in that Channel do not run:
To prove then who advised for the best,
Thus I thought fit to put it to the Test.
I further thought, if now I did deny
Those that would have it, thus to gratifie;
I did not know, but hinder *them I might*
Of that which would to them be great delight.
For those which were not for its coming forth;
I said to them, Offend you I am loth:
Yet since your Brethren pleased with it be,
Forbear to judge, till you do further see.
If that thou wilt not read, let it *alone,*
Some love the Meat, some love to pick the Bone,
Yea that I might them better moderate
I did too with them thus Expostulate.
May I not write in such a style as this?
In such a Method *too, and yet not miss*
My *end,* thy *good? why may it not be done?*
Dark clouds bring waters, when the bright bring none:
Yea, dark *or* bright, *if they their* Silver drops
Cause to descend, the earth, by yielding Crops,
Gives praise to both, and carpeth not at either,
But treasures up the Fruit they yield together;

Yea, so commixes both, that in her Fruit
None can distinguish this from that; they suit
Her well when hungry: But if she be full,
She spues out both, and makes their blessings null.
You see the ways the Fisher-man *doth take*
To catch the Fish; what Engines doth he make?
Behold! How he engageth all his wits;
Also his snares, lines, angles, hooks, and nets:
Yet Fish there be, that neither Hook nor Line,
Nor Snare, nor Net, nor Engine can make thine:
They must be grop'd for, and be tickled too,
Or they will not be catcht, what e'er you do.
How does the Fowler *seek to catch his game*
By divers means, all which one cannot name?
His gun, his nets, his lime-twigs, light and bell:
He creeps, he goes, he stands; yea who can tell
Of all his postures? yet there's none of these
Will make him Master of what Fowls he please.
Yea, he must Pipe and Whistle to catch this,
Yet if he does so, that Bird he will miss.
If that a Pearl may in a Toads-head *dwell,*
And may be found too in an Oyster-shell;
If things that promise nothing, do contain
What better is than Gold; who will disdain,
That have an inkling of it, there to look,
That they may find it? Now my little Book
(Tho void of all these paintings that may make
It with this or the other man to take)
Is not without those things that do excel
What do in brave, but empty Notions dwell.
Well, yet I am not fully satisfy'd
That this your Book will stand, when soundly try'd.
Why what's the matter? It is dark, *what tho?*
But it is feigned: *What of that? I tro,*
Some men by feigned words, as dark as mine,
Make truth to spangle, and its Rays to shine.
But they want solidness: *speak man thy mind:*
They drown'd the weak Metaphors make us blind.
Solidity, indeed becomes the Pen
Of him that writeth things Divine to Men:

But must I needs want solidness, because
By Metaphors *I speak? were not Gods Laws,*
His Gospel-Laws, in olden times held forth
By Types, Shadows and Metaphors? *Yet loth*
Will any sober Man be to find fault
With them, lest he be found for to assault
The highest Wisdom: No, he rather stoops,
And seeks to find out what by Pins and Loops,
By Calves, and Sheep, by Heifers, and by Rams.
By Birds and Herbs, and by the blood of Lambs,
God speaketh to him; and happy is he
That finds the Light and Grace that in them be.
Be not too forward therefore to conclude,
That I want solidness; that I am rude:
All things solid in Shew, not solid be;
All things in Parables despise not we,
Lest things most hurtful lightly we receive;
And things that good are, of our Souls bereave.
My dark and cloudy words, they do but hold
The truth, as Cabinets inclose the Gold.
The Prophets used much by Metaphors
To set forth Truth; Yea, who so considers
Christ his Apostles too, shall plainly see,
That Truths, to this day, in such Mantles be.
Am I afraid to say that Holy Writ,
Which for its Stile and Praise puts down all wit,
Is every where so full of all these things,
(Dark Figures, Allegories) yet there springs
From that same Book, that lustre, and those rays
Of light, that turns our darkest nights to days.
Come let my Carper, to his Life *now look,*
And find there darker Lines than in my Book
He findeth any: Yea, and let him know,
That in his best things *there are* worse *lines too.*
May we but stand before Impartial Men,
To his poor One, I dare adventure Ten,
That they will take my *meaning in these lines,*
Far better than his lyes in Silver Shrines.
Come, Truth, altho in Swadling-clouts, I find,
Informs the Judgment, rectifies the Mind;

Pleases the Understanding, makes the Will
Submit; The Memory too it doth fill
With what doth our Imaginations please;
Likewise, it tends our Troubles to appease.
Sound words I know Timothy *is to use,*
And old Wives Fables he is to refuse;
But yet grave Paul *him no where did forbid*
The use of Parables: in which lay hid
That gold, those pearls, and precious stones that were
Worth digging for, and that with greatest care.
Let me add one word more, O Man of God:
Art thou offended? Dost thou wish I had
Put forth my Matter in another dress,
Or that I had in things been more express?
To those that are my betters, (as is fit)
Three things let me propound, then I submit.
1. *I find not that I am deny'd the use*
Of this my Method, so I none abuse.
Put on the Words, Things, Readers, or be rude
In handling Figure or Similitude,
In application; but all that I may,
Seek the advance of Truth, this or that way:
Denyed, did I say? Nay, I have leave,
(Examples too, and that from them that have
God better pleased by their Words or Ways,
Than any Man that breatheth now adays)
Thus to express my mind, thus to declare
Things unto thee that Excellentest are.
2. *I find that Men (as high as Trees) will write*
Dialogue-wise; yet no man doth them slight,
For writing so: Indeed if they abuse
Truth, cursed be they, and the craft they use
To that intent; but yet let Truth be free
To make her Sallys upon Thee, and Me,
Which way it pleases God: for who knows how,
Better than he that taught us first to Plow,
To Guide our Mind and Pens for his Design?
And he makes base things usher in Divine.
3. *I find that Holy Writ in many places,*
Hath semblance with this method, where the cases

Do call for one thing, to set forth another;
Use it I may then, and yet nothing smother
Truths Golden Beams: Nay, by this method may
Make it cast forth its Rays as light as day.
And now before I do put up my Pen,
I'll shew the profit of my Book, and then
Commit both thee and It unto that hand
That pulls the strong down, and makes weak ones stand.
This Book it chalketh out before thine eyes
The Man that seeks the everlasting Prize:
It shews you whence he comes, whither he goes;
What he leaves undone; also what he does:
It also shews you how he runs, and runs,
Till he unto the Gate of Glory comes.
It shews too, who sets out for Life amain,
As if the lasting Crown they would attain:
Here also you may see the reason why
They lose their Labour and like fools do die.
This Book will make a Traveller of thee;
If by its Counsel thou wilt ruled be;
It will direct thee to the Holy-Land,
If thou wilt its directions understand:
Yea, it will make the slothful active be
The blind also delightful things to see.
Art thou for something rare, and profitable?
Wouldest thou see a Truth within a Fable?
Art thou forgetful? wouldest thou remember
From New-years day *to the last of* December?
Then read my Fancies, they will stick like Burrs,
And maybe to the helpless Comforters.
This Book is writ in such a Dialect,
As may the minds of listless Men affect:
It seems a Novelty, and yet contains
Nothing but sound and honest Gospel strains.
Wouldst thou divert thy self from Melancholy?
Wouldst thou be pleasant, yet be far from folly?
Wouldst thou read Riddles, and their Explanation,
Or else be drowned in thy Contemplation?
Dost thou love picking-meat? or wouldst thou see
A Man i'th'Clouds, and hear him speak to thee?

FOR HIS BOOK

Wouldst thou be in a Dream, and yet not sleep?
Or wouldst thou in a moment laugh and weep?
Wouldst thou lose thy self, and catch no harm?
And find thy self again without a charm?
Wouldst read thy self, and read thou knowest not what,
And yet know whether thou art blest or not,
By reading the same Lines? O then come hither,
And lay my Book, thy Head, and Heart together.

JOHN BUNYAN.

THE

Pilgrim's Progress:

In the Similitude of a

DREAM.

AS I walked through the Wilderness of this World, I lighted on a certain Place where was a *Den: and I laid me down in *that* place to sleep: And as I slept I dreamed a Dream. I dreamed, and behold, *I saw a Man* †*cloathed with Rags, standing in a certain place, with his Face from his own House, a Book in his hand, and a great Burden upon his Back,* I looked, and saw him open the Book, and read therein, and as he read he wept and trembled, and not being able longer to contain, he brake out with a lamentable Cry, saying, **What shall I do?*

* *The Goal.*

† Isa. 64. 6.
Luke 14. 33.
Ps. 38. 4.
Hab. 2. 2.
Acts 16. 31.

His Out-cry.

* Acts 2. 27.

In this plight therefore he went home, and refrained himself as long as he could, that his Wife and Children should not perceive his Distress, but he could not be silent long, because that his trouble increased: wherefore at length he brake his mind to his Wife and children; and thus he began to talk to them. *O my dear Wife,* said he, *and you the Children of my Bowels, I your dear Friend am in my self undone, by reason of a burden that lieth hard upon me: moreover I am for certain informed, that* **this our City will be burned with Fire from Heaven, in which fearful overthrow, both*

* *This World.*

my self, with thee my Wife, and you my sweet Babes, shall miserably come to ruin; *except* (*the which* †*yet I see not*) *some way of escape can be found, whereby we may be delivered.* At this, His Relations were sore amazed; not for that they believed that what he had said to them was true, but because they thought that some frenzy Distemper had got into his Head: therefore, it drawing towards night, and they hoping that sleep might settle his brains, with all haste they got him to Bed; but the night was as troublesome to him as the day; wherefore, instead of sleeping, he spent it in sighs and tears. So when the morning was come, they would know how he did; he told them *worse* and *worse*; He also set to talking to them again, but they began to be hardned. *They also thought to drive away his distemper by harsh and surly carriages to him: Sometimes they would deride, sometimes they would chide, and sometimes they would quite neglect him: wherefore he began to retire himself to his Chamber to pray for, and pity them; and also to condole his own misery; he would also walk solitarily in the Fields, sometimes reading, and sometimes praying; and thus for some days he spent his time.

† *He knows no way of escape as yet.*

* *Carnal Physick for a sick Soul.*

Now, I saw, upon a time, when he was walking in the Fields, that he was (as he was wont) reading in this Book, and greatly distressed in his Mind; and as he read he burst out, as he had done before, crying, **What shall I do to be saved?*

* *Acts* 16. 30, 31.

I saw also that he looked *this* way, and *that* way, as if he would run; yet he stood still, because (as I perceived) he could not tell which way to go, I looked then, and saw a man named *Evangelist*, coming to him, and asked, *Wherefore dost thou cry?* He answered, Sir, I perceive by the Book, in my hand, that I am condemned to die, and †after that to come to Judgment, and I find that I am not *willing to do the first, nor †able to do the second.

† *Heb.* 9. 27.

* *Job* 26. 21, 22.

† *Exod.* 22. 14.

Then said *Evangelist*, Why not willing to die; since this Life is attended with so many Evils? The Man answered, because I fear that this burden that is upon my back, will sink me lower than the Grave; and I shall fall into **Tophet*. And, Sir, if I be not fit to go to Prison, I am not fit to go to Judgment, and from thence to Execution; and the thoughts of these things make me cry.

* *Isa.* 30. 33.

Then said *Evangelist*, if this be thy Condition, why standest thou still? He answered, because I know not whither to go. Then he gave him a †*Parchment Roll*, and there was written within, **Fly from the Wrath to come.*

† *Conviction of the necessity of flying.*

* Mat. 3. 7.

The Man therefore read it, and looking upon *Evangelist* very carefully, said, Whither must I fly? Then said *Evangelist*, pointing with his Finger over a very wide Field, Do you see yonder *Wicket-Gate*? The Man said, No*; Then said the other, Do you see yonder †shining Light? He said, I think I do. Then said *Evangelist*, Keep that Light in your Eye, and go up directly thereto, *so shalt thou see the Gate; at which when thou knockest, it shall be told thee what thou shalt do.

* Mat. 7.
Psal. 119. 105.
2 Pet. 2. 29.

† *Christ, and the way to him cannot be found without the word.*

* Luke 14. 16.

So I saw in my Dream, that the Man began to run; now he had not run far from his own Door, but his Wife and Children perceiving it, began to cry after him to return; †but the man put his Fingers in his Ears, and ran on crying, Life, Life, Eternal Life: so he loooked not behind him *but fled towards the middle of the Plain.

† Gen. 19. 17.

* *They that fly from the wrath to come, are a gazing stock to the world.*

The Neighbours also came out to †see him run, and as he ran, some mocked, others threatned, and some cried after him to return; And among those that did so, there were two that were resolved to fetch him back by force. *The Name of the one was *Obstinate*, and the Name of the other *Pliable*. Now by this time the Man was got a good distance from them; but however they were resolved to pursue him; which they did, and in a little time they overtook him. Then said the Man, Neighbours, *Wherefore are you come?* They said, to perswade you to go back with us; but he said, that can by no means be? You dwell, (said he) in the City of Destruction, (the place also where I was born) I see it to be so; and dying there, sooner or later, you will sink

† Jer. 20. 10.

* Obstinate *and* Pliable *follow him.*

lower than the Grave, into a Place that burns with Fire and Brimstone; be content good Neighbours, and go along with me.

*What, said *Obstinate*, and leave our Friends and our Comforts behind us!

* *Obstinate.*

†Yes, said *Christian* (for that was his name) because, that *all, which you shall forsake*, is not *worthy to be compared with a *little* of that that I am seeking to enjoy; and if you will go along with me, *and hold it*, you shall fare as I my self; for there where I go is †enough and to spare; Come away, and prove my Words.

† *Christian.*

* 2 Cor. 4. 18.

† Luke 15. 17.

Obst. What are the things you seek, since you leave *all* the world to find them?

Chr. I seek an **Inheritance, incorruptible, undefiled, and that fadeth not away*; and it is laid up in Heaven, †and safe there, to be bestowed, at the time appointed, on them that diligently seek it. Read it so, if you will, in my Book.

* 1 Pet. 1. 4.

† Heb. 11. 16.

Obst. *Tush, said* Obstinate, *away with your Book; will you go back with us, or no?*

Chr. No, not I, said the other; because I have laid my hand to the *Plow.

* Luke 9. 62.

Obst. *Come then, Neighbour* Pliable, *let us turn again, and go home without him; there is a Company of these Craz'd-headed Coxcombs, that when they take a Fancy by the end, are wiser in their own Eyes than seven men that can render a reason.*

Pli. Then said *Pliable*, don't revile; if what the good *Christian* says, is true, the things he looks after are better than ours; my heart inclines to go with my Neighbour.

Obst. *What! more fools still? Be ruled by me, go back; who knows whither such a brain-sick fellow will lead you? Go back, go back, and be wise.*

Chr. Nay, but do thou *come with thy Neighbour, *Pliable*, there are such things to be had which I spoke of, and many more Glories besides; if you believe not me, read here in this Book; and for the truth of what is exprest therein, behold all is confirmed by the †blood of him that made it.

* Christian *and* Obstinate *pull for* Pliable'*s Soul.*

† Heb. 9. 17, 18, 19, 20, 21.

Pli. *_Well Neighbour_ Obstinate, (_saith_ Pliable) _I begin to come to a point, I intend to go along with this good man, and to cast in my lot with him: but my good Companion, do you know the way to this desired place?_

* Pliable _contented to go with_ Christian.

Chr. I am directed by a man whose name is _Evangelist_, to speed me to a little Gate that is before us, where we shall receive instructions about the way.

Pli. _Come then, good Neighbour, let us be going, then they went both together._

Obst. And I will go back to my place, said _Obstinate_: †I will be no Companion of such mis-led fantastical Fellows.

† Obstinate _goes railing back._

Now I saw in my Dream, that when _Obstinate_ was gon back, _Christian_ and _Pliable_ went *talking over the Plain, and thus they began their Discourse.

* _Talk between_ Christian _and_ Pliable.

Chr. Come Neighbour _Pliable_, how do you do? I am glad you are perswaded to go along with me; had even _Obstinate_ himself but felt what I have felt of the powers and terrors of what is yet unseen, he would not thus lightly have given us the back.

Pli. _Come Neighbour_ Christian; _since there is none but us two here, tell me now further, what the things are: and how to be enjoyed, whither we are going._

Chr. I can *better conceive of them with my mind, than speak of them with my Tongue: But yet since you are desirous to know, I will read of them in my Book.

* _Gods things unspeakable._

Pli. _And do you think that the words of your Book are certainly true?_

Chr. Yes verily, for it was made by him that †cannot lie.

Pli. _Well said, what things are they?_

† Tit. 1. 2.

Chr. There is an *endless Kingdom to be inhabited, and everlasting Life to be given us; that we may inhabit that Kingdom for ever.

* Isa. 45. 17. John 10. 27, 28, 29.

Pli. _Well said, and what else?_

Chr. There are Crowns of Glory to be given us; †and Garments that will make us shine like the Sun in the Firmament of Heaven.

Pli. _This is very pleasant; and what else?_

† 2 Tim. 4. 8. Rev. 23. 4. Matth. 13.[43.]

Chr. There shall be no more crying; *nor Sorrow, for he that is owner of the place will wipe all Tears from our Eyes.

* Isa. 15. 8. Rev. 7. 16, 17. ch. 21. 4.

Pli. *And what Company shall we have there?*

Chr. There we shall be with *Seraphims*, *and *Cherubims*, Creatures that will dazle your Eyes to look on them: There also you shall meet with thousands, and ten thousands that have gone before us to that place; none of them are hurtful, but loving and holy, every one walking in the sight of God, and standing in his Presence with acceptance for ever: In a Word, there we shall see the †Elders with their Golden Crowns: There we shall see the Holy *Virgins with their Golden Harps. There we shall see †Men that, by the World, were cut in pieces, burnt in Flames, eaten of Beasts, drowned in the Seas, for the Love that they bare to the Lord of the place; all well, and cloathed with *Immortality, as with a Garment.

* Isa. 6. 2. 1 Thes. 4. 16, 17. Rev. 5. 11.

† Rev. 4. 5.

* Ch. 14. 1, 2, 3, 4, 5.

† John 12. 25.

* 2 Cor. 5. 2, 3, 5.

Pli. *The hearing of this is enough to ravish ones Heart; but are these things to be enjoyed? how shall we get to be Sharers thereof?*

Chr. The Lord, the Governour of the Country, hath recorded *that* †in this Book the substance of which is, if we be truly willing to have it, he will bestow it upon us freely.

† Isa. 55. 12. John 7. 37. *ch.* 6. 37. Rev. 21. 6. *ch.* 22. 17.

Pli. *Well, my good Companion, glad am I to hear of these things, come on, let us mend our pace.*

Chr. I cannot go so fast as I would by reason of this burden that is on my Back.

Now I saw in my Dream, that just as they had ended this talk, they drew near to a very *Miry* **Slough* that was in the midst of the Plain, and they being heedless, did both fall suddenly into the Bog. The name of the Slough was *Despond.* Here therefore they wallowed for a time, being grievously bedaubed with Dirt; And *Christian*, because of the Burden that was on his Back, began to sink in the Mire.

* *The Slough of Despond.*

Pli. *Then said* Pliable, *Ah, Neighbour* Christian, *where are you now?*

Chr. Truly, said *Christian*, I do not know.

Pli. At that *Pliable* began to be offended; and angerly said to his Fellow, *Is this the happiness you have told me all this while of? If we have such ill speed at our first setting out, what may we expect 'twixt this and our journeys end? †May I get out again with my Life, you shall possess the brave Country alone for me.* And with that he gave a desperate struggle or two, and got out of the Mire, on that side of the Slough which was next to his own house; so away he went, and *Christian* saw him no more.

† *It is not enough to be pliable.*

Wherefore *Christian* was left to tumble in the Slough of *Despond* alone; but still he endeavoured to struggle to that side of the Slough, that was further *from his own House, and next to the Wicket-gate; the which he did, but could not get out because of the Burden that was upon his Back: But I beheld in my Dream, that a Man came to him, whose name was *Help*, and asked him, *What he did there?*

* Christian *in trouble, seeks still to get farther from his own house.*

Chr. Sir, said *Christian*, I was bid go this way, by a Man called *Evangelist*, who directed me also to yonder Gate, that I might escape the Wrath to come. And as I was going thither, I fell in here.

Help. *But why did not you look for *the steps?*

* *The Promises.*

Chr. Fear followed me so hard, that I fled the next way, and fell in.

Help. *Then*, said he, †*Give me thy hand; so he gave him his hand*, and *he drew him out, and set him upon sound ground, and bid him go on his way.

† Help *lifts him out.*

* Psal. 40. 2.

Then I stepped to him that pluckt him out, and said, Sir, wherefore, since over this place is the way from the City of *Destruction*, to yonder *Gate*, is it that *this* Plat is not mended, that poor Travellers might go thither with more security? And he said unto me, this *miry Slough*, is such a place as cannot be mended: It is the descent whither the scum and filth that attends conviction *for sin doth continually run, and therefore it was called the *Slough* of *Despond*: for still as the sinner is awakened about his lost condition, there ariseth in his Soul many Fears and Doubts, and discouraging Appre-

* *What makes the Slough of Despond.*

hensi ons, which all of them get together, and settle in this place: And this is the reason of the badness of this Ground.

It is not the †Pleasure of the King that this place should remain so bad, his Labourers also, have by the directions of His Majesties Surveyors, been for above this sixteen hundreds years imployed about *this patch* of Ground, if perhaps it might have been mended: Yea, and to my Knowledge, said he, *Here* hath been swallowed up at least twenty thousand Cart-loads; yea millions of wholsome Instructions, that have at all seasons been brought from all places of the Kings Dominions, (and they that can tell, say, they are the best materials to make good ground of the place,) if so be it might have been mended, but it is the *Slough of Despond still*; and so will be, when they have done what they can.

† Isa. 35. 3, 4.

True, there are, by the direction of the Law-giver, certain good and substantial *Steps, placed even through the very midst of this *Slough*; but at such time as this place doth much spue out it's Filth, as it doth against change of Weather, these Steps are hardly seen, or if they be, men, through the dizziness of their Heads, step besides; and then they are bemired to purpose, notwithstanding the Steps be there, but the Ground is †good when they are once got in at the Gate.

* *The Promises of Forgiveness and Acceptance to life by Faith in Christ.*

† 1 *Sam.* 12. 23.

Now I saw in my Dream, that by this time **Pliable* was got home to his House. †So his Neighbours came to visit him: and some of them called him *wise Man* for coming back; and some called him *Fool* for hazarding himself with *Christian*; others again did mock at his *Cowardliness*; saying, *Surely since you began to venture, I would not have been so base to have given out for a few Difficulties*: So *Pliable* sat sneaking among them. But at last he got more Confidence, and then they all turned their Tales, and began to deride poor *Christian* behind his Back. And thus much concerning *Pliable*.

* Pliable *is got home, and is visited by his Neighbours.*

† *His Entertainment by them at his return.*

Now as *Christian* was walking solitarily by himself, he espied one afar off, come crossing over the Field *to meet him, and their hap was to meet *just as they were crossing the way of each other*. The Gentleman's Name that met him was Mr. *Worldly*

* Worldly Wiseman *meets with* Christian.

Wiseman, he dwelt in the Town of *Carnal Policy*, a very great Town, and also hard by from whence *Christian* came. This Man then meeting with *Christian*, and having some incling of him (for *Christian*'s setting forth from the City of *Destruction* was much noised abroad, not only in the Town where he dwelt, but also it began to be the *Town Talk* in some other places.) Master *Worldly Wiseman* therefore, having some guess of him, by beholding his laborious going, by observing his Sighs and Groans, and the like; began thus to enter into some Talk with *Christian*.

Talk between Mr. Worldly Wiseman *and* Christian.

Worl. *How now, good Fellow, whither away after this burdened manner?*

Chr. A burdened manner indeed, as ever, I think, poor Creature had. And whereas you ask me, *Whither away*, I tell you, Sir, I am going to yonder Wicket-gate before me; for there, as I am informed, I shall be put into a way to be rid of my heavy burden.

Worl. *Hast thou a wife and Children?*

Chr. Yes; but I am so laden with this Burden, that I cannot take that Pleasure in them as formerly: methinks, I am *as if I had none.*

Worl. *Wilt thou hearken to me if I give thee Counsel?*

Chr. If it be good I will, for I stand in need of good Counsel.

Worl. **I would advise thee then that thou with all speed get thy self rid of thy Burden; for thou wilt never be settled in thy mind till then: nor canst thou enjoy the benefits of the blessing which God hath bestowed upon thee, till then.*

* Worldly Wiseman's *Counsel to* Christian.

Chr. That is that which I seek for, even to be rid of this heavy burden; but get it off my self I cannot: nor is there any man in our Country that can take it off my shoulders; therefore am I going this way, as I told you, that I may be rid of my burden.

Worl. *Who bid you go this way to be rid of your burden?*

Chr. A man that appeared to me to be a very great and honorable Person; his Name, as I remember, is *Evangelist*.

† *Mr.* Worldly Wiseman *condemned* Evangelists *Counsel.*

Worl. †*I beshrew him for his Counsel, there is not a more dangerous and troublesome way in the World, than is that unto which he hath directed thee, and that thou shalt find, if thou wilt be ruled by his Counsel; Thou hast met with something (as I perceive) already; for I see the dirt of the* Slough of Despond *is upon thee, but that* Slough *is the beginning of the sorrows that do attend those that go on in that way: hear me, I am older than thou, thou art like to meet with in the way which thou goest, Wearisomness, Painfulness, Hunger, Perils, Nakedness, Sword, Lions, Dragons, Darkness, and in a word Death, and what not. These things are certainly true, having been confirmed by many Testimonies. And should a man so carelesly cast away himself, by giving heed to a stranger?*

Chr. Why, Sir, this burden upon my back is more terrible to me than are all these things which you have mentioned: *nay, methinks I care not what I meet with in the way, if so be I can also meet with deliverance from my burden.

* *The frame of the heart of a young* Christian.

Worl. *How camest thou by the burden at first?*

Chr. By reading this Book in my Hand.

Worl. †*I thought so; and it is happened unto thee as to other weak men, who medling with things too high for them, do suddenly fall into thy distractions; which distractions do not only unman men, (as thine I perceive has done thee) but they run them upon desperate ventures, to obtain they know not what.*

† Worldly Wiseman *does not like that Man should be serious in reading the Bible.*

Chr. I know what I would obtain: it is ease for my heavy burden.

Worl. *But why wilt thou seek for ease this way, seeing so many dangers attend it, especially, since (hadst thou but patience to hear me) I could direct thee to the obtaining of what thou desirest, without the dangers that thou in this way wilt run thy self into: yea, and the remedy is at hand. Besides, I will add, that instead of those dangers, thou shalt meet with much Safety, Friendship, and Content.*

Chr. Sir, I pray open this secret to me.

Worl. **Why in yonder Village, (the Village is named* Morality) *there dwells a Gentleman, whose name is* Legality, *a very judicious man, (and a man of a very good Name) that has skill to help men off with such Burdens as thine are, from their Shoulders, yea, to my Knowledge, he hath done a great deal of good this way: Ay, and besides, he hath skill to cure those that are somewhat crazed in their wits with their Burdens. To him, as*

* *Whether Mr.* Worldly *prefers Morality before the straight Gate.*

I said, thou mayest go, and be helped presently. His house is not quite a Mile from this place; and if he should not be at home himself, he hath a pretty young Man to his Son, whose Name is Civility *that can do it (to speak on) as well as the old Gentleman himself: There, I say, thou mayest be eased of thy Burden, and if thou art not minded to go back to thy former Habitation, as indeed I would not wish thee, thou mayest send for thy Wife and Children to thee to this Village, where there are Houses now stand empty, one of which thou mayest have at reasonable rates: Provision is there also cheap and good, and that which will make thy Life the more happy, is, to be sure there thou shalt live by honest Neighbours, in Credit and good Fashion.*

*Now was *Christian* somewhat at a stand; but presently he concluded, if this be true which this Gentleman hath said, my wisest course is to take his Advice; and with that he thus farther spoke.

* Christian *snared by Mr.* Worldly Wisemans *word.*

Chr. Sir, which is my way to this honest Man's house?

† *Mount* Sinai.

Worl. *Do you see yonder †high hill?*

Chr. Yes, very well.

Worl. By that Hill you must go, and the first house you come at is his.

So *Christian* turned out of his way to go to Mr. *Legality*'s House for help: but behold, when he was got now hard by the Hill, it seemed so high, and also that side of it that was next the way side, did hang so much over, that *Christian* was *afraid to venture further, lest the Hill should fall on his Head; wherefore there he stood still; and wotted not what to do. Also his burden *now* seemed heavier to him than while he was in his way. There came also †flashes of fire out of the Hill that made **Christian* afraid that he should be burned: here therefore he sweat, and did quake for †fear. And now he began to be sorry that he had taken Mr. *Worldly Wiseman*'s Counsel; and with that he saw **Evangelist* coming to meet him; at the sight also of whom he began to blush for shame. So *Evangelist* drew nearer and nearer, and coming up to him, he looked upon him with a severe and dreadful Countenance, and thus began to reason with *Christian*.

* Christian *afraid that Mount* Sinai *would fall on his head.*

† Exod. 19. 18.

* Ver. 16.

† Heb. 12. 11.

* Evangelist *findeth* Christian *under Mount* Sinai, *and looketh severely upon him.*

Evan. †What dost thou here *Christian*? said he; at which words *Christian* knew not what to answer: wherefore at present he stood speechless before him. Then said *Evangelist* farther, *Art not thou the man that I found crying without the Walls of the City of* Destruction?

† Evangelist *reasons refresh with* Christian.

How is it then that thou art so quickly turned aside, for thou art now out of the way?

Chr. I met with a Gentleman so soon as I had got over the *Slough of Despond*, who perswaded me, that I might in the *Village* before me, find a Man that could take off my burden.

Evan. *What was he?*

Chr. He looked like a Gentleman, and talked much to me, and got me at last to yield; so I came hither: But when I beheld this Hill, and how it hangs over the way, I suddenly made a stand, lest it should fall on my head.

Evan. *What said that Gentleman to you?*

Chr. Why, he asked me whither I was going, and I told him.

Evan. *And what said he then?*

Chr. He asked me if I had a Family, and I told him: but said I, I am so loaden with the Burden that is on my back, that I cannot take Pleasure in them as formerly.

Evan. *And what said he then?*

Chr. He bid me with speed get rid of my burden, and I told him 'twas ease that I sought: And, said I, I am therefore going to yonder *Gate* to receive further direction how I may get to the place of Deliverance. So he said that he would shew me a better way, and short, not so attended with difficulties, as the way, Sir, that you set me in: which way, said he, will direct you to a Gentlemans house that hath skill to take off these Burdens: so I believed him, and turned out of *that* way, into *this*, if haply I might be soon eased of my Burden: but when I came to this place, and beheld things as they are, I stopped for fear (as I said) of danger: but I now know not what to do.

Evan. *Then* (said Evangelist) *stand still a little, That I may shew thee the words of God.* So he stood trembling. *Then* (said Evangelist) **See that ye refuse not him that speaketh; for if they escaped not who refused him that spake on*

* Heb. 12.22.

Earth, †*much more shall not we escape, if we turn away from him that speaketh from Heaven.* He said moreover, **Now the just shall live by Faith, but if any man draws back, my Soul shall have no pleasure in him.* He also did thus apply them: *Thou art the man that art running into this misery, thou hast begun to reject the Counsel of the most high, and to draw back thy foot from the way of peace, even almost to the hazarding of thy Perdition.*

† Evangelist *convinces* Christian *of his Error.*

* Chap. 10. 38.

Then *Christian* fell down at his foot as dead, crying, Wo is me, for I am undone: at the sight of which, *Evangelist* caught him by the right hand, saying, All manner of Sin and Blasphemies shall be forgiven unto men; be not faithless, but believing; then did *Christian* again a little revive, and stood up trembling, as at first, before *Evangelist*.

Then *Evangelist* proceeded, saying, *Give more earnest heed to the things that I shall tell thee of.* I will now shew thee who it was that deluded thee, and who it was also to whom he sent thee. †The Man that met thee is one *Worldly Wiseman*, and rightly is he so called; partly, *because he savoureth only the Doctrine of this World, (therefore he always goes to the Town of *Morality* to Church) and partly, †because he loveth that Doctrine best; for it saveth him best from the Cross; and because he is of this carnal temper, therefore he seeketh to pervert my ways, though right.

† *Mr.* Worldly Wiseman *described by* Evangelist.

* 1 John 4. 5.

† Col. 6. 12.

*Now there are three things in this mans Counsel that thou must utterly abhor.

* Evangelist *discovers the deceit of Mr.* Worldly Wiseman.

1. His turning thee out of the way.

2. His labouring to render the Cross odious to thee.

3. And his setting thy feet in that way that leadeth unto the administration of Death.

First, Thou must abhor his turning thee out of the way; yea, and thine own consenting thereto; because this is to reject the Counsel of God for the sake of the Counsel of a *Worldly Wiseman.* The Lord says, †*strive to enter in at the strait Gate*, the Gate to which I send thee, **for strait is the Gate that leadeth unto Life, and few there be that find it.* From this little Wicket-

† Luke 13. 24.

* Mat. 7. 13, 14.

gate, and from the way thereto, hath this wicked Man turned thee, to the bringing of thee almost to Destruction; hate therefore his turning thee out of the way, and abhor thy self for hearkning to him.

Secondly, Thou must abhor his labouring to render the Cross odious unto thee; for thou art to †*prefer it before the Treasures in Egypt*: besides, the King of Glory hath told thee, *that he that will save his Life shall lose it: and †*he that comes after him, and hates not his Father and Mother, and Wife, and Children, and Brethren, and Sisters, yea, and his own Life also, he cannot be my Disciple*, I say therefore, for man to labour to perswade thee, that that shall be thy Death, without which, the Truth hath said, thou canst not have eternal life: this Doctrine thou must abhor.

† Heb. 11. 25, 26.

* Mark 8. 34. John 13. 25. Mat. 10. 39.

† Luk. 14. 16.

Thirdly, Thou must hate his setting of thy feet in the way that leadeth to the ministration of Death. And for this, thou must consider to whom he sent thee, and also how unable that Person was to deliver thee from thy burden.

He to whom thou wast sent for ease, being by name *Legality*, is the Son of the *Bond-woman which now is, and is in Bondage with her Children, and is in a Mystery this †Mount *Sinai*, which thou hast feared will fall on thy head. Now if she with her Children are in Bondage, how canst thou expect by them to be made free? This *Legality* therefore is not able to set thee free from thy Burden. No man was as yet ever rid of his Burden to him, no, nor ever is like to be: ye cannot be justified by the works of the Law; for by the deeds of the Law no man living can be rid of his Burden: therefore Mr. *Worldly Wiseman* is an Alien, and Mr. *Legality* is a Cheat: and for his Son *Civility*, notwithstanding his *simpering* looks, he is but an Hypocrite, and cannot help thee. Believe me, there is nothing in all this noise, that thou hast heard of these sottish men, but a design to beguile thee of thy Salvation, by turning thee from the way in which I had set thee. After this *Evangelist* called aloud to the Heavens for Confirmation of what he had said; and with that there came words and fire out of the Mountain under which poor Christian stood, that made the hair of his Flesh stand up.

* Gal. 4. 21, 22, 23, 24, 25, 26, 27.

† *The Bond-woman.*

The words were thus pronounced, *As many as are of the works of the Law, are under the curse*; *for it is written, cursed is every one that continueth not in all things which are written in the Book of the Law to do them.*

Gal. 3. 10.

Now Christian looked for nothing but Death, and began to cry out lamentably: even cursing the time in which he met with Mr. *Worldly Wiseman*; still calling himself a thousand Fools for hearkening to his Counsel: he also was greatly ashamed to think that this Gentlemans Arguments, flowing only from the flesh, should have the Prevalency with him as to cause him to forsake the right way. This done, he applied himself again to *Evangelist* in words and sence as follows.

Chr. *Sir, what think you? is there hopes? may I now go back; and go up to the *Wicket-Gate*, shall I not be abandoned for this, and sent back from thence ashamed? I am sorry I have hearkened to this mans counsel, but may my sins be forgiven?

* Christian *enquired if he may yet be happy.*

Evan. Then said *Evangelist* to him, Thy sin is very great, for by it thou hast committed two evils; thou hast forsaken the way that is good, to tread in forbidden paths: †yet will the man at the Gate receive thee, for he has *good will* for men; only, said he, take heed that thou turn not aside again, lest thou perish from the way, when his wrath is *kindled but a little. Then did *Christian* address himself to go back, and *Evangelist*, after he had kist him, gave him one smile, and bid him God speed: so he went on with haste, neither spake he to any man by the way; nor if any asked him, would he vouchsafe them an answer. He went like one that was all the while treading on forbidden ground, and could by no means think himself safe, till again he was got into the way which he left to follow Mr. *Worldly Wiseman*'s Counsel: so in process of time *Christian* got up to the Gate. Now over the Gate there was written, *Knock and it shall be opened to you*†. He knocked therefore more than once or twice, saying,

† Evangelist *comforts him.*

* *Psal.* 2. last.

† Mat. 7. 8.

May I now enter here? will he within
Open to sorry me, though I have been
An undeserving Rebel? then shall I
Not fail to sing his lasting Praise on high.

At last there came a grave Person to the Gate, named *Good-will*, who asked *who was there? and whence he came? and what he would have?*

Chr. Here is a poor burdened Sinner, I come from the City of *Destruction*, but am going to Mount *Zion*, that I may be delivered from the Wrath to come; I would therefore, Sir, since I am informed that by this Gate is the way thither, know if you are *willing* to let me in.

Good-will. *I am willing with all my Heart, said he; and with that he opened the Gate.

* *The Gate will be opened to broken hearted sinners.*

So when *Christian* was stepping in, the other gave him a Pull: then said *Christian*, What means that? the other told him, A little distance from this Gate, there is erected a strong Castle, of which **Beelzebub* is the Captain; from thence both he, and them that are with him, shoot Arrows at those that come up to this Gate: if happily they may die before they can enter in. Then said *Christian*, †I rejoyce and tremble. So when he was got in, the Man of the Gate asked him, who directed him thither?

* *Satan envies those that enter the straight Gate.*

† Christian *entred the Gate with Joy and Trembling.*

Chr. *Evangelist* †bid me come hither and knock, (as I did;) and he said, that you, Sir, would tell me what I must do.

† *Talk between* Goodwill *and* Christian.

Good-will. *An open door is set before thee, and no man can shut it.*

Chr. Now I begin to reap the Benefits of my Hazards.

Good-will. *But how is it that you came alone?*

Chr. Because none of my Neighbours saw their danger as I saw mine.

Good-will. *Did any of them know of your coming?*

Chr. Yes, My Wife and Children saw me at the first, and called after me to turn again: also some of my Neighbours stood crying and calling after me to return; but I put my Fingers in my Ears, and so came on my way.

Good-will. *But did none of them follow you to perswade you to go back?*

Chr. Yes, both *Obstinate* and *Pliable*: But when they saw that they could not prevail, *Obstinate* went railing back: but *Pliable* came with me a little way.

Good-will. *But why did he not come through?*

Chr. We indeed came both together, until we came at the *Slough of Despond*, into the which we also suddenly fell. And then was my Neighbour *Pliable* discouraged, and would not adventure farther. *Wherefore, getting out again, on *that side* next to his own House, he told me, I should possess the brave Country alone for him: So he went *his* way, and I came *mine*. He after *Obstinate*, and I to this Gate.

* *A Man may have company when he sets out for Heaven, and yet go thither alone.*

Good-will. Then said *Good-will*, Alas poor Man, is the Cœlestial Glory of so small esteem with him, that he counteth it not worth running the hazard of a few Difficulties to obtain it?

Chr. Truly, said *Christian*, I have said the Truth of *Pliable*, and if I should also say all the truth of my self, it will appear there is †no betterment 'twixt him and my self. 'Tis true, he went back to his own house, but I also turned aside to go into the way of Death, being perswaded thereto by the carnal Argument of one Mr. *Worldly-wiseman*.

† Christian *accuseth himself before the Man at the Gate.*

Good-will. Oh, did he light upon you? What, he would have had you a sought for ease at the hands of Mr. *Legality*; they are both of them a very cheat: but did you take his Counsel?

Chr. Yes, as far as I durst, I went to find out Mr. *Legality*, untill I thought that the Mountain that stands by his house, would have fallen upon my head, wherefore there I was forced to stop.

Good-will. That Mountain has been the death of many, and will be the death of many more: 'tis well you escaped being by it dash'd in pieces.

Chr. Why, truly, I do not know what had become of me there, had not *Evangelist* happily met me again as I was musing in the midst of my *Dumps*: but 'twas God's Mercy that he came to me again, for else I had never come hither. But now I am come, such a one as I am, more fit indeed for death, by that Mountain, than thus to stand talking with my Lord: But oh! what a favour is this to me, that yet I am admitted entrance here.

Good-will. *We make no Objections against any, notwithstanding all that they have done before they come hither, †*they in no wise are cast out*; and therefore, good *Christian*, come a little way with me, and I will teach thee about the way thou must go. *Look before thee; dost thou see this narrow way? *THAT* is the way thou must go. It was cast up by the Patriarchs, Prophets, Christ, and his Apostles, and it is as streight as a *Rule* can make it: This is the way thou must go.

* Christian is *comforted again.*

† Joh. 6. 37.

* Christian *directed yet on his way.*

Chr. But said *Christian*, *is there no turnings nor windings, by which a Stranger *may lose his way?*

Good-will. Yes, there are many ways *BUTT* down upon this: and they are crooked and wide: But *thus* thou may'st distinguish the right from the wrong, *the* right only being †streight and narrow.

* Christian *afraid of losing his way.*

† Mat. 7. 14.

Then I saw in my Dream, *That *Christian* asked him further, if he could not help him off with his Burden that was upon his back; for as yet he had not got rid thereof, nor could he by any means get it off without help.

* Christian *weary of his Burthen.*

He told him, as to thy burden, be content to bear it, untill thou comest to the *place of* †Deliverance; for there it will fall from thy back of it self.

Then *Christian* began to gird up his Loins, and to address himself to his Journey. So the other told him, that by that he was got some distance from the Gate, he would come at the house of the Interpreter, at whose door he should knock, and he would shew him excellent things. Then *Christian* took his leave of his friend, and he again bid him God-speed.

† *There is no deliverance from the guilt and burden of Sin but by the Death and Blood of Christ.*

Then he went on, till he came at the house of the **Interpreter*, where he *knocked* over and over; at last one came to the door, and asked, *Who was there?*

Chr. Sir, here is a Traveller, who was bid by an Acquaintance of the good Man of this House, to call here for my Profit; I would therefore speak with

* Christian *comes to the House of the Interpreter.*

the Master of the House: so he called for the Master of the House; who after a little time came to *Christian*, and asked him what he would have.

Chr. Sir, said *Christian*, I am a Man that am come from the City of *Destruction*, and am going to the Mount *Zion*, and I was told by the Man that stands at the Gate at the head of this way, that if I called here, you would shew me excellent things, such as would be an help to me in my Journey.

Interp. Then said the *Interpreter*, *Come in, I will shew thee that which will be profitable to thee. So he commanded his Man to †light the Candle, and bid *Christian* follow him, so he had him into a private Room, and bid his Man open a door; the which when he had done, *Christian saw the picture of a very grave Person hang up against the Wall, and this was the fashion of it, †*It had Eyes lifted up to Heaven*, *the best of Books in his hand*, *the Law of Truth was written upon its Lips*, *the World was behind his Back*; *it stood as if it pleaded with Men*, *and a Crown of Gold did hang over its Head.*

* *He is entertained.*

† *Illumination.*

* Christian *sees a brave Picture.*

† *The fashion of the Picture.*

Chr. *Then said* Christian, *What meaneth this?*

Inter. The Man whose Picture this is, is one of a thousand; he can *beget Children, travel in Birth with Children, and †nurse them himself when they are born. And whereas thou seest *him with his Eyes lift up to Heaven, the best of Books in his hand, and the Law of Truth writ on his Lips; it is to shew thee, that his Work is to know and unfold dark things to Sinners; even as also thou †seest him stand as if he pleaded with men; and whereas thou see'st the World as cast behind him, and that a Crown hangs over his head; that is to shew thee, that slighting and despising the things that are present, for the love that he hath to his Master's Service, he is sure in the World that comes next, to have Glory for his Reward. Now, said the *Interpreter*, I have shewed thee *this* Picture first, *because the Man whose Picture this is, is the only Man, whom the Lord of the place whither thou art going, hath authorized to be thy Guide in all difficult Places thou mayest meet with in the

* 1 Cor. 4. 15.

† Gal. 4. 19.

† *The meaning of the Picture.*

* *Why he shewed him the Picture first.*

way: wherefore take good heed to what I have shewed thee, and bear well in thy mind what thou hast seen; lest in thy Journey thou meet with some that pretend to lead thee right, but their way goes down to Death.

Then he took him by the Hand, and led him into a very large *Parlor* that was full of Dust, because never swept; the which, after he had reviewed a little while, the *Interpreter* called for a Man to *sweep*: Now when he began to sweep, the Dust began so abundantly to fly about, that *Christian* had almost therewith been choaked. Then said the *Interpreter* to a *Damsel* that stood by, bring hither Water, and sprinkle the Room; the which when she had done, it was swept, and cleansed with Pleasure.

Chr. *Then said* Christian, *What means this?*

Int. The *Interpreter* answered, This *Parlor* is the Heart of a Man that was never sanctified by the sweet Grace of the Gospel: The *Dust*, is his original Sin, and inward Corruptions that have defiled the whole Man. He that began to sweep at first is the Law; but she that brought Water, and did sprinkle it, is the Gospel. Now, whereas thou sawest that so soon as the first began to sweep, the Dust did so fly about, that the Room by him could not be cleansed, but that thou wast almost choaked therewith: this is to shew thee, that the Law, instead of cleansing the Heart (by its working) from Sin, *doth revive, put †strength into, and *increase it in the Soul, even as it doth discover and forbid it, for it doth not give power to subdue.

* Rom. 7. 9.

† 1 Cor. 15. 56.

* Rom. 5. 20.

Again, as thou sawest the *Damsel* sprinkle the Room with Water, upon which it was cleansed with pleasure; this is to shew thee, that when the Gospel comes in the sweet and precious influences thereof to the Heart, then I say, even as thou sawest the Damsel lay the Dust by sprinkling the Floor with Water, so is sin vanquished and subdued, and the Soul made clean, through the Faith of it, and consequently †fit for the King of Glory to inhabit.

† John 15. 3. Eph. 5. 16. Acts 15. 9. Rom. 16. 25, 26. John 15. 13.

I saw moreover in my Dream, *that the *Interpreter* took him by the hand, and had him into a little Room, where sat two little Children, each one in his chair. The Name of the eldest was *Passion*,

* *He shewed him* Passion *and* Patience.

and the Name of the other *Patience*. *Passion* seemed to be much discontented, but *Patience* was very quiet. Then *Christian* asked, What is the reason of the Discontent of *Passion*? The *Interpreter* answered, the Governour of them would have him stay for his best things, till the beginning of the next Year; but he will have all now: *But *Patience* is willing to wait.

Passion *will have it now.*

* Patience *is for waiting.*

Then I saw that one came to †*Passion*, and brought him a Bag of Treasure, and poured it down at his Feet; the which he took up and rejoyced therein, and withall laughed *Patience* to scorn: But I beheld but a while, and he had *lavished all away, and had nothing left him but Rags.

† Passion *hath his desire,*

* *And quickly lavishes all away.*

Chr. *Then said* Christian *to the* Interpreter, †*Expound this matter more fully to me.*

† *The Matter expounded.*

Inter. So he said, These two Lads are Figures, *Passion*, of the men of this world; and *Patience*, of the men of that which is to come: For as here thou see'st, *Passion will have all now*, this year; that is to say, in this World; so are the Men of this World: They must have all their good things now, they cannot stay till next year, that is, untill the next World, for their Portion of good. That Proverb, **A Bird in the Hand is worth two in the Bush*, is of more Authority with them, than are all the Divine Testimonies of the good of the World to come. But as thou sawest, that he had quickly lavished all away, and had presently left him nothing but Rags; so will it be with all such Men at the end of this world.

* *The Worldly man for a Bird in the hand.*

Chr. *Then said* Christian; *Now I see that* Patience *has the best* †*Wisdom, and that upon many Accounts.* 1. *Because he stays for the best things.* 2. *And also because he will have the Glory of his, when the other had nothing but Rags.*

† Patience *had the best Wisdom.*

Int. Nay, you may add another, to wit, the Glory of the *next* World will never wear out; but these are suddenly gone. Therefore *Passion* had not so much reason to laugh at *Patience*, because he had his good things first, as *Patience* will have to laugh at *Passion*, *because he had his best things *last*; for *first* must give place to *last*, because *last* must have his time to come: but *last* gives place to nothing; for there is not another to Succeed: he therefore that hath his Portion *first*, must needs have a time to spend it, but he that has his Portion *last*, must have it lastingly; Therefore it is said of †*Dives, in thy life-time thou receivedst thy good things; and likewise* Lazarus *evil things, but now he is comforted, and thou art tormented.*

* *Things that are first must give place, but things that are last are lasting.*

† Luke 16. Dives *had his good things first.*

Chr. *Then I perceive, 'tis not best to covet things that are* now, *but to wait for things to* come.

Int. You say truth, **for the things that are seen, are* Temporal; *but the things that are not seen, are* Eternal: But tho' this be so, yet since things present, and our fleshly Appetite, *are such near Neighbours one to another*; and again, because Things to come, and carnal sense are such Strangers one to another: Therefore it is, that the first of these so suddenly fall into *amity*, and that *distance* is so continually between the second.

* 2 Cor. 4. 18. *The first things are but Temporal.*

Then I saw in my Dream, that the *Interpreter* took *Christian* by the Hand, and led him into a Place where was a Fire burning against a Wall, and one standing by it, alwayes casting much Water upon it to quench it; Yet did the Fire burn higher and hotter.

Then said Christian, *What means this?*

The *Interpreter* answered, This Fire is the Work of Grace that is wrought in the Heart; he that casts Water upon it, to extinguish and put it out, is the *Devil*: but in that thou seest the Fire notwithstanding burn higher and hotter, thou shalt also see the reason of that: So he had him about to the backside of the Wall, where he saw a man with a Vessel of Oyl in his hand, of the which he did also continually cast (but secretly) into the Fire.

Then said Christian, *What means this?*

The *Interpreter* answered, This is *Christ*, who continually with the Oyl of his Grace, maintains the Work already begun in the Heart; by the means of which, notwithstanding what the Devil can do, the Souls of his people prove Gracious still. And in that thou sawest, that the

2 Cor. 12. 9.

Man stood behind the Wall to maintain the Fire; this is to teach thee, that it is hard for the Tempted to see how this work of Grace is maintained in the Soul.

I saw also, that the *Interpreter* took him again by the hand, and led him into a pleasant place, where was builded a stately Palace, beautiful to behold; at the sight of which, *Christian* was greatly delighted; he saw also upon the top thereof, certain Persons walking, who were cloathed all in Gold.

Then said *Christian*, May we go in thither?

Then the *Interpreter* took him, and led him up toward the Door of the Palace; and behold, at the Door stood a great Company of men, as desirous to go in, but durst not. There also sat a Man, at a little distance from the Door, at a Table side, with a Book, and his Ink-horn before him, to take the Name of him that should enter therein: He saw also, that in the door-way stood many Men in Armour to keep it, being resolved to do to the Men that would enter what hurt and mischief they could. Now was *Christian* somewhat in amaze: at last, when every man started back for fear of the armed men, *Christian* saw a Man of a very stout Countenance come up to the Man that sat there to write, saying, * *Set down my Name, Sir*: the which when he had done, he saw the Man draw his Sword, and put an Helmet upon his Head, and rush toward the Door upon the armed Men, who laid upon him with deadly force: but the man, not at all discouraged, fell to cutting and hacking most fiercely, so after he had †received and given many Wounds to those that attempted to keep him out, he cuts his way through them all, and pressed forward into the Palace: at which there was a pleasant Voice heard from those that were within, even of those that walked upon the top of the Palace, saying,

* *The Valiant man.*

† Acts 14. 22.

Come in, come in;
Eternal Glory thou shalt win.

So he went in, and was cloathed with such Garments as they. Then *Christian* smiled, and said, I think verily I know the meaning of this.

Now, said *Christian*, let me go hence. Nay stay (said the *Interpreter*) till I have shewed thee a little more, and after that thou shalt go on thy way. So he took him by the hand again, and led him into a very dark Room, where there sat a Man in an Iron *Cage.

Now the Man, to look on, seemed very sad: he sat with his Eyes looking down to the Ground, his hands folded together; and he sighed as if he would break his Heart. Then said *Christian*, *What means this?* At which the *Interpreter* bid him talk with the Man.

* Despair *like an Iron Cage.*

Chr. Then said *Christian* to the Man, *What art thou?* The Man answered, *I am what I was not once.*

Chr. *What wast thou once?*

Man. The *Man* said, I was once a fair †and flourishing Professor, both in mine own Eyes, and also in the Eyes of others: I once was, as I thought, fair for the Cœlestial City, and had then even joy at the thoughts that I should get thither.

† Luke 8. 18.

Chr. *Well, but what art thou now?*

Man. I am *now* a Man of *Despair*, and am shut up in *it*, as in *this* Iron Cage. I cannot get out; O *now* I cannot.

Chr. *But how camest thou in this Condition?*

Man. I left off to watch, and be sober, I laid the Reins upon the neck of my Lusts; I sinned against the light of the Word, and the goodness of God: I have grieved the Spirit, and he is gone; I tempted the Devil, and he is come to me; I have provoked God to anger, and he has left me; I have so hardened my Heart, that I *cannot* Repent.

Then said *Christian* to the *Interpreter*, But is there no hopes for such a Man as this? Ask him, said the *Interpreter*.

Chr. Then said *Christian*, *Is there no hope*, *but you must be kept in the Iron Cage of Despair?*

Man. No, none at all.

Chr. *Why? The Son of the blessed is very pitiful?*

Man. I have *Crucified him to my self afresh, I have despised his Person, I have despised †his Righteousness, I have counted his Blood an unholy thing, I have done despite *to the Spirit of Grace: Therefore I have shut my self out of all the Promises, and there now remains to me nothing but threatnings, dreadful threatnings, faithful threatnings, of

* Heb. 6. 6.

† Luke 19. 14.

* Heb. 10. 28, 29.

certain Judgment and fiery Indignation, which shall devour me as an Adversary.

Chr. *For what did you bring your self into this Condition?*

Man. For the Lusts, Pleasures, and Profits of this World; in the enjoyment of which, I did then promise my self much Delight: but now every one of those things also bite me, and gnaw me like a burning Worm.

Chr. *But canst thou not now repent and turn?*

Man. God hath denied me Repentance; his Word gives me no Encouragement to believe, yea himself hath shut me up in this Iron Cage: nor can all the Men in the World let me out. O Eternity; Eternity! How shall I grapple with the Misery that I must meet with in Eternity?

Int. Then said the *Interpreter* to *Christian*, Let this Man's Misery be remembred by thee, and be an everlasting Caution to thee.

Chr. Well, said *Christian*, this is fearful; God help me to watch and be sober; and to pray, that I may shun the cause of this Man's Misery. Sir, is it not time for me to go on my way now?

Int. Tarry till I shall shew thee one thing more, and then thou shalt go on thy way.

So he took *Christian* by the hand again, and led him into a Chamber, where there was one rising out of Bed; and as he put on his Raiment he shook and trembled. Then said *Christian*, Why doth this Man thus tremble? The *Interpreter* then bid him tell to *Christian* the reason of his so doing: So he began, and said, This Night as I was in my Sleep I dreamed, and behold the Heavens grew exceeding black; also it thundred and lightned in most fearful wise, that it put me into an Agony. So I looked up in my Dream, and saw the Clouds rack at an unusual rate, upon which I heard a great Sound of a Trumpet, and saw also a Man sit upon a Cloud attended with the thousands of Heaven; they were all in flaming Fire, also the Heavens were on a burning Flame. I heard then a Voice, saying, *Arise ye dead, and come to Judgment*; and with that the Rocks rent, the Graves opened, and the Dead that were therein came forth; some of them were exceeding glad, and

1 Cor. 15.
1 Thess. 4.
Jude 15.
John 5. 28.
2 Thess. 1. 8.
Reve. 20. 11, 12, 13, 14.
Isa. 26. 21.
Mich. 7. 16, 17.
Psal. 5. 1, 2, 3.

looked upward; and some sought to hide themselves under the Mountains: Then I saw the Man that sate upon the Cloud, open the Book, and bid the World draw near. Yet there was, by reason of a fierce Flame that issued out and came before him, a convenient distance betwixt him and them, as betwixt the Judge and the Prisoners at the Bar. I heard it also proclaimed to them that attended on the Man that sat on the Cloud, **Gather together the Tares, the Chaff and Stubble, and cast them into the burning Lake*; and with that the bottomless Pit opened, just whereabout I stood: out of the Mouth of which there came in an abundant manner Smoke, and Coals of Fire, with hideous Noises. It was also said to the same Persons, †*Gather my Wheat into the Garner.* And with that I saw many catch'd up *and carried away into the Clouds, but I was left behind. I also sought to hide my self, but I could not, for the Man that sat upon the Cloud still kept his eye upon me: my Sins also came in my mind, and my Conscience did accuse me on every side. Upon this I awaked from my Sleep.

Mal. 3. 2, 3.
Dan. 7. 9, 10.

* Mark 3. 13.
Ch. 13. 30.
Mal. 4. 1.

† Luke 3. 17.

* 1 Thess. 7. 16, 17.

Rom. 2. 14, 15.

Chr. *But what was it that made you so afraid of this sight?*

Man. Why, I thought that the day of Judgment was come, and that I was not ready for it: but this frighted me most, that the Angels gathered up several, and left me behind; also the Pit of Hell opened her Mouth just where I stood: my Conscience too afflicted me; and (as I thought) the Judge had always his eye upon me, shewing Indignation in his Countenance.

Then said the *Interpreter* to *Christian*, *Hast thou considered all these things?*

Chr. Yes, and they put me in *hope* and *fear*.

Int. Well, keep all things so in thy mind, that they may be as a *Goad* in thy sides, to prick thee forward in the way thou must go. Then *Christian* began to gird up his Loins, and to address himself to his Journey. Then said the *Interpreter*, the Comforter be always with thee, good *Christian*, to guide thee in the way that leads to the City.

So *Christian* went on his way, saying,

Here I have seen things rare and profitable,
Things pleasant, dreadful, things to make me stable
In what I have began to take in hand:
Then let me think on them, and understand
Wherefore they shew'd me were, and let me be
Thankful, O good Interpreter, to thee.

Now I saw in my Dream, that the highway up which *Christian* was to go, was fenced on either side with a Wall, and that Wall was called **Salvation.* Up this way therefore did burdened *Christian* run, but not without great difficulty, because of the Load on his Back.

* Isa. 36. 1.

He ran thus till he came at a Place somewhat ascending; and upon that place stood a *Cross*, and a little below in the bottom, a Sepulchre. So I saw in my Dream, that just as *Christian* came up with the *Cross*, his Burden loosed from off his Shoulders, and fell from off his Back, and began to tumble; and so continued to do, till it came to the mouth of the Sepulchre, where it fell in, and I saw it no more.

Then was *Christian* glad and lightsome, and said with a merry heart, *He hath given me Rest, by his Sorrow; and Life, by his Death.* Then he stood still a while, to look and wonder; for it was very surprizing to him, that the sight of the Cross should thus ease him of his Burden. He looked therefore, and looked again, even till the springs that were in his Head sent the †Waters down his Cheeks. Now as he stood looking and weeping, behold three shining ones came to him, and saluted him, with *Peace be to thee*; so the first said to him, **Thy sins be forgiven thee*; The second *stript him of his Rags*, and †cloathed him with change of Raiment. The third also *set *a mark in his Forehead*, and gave him a Roll, with a Seal upon it, which he bid him look on as he ran, and that he should give it in at the Cœlestial Gate: so they went their way. Then *Christian* gave three leaps for joy, and went on singing,

When God releases us of our guilt and burden, we are as those that leap for Joy.

† Zech. 12. 10.

* Mark 2. 2.

† Zech. 3. 4.

* Eph. 1. 8. 13.

Thus far I did come loaden with my sin,
Nor could ought ease the grief that I was in,

Till I came hither: What a Place is this!
Must here be the beginning of my Bliss?
Must here the Burden fall from off my Back?
Must here the strings that bound it to me crack?
Bless'd Cross! bless'd Sepulchre! bless'd rather be
The man that there was put to shame for me.

A Christian can sing tho' alone when God doth give him the joy of his heart.

I saw then in my Dream that he went on *thus*, even untill he came at a Bottom, where he saw, a little out of the way, three men fast asleep, with Fetters upon their heels. The name of the one was **Simple*, another *Sloth*, and the third *Presumption.*

* *Simple, Sloth*, and *Presumption.*

Christian then seeing them lye in this case, went to them, if peradventure he might awake them. And cried, You are like them that sleep on the top of †a Mast, for the dead Sea is under you, a Gulf that hath no bottom: Awake therefore, and come away, *be willing also*, and I will help you off with your Irons. He also told them, If he that goeth about like **a roaring Lion*, comes by, you will certainly become a Prey to his Teeth. With that they look'd upon him, and began to reply in this sort†: *Simple* said, *I see no Danger*, *Sloth* said, *Yet a little more Sleep, and Presumption* said, *Every Fat must stand upon his own bottom.* And so they lay down to sleep again, and *Christian* went on his way.

† Prov. 23. 24.

* 1 Pet. 5. 8.

† *There is no perswasion will do, if God openeth not the eyes.*

Yet was he troubled to think, that Men in that danger should so little esteem the kindness of him that so freely offered to help them, both by awakening of them, counselling of them, and proffering to help them off with their Irons. And as he was troubled thereabout, he espied two men come tumbling over the Wall, on the left hand of the narrow way; and they made up apace to him. The name of the one was *Formalist*, and the name of the other *Hypocrisie.* So as I said, they drew up unto him, who thus entred with them into Discourse.

Chr. **Gentlemen, whence came you, and whither go you?*

Form. and *Hyp.* We were born in the Land of *Vain-Glory*, and are going for Praise to Mount *Sion.*

* Christian *talked with them.*

Chr. *Why came you not in at the Gate which*

standeth at the beginning of the way? Know you not that it is written, †*That he that cometh not in by the Door, but climbeth up some other way, the same is a Thief and a Robber.*

† John 10. 1.

Form. and *Hyp.* They said, that to go to the Gate for Entrance, was by all their Country-men counted too far about, and that therefore their usual way was to make a short cut of it, and to Climb over the Wall as they had done.

Chr. *But will it not be counted a Trespass against the Lord of the City whither we are bound, thus to violate his revealed Will?*

Form. and *Hyp.* They told him, *That as for that, he needed not trouble his head thereabout: for what they did they had custom for, and could produce (if need were) Testimony that would witness it, for more than a thousand Years.

* *They that come into the way, but not by the door, think that they can say something in vindication of their own Practice.*

Chr. *But, said* Christian, *will it stand a Tryal at Law?*

Form. and *Hyp.* They told him that *custom*, it being of so long a standing as above a thousand Years, would doubtless now be admitted as a thing legal, by an impartial Judge. And besides, say they, if we get into the way, what's matter which way we get in? if we are in we are in: thou art but in the way, who as we perceive, came in at the Gate; and we are also in the way that came tumbling over the Wall; Wherein now is thy Condition better than ours?

Chr. I walk by the *Rule* of my Master, you walk by the rude working of your Fancies. You are counted Thieves already, by the Lord of the way, therefore I doubt you will not be found true men at the end of the way. You come in by your selves, without his Direction, and shall go out by your selves, without his Mercy.

To this they made him but little Answer; only they bid him look to himself. Then I saw that they went on; every man in his Way, without much conference one with another; save that these two men told *Christian*, That, as to *Laws* and *Ordinances*, they doubted not but they should as conscientiously do them as he. Therefore, said they, We see not wherein thou differest from us, but by the *Coat* that is on thy Back, which was as we tro, given thee by some of thy Neighbours, to hide the shame of thy Nakedness.

Chr. By *Laws and Ordinances you will not be saved, since you came not in by the door. And as for this *Coat* that is on my back, it was given me by the Lord of the place whither I go; and that, as you say, to cover my nakedness with. And I take it as a token of kindness to me, for I had nothing but rags before; and besides, †thus I comfort my self as I go; Surely, think I, when I come to the Gate of the City, the Lord thereof will know me for good, since I have his *Coat* on my Back! a *Coat* that he gave me freely in the day that he stript me of my Rags. I have moreover a mark in my forehead, of which perhaps you have taken no notice, which one of my Lords most intimate Associates fixed there in the day that my Burden fell off my Shoulders. I will tell to you moreover, that I had then given me a Roll sealed, to comfort me by reading, as I go on the way; I was also bid to give it in at the Cœlestial Gate, in token of my certain going in after it; all which things I doubt you want, and want them because you came not in at the Gate.

* Gal. 1. 16.

† Christian *has got his Lords Coat on his back and is comforted therewith, he is comforted also with his Mark and his Roll.*

To these things they gave him no answer, only they looked upon each other, and *laughed.* Then I saw that they went on all, save that *Christian* kept *before, who had no more talk but with himself, and that sometimes sighingly, and sometimes comfortably: also he would be often reading in the Roll, that one of the shining ones gave him, by which he was refreshed.

* Christian *has talk with himself.*

I beheld then, that they all went on till they came to the foot of the Hill †*Difficulty*, at the bottom of which was a Spring. There was also in the same place two other wayes, besides that which came straight from the Gate; one turned to the left hand, and the other to the right, at the bottom of the Hill: but the narrow way lay right up the Hill, (and the name of the going up the side of the Hill, is called *Difficult*;) *Christian* went now to the †Spring, and drank thereof to refresh himself, and then began to go up the Hill, saying,

† *He comes to the Hill* Difficulty.

† Isa. 49. 10.

The Hill, though high, I covet to ascend,
The Difficulty will not me offend.
For I perceive the way to Life lies here;

Come, pluck up, Heart, let's neither faint nor fear.
Better, tho difficult, the right way to go,
Than wrong, though easie, where the end is Woe.

The other two also came to the Foot of the Hill; but when they saw that the Hill was steep and high, and that there was two other wayes to go; and supposing also that these two wayes might meet again with that up which *Christian* went, on the other side of the Hill: Therefore they were resolved to go in those wayes, (now the name of one of those wayes was *Danger*, and the name of the other *Destruction.*) So *the one took the way which is called *Danger*, which did lead him into a great Wood, and the other took directly up the way to *Destruction*, which led him into a wide Field, full of dark Mountains, where he stumbled and fell, and rose no more.

* *The Danger of turning out of the way.*

I looked then after *Christian*, to see him go up the Hill, where I perceived he fell from running to going, and from going to clambering upon his Hands and his Knees, because of the steepness of the place. Now about the mid-way to the top of the Hill, was a pleasant **Arbor*, made by the Lord of the Hill, for the refreshing of weary Travellers. Thither therefore *Christian* got, where also he sat down to rest him. Then he pull'd his Roll out of his Bosom, and read therein to his comfort; he also now began afresh to take a review of the Coat or Garment that was given him as he stood by the Cross. Thus pleasing himself a while, he at last fell into a Slumber, and thence into a fast Sleep, which detained him in that place untill it was almost Night; and in his Sleep *his Roll fell out of his hand. Now as he was sleeping, there came one to him and awaked him, saying, †*Go to the Ant thou Sluggard, consider her ways, and be wise*: and with that *Christian* suddenly started up, and sped him on his way, and went apace till he came to the top of the Hill.

* *A Ward of Grace.*

* *He that sleeps is a loser.*

† Prov. 6. 6.

Now when he was got up to the top of the Hill, there came two men running to meet him amain; the name of the one was **Timorous*, and the other *Mistrust*: to whom *Christian* said, Sirs, what's the matter you run the wrong way? *Timorous*

* Christian *meets with* Mistrust *and* Timorous.

answered, That they were going to the City of *Zion*, and had got up that *Difficult* place; but said he, the further we go, the more danger we meet with, wherefore we turned, and are going back again.

Yes, said *Mistrust*, for just before us lies a couple of Lions in the way, (whether sleeping or waking we know not) and we could not think, if we came within reach but they would presently pull us in pieces.

Chr. *Then said* Christian, *you make me afraid, but whither shall I fly to be safe? If I go back to mine own Countrey,* That *is prepared for Fire and Brimstone, and I shall certainly perish there. If I can go to the Cœlestial City, I am sure to be in safety there,* **I must venture; To go back is nothing but death, to go forward is fear of death, and life everlasting beyond it. I will yet go forward. So* Mistrust *and* Timorous *ran down the Hill, and* Christian *went on his way. But thinking again of what he heard from the men, he felt in his Bosom for his Roll, that he might read therein and be comforted; but he felt and found* †*it not. Then was* Christian *in great distress, and knew not what to do, for he wanted that which used to relieve him; and that which should have been his Pass into the Cœlestial City. Here therefore he began to be much* **perplexed, and knew not what to do; at last he bethought himself that he had slept in the* Arbor *that is on the side of the Hill; and falling down upon his knees, he asked God forgiveness for that foolish fact, and then went back to look for his Roll. But all the way he went back, who can sufficiently set forth the sorrow of* Christians *heart? Sometimes he sighed, sometimes he wept, and oftentimes he chid himself, for being so foolish to fall asleep in that place which was erected only for a little refreshment for his weariness. Thus therefore he went back, carefully looking on this side, and on that, all the way as he went, if happily he might find the Roll, that had been his comfort so many times in his Journey. He went thus till he came again within sight of the* Arbor *where he sat and slept; but that sight renewed* †*his sorrow the more, by bringing again, even afresh, his evil of sleeping unto his mind. Thus therefore he now went on bewailing his sinful sleep, saying,* O wretched man

* Christian *shakes for fear.*

† Christian *missed his Roll wherein he used to take comfort.*

* *He is perplexed for his Roll.*

† Christian *bewails his foolish sleeping,* Rev. 2. 2. 2 Thes. 5. 7, 8.

that I am, *that I should sleep in the day time, that I should sleep in the midst of difficulty! that I should so indulge the flesh as to use that rest for ease to my flesh, which the Lord of the Hill hath erected only for the relief of the Spirits of Pilgrims! How many steps have I took in vain! (Thus it happened to* Israel *for their sin they were sent back again by the way of the red Sea) and I am made to tread those steps with sorrow, which I might have trod with delight, had it not been for this sinful sleep. How far might I have been on my way by this time! I am made to tread those steps thrice over, which I needed not to have trod but once: Yea now also I am like to be benighted, for the day is almost spent. O that I had not slept! Now by this time he was come to the* Arbor *again, where for a while he sat down and wept; but at last (as* Christian *would have it) looking sorrowfully down under the Settle, there he *espied his Roll; the which he with trembling and haste catch'd up and put into his Bosom; but who can tell how joyful this man was, when he had gotten his Roll again? For this Roll was the assurance of his Life, and acceptance at the desired Haven. Therefore he laid it up in his Bosom, gave thanks to God for directing his Eye to the place where it lay, and with Joy and Tears betook himself again to his Journey. But oh, how nimbly did he go up the rest of the Hill! Yet before he got up, the Sun went down upon* Christian; *and this made him again recall the Vanity of his sleeping to his remembrance; and thus he again began to condole with himself*; O thou sinful sleep! how for thy sake am I like to be benighted in my Journey! I must walk without the Sun, darkness must cover the path of my feet, and I must hear the noise of the doleful Creatures, because of my sinful sleep! *Now also he remembred the story that* Mistrust *and* Timorous *told him of, how they were frighted with the sight of the Lions. Then said* Christian *to himself again, These Beasts range in the night for their prey, and if they should meet with me in the dark, how should I shift them? how should I escape being by them torn in pieces? Thus he went on, but while he was bewailing his unhappy miscarriage, he lift up his Eyes, and behold there was a very stately Palace before him, the name of which was* Beautiful, *and it stood by the High-way side.*

* Christian *findeth his Roll where he lost it.*

So I saw in my Dream, that he made haste and went forward, that if possible he might get Lodging there; Now before he had gone far, he entred into a very narrow passage, which was about a furlong off the Porters Lodge, and looking very narrowly before him as he went, he espied two Lions in the way. Now thought he, I see the dangers that *Mistrust* and *Timorous* were driven back by. (The Lions were chained, but he saw not the Chains.) Then he was afraid, and thought also himself to go back after them, for he thought nothing but Death was before him: But the *Porter* at the Lodge, whose Name is *Watchful*, perceiving that *Christian* made a halt, as if he would go back, cryed unto him, saying, Is thy strength so small? fear not the Lions, for they are chained, and are placed there for tryal of Faith, where it is; and for discovery of those that have none: keep in the midst of the Path, and no hurt shall come unto thee.

* Mark 13. 14.

Then I saw that he went on, trembling for fear of the Lions; but taking good heed to the directions of the *Porter*, he heard them roar, but they did him no harm. Then he clapt his hands, and went on till he came and stood before the Gate where the *Porter* was. Then said *Christian* to the *Porter*, Sir, What House is this, and may I lodge here to night? The *Porter* answered, This House was built by the Lord of the Hill, and he built it for the Relief and Security of Pilgrims. The *Porter* also asked whence he was, and whither he was going?

Chr. I am come from the City of *Destruction*, and am going to Mount *Zion*, but because the Sun is now set, I desire, if I may to lodge here to night.

Por. *What is your Name?*

Chr. My Name is now *Christian*, but my Name at the first was *Graceless*: I came of the Race of * *Japhet*, whom God will perswade to dwell in the Tents of *Shem*.

* Gen. 9. 27.

Por. *But how doth it happen you come so late, the Sun is set?*

Chr. I had been here sooner, but that, wretched man that I am! I slept in the *Arbor* that stands on the Hill-side; nay, I had notwithstanding that, been here much sooner, but that in my sleep I lost my evidence, and came without it to the brow of the Hill, and then feeling for it, and finding it not, I was forced, with sorrow of Heart, to go back to the place where I slept my sleep, where I found it, and now I am come.

Por. Well, I will call out one of the Virgins of this place, who will (if she like your talk) bring you into the rest of the Family, according to the Rules of the House. So *Watchful* the *Porter* rang a Bell, at the sound of which came out at the door of the House a grave and beautiful Damsel named *Discretion*, and asked why she was called?

The *Porter* answered, This Man is in a Journey from the City of *Destruction* to Mount *Zion*, but being weary and benighted, he asked me if he might lodge here to night? so I told him I would call for thee, who, after discourse had with him, mayest do as seemeth thee good, even according to the Law of the House.

Then she asked him whence he was, and whither he was going? and he told her. She asked also, how he got in the way? and he told her. Then she asked him, What he had seen and met with in the way? and he told her. And last, she asked his Name? so he said, It is *Christian*, and I have so much the more a desire to lodge here to night, because, by what I perceive, this place was built by the Lord of the Hill, for the relief and security of Pilgrims: So she smiled, but the water stood in her Eyes: And after a little pause, she said, I will call forth two or three more of the Family. So she ran to the Door and called out *Prudence*, *Piety*, and *Charity*, who after a little more discourse with him, had him into the Family; and many of them meeting him at the threshold of the house, said, Come in, thou blessed of the Lord; this house was built by the Lord of the Hill, on purpose to entertain such Pilgrims in. Then he bowed his head and followed them into the House: so when he was come in, and sat down, they gave him something to drink; and consented together that until supper was ready, some of them should have some particular discourse with *Christian*, for the best improvement of time, and they appointed *Piety* and *Prudence*, and *Charity* to discourse with him: and thus they began.

Piety *dis-courses him.*

Piety. *Come, good* Christian, *since we have been so loving to you, to receive you into our house this night; let us, if perhaps we may better our selves thereby, talk with you of all things that have hapned to you in your Pilgrimage?*

Chr. With a very good will, and I am glad that you are so well disposed.

Piety. *What moved you at first to betake your self to a Pilgrims life?*

Chr. I was *driven out of my Native Country by a dreadful sound that was in mine Ears, *to wit*, That unavoidable destruction did attend me, if I abode in that place where I was.

* *How* Christian *was driven out of his own Country.*

Piety. *But how did it happen that you came out of your Country this way?*

Chr. It was as God would have it; for when I was under the fears of destruction, I did not know whither to go; but by chance there came a man, even to me, (as I was trembling and weeping) whose name is †*Evangelist*, and he directed me to the Wicket Gate, which else I should never have found, and so set me into the way that hath led me directly to this House.

† *How he goes into the way to* Zion.

Piety. *But did you not come by the House of the Interpreter?*

Chr. Yes, and did see such things there, the remembrance of which will stick by me as long as I live: especially three things, *to wit, How Christ, in despite of Satan, maintains his work of Grace in the heart: how the man had sinned himself quite out of hopes of Gods mercy, and also the dream of him that thought in his sleep the day of Judgment was come.

* *A rehearsal of what he saw in the way.*

Piety. *Why? did you hear him tell his Dream?*

Chr. Yes, and a dreadful one it was, I thought; it made my heart ake as he was telling of it, but yet I am glad I heard it.

Piety. *Was that all you saw at the house of the Interpreter?*

Chr. No, he took me and had me where he shewed me a stately Palace, and how the People were clad in Gold that were in it; and how there came a venturous Man, and cut his way through the Armed men that stood in the Door to keep him out; and how he was bid to come in, and win eternal Glory; Me thought those things did ravish my heart; I would have staid at that good Mans house a twelve month, but that I knew I had further to go.

Piety. *And what saw ye else in the way?*

Chr. Saw! Why, I went but a little further, and I saw one, as I thought in my mind, hang bleeding upon the Tree;

and the very sight of him made my Burden fall off my back (for I groaned under a very heavy burden) but then it fell down from off me. 'Twas a strange thing to me, for I never saw such a thing before; Yea, and while I stood looking up (for then I could not forbear looking) three shining ones came to me: one of them testified that my sins were forgiven me; another stript me of my Rags, and gave me this broidered Coat which you see; and the third set the mark which you see in my fore-head, and gave me this sealed Roll (and with that he plucked it out of his Bosome.)

Piety. *But you saw more than this, did you not.*

Chr. The things that I have told you were the best, yet some other matter I saw, as namely, I saw three Men, *Simple*, *Sloth*, and *Presumption*, lie a sleep a little out of the way as I came, with Irons upon their heels; but do you think I could awake them? I also saw *Formality* and *Hypocrisie* come tumbling over the Wall to go (as they pretended) to *Zion*, but they were quickly lost; even as my self did tell them, but they would not believe: but, above all, I found it hard work to get up this Hill, and as hard to come by the Lions Mouth; and truly if it had not been for the good Man, the Porter that stands at the Gate, I do not know, but that after all, I might have gone back again: but I thank God I am here, and I thank you for receiving of me.

Then *Prudence* thought good to ask him a few Questions, and desired his answer to them.

Prudence *discourses him.*

Pru. *Do you not think sometimes of the Countrey from whence you came?*

* Christian's *thoughts of his Native Country.*

Heb. 11. 15, 16.

Chr. Yes, *but with much shame and detestation; *Truly, if I had been mindful of that Countrey from whence I came out, I might have had opportunity to have returned; but now I desire a better Countrey, that is an heavenly.*

Pru. *Do you not yet bear away with you some of the things that then you were conversant withall?*

† Christian *distasted with carnal cogitations.*

Chr. Yes, but greatly against my will, especially my inward and †carnal cogitations; with which all my Country-men, as well as my self, were delighted; but now all those things are my grief, and might I but chuse mine own things, I would *chuse never to think of those things more: but when I would be a doing of that which is best, †that which is worst is with me.

* Christian's *choice.*

† Rom. 7.

Pru. *Do you not find sometimes, as if those things were vanquished, which at other times are your perplexity?*

Chr. Yes, but that is but seldom; but they are to me *golden hours, in which such things happen to me.

* Christian's *golden hours.*

Pru. *Can you remember by what means you find your annoyances at times, as if they were vanquished?*

Chr. Yes, when †I think what I saw at the Cross, that will do it; and when I look upon my Broidred Coat, that will do it; and when I look into the Roll that I carry in my Bosom, that will do it; and when my thoughts wax warm about whither I am going, that will do it.

† *How* Christian *gets power against his Corruptions.*

Pru. *And what is it that makes you so desirous to go to Mount* Zion*?*

Chr. Why, *there I hope to see him *alive*, that did hang *dead* on the Cross; and there I hope to be rid of all those things, that to this day are in me an annoyance to me; there, they say, there is no †death, and there I shall dwell with such Company as I like best. For to tell you truth, I love him, because I was by him eased of my burden, and I am weary of my inward sickness: I would fain be where I shall die no more, and with the Company that shall continually cry, **Holy, Holy, Holy.*

* *Why* Christian *would be at Mount* Zion.

† Isa. 25. 8. Rev. 21. 4.

Then said *Charity* to *Christian, Have you a Family? Are you a married man?*

* Charity *discourses him.*

Chr. I have a Wife and four small Children.

Cha. *And why did you not bring them along with you?*

Chr. Then *Christian* *wept, and said, Oh, how willingly would I have done it, but they were all of them utterly averse to my going on Pilgrimage.

* Christian's *love to his Wife and Children.*

Cha. *But you should have talked to them, and have endeavoured to have shown them the danger of being behind.*

Chr. So I did, and told them also what God had shewed

to me of the Destruction of our City: but I seemed to them as one that mocked; and they believed me not.

Gen. 19. 14.

Cha. *And did you pray to God that he would bless your Counsel to them?*

Chr. Yes, and that with much affection; for you must think that my Wife and poor Children were very dear unto me.

Cha. *But did you tell them of your own sorrow, and fear of destruction? for I suppose that destruction was visible enough to you?*

Chr. Yes, over, and over, and over. They might also †see my fears in my Countenance, in my Tears, and also in my trembling under the apprehension of the Judgment that did hang over our heads; but all was not sufficient to prevail with them to come with me.

† Christian's *fear of perishing might be read in his very countenance.*

Cha. *But what could they say for themselves, why they came not?*

Chr. Why, *my Wife was afraid of losing this World; and my Children were given to the foolish delights of youth: so what by one thing and what by another, they left me to wander in this manner alone.

* *The cause why his Wife and Children did not go with him.*

Cha. *But did you not with your vain life damp all that you by words used by way of perswasion to bring them away with you?*

Chr. Indeed I cannot commend my life, for I am conscious to my self of many failings therein: I know also that a man by his Conversation may soon overthrow what by Argument or Persuasion he doth labour to fasten upon others for their good. Yet, this I can say, I was very wary of giving them occasion, by any unseemly action, to make them averse to going on Pilgrimage. Yea, for this very thing, they would tell me I was too precise, and that I denied my self of things (for their sakes) in which they saw no evil. Nay, I think I may say, that if what they saw in me did hinder them, it was my great tenderness in sinning against God, or of doing any wrong to my Neighbour.

Christians *good conversation before his Wife and Children.*

Cha. *Indeed* *Cain *hated his Brother*, *because his own works were evil*, *and his Brothers righteous*; *and if thy Wife and Children have been offended with thee for this*, *they thereby shew themselves to be implacable to good*, * *and thou hast delivered thy Soul from their blood*.

* Christian *clear of their Blood*, *if they perish.*

* Ezek. 4. 19.

Now I saw in my Dream, that thus they sat talking together until Supper was ready. So when they had made ready, they sat down to meat: Now the Table was furnished with *fat things, and with Wine that was well refined, and all their †talk at the Table was about the LORD of the Hill: as namely, about that HE had done, and whereof HE did what HE did, and why he had builded that House: and by what they said, I perceived that HE had been a *great Warriour*, and had fought with, and slain *him that had the power of Death, but not without great danger to himself: which made me love him the more.

* *What* Christian *had to his Supper.*

† *Their Talk at Supper time.*

* Heb. 2. 14, 15.

For, as they said, and as I believe (said *Christian*) he did it with the loss of much blood: but that which put glory of Grace into all he did, was, that he did it out of pure love to this Countrey. And beside, there were some of them of the Houshold that said, they had been and spoke with him since he did dye on the Cross; and they have attested, that they had it from his own lips, that he is such a lover of poor Pilgrims, that the like is not to be found from the East to the West.

They moreover gave an instance of what they affirm'd, and that was, He had stript himself of his glory, that he might do this for the Poor; and that they heard him say and affirm, *That he would not dwell in the Mountain of* Zion *alone*. They said moreover, That he had made many Pilgrims *Princes, though by nature they were Beggars born, and their original had been the Dunghil.

* *Christ makes Princes of Beggars.*

1 Sam. 2. 8.

Psal. 113. 7.

Thus they discoursed together till late at night, and after they had committed themselves to their Lord for Protection, they betook themselves to rest: The Pilgrim they laid in a large upper *Chamber, whose Window opened towards the Sun-rising: the name of the Chamber was *Peace*, where he slept till break of day, and then he awoke, and sung,

* Christians *Bed-Chamber.*

Where am I now! is this the love and care
Of Jesus, for the men that Pilgrims are
Thus to provide! That I should be forgiven!
And dwell already the next door to Heaven.

So in the morning they all got up, and after some more discourse, they told him that he should not depart till they had shew'd him the *Rarities* of that place. And first they had him into the Study, *where they shewed Records of the greatest Antiquity; in which, as I remember my Dream, they shewed him the first *Pedegree* of the Lord of the Hill, that he was the Son of the Ancient of Days, and came by that eternal Generation. Here also was more fully Recorded the Acts that he had done, and the names of many hundreds that he had taken into his Service; and how he had placed them in such Habitations that could neither by length of Days, nor decays of Nature be dissolved.

* Christian *had into the Study, and what he saw there.*

Then they read to him some of the worthy Acts that some of his Servants had done. As how they had subdued Kingdoms, wrought Righteousness, obtained Promises, stopped the mouths of Lions, quenched the †violence of Fire, escaped the edge of the Sword, out of weakness were made strong, waxed valiant in fight, and turned to flight the Armies of the *Aliens*.

† Heb. 11. 33, 34.

Then they read again in another part of the Records of the House, where it was shewed how willing their Lord was to receive into his favour, any, even any, though they in time past had offered great affronts to his Person and Proceedings. Here also were several other Histories of many other famous things, of all which *Christian* had a view: as of things both Ancient and Modern, together with Prophecies and Predictions of things that have their certain accomplishment, both to the dread and amazement of Enemies, and the comfort and solace of Pilgrims.

The next day they took him, and had him into the †Armory, where they shewed him all manner of Furniture, which their Lord had provided for Pilgrims, as Sword, Shield, Helmet, Brest-plate, *All Prayer*, and Shoes that would not wear out. And there was here enough of this to harness out as many men

† Christian *had into the Armory.*

for the service of their Lord, as there be Stars in the Heaven for multitude.

They also shewed him some of the Engines with which some of his Servents had done wonderful things. *They shewed him *Moses*'s Rod, the Hammer and Nail with which *Jael* slew *Sisera*, the Pitchers, Trumpets, and Lamps too, with which *Gideon* put to flight the Armies of *Midian*. Then they shewed him the Oxes Goad wherewith *Shamgar* slew six hundred men. They shewed him also the Jaw-bone with which *Sampson* did such mighty feats; they shewed him moreover the Sling and Stone with which *David* slew *Goliah* of *Gath*: and the Sword also with which their Lord will kill the man of Sin in the day that he shall rise up to the Prey. They shewed him besides, many excellent things, with which *Christian* was much delighted. This done, they went to their rest again.

* Christian *is made to see ancient things.*

Then I saw in my Dream, that on the morrow he got up to go forwards, but they desired him to stay till the next day also; and then said they, we will (if the day be clear) shew you the *delectable Mountains, which they said, would yet further add to his comfort, because they were nearer the desired Heaven, than the place where at present he was. So he consented and staid. When the morning was up, they had him to the top of the House, †and bid him look South, so he did: and behold at a great distance he saw a most pleasant Mountainous Country, beautified with Woods, Vine-yards, Fruits of all sorts; Flowers also, with Springs and Fountains, very delectable to behold. Then he asked the name of the Country; they said it was *Immanuels Land*: and it is as Common, say they, as this Hill is, to and for all the Pilgrims. And when thou comest there, from thence thou mayest see to the Gate of the Cœlestial City; as the Shepherds that live there will make appear.

* Christian *shewed the delectable Mountains.*

† Isa. 33. 16, 17.

Now he bethought himself of setting forward, *and they were willing he should: but first, said they, let us go again into the Armory; so they did, and when he came there, they †harnessed him from head to foot, with what was of proof, lest perhaps he should meet with assaults in the way. He being therefore thus accoutred, walketh out with

* Christian *set forward.*

† Christian *sent away armed.*

his Friends to the Gate, and there he asked the Porter if he saw any Pilgrims pass by; then the Porter answered, Yes.

Chr. *Pray did you know him? said he.*

Por. I asked his name, and he told me it was *Faithfull.*

Chr. O said *Christian, I know him, he is my Towns-man, my near Neighbour, he comes from the place where I was born; how far do you think he may be before?*

Por. He is got by this time below the Hill.

Chr. *Well,* *said Christian, *good Porter, the Lord be with thee, and add to all thy blessings much increase of the kindness that thou hast shewed to me.*

* *How* Christian *and the* Porter *greet at parting.*

Then he began to go forward, but *Discretion, Piety, Charity,* and *Prudence* would accompany him down to the foot of the Hill. So they went on together, reiterating their former discourses till they came to go down the Hill. Then said *Christian,* as it was *difficult* coming up, so (so far as I can see) it is *dangerous* going down. Yes, said *Prudence,* so it is: for it is an hard matter for a man to go down into the Valley of *Humiliation,* as thou art now, and to catch no slip by the way: Therefore, said they, are we come out to accompany thee down the Hill. So he began to go down; but very warily, yet he caught a slip or two.

The Valley of Humiliation.

Then I saw in my Dream, that these good Companions (when *Christian* was gone down to the bottom of the Hill) gave him a Loaf of Bread, a Bottle of Wine and a Cluster of Raisins, and then he went on his way.

But now in this Valley of *Humiliation* poor *Christian* was hard put to it, for he had gone but a little way before he espied a foul *Fiend* coming over the Field to meet him; his name is *Apollyon.* Then did *Christian* begin to be afraid, and cast in his mind whether to go back or to stand his ground. But he considered again, that he had no Armour for his Back, and therefore thought that to turn the Back to him might give him greater advantage with ease to pierce him with his Darts; therefore he resolved to venture, and stand his ground. For, thought he, *had I no more in mine eye than the saving of my life, 'twould be the best way to stand.

Christian *no Armour for his Back.*

* Christian's *resolution in the approach of* Apollyon.

So he went on, and *Apollyon* met him: now the Monster was hideous to behold, he was cloathed with scales like a Fish; (and they are his pride) he had Wings like a Dragon, Feet like a Bear, and out of his Belly came Fire and Smoke, and his Mouth was as the Mouth of a Lyon. When he was come up to *Christian*, he beheld him with a disdainful countenance, and thus began to question with him.

Apol. *Whence come you, and whither are you bound?*

Chr. I am come from the City of *Destruction* †which is the place of all evil, and am going to the City of *Zion.*

† *Discourse betwixt* Christian *and* Apollyon.

Apol. *By this I perceive thou art one of my Subjects, for all that Country is mine, and I am the Prince and God of it. How is it then that thou hast run away from thy King? Were it not that I hope thou mayest do me more service, I would strike thee now at one blow to the Ground.*

Chr. I was born indeed in your Dominions, but your service was hard, and your Wages such as a man could not live on, **for the Wages of sin is death*; therefore when I was come to years, I did as other considerate Persons do, look out, if perhaps I might mend my self.

* Rom. 6. 23.

Apol. *There is no Prince that will thus lightly lose his Subjects, neither will I as yet lose thee; but since thou complainest of thy Service and Wages, †be content to go back, what our Countrey will afford, I do here promise to give thee.*

† Apollyon's *flattery.*

Chr. But I have let my self to another, even to the King of Princes, and how can I with fairness go back with thee?

Apol. *Thou hast done in this according to the Proverb,* †change a bad for a worse: *but it is ordinary for those that have professed themselves his Servants, after a while to give him the slip, and return again to me: do thou so too, and all shall be well.*

† Apollyon *undervalues Christs service.*

Chr. I have given him my Faith, and sworn my Allegiance to him, how then can I go back from this, and not be hanged as a Traitor?

Apol. *Thou didst the same by me, and yet I am willing to pass by all, if now thou wilt yet turn again, and go back.*

Chr. What I promised thee was in my non-age, and besides, I count that the Prince under whose Banner now I stand, is able to absolve me, yea, and to pardon also what I did as to my complyance with thee: and besides (O thou destroying *Apollyon*) to speak truth, I like his Service, his wages, his Servants, his Government, his Company, and Country, better than thine: and therefore leave off to perswade me further, I am his Servant, and I will follow him.

Apollyon *pleads the grievous end of Christians, to disswade* Christian *from persisting in his way.*

Apol. *Consider again, when thou art in cool blood, what thou art like to meet with in the way that thou goest. Thou knowest, that for the most part, his Servants come to an ill end, because they are Transgressors against me and my way; how many of them have been put to shamefull death? and besides, thou countest his Service better than mine; whereas he never came yet from the place where he is, to deliver any that served him out of their hands: but as for me, how many times, as all the World very well knows, have I delivered, either by power or fraud, those that have faithfully served me, from him and his; though taken by them; and so I will deliver thee.*

Chr. His forbearing at present to deliver them, is on purpose to try their love, whether they will cleave to him to the end: and as for the ill end thou sayest they come to, that is most glorious in their account: For, for present deliverance, they do not much expect it; for they stay for their Glory, and then they shall have it, when their Prince comes in his, and the Glory of the Angels.

Apol. *Thou hast already been unfaithful in thy service to him, and how dost thou think to receive Wages of him?*

Chr. Wherein, O *Apollyon*, have I been unfaithful to him?

Apollyon *pleads* Christians *infirmities against him.*

Apol. *Thou didst faint at first setting out, when thou wast almost choaked in the Gulf of* Despond, *thou diddest attempt wrong ways to be rid of thy Burden, whereas thou shouldest have stayed till thy Prince had taken it off. Thou didst sinfully sleep and lose thy choice things: thou wast also almost perswaded to go back at the sight of the Lions: and when thou talkest of thy Journey and of what thou hast heard, and seen, thou art inwardly desirous of vain Glory in all that thou sayest or doest.*

Chr. All this is true, and much more, which thou hast left out; but the Prince whom I serve and honour, is merciful, and ready to forgive: but besides, these infirmities possessed me in thy Country, for there I suck'd them in, and I have groaned under them, being sorry for them, and have obtained Pardon of my Prince.

Apol. Then *Apollyon* broke out into a grievous rage, saying, *I am an Enemy to this Prince; I hate his Person, his Laws, and People; I am come out on purpose to withstand thee.*

Apollyon *in a rage falls upon* Christian.

Chr. *Apollyon*, beware what you do, for I am in the Kings High-way, the way of Holiness, therefore take heed to your self.

Apol. Then *Apollyon* stradled quite over the whole breadth of the way, and said, I am void of fear in this matter, prepare thy self to die, for I swear by my Infernal Den, that thou shalt go no further, here will I spill thy Soul; and with that he threw a flaming Dart at his Breast, but *Christian* had a shield in his hand, with which he caught it, and so prevented the danger of that. Then did *Christian* draw, for he saw 'twas time to bestir him, and *Apollyon* as fast made at him, throwing Darts as thick as Hail; by the which, notwithstanding all that Christian could do to avoid it, †*Apollyon* wounded him in his *head*, his *hand* and *foot*, this made *Christian* give a little back; *Apollyon* therefore followed his work amain, and *Christian* again took courage, and resisted as manfully as he could. This sore Combat lasted for above half a day, even till *Christian* was almost quite spent. For you must know that *Christian*, by reason of his Wounds, must needs grow weaker and weaker.

† Christian *wounded in his under-standing, Faith, and Conversation.*

Then *Apollyon* espying his opportunity, began to gather up close to *Christian*, and wrestling with him, gave him a dreadful fall, and with that *Christians* Sword flew out of his hand. Then said *Apollyon*, *I am sure of thee now*; and with that he had almost prest him to death; so that *Christian* began to despair of Life. But as God would have it, while *Apollyon* was fetching his last blow, thereby to make a full end of this good man, *Christian* nimbly stretched out his hand for his Sword, and caught it, saying, †*Rejoyce not against me, O mine Enemy, when I fall I shall arise*, and with that gave him a deadly thrust, which made him give back, as one that had received his

Apollyon *casteth* Christian *down to the Ground.*

Christians *victory over* Apollyon.

† Mich. 7. 8.

mortal wound: *Christian* perceiving that, made at him again, saying, †*Nay in all these things we are more than conquerours, through him that loved us.* And with that *Apollyon* spread forth his Dragons wings, and sped him away, that *Christian* saw him no more.

† Rom. 8. 8, 9.
Jam. 4. 7.

A brief relation of the combat by the Spectator.

In this combat no man can imagine, unless he had seen and heard, as I did, what yelling and hideous roaring *Apollyon* made all the time of the fight, he spake like a Dragon: and on the other side, what sighs and groans burst from *Christians* heart. I never saw him all the while give so much as one pleasant look, till he perceived he had wounded *Apollyon* with his two edg'd Sword, then indeed he did smile, and look upward; but 'twas the dreadfullest sight that ever I saw.

Christian *gives God thanks for his deliverance.*

So when the battel was over, *Christian* said, I will here give thanks to him that hath delivered me out of the mouth of the Lion; to him that did help me against *Apollyon*: and so he did, saying,

Great Beelzebub, *the Captain of this Fiend,*
Design'd my ruine, therefore to this end
He sent him harnest out; and he with rage,
That hellish was, did fiercely me engage:
But blessed Michael *helped me, and I*
By dint of Sword did quickly make him fly:
Therefore to him let me give lasting praise,
And thanks, and bless his holy Name always.

Then there came to him an hand with some of the Leaves of the Tree of Life, the which *Christian* took and applied to the wounds *that* he had receiv'd in the Battel, and was healed immediately. He also sat down in *that* place to eat bread, and to drink of the *Bottle that* was given him a *little* before; so being refreshed, he addressed himself to his Journey, with *his Sword drawn in his hand, for he said, I know not but some other enemy may be at hand, but he met with no other affront from *Apollyon*, quite *thorow this* Valley.

* Christian *goes on his journey with his Sword drawn in his hand.*

The Valley of the shadow of Death.

Now at the *end* of *this Valley* was another, call'd *the Valley of the shadow of Death*, and Christian must needs go *through* it, because the *way* to the Cœlestial *City* lay through the midst of it: Now *this Valley* is a very solitary place. The Prophet †*Jeremiah* thus describes it; *A Wilderness, a Land of desarts, and of Pits, a Land of Drought, and of the shadow of Death, a Land that no man* (but a Christian) *passeth through, and where no man dwelt.*

† Jer. 2. 6.

Now here Christian was worse put to it than in his fight with *Apollyon*, as by the sequel you shall see.

I saw then in my Dream, *that when* Christian *was got on the borders of the shadow of* Death, there met him *two Men*, **Children of them that brought up an* †evil report *of the* good Land, making haste to go back, to whom *Christian* spake as follows.

* *The children of the Spies go back.*

Chr. *Whither are you going?*

† Numb. 13.

Men. They said, Back, back, and we would have you do so to, if either Life or Peace is prized by you.

Chr. *Why? what's the matter? said* Christian.

Men. Matter, said they, we were going that way as you are going, and went as far as we durst, and indeed we were almost past coming back, for had we gone a little further, we had not been here to bring the News to thee.

Chr. *But what have you met with, said* Christian.

Men. Why! we were almost in the Valley of the shadow of Death, but that by good hap we looked before us, and saw the danger before we came to it.

Psal. 4. 19.

Chr. *But what have you seen? said* Christian.

Psal. 117. 19.

Men. Seen! Why, the Valley it self, which is as dark as pitch; we also saw there the Hobgoblins, Satyrs, and Dragons of the Pit: we heard also in that Valley a continual howling and yelling, as of a People under unutterable misery, who were sat down in affliction and Irons: and over that Valley hangs the discouraging *Clouds of confusion, Death also doth alwayes spread his Wings over it. In a word, it is every whit dreadful, being utterly without order.

* Job 3. 5. chap. 10. 2.

Chr. *Then said* Christian, *I perceive not yet, by what you have said, but that* **this is my way to the desired Heaven.*

* Jer. 2. 6.

Men. Be it thy way, we will not chuse it for ours: so

they parted, and *Christian* went on his way but still with his Sword drawn in his hand for fear lest he should be assaulted.

I saw then in my Dream so far as this Valley reached, there was on the right hand a very deep Ditch, that Ditch is it into which the Blind hath led the Blind in all Ages, and have both there miserably perished. Again, behold on the left hand there was a very dangerous Quagg, into which, if even a good man falls, he finds no bottom for his foot to stand on: Into this Quagg King *David* once *did fall*, and had no doubt there been smothered, had not he that is able pluckt him out.

Psal. 69. 14.

The Path-way was here also exceeding narrow, and therefore good *Christian* was the more put to it; for when he sought in the dark to shun the Ditch on the one hand, he was ready to tip over into the mire on the other; also when he sought to escape the mire, without great carefulness, he would be ready to fall into the Ditch, thus he went on, and I heard him here sigh bitterly; for besides the danger mentioned above, the Path-way was here so dark, that oft-times when he lift up his foot to go forward, he knew not where, nor upon what he should set it next.

About the midst of this Valley, I perceived the Mouth of Hell to be, and it stood also hard by the way-side: Now thought *Christian*, what shall I do? And ever and anon the Flame and Smoke would come out in such abundance, with sparks and hideous noises, (things that cared not for *Christian's* Sword, as did *Apollyon* before) that he was forced to put up his Sword, and betake himself to another weapon called **All prayer*; so he cried in my hearing, **O Lord I beseech thee deliver my Soul.* Thus he went on a great while, yet still the flames would be reaching towards him: also he heard doleful Voices, and rushings to and fro, so that sometimes he thought he should be torn in pieces, or trodden down like mire in the Streets. This frightful sight was seen, and these dreadful noises were heard by him for several miles together, and coming to a place, where he thought he heard a company of *Fiends* coming forward to meet him, he stopt, and began to muse what he had best to do. Sometimes he had half a thought to go back. Then again he thought he might be

* Ephes. 6. 18.
* Psal. 116. 3.

Christian *put to a stand but for a while.*

half way through the Valley: he remembred also how he had already vanquished many a danger: and that the danger of going back might be much more than for to go forward; so he resolved to go on; Yet the *Fiends* seemed to come nearer and nearer; but when they were come even almost at him, he cryed out with a most vehement voice, *I will walk in the strength of the Lord God*; so they gave back, and came no further.

One thing I would not let slip, I took notice that now poor Christian *was so confounded, that he did not know his own voice; and thus I perceived it; Just when he was come over against the mouth of the burning Pit, one of the wicked ones got behind him, and stept up softly to him, and whisperingly suggested many grievous blasphemies to him,* **which he verily thought had proceeded from his own mind. This put* Christian *more to it than any thing that he met with before, even to think that he should now blaspheme him, that he loved so much before; yet, if he could have helped it, he would not have done it; but he had not the discretion neither to stop his Ears, nor to know from whence those blasphemies came.*

* *Christian* made believe that he spake blasphemies, when 'twas Satan that suggested them into his mind.

When *Christian* had travelled in this disconsolate condition some considerable time, he thought he heard the Voice of a man, going before him, saying, *Though I walk through the Valley of the shadow of Death, I will fear none ill, for thou art with me.*

Psal. 23. 4.

Then was he glad: and that for these reasons:

First, because he gathered from thence, That some who feared God, were in this Valley as well as himself.

Secondly, For that he perceived God was with them, though in that dark and dismal state, and why not, thought he, with me, though by reason of the Impediment that attends this place I cannot perceive it.

Job 9. 10.

Thirdly, For that he hoped (could he overtake them) to have company by and by, so he went on, and called to him that was before, but he knew not what to answer: for that he also thought himself to be alone: And by and by the day broke: Then said Christian, **He hath turned the shadow of Death into the Morning.*

* Amos 5. 8.

Now Morning being come, he looked back, not of desire to return, but to see, by the light of the day, what hazards he had gone through in the dark. So he saw more perfectly the Ditch that was on the one hand, and the Quag that was on the other; also how narrow the way was which led betwixt them both; also now he saw the Hobgoblings, and Satyrs, and Dragons of the Pit, but all afar off; for after break of day they came not nigh, yet they were discovered to him, according to that which is written, *He discovereth deep things out of darkness, and bringeth out to light the shadow of death.*

Christian glad at break of day.

* Job 12. 22.

Now was *Christian* much affected with his deliverance from all the dangers of his solitary way, which dangers, though he feared them more before, yet he saw them more clearly now, because the light of the day made them conspicuous to him; and about this time the Sun was rising, and this was another mercy to *Christian*, for you must note, that though the first part of the Valley of the shadow of death was dangerous, *yet this second part which he was yet to go, was (if possible) far more dangerous: for, from the place where he now stood, even to the end of the Valley, the way was all along set so full of Snares, Traps, Gins, and Nets here, and so full of Pits, Pitfals, deep holes and shelvings down there, that had it now been dark, as it was when he came the first part of the way, had he had a thousand Souls, they had in reason been cast away; but as I said just now the Sun was rising. Then said he, **his Candle shineth on my head*, *and by his light I go through darkness.*

* *The second part of this Valley very dangerous.*

* Job 29. 3.

In this light therefore he came to the end of the Valley. Now I saw in my Dream, that at the end of this Valley lay blood, bones, ashes and mingled bodies of Men, even of Pilgrims, that had gone this way formerly: And while I was musing what should be the reason, I espied a little before me a Cave, where two Giants, *Pope* and *Pagan*, dwelt in old time, by whose Power and Tyranny the Men whose bones, blood, Ashes, *&c.* lay there, were cruelly put to death. But by this place *Christian* went without much danger, whereat I somewhat wondered, but I have learnt since, that *Pagan* has been dead many a day, and as for the other, though he be yet alive, he is by reason of age, and also of the many shrewd brushes that he met with in his younger days, grown so crazy and stiff in his joynts, that he can now do little more than sit in his Caves mouth, grinning at Pilgrims as they go by, and biting his nails, because he cannot come at them.

So I saw that *Christian* went on his way, yet at the sight of the *old Man* that sat in the Mouth of the Cave, he could not tell what to think, especially because he spake to him, though he could not go after him; saying, *You will never mend, till more of you be burned*: but he held his peace, and set a good face on't, and so went by: and catcht no hurt. Then sang *Christian.*

O world of wonders! (I can say no less)
That I should be preserv'd in that distress
That I have met with here! O blessed be
That hand that from it hath deliver'd me!
Dangers in darkness, Devils, Hell and Sin,
Did compass me while I this Vale was in:
Yea Snares & Pits, & Traps & Nets did lie
My Path about, that worthless silly I
Might have been catch't intangled, and cast down:
But since I live, let JESUS wear the Crown.

Now as *Christian* went on his way, he came to a little ascent, which was cast up on purpose, that Pilgrims might see before them up there, therefore *Christian* went, and looking forward, he saw *Faithful* before him upon his Journey. Then said *Christian* aloud, Ho, ho, So ho; stay, and I will be your Companion. At that *Faithful* looked behind him, to whom *Christian* cryed, Stay, stay, till I come up to you: but *Faithful answered*, *No*, I am upon my Life, and the Avenger of Blood is behind me. At this *Christian* was somewhat moved, and putting to all his strength, he quickly got up with *Faithful*, and did also over-run him, so the *last was first*. Then did *Christian* vain-gloriously smile, because he had gotten the start of his Brother, but not taking good heed to his feet, he suddenly stumbled and fell, and could not rise again, until *Faithful* came up to help him.

Christian *overtakes* Faithful.

Then I saw in my dream they went very lovingly on together; and had sweet discourse of all things that had hapned to them in their Pilgrimage; and thus *Christian* began.

Christian's *fall makes* Faithful *and he go lovingly together.*

Chr. *My honoured and well beloved Brother* Faithful, *I am glad that I have overtaken you, and that God has so tempred our Spirits, that we can walk as companions in this so pleasant a Path.*

Faith. I had thought dear Friend, to have had your company quite from our Town, but you did get the start of me: wherefore I was forced to come thus much of the way alone.

Chr. *How long did you stay in the City of* Destruction, *before you set out after me on your Pilgrimage?*

Faith. Till I could stay no longer: for there was great talk presently after you were gone out, that our City would in short time with Fire from Heaven be burned down to the Ground.

Their talk about the Country *from whence they came.*

Chr. *What? Did your Neighbors talk so?*

Faith. Yes, 'twas for a while in every bodies mouth.

Chr. *What, and did no more of them but you come out to escape the danger?*

Faith. Though there was, as I said, a great talk thereabout, yet I do not think they did firmly believe it. For in the heat of the discourse I heard some of them deridingly speak of you, and of your desperate Journey, (for so they called this your Pilgrimage;) but I did believe, and do still, that the end of our City will be with Fire and Brimstone from above: and therefore I have made my escape.

Chr. *Did you hear no talk of Neighbour* Pliable.

Faith. Yes *Christian*, I heard that he followed you till he came at the Slough of *Despond*; where, as some said, he fell in; but he would not be known to have so done: but I am sure he was soundly bedabled with that kind of dirt.

Chr. *And what said the Neighbours to him?*

Faith. He hath since his going back been had greatly in derision, and that among all sorts of People; some do mock and despise him, and scarce will any set him on work. He is now seven times worse than if he had never gone out of the City.

How Pliable *was accounted of when he got home.*

Chr. *But why should they be so set against him, since they also despise the way that he forsook?*

Faith. Oh, they say, hang him; he is a turn Coat, he was not true to his profession; I think God has stirred up even his Enemies to hiss at him, and make him a Proverb, because he hath forsaken the way.

Jer. 28. 18, 19.

Chr. *Had you no talk with him before you came out?*

Faith. I met him once in the Streets, but he leered away on the other side, as one ashamed of what he had done: so I spake not to him.

Chr. *Well, at my first setting out, I had hopes of that man: but now I fear he will perish in the Overthrow of the* City, *For it is hapned to him according to the true Proverb, The Dog is turned to his vomit again, and the Sow that was washed, to her wallowing in the Mire.

* 2 Pet. 2. 22.

The Dog and Sow.

Faith. They are my fears of him too, but who can hinder that which will be?

Chr. Well, Neighbour *Faithful*, said Christian, let us leave him, and talk of things that more immediately concern our selves, *Tell me now, what you have met with in the way as you came: for I know you have met with some things, or else it may be writ for a wonder.*

Faith. I escaped the Slough that I perceiv'd you fell into, and got up to the Gate without that danger; only I met with one whose Name was *Wanton*, that had like to have done me a mischief.

Faithful *assaulted by* Wanton.

Chr. *'Twas well you escaped her Net*; *Joseph *was hard put to it by her, and he escaped her as you did, but it had like to have cost him his Life. But what did she do to you?*

* Gen. 39. 11, 12, 13.

Faith. You cannot think (but that you know something) what a flattering tongue she had, she lay at me hard to turn aside with her, promising me all manner of content.

Chr. *Nay, she did not promise you the content of a good Conscience.*

Faith. You know that I mean, all carnal and fleshly content.

Chr. *Thank God you have escaped her; The* **abhorred of the Lord shall fall into her Ditch.*

* Prov. 22. 24.

Faith. Nay, I know not whether I did wholly escape her or no.

Chr. *Why I tro, you did not consent to her desires?*

Faith. No not to defile my self; for I remembred an old writing that I had seen, which said, *Her Steps take hold of Hell.* So I shut mine Eyes, because I would not be bewitcht with her looks; then she railed on me, and I went my way.

Prov. 5. 5.
Job 31. 1.

Chr. *Did you meet with no other assault as you came?*

Faith. When I came to the foot of the Hill called *Difficulty*, I met with a very aged Man, who asked me, *What I was, and whither bound?* I told him that I am a Pilgrim, going to the Cœlestial City: Then said the old man, *Thou lookest like an honest fellow, wilt thou be content to dwell with me, for the wages that I shall give thee?* Then I askt him his name and where he dwelt? He said his Name was *Adam the First, and that he dwelt in the Town of * Deceit.* I asked him then, what was his work? and what the wages that he would give; He told me that his work was *many delights, and his wages, that I should be his Heir at last.* I further askt him, what House he kept, and what other Servants he had? so he told me, *That his House was maintained with all the dainties in the world, and that his Servants were those of his own begetting.* Then I asked how many Children he had? He said that he had but three Daughters; *The * lust of the Flesh, the lust of the Eyes, and the pride of Life*: and that I should marry them if I would. Then I asked how long time he would have me to live with him? And he told me, *as long as he lived himself.*

He is assaulted by Adam *the First.*

* Eph. 4. 22.

* 1 John 2. 16.

Chr. *Well, and what conclusion came the* Old man *and you to at last?*

Faith. Why at first I found my self somewhat inclinable to go with the Man, for I thought he spake very fair; but looking in his forehead, as I talked with him, I saw there written, *Put off the old Man with his Deeds.*

Chr. *And how then?*

Faith. Then it came burning hot into my mind: whatever he said, and however he flattred, when he got me home to his house, he would sell me for a slave. So I bid him forbear to talk, for I would not come near the door of his House. Then he revil'd me, and told me, that he would send such a one after me, that should make my way bitter to my Soul; So I turned to go away from him; but just as I turned my self to go thence, I felt him take hold of my flesh, and give me such a deadly twitch back, that I thought he had pulled part of me after himself: This made me cry, **O wretched man!* So I went on my way up the Hill.

* Rom. 7. 24.

Now when I had got about half way up, I looked behind me, and saw one coming after me, swift as the wind; so he overtook me just about the place where the Settle stands.

Chr. *Just there, said* Christian, *did I sit down to rest me; but being overcome with sleep, I there lost this Roll out of my bosome.*

Faith. But good Brother hear me out: So soon as the man overtook me, he was but a word and a blow; for down he knockt me, and laid me for dead. But when I was a little come to my self again, I asked him wherefore he served me so? he said, because of my secret inclining to *Adam the First*: and with that he struck me another deadly blow on the Breast, and beat me down backward; so I lay at his foot as dead as before. So when I came to my self again, I cried him mercy, but he said I know not how to shew mercy, and with that knockt me down again. He had doubtless made an end of me, but that one came by, and bid him forbear.

Chr. *Who was that that bid him forbear?*

Faith. I did not know him at first, but as he went by, I perceived the holes in his hands and in his side, then I concluded that he was our Lord. So I went up the Hill.

Chr. *That Man that overtook you was* Moses, **he spareth none, neither knoweth he how to shew mercy to those that transgress his Law.*

* *The Thunder of* Moses.

Faith. I know it very well, it was not the first time that he has met with me. 'Twas he that came to me when I dwelt securely at home, and that told me he would burn my house over my head, if I staid there.

Chr. *But did you not see the house that stood there on the top of the hill on the side of which* Moses *met you?*

Faith. Yes, and the Lions too, before I came at it; but for the Lions, I think they were asleep, for it was about Noon;

and because I had so much of the day before me, I passed by the Porter, and came down the Hill.

Chr. *He told me indeed that he saw you go by, but I wish you had called at the house; for they would have shewed you so many Rarities, that you would scarce have forgot them to the day of your death. But pray tell me, did you meet no body in the Valley of* Humility?

Faithful *assaulted by* Discontent.

Faith. Yes, I met with one *Discontent*, who would willingly have perswaded me to go back again with him; his reason was, for that the Valley was altogether without *Honour*; he told me moreover, that there to go, was the way to disobey all my Friends, as *Pride*, *Arrogancy*, *Self-conceit*, *Worldly Glory*, with others, who he knew, as he said, would be very much offended, if I made such a fool of my self as to wade through this Valley.

Chr. *Well, and how did you answer him?*

Faithful's *answer to* Discontent.

Faith. I told him, that although all these that he named might claim Kindred of me, and that rightly, (for indeed they were my Relations, *according to the flesh*) yet since I became a Pilgrim, they have disowned me, and I also have rejected them: and therefore they were to me now no more than if they had never been of my Linage: I told him moreover, That as to this Valley he had quite mis-represented the thing: *for before Honour is Humility, and a haughty Spirit before a fall.* Therefore said I, I had rather go through this Valley to the Honour that was so accounted by the wisest, than chuse that which he esteemed most worthy our affections.

Chr. *Met you with nothing else in that Valley?*

He is assaulted with Shame.

Faith. Yes, I met with *Shame*, but of all the men that I met with in my Pilgrimage, he I think, bears the wrong name: the other would be said nay, after a little argumentation (and somewhat else,) but this bold-faced *Shame* would never have done.

Chr. *Why, what did he say to you?*

Faith. What! why he objected against Religion it self: he said 'twas a pitiful, low, sneaking business for a man to mind Religion: he said that tender Conscience was an unmanly thing: and that for a man to watch over his words and waies,

so as to tie up himself from that hectoring Liberty, that the brave Spirits of the times accustom themselves unto would make him the Ridicule of the times. He objected also, that but few of the Mighty, Rich, or Wise, were ever of my opinion: nor
any of them neither, before they were perswaded 1 Cor. 1. 26.
to be Fools, and to be of a voluntary fondness, to Chap. 3. 18.
venture the loss of all, *for no body knows what.* Phil. 3. 7, 9.
He moreover objected *the base and low estate * John 7. 48.
and condition of those that were chiefly the
Pilgrims of the times in which they lived: also their Ignorance, and want of understanding in all natural Science. Yea, he did hold me to it at that rate also, about a great many more things than here I relate: as that it was a shame to sit whining and mourning under a Sermon, and a shame to come sighing and groaning home. That it was a shame to ask my Neighbour forgiveness for petty faults, or to make restitution where I have taken from any. He said also that Religion made a man grow strange to the great, because of a few Vices (which is called by finer names) and made him own and respect the base, because of the same Religious fraternity: And is not this, said he, a shame?

Chr. *And what did you say to him?*

Faith. Say! I could not tell what to say at first. Yea, he put me so to it, that my Blood came up in my Face: even this *Shame* fetch't it up, and had almost beat me quite off. But at
last I began to consider, **That that which is* * Luk. 16. 15.
highly esteemed among Men, is had in an abomination with God. And I thought again, this *Shame* tells me what Men are, but it tells me nothing what *God* or the *Word* of God is. And I thought moreover, that at the day of doom we shall not be doomed to Death or Life, according to the hectoring Spirits of the World: but according to the Wisdom and Law of the highest. Therefore thought I, what God says is best indeed, is best, though all men in the World are against it. Seeing then that God prefers his Religion, seeing God prefers a tender Conscience, seeing they that make themselves Fools for the Kingdom of Heaven are wisest: and that the poor man that loveth Christ, is richer than the greatest man in the World that hates him: *Shame* depart, thou art an Enemy to my

Salvation: shall I entertain thee against my Sovereign Lord? How then shall I look him in the face at his coming? should I now be ashamed of his Ways and Servants, how can I expect the blessing? but indeed this *Shame* was a bold Villain; I could scarce shake him out of my Company; yea, he would be haunting of me, and continually whispering me in the Ear, with some one or other of the Infirmities that attend Religion: But at last I told him, 'twas but in vain to attempt further in this business; for those things that he disdained, in those did I see most glory: And so at last I got past this *importunate* one.

Mark 8. 3.

And when I had shaken him off, then I began to sing;

The Tryals that those men do meet withal,
That are obedient to the heavenly call,
Are manifold and suited to the flesh,
And come, and come, and come again afresh;
That now or sometimes else, we by them may
Be taken, overcome, and cast away.
O let the Pilgrims, let the Pilgrims then,
Be vigilant, and quit themselves like Men.

Chr. I am glad my Brother, that thou didst withstand this Villain so bravely; for of all, as thou sayest, I think he has the wrong Name, for he is so bold as to follow us in the Streets, and to attempt to put us to shame before all men; that is, to make us ashamed of that which is good; but if he was not himself audacious, he would never attempt to do as he does; but let us still resist him; for notwithstanding all his bravadoes, he promoted the Fool, and none else. *The Wise shall inherit Glory, said* Solomon, *but shame shall be the promotion of Fools.*

Prov. 3. 35.

Faith. *I think we must cry to him for help against* shame, *that would have us be valiant for Truth upon the Earth.*

Chr. You say true, But did you meet no body else in that Valley?

Faith. *No not I, for I had Sun-shine all the rest of the way, through that, and also through the Valley of the shadow of death.*

Chr. 'Twas well for you, I am sure it fared far otherwise with me. I had for a long Season, as soon almost as I entred into that Valley, a dreadful Combate with that foul Fiend *Apollyon*: Yea, I thought verily he would have killed me: especially when he got me down, and crush'd me under him, as if he would have crush'd me to pieces. For as he threw me, my sword flew out of my hand; nay he told me, *He was sure of me*: but *I cryed to God, and he heard me, and delivered me out of all my troubles.* Then I entred into the Valley of the shadow of death, and had no light for almost half the way through it. I thought I should have been kill'd there, over and over: but at last, day broke, and the Sun rose, and I went through that which was behind with far more ease and quiet.

Moreover I saw in my dream, that as they went on, *Faithful*, as he chanced to look on one side, saw a man whose Name is *Talkative*, walking at a distance besides them (for in this place there was room enough for them all to walk:) *He was a tall man, and something more comely at a distance than at hand*: To this man, *Faithful* addressed himself in this manner:

Talkative *described.*

Faith. *Friend, Whither away? Are you going to the Heavenly Country?*

Talk. I am going to the same place.

Faith. *That is well: Then I hope we shall have your good company.*

Talk. With a very good will, will I be your companion.

Faith. *Come on then, and let us go together, and let us spend our time in discoursing of things that are profitable.*

Faithful *and* Talkative *enter discourse.*

Talk. To talk of things that are good, to me is very acceptable; with you, or with any other; and I am glad that I have met with those that incline to so good a work. For to speak the truth; there are but few that care thus to spend their time (as they are in their travels) but chuse much rather to be speaking of things to no profit, and this hath been a trouble to me.

Talkative'*s dislike of bad discourse.*

Faith. *That is indeed a thing to be lamented; for what thing so worthy of the use of the tongue and mouth of men on Earth, as are the things of the God of Heaven?*

Talk. I like you wonderful well, for your sayings are full of conviction; and I will add, what thing is so pleasant, and what so profitable, as to talk of the things of God:

What things so pleasant? (that is, if a man hath any delight in things that are wonderful) for instance: If a man doth delight to talk of the History, or the Mystery of things, or if a man doth love to talk of Miracles, Wonders or Signs, where shall he find things recorded so delightful, and so sweetly penned as in the holy Scripture?

Faith. *That's true: but to be profited by such things in our talk should be our chief design.*

Talk. That is it that I said; for to talk of such things is most profitable, for by so doing, a man may get knowledge of many things: as of the vanity of earthly things, and the benefit of things above: (thus in general) but more particular, By this a man may learn the necessity of the New Birth, the insufficiency of our works, the need of Christ's righteousness, *&c.* Besides, by this a man may learn what it is to repent, to believe, to pray, to suffer, or the like: by this also a man may learn what are the great Promises and Consolations of the Gospel, to his own comfort. Further, by this a man may learn to refuse false Opinions, to vindicate the truth, and also to instruct the ignorant.

Talkative's *fine discourse.*

Faith. *All this is true, and glad am I to hear these things from you.*

Talk. Alas, the want of this is the cause that so few understand the need of Faith, and the necessity of a work of Grace in their Soul, in order to eternal Life, but ignorantly live in the works of the Law, by which a man can by no means obtain the Kingdom of Heaven.

Faith. *But by your leave, heavenly knowledge of these is the gift of God; no man attaineth to them by humane industry, or only by the talk of them.*

Talk. All that I know very well. For a man can receive nothing except it be given him from Heaven; all is of Grace, not of works: I could give you an hundred Scriptures for the confirmation of this.

O brave Talkative.

Faith. *Well then, said* Faithful: *what is that one thing, that we shall at this time found our discourse upon?*

Talk. What you will: I will talk of things heavenly, or things earthly; things Moral, or things Evangelical; things sacred, or things prophane; things past, or things to come; things foreign, or things at home; things more essential, or things circumstantial; provided that all be done to our profit.

O brave Talkative.

Faith. Now did *Faithful* begin to wonder, *and stepping to* Christian *(for he walked all this while by himself) he said to him, but softly, what a brave companion have we got! Surely this man will make a very excellent Pilgrim.*

Faithful *beguiled by* Talkative.

Chr. At this *Christian* modestly smiled, and said, this man with whom you are so taken, will beguile with this tongue of his twenty of them that know him not.

Christian *makes a discovery of* Talkative, *telling* Faithful *who he was.*

Faith. *Do you know him then?*

Chr. Know him! Yes, better than he knows himself.

Faith. *Pray what is he?*

Chr. His name is *Talkative*, he dwelleth in our Town; I wonder that you should be a stranger to him, only I consider that our Town is large.

Faith. *Whose Son is he? and whereabout doth he dwell.*

Chr. He is the Son of one *Say-well*, he dwelt in *Prating-row*, and he is known of all that are acquainted with him, by the name of *Talkative* in *Prating-row*, and notwithstanding his fine tongue, he is but a sorry fellow.

Faith. *Well, he seems to be a very pretty man.*

Chr. That is to them that have not through acquaintance with him, for he is best abroad, near home he is ugly enough: your saying that he is a *pretty man*, brings to my mind what I have observed in the work of the Painter, whose Pictures shew best at a distance, but very near, more unpleasing.

Faith. *But I am ready to think you do but jest, because you smiled.*

Chr. God forbid that I should jest, (though I smiled) in this matter, or that I should accuse any falsly; I will give you a further discovery of him. This man is for any company, and for any talk; as he talketh now with you, so will he talk when he is on the Ale-bench; And the more Drink he hath in his Crown, the more of these things he hath in his mouth: Religion hath no place in his heart, or house, or conversation; all he hath lieth in his tongue, and his Religion is to make a noise therewith.

Faith. *Say you so! then am I in this man greatly deceived.*

Chr. Deceived! you may be sure of it. Remember the Proverb, *They say, and do not: but the Kingdom of God is not in Word, but in Power.* He talketh of Prayer, of Repentance, of Faith, and of the New birth: but he knows but only to talk of them. I have been in his Family, and have observed him both at home and abroad; and I know what I say of him is the truth. His house is as empty of Religion, *as the white of an Egg is of savour.* There is there neither Prayer, nor sign of Repentance for sin: Yea, the brute in his kind serves God far better than he. He is the very stain, reproach and shame of Religion to all that know him; it can hardly have a good word in all that end of the Town where he dwells, through him. Thus say the common People that know him, *A Saint abroad, and a Devil at home.* His poor family finds it so, he is such a churle, such a railer at, and so unreasonable with his Servants, that they neither know how to do for, or to speak to him. Men that have any dealings with him, say, it's better to deal with a *Turk* than with him, for fairer dealing they shall have at their hands. This *Talkative* (if it be possible) will go beyond them, defraud, beguile, and over-reach them. Besides, he brings up his Sons to follow his steps, and, if he finds in any of them *a foolish timorousness*, (for so he calls the first appearance of a tender conscience) he calls them fools and blockheads, and by no means will employ them in much, or speak to their Commendations before others. For my part I am of opinion, that he has, by his wicked life caused many to stumble and fall, and will be, if God prevents not, the ruin of many more.

Mat. 23.
1 Cor. 4. 2.
Talkative *talks but does not.*

His House is empty of Religion.

He is a stain to Religion.
Rom. 2. 24, 25.
The Proverb that goes of him.

Men shun to deal with him.

Faith. *Well, my Brother, I am bound to believe you; not only because you say you know him, but also because like a Christian, you make your reports of men. For I cannot think that you speak these things of ill will, but because it is even so as you say.*

Chr. Had I known him no more than you, I might

perhaps, have thought of him as at the first you did: Yea, had he received this report at their hands only that are enemies to Religion, I should have thought it had been a slander. (A lot that often falls from bad mens mouths upon good mens names and professions:) But all these things, yea, and a great many more as bad, of my own knowledge I can prove him guilty of. Besides, good men are ashamed of him, they can neither call him *Brother* nor *Friend*; the very naming of him among them, makes them blush if they know him.

Faith. *Well, I see that* saying *and* doing *are two things, and hereafter I shall better observe this distinction.*

Chr. They are two things indeed, and are as diverse, as are the Soul and the Body: For as the Body without the Soul is but a dead Carkass; so *Saying*, if it be alone, is but a dead Carkass also. The Soul of Religion is the practick part. *Pure Religion and undefiled before God and the Father, is this, to visit the fatherless and widows in their affliction, and to keep himself unspotted from the World*, This *Talkative* is not aware of, he thinks that *hearing* and saying will make a good Christian: and thus he deceiveth his own Soul. Hearing is but as the sowing of the Seed; talking is not sufficient to prove that fruit is indeed in the heart and life; and let us assure our selves, that at the day of Doom men shall be judged according to their fruit. It will not be said then, *Did you believe?* but were you *Doers*, or *Talkers* only? and accordingly shall they be judged. The end of the world is compared to our Harvest, and you know men at harvest regard nothing but fruit. Not that any thing can be accepted that is not of Faith: But I speak this to shew you how insignificant the Profession of *Talkative* will be at that day.

The Carkass of Religion.

James 1. 27. *see ver.* 2, 3, 24, 25, 26.

See Matth. 14. 25.

Faith. *This brings to my mind that of* Moses, *by which he describeth the Beast that is clean. He is such an one that parteth the hoof, and cheweth the Cud; not that parteth the hoof only, or that cheweth the Cud only. The Hare cheweth the Cud, but yet is unclean because he parteth not the hoof. And this truly resembleth* Talkative: *he cheweth the Cud, he seeketh knowledge, he cheweth upon the Word, but*

Lev. 11. Deut. 14.

Faithful convinced of the badness of *Talkative.*

he divideth not the hoof, he parteth not with the way of sinners; but as the Hare, he retaineth the foot of a dog or bear, and therefore is unclean.

Chr. You have spoken, for ought I know, the true Gospel sense of those Texts; and I will add another thing: *Paul* calleth some men, yea, and those great Talkers too, *Sounding-brass*, and *tinkling Cymbals*: that is, as he expounds them in another place, *Things without life giving sound.* Things without life, that is, without the true Faith and Grace of the Gospel; and consequently, things that shall never be placed in the Kingdom of Heaven among those that are the Children of Life: Though their *sound* by their *talk* be as if it were the Tongue or Voice of an Angel.

1 Cor. 13. 1, 2, 3. ch. 14. 7. *Talkative* like two things that sound without life.

Faith. *Well, I was not so fond of his Company at first, but I am as sick of it now. What shall we do to be rid of him?*

Chr. Take my advice, and do as I bid you, and you shall find that he will soon be sick of your company too, except God shall touch his heart and turn it.

Faith. *What would you have me to do?*

Chr. Why, go to him, and enter into some serious discourse about the *power of Religion*; and ask him plainly (when he has approved of it, for that he will) whether this thing be set up in his Heart, House or Conversation.

Faith. Then *Faithful* stept forward again, and said to *Talkative*: *Come, what chear? how is it now?*

Talk. Thank you, well. I thought we should have had a great deal of talk by this time.

Faith. *Well, if you will we will fall to it now, and since you left it with me to state the question, let it be this: How doth the saving Grace of God discover it self, when it is in the heart of man?*

Talk. I perceive then that our talk must be *about the power of things*; Well, 'tis a very good question, and I shall be willing to answer you. And take my answer in brief thus. First, *Where the Grace of God is in the Heart, it causeth there a great out-cry against sin.* Secondly,———

Talkative's *false discovery of a work of grace.*

Faith. *Nay, hold, let us consider of one at once, I think you should rather say, It shows it self by inclining the Soul to abhor its sin.*

Talk. Why, what difference is there between crying out against, and abhorring of sin?

Faith. *Oh! a great deal; a man may cry out against sin of policy, but he cannot abhor it, but by vertue of a godly antipathy against it: I have heard many cry out against sin in the Pulpit, who yet can abide it well enough in the heart, house and conversation.* Joseph's *Mistress cryed out with a loud voice, as if she had been very holy; but she would willingly, notwithstanding that, have committed uncleanness with him. Some cry out against sin, even as the mother crys out against her Child in her lap, when she calleth it Slut, and naughty Girl, & then falls to hugging & kissing it.*

The crying out against sin, no sign of grace.

Gen. 39. 15.

Talk. You lie at the catch I perceive.

Faith. *No not I, I am only for setting things right. But what is the second thing whereby you will prove a discovery of a work of grace in the heart?*

Talk. *Great Knowledge* of Gospel-Mysteries.

Faith. *This sign should have been first, but first or last, it is also false; for knowledge, great knowledge may be obtained in the Mysteries of the Gospel, and yet no work of grace in the Soul. Yea, if a man have all knowledge, he may yet be nothing; and so consequently be no child of God. When Christ said,* Do you know all these things? *And the Disciples had answered, Yes: He added,* Blessed are ye if ye do them. *He doth not lay the Blessing in the knowing of them, but in the doing of them. For there is a knowledge that is not attended with doing:* He that knoweth his Masters will, and doeth it not. *A man may know like an Angel, and yet be no Christian: Therefore your sign of it is not true. Indeed to know is a thing that pleaseth Talkers and Boasters; but to do, is that which pleaseth God. Not that the heart can be good without knowledge; for without that the heart is naught: There is therefore knowledge, and knowledge. Knowledge that resteth in the bare speculation of things, and knowledge that is accompanied with the grace of faith and love, which puts a man upon doing even the will of God from the heart: The first of these will serve the Talker, but without the other the true Christian is not*

Great knowledge no sign of Grace.

1 Cor. 13.

Knowledge and knowledge.

content. Give me understanding and I shall keep thy Law, yea, shall I observe it with my whole heart, *Psal.* 119. 34.

True Knowledge attended with endeavours.

Talk. You lie at the catch again, this is not for edification.

Faith. *Well if you please, propound another sign how this work of grace discovereth it self where it is.*

Talk. Not I, for I see we shall not agree.

Faith. *Well, if you will not, will you give me leave to do it?*

Talk. You may use your liberty.

Faith. *A work of grace in the soul discovereth it self, either to him that hath it, or to standers by.*

One good sign of grace.

John 16. 8.
from 7. 24.
John 16. 9.
Mark 16. 16.
Psal. 38. 18.
Jer. 31. 19.
Gal. 2. 15.
Acts 4. 12.
Matth. 5. 6.
Rev. 1. 6.

To him that hath it, thus it gives him conviction of sin, especially of the defilement of his nature, and the sin of unbelief, (for the sake of which he is sure to be damned, if he findeth not mercy at God's hand by faith in Jesus Christ). This sight and sense of things worketh in him sorrow and shame for sin; he findeth moreover revealed in him the Saviour of the World, and the absolute necessity of closing with him for life, at the which he findeth hungrings and thirstings after him, to which hungrings, &c. *the Promise is made. Now according to the strength or weakness of his Faith in his Saviour, so is his joy and peace, so is his love to holiness, so are his desires to know him more, and also to serve him in this World. But though I say it discovereth it self thus unto him; yet it is but seldom that he is able to conclude, that this is a work of Grace, because his corruptions now, and his abused reason makes his mind to mis-judge in this matter; therefore in him that hath this work there is required a very sound Judgment, before he can with steddiness conclude that this is a work of Grace.*

Rom. 10. 10.
Phil. 1. 27.
Matth. 5. 9.
John 24. 15.
Psal. 50. 20.
Job 42. 5, 6.
Ezek. 29. 43.

To others it is thus discovered.

1. *By an experimental confession of his faith in Christ.* 2. *By a life answerable to that confession, to wit, a life of holiness; heart-holiness, family-holiness, (if he hath a family) and by Conversation holiness in the world: which in the general teacheth him inwardly to abhor his sin, and himself for that in secret, to*

suppress it in his Family, and to promote holiness in the World; not by talk only, as an Hypocrite or Talkative person may do: but by a practical subjection in faith and love to the power of the Word: and now Sir, as to this brief description of the work of Grace, and also the discovery of it, if you have ought to object, object: if not, then give me leave to propound to you a second question.

Talk. Nay, my part is not now to object, but to hear, let me therefore have your second question.

Faith. It is this, *Do you experience this first part of this description of it? and doth your life and conversation testifie the same? or standeth your Religion* in word or tongue, and *not in* Deed *and* Truth: *pray if you incline to answer me in this, say no more than you know the God above will say* Amen *to*; *and also, nothing but what your Conscience can justifie you in.* For not he that commendeth himself is approved, but whom the Lord commendeth. *Besides, to say I am thus and thus, when my Conversation, and all my Neighbours tell me I lie, is great wickedness.*

Another good sign of grace.

Talk. Then *Talkative* at first began to blush, but recovering himself, thus he replied. You come now to experience, to Conscience, and God: and to appeal to him for Justification of what is spoken: This kind of discourse I did not expect, nor am I disposed to give an answer to such questions, because, I count not my self bound thereto, unless you take upon you to be a *Catechiser*; and though you should so do, yet I may refuse to make you my Judg. But I pray will you tell me, why you ask me such questions?

Talkative *not pleased with* Faithful's *question.*

Faith. *Because I saw you forward to talk, and because I knew not that you had ought else but notion. Besides, to tell you all the truth, I have heard of you, that you are a man whose Religion lies in talk, and that your conversation gives this your Mouth-profession the lie. They say you are a spot among Christians, and that Religion fareth the worse for your ungodly conversation, that some already have stumbled at your wicked waies, and that more are in danger of being destroyed thereby; your Religion and an Ale-house, and Covetousness, and Uncleanness, and Swearing, and Lying, and vain Company-keeping,* &c. *will stand together. The Proverb is true of you, which it said*

The reasons why Faithful *put him to that question.*

Faithful's *plain dealing to* Talkative.

of a Whore; *to wit*, *That she is a shame to all women*, *so you are a shame to all Professors.*

Talk. Since you are ready to take up reports, and to judg so rashly as you do; I cannot but conclude you are some peevish or melancholick man, not fit to be discoursed with, and so adieu.

Talkative *flings away from* Faithful.

Chr. Then came up *Christian*, and said to his Brother, I told you how it would happen, your words and his lust could not agree; he had rather leave your company than reform his life: but he is gone, as I said, let him go; the loss is no mans but his own, he has saved us the trouble of going from him: for he continuing (as I suppose he will do) as he is, he would have been but a blot in our company: besides, the Apostle saies, *From such withdraw thy self.*

A good riddance.

Faith. *But I am glad we had this little discourse with him*, *it may happen that he will think of it again*; *however I have dealt plainly with him*; *and so am clear of his blood if he perisheth.*

Chr. You did well to talk so plainly to him as you did; there is but little of this faithful dealing with men now-a-days, and that makes Religion to stink so in the Nostrils of many, as it doth; for they are these Talkative Fools, whose Religion is only in word, and are debauched and vain in their Conversation, that (being so much admitted into the fellowship of the godly) do puzzle the World, blemish Christianity, and grieve the sincere. I wish that all men would deal with such as you have done, then should they be either made more conformable to Religion, or the company of Saints would be too hot for them. Then did *Faithful* say,

How Talkative *at first lifts up his Plumes!*
How bravely doth he speak! how he presumes
To drive down all before him! but so soon
As Faithful *talks of* Heart-work *like the Moon*,
That's past the full, *into the Wane he goes:*
And so will all, *but he that* Heart-work *knows.*

Thus they went on talking of what they had seen by the way; and so made that way easie, which would otherwise no doubt have been tedious to them: for now they went through a Wilderness.

Now when they were got almost quite out of this Wilderness, *Faithful* chanced to cast his eye back, and espied one coming after them, and he knew him. Oh! said *Faithful* to his Brother, who comes yonder? Then *Christian* looked, and said, it is my good friend *Evangelist*, Ai, and my good friend too, said *Faithful*; for 'twas he that set me the way to the Gate. Now was *Evangelist* come up unto them, and thus saluted them.

Evangelist *overtakes them again.*

Evan. Peace be with you, dearly beloved, and peace be to your helpers.

Chr. *Welcome, welcome, my good* Evangelist, *the sight of thy countenance brings to my remembrance, thy ancient kindness, and unwearied labouring for my eternal good.*

They are glad at the sight of him.

Faith. *And a thousand times welcome, said good* Faithful; *thy company, O sweet* Evangelist, *how desireable is it to us poor Pilgrims!*

Evan. Then said *Evangelist*, how hath it fared with you my friends, since the time of our last parting? what have you met with; and how have you behaved your selves?

Chr. *Then* Christian *and* Faithful *told him of all things that had happened to them in the way, and how, and with what difficulty they had arrived to that place.*

Evan. Right glad am I, said *Evangelist*; not that you have met with Trials, but that you have been Victors; and for that you have (notwithstanding many weaknesses) continued in the way to this very day.

His Exhortation to them.

I say, right glad am I of this thing, and that for mine own sake and yours; I have sowed, and you have reaped, and the day is coming when both he that sowed, and they that reaped shall rejoice together; that is, if you hold out; for in due time ye shall reap, if ye faint not. The Crown is before you, and it is an incorruptible one; so run that you may obtain it. Some there be that set out for this Crown, and after they have gone far for it, another comes in and takes it from them: hold fast therefore that you have, let no man take your Crown; you are not yet out of the Gun-shot of the Devil: you have not resisted unto blood, striving against sin.

John 4. 36. Gal. 6. 9. 1 Cor. 9. 24, 25, 26, 27. Rev. 3. 11.

Let the Kingdom be always before you, and believe stedfastly concerning things that are invisible. Let nothing that is on this side the other world get within you; and above all look well to your own hearts, and to the lusts thereof; for they are deceitful above all things, and desperately wicked: set your faces like a flint, you have all power in heaven and earth on your side.

They do thank him for his exhortations.

Chr. *Then* Christian *thanked him for his exhortation, but told him withal, that they would have him speak farther to them for their help the rest of the way; and the rather for that they well knew that he was a Prophet, and could tell them of things that might happen unto them; and also how they might resist and overcome them. To which request* Faithful *also consented. So* Evangelist *began as followeth.*

** He predicteth what troubles they shall meet with in* Vanity-Fair, *and encourageth them to stedfastness.*

Evan. *My Sons, you have heard in the words of the truth of the Gospel, that you must through many Tribulations enter into the Kingdom of Heaven. And again, that in every City, bonds and afflictions abide on you; and therefore you cannot expect that you should go long on your Pilgrimage without them in some sort or other. You have found something of the truth of these testimonies upon you already, and more will immediately follow: For now as you see, you are almost out of this Wilderness, and therefore you will soon come into a Town that you will by and by see before you: and in that Town you will be hardly beset with enemies, who will strain hard but they will kill you: and be you sure, that one or both of you must seal the testimony which you hold, with blood: but be you faithful unto death, and the King will give you a Crown of Life. *He that shall die there, although his Death will be unnatural, and his pain perhaps great, he will yet have the better of his fellow; not only because he will be arrived at the Celestial City soonest, but because he will escape many miseries that the other will meet with in the rest of his Journey. But when you are come to the Town, and shall find fulfilled what I have here related, then remember your friend, and quit your selves like men; and

** He whose lot it will be there to suffer will have the better of his brother.*

commit the keeping of your souls to your God in well doing, as unto a faithful Creator.

Then I saw in my Dream, that when they were got out of the wilderness, they presently saw a Town before them, and the name of that Town is *Vanity*; and at the Town there is a Fair kept called *Vanity-Fair*; it is kept all the year long, it beareth the name of *Vanity-Fair*, because the Town where it is kept *is lighter than Vanity*; and also, because all that is there sold, or that cometh thither, is *Vanity*. As is the saying of the wise, *All that cometh is Vanity*.

Isa. 40. 7. Eccles. 1. ch. 2. 11, 17.

This Fair is no new erected business, but a thing of ancient standing; I will shew you the original of it.

Almost five thousand years agone, there were Pilgrims, walking to the Celestial City, as these two honest persons are; and *Belzebub*, *Apollyon* and *Legion*, with their Companions, perceiving by the Path that the Pilgrims made, that their way to the City lay through this *Town of Vanity*, they contrived here to set up a Fair; a Fair wherein should be sold of all sorts of *Vanity*, and that it should last all the year long. Therefore at this Fair are all such Merchandize sold, as Houses, Lands, Trades, Places, Honours, Preferments, Titles, Countries, Kingdoms, Lusts, Pleasures, and Delights of all sorts, as Whores, Bawds, Wives, Husbands, Children, Masters, Servants, Lives, Blood, Bodies, Souls, Silver, Gold, Pearls, precious Stones, and what not?

The Antiquity of this Fair.

The Merchandize of this Fair.

And moreover, at this Fair there is at all times to be seen Jugglings, Cheats, Games, Plaies, Fools, Apes, Knaves, and Rogues, and that of every kind.

Here are to be seen too, and that for nothing, Thefts, Murders, Adulteries, False Swearers, and that of a blood red colour.

And as in other Fairs of less moment, there are several Rows and Streets under their proper Names where such Wares are vended; So here likewise, you have the proper Places, Rows, Streets, (*viz.* Countries and Kingdoms) where the Wares of this Fair are soonest to be found: Here is the *Brittan* Row, the *French* Row, the *Italian* Row, the *Spanish* Row, the *German* Row, where several sorts of Vanities are to be sold. But as in other *Fairs*,

The Streets of the Fair.

some one Commodity is as the chief of all the Fair, so the Ware of *Rome* and her Merchandize is greatly promoted in this Fair: only our *English* Nation, with some others, have taken a dislike thereat.

Now as I said, the way to the Cœlestial City lies just through this *Town*, where this lusty Fair is kept; and he that will go to the City and yet not go through this Town must needs *go out of the World*. The Prince of Princes himself, when here, went through this Town to his own Countrey, and that upon a *fair-day* too: yea, and as I think, it was *Belzebub*, the chief Lord of this *Fair*, that invited him to buy of his *Vanities*; yea, would have made him Lord of the *Fair*, would he but have done him Reverence as he went through the *Town*. Yea, because he was such a person of honour *Belzebub* had him from *Street* to *Street*, and shewed him all the Kingdoms of the world in a little time, that he might (if possible) allure that Blessed One, to cheapen and buy some of his *Vanities*. But he had no mind to the Merchandice, and therefore left the *Town*, without laying out so much as one farthing upon these *Vanities*. This *Fair* therefore is an ancient thing, of long standing, and a very great *Fair*.

1 Cor. 5. 10. *Christ went through this Fair.* Matth. 7. 8. Luk. 4. 5, 6, 7.

Christ bought nothing in this Fair.

Now these Pilgrims, as I said, must needs go through this *Fair*. Well so they did; but behold, even as they entred into the *Fair*, all the People in the *Fair* were moved, and the Town it self as it were in a Hubbub about them; and that for several reasons: For

The Pilgrims enter the Fair.

The Fair in a hubbub about them.

First, The Pilgrims were cloathed with such kind of *Raiment*, as was diverse from the *Raiment* of any that traded in that *Fair*. The People therefore of the *Fair* made a great gazing upon them: Some said they were fools, some they were Bedlams, and some they were outlandish men.

The first cause of the hubbub.

Secondly, and as they wondred at their *Apparel*, so they did likewise at their *Speech*; for few could understand what they said, they naturally spoke the Language of *Canaan*; but they that kept the *Fair*, were the men of this world: so that from one end

1 Cor. 2. 7, 8. *The second cause of the hubbub.*

of the *Fair* to the other, they seemed *Barbarians* each to the other.

Thirdly, But that which did not a little amuse the Merchandisers, was, that these Pilgrims set very light by all their Wares, they cared not so much as to look upon them: And if they called upon them to buy, they would put their fingers in their ears and cry, *Turn away mine eyes from beholding Vanity*; and look upwards, signifying that their Trade and Traffick was in Heaven.

Third cause of the hubbub.

Psal. 119. 37.
Phil. 3. 19, 20.

One chanced mockingly, beholding the carriages of the men, to say unto them, *What will ye buy?* but they looking gravely upon him, said, *We buy the Truth.* At that, there was an occasion taken to despise the men the more; some mocking, some taunting, some speaking reproachfully, and some calling upon others to smite them. At last things came to an hubbub, and great stir in the *Fair*; insomuch that all order was confounded. Now was word presently brought to the *great one of the Fair*, who quickly came down, and deputed some of his most trusty Friends to take those men into examination, about whom the *Fair* was almost overturned. So the men were brought to examination; and they that sat upon them, asked them whence they came, whither they went, and what they did there in such an unusual Garb? *The men told them, that they were Pilgrims and Strangers in the world, and that they were going to their own Countrey*, which was the heavenly *Jerusalem*, and that they had given no occasion to the men of the Town, nor yet to the Merchandizers, thus to abuse them, and to let them in their Journey: except it was, for that, when one asked them what they would buy, they said, they would *buy the Truth.* But they that were appointed to examine them, did not believe them to be any other than Bedlams and mad, or else such as came to put all things into a confusion in the *Fair*. Therefore they took them and beat them, and besmeared them with dirt, and then put them into the Cage, that they might be made a

Fourth cause of the hubbub.

Prov. 23. 23.

They are mocked.

The Fair in a hubbub.

They are examined.

* *They tell who they are, and whence they came.*

* Heb. 11. 12, 13, 14, 15, 16.

They are not in the cage.

spectacle to all the men of the *Fair*. There therefore they lay for some time, and were made the objects of any man's sport, or malice, or revenge. The great one of the *Fair* laughing still at all that befell them. But the men being patient, and not rendring railing for railing, but contrariwise blessing, and giving good words for bad, and kindness for injuries done: Some men in the *Fair* that were more observing, and less prejudiced than the rest, began to check and blame the baser sort for their continual abuses done by them to the men: They therefore in angry manner let fly at them again, counting them as bad as the men in the Cage, and telling them that they seemed confederates, and should be made partakers of their Misfortunes. The other replied, that for ought they could see, the men were quiet and sober, and intended no body any harm; and that there were many that traded in their *Fair*, that were more worthy to be put into the Cage, yea, and Pillory too, than were the men that they had abused. Thus, after divers words had passed on both sides (the men behaving themselves all the while very wisely and soberly before them,) they fell to some blows among themselves, and did harm one to another. Then were these two poor men brought before their Examiners again, and there charged as being guilty of the late hubbub that had been in the *Fair*. So they beat them pitifully, and hanged Irons upon them, & led them in Chains up and down the *Fair*, for an Example and Terror to others, lest any should speak in their behalf, or joyn themselves unto them. But *Christian* and *Faithful* behaved themselves yet more wisely; and received the Ignomy and shame that was cast upon them, with so much meekness and patience, that it won to their side (though but few in comparison of the rest) several of the men in the *Fair*. This put the other party yet into a greater rage, insomuch that they concluded the death of these two men. Wherefore they threatned that neither the Cage, nor Irons should serve their turn, but that they should die for the

They are put in the Cage.

Their behaviour in the Cage.

The men of the Fair do fall out among themselves about these two men.

They are made the Authors of this disturbance.

They are led up and down the Fair in Chains, for a terror to others.

Some of the men of the Fair won to them.

Their Adversaries resolve to kill them.

abuse they had done, and for deluding the men of the *Fair*.

Then were they remanded to the Cage again, until further order should be taken with them. So they put them in, and made their feet fast in the stocks.

They are again put into the Cage, and after brought to Tryal.

Here therefore they called again to mind what they had heard from their faithful friend *Evangelist*, and were the more confirmed in their way and sufferings, by what he told them would happen to them. They also now comforted each other, that whose lot it was to suffer, even he should have the best on't, therefore each man secretly wished that he might have that Preferment: But committing themselves to the all-wise dispose of him that ruleth all things, with much content they abode in the condition in which they were until they should be otherwise disposed of.

Then a convenient time being appointed, they brought them forth to their Tryal, in order to their Condemnation. When the time was come, they were brought before their enemies and Arraigned; the Judges name was Lord *Hate-good*: Their Indictment was one and the same in substance, though somewhat varying in form; the Contents whereof was this.

That they were enemies to, and disturbers of their Trade, that they had made Commotions and Divisions in the Town, and had won a party to their own most dangerous Opinions, in contempt of the Law of their Prince.

Their Indictment.

Then *Faithful* began to answer, that he had only set himself against that which had set it self against him that is higher than the highest. And said he, as for disturbance I make none, being my self a man of Peace; the parties that were won to us, were won by beholding our Truth and Innocence, & they are only turned from the worse to the better. And as to the King you talk of, since he is *Belzebub*, the Enemy of our Lord, I defie him and all his Angels.

Faithfuls *answer for himself.*

Then Proclamation was made, that they that had ought to say for their Lord the King against the Prisoner at the Bar, should forthwith appear, and give in their Evidence. So there came in three Witnesses, to wit, *Envy*, *Superstition* and *Pickthank*; They were then asked, If they knew the Prisoner at the Bar? And what they had to say for their Lord the King against him?

Then stood forth **Envy*, and said to this effect; My Lord, I have known this man a long time, and will attest upon my Oath before this Honourable Bench, that he is——

* Envy *begins.*

Judge. Hold, give him his Oath: So they sware him: Then he said, My Lord, this man, notwithstanding his plausible name, is one of the vilest men in our Countrey; he neither regardeth Prince nor People, Law nor Custom; but doth all that he can to possess all men with certain of his disloyal notions, which he in the general calls Principle of Faith and Holiness. And in particular, I heard him once my self affirm, *That Christianity and the Customs of our town of* Vanity, *were diametrically opposite, and could not be reconciled.* By which saying, my Lord, he doth at once, not only condemn all our laudable doings, but us in the doing of them.

Judg. Then did the Judge say unto him, hast thou any more to say?

Envy. My Lord, I could say much more, only I would not be tedious to the Court. Yet if need be, when the other Gentlemen have given in their Evidence, rather than any thing shall be wanting that will dispatch him, I will enlarge my Testimony against him. So he was bid stand by. Then they called *Superstition*, and bid him look upon the Prisoner; they also asked, what he could say for their Lord the King against him? Then they sware him, so he began.

Super. My Lord, I have no great acquaintance with this man, nor do I desire to have farther knowledge of him; however this I know, that he is a very pestilent fellow, from some discourse that the other day I had with him in this *Town*; for then talking with him, I heard him say, That our Religion was nought, and such by which a man could by no means please God: Which saying of his, my Lord, your Lordship very well knows, what necessarily thence will follow, to wit, that we still do worship in vain, are yet in our sins, and finally shall be damned; and this is that which I have to say.

Superstition *follows.*

Then was *Pickthank* sworn, and did say what he knew, in behalf of their Lord the King against the Prisoner at the Bar.

Pick. My Lord, and you Gentlemen all, this fellow I have known of a long time, and have heard him speak things that ought not to be spoke. For he hath railed on our noble Prince *Belzebub*, and hath spoken contemptible of his honourable Friends, whose Names are, the Lord *Old-Man*, the Lord *Carnal delight*, the Lord *Luxurious*, the Lord *Desire of vain glory*, my old Lord *Letchery*, Sir *Having Greedy*, with all the rest of our Nobility; and he hath said moreover, that if all men were of his mind, if possible, there is not one of these Noble men should have any longer a being in this Town. Besides, he hath not been afraid to rail on you my Lord, who are now appointed to be his Judge, calling you an ungodly Villain, with many other such like villifying terms, with which he hath bespattered most of the Gentry of our Town. When this *Pickthank* had told his Tale, the Judge directed his Speech to the Prisoner at the Bar, saying, thou Runagate, Heretick, and Traytor, hast thou heard what these honest Gentlemen have witnessed against thee?

Pickthank's *Testimony.*

Sins are all Lords and great ones.

Faith. *May I speak a few words in my own defence.*

Judge. Sirrah, Sirrah, thou deservest to live no longer, but to be slain immediately upon the place; yet that all men may see our gentleness towards thee, let us hear what thou vile Runagate hast to say.

Faith. 1. I say then in answer to what Mr. *Envy* hath spoken, I never said ought but this, *That what Rule, or Laws, or Custom, or People were flat against the Word of God, are diametrically opposite to Christianity.* If I have said amiss in this convince me of my errour, and I am ready here before you to make my recantation.

Faithful's *defence of himself.*

2. As to the second, to wit, Mr. *Superstition* and his charge against me, I said only this, *That in the worship of God there is required a Divine Faith, but there can be no divine faith without a divine revelation of the will of God. Therefore whatever is thrust into the Worship of God, that is not agreeable to divine Revelation, cannot be done but by an humane Faith, which Faith will not be profitable to Eternal Life.*

3. As to what Mr. *Pickthank* hath said, I say (avoiding terms, as that I am said to rail, and the like) that the Prince of

this Town, with all the rabblement his Attendants, by this Gentleman named, are more fit for being in Hell, than in this Town and Countrey; *and so the Lord have mercy upon me.*

Then the Judge called to the Jury (who all this while stood by, to hear and observe;) Gentlemen of the Jury, you see this man about whom so great an uproar hath been made in this Town: you have also heard what these worthy Gentlemen have witnessed against him; also you have heard his reply and confession: It lieth now in your breast to hang him, or save his life: but yet I think meet to instruct you in our Law.

The Judge his speech to the Jury.

There was an act made in the days of *Pharaoh* the Great, Servant to our Prince, that, lest those of a contrary Religion should multiply and grow too strong for him, their Males should be thrown into the River. There was an Act also made in the days of *Nebuchadnezzar* the Great, another of his Servants, that whoever would not fall down and worship his golden Image, should be thrown into a Fiery Furnace. There was also an Act made in the days of *Darius*, that who so for some time called upon any God but him should be cast into the Lions Den. Now the substance of these Laws this Rebel has broken; not only in thought (which is not to be born) but also in word and deed; which must therefore needs be intollerable.

Exod. 1.

Dan. 3.

Dan. 6.

For that of *Pharaoh*, his Law was made upon supposition, to prevent mischief; no Crime yet being apparent; but here is a Crime apparent. For the second and third, you see he disputeth against our Religion; and for the Treason he hath confessed, he deserveth to die the death.

Then went the Jury out, * whose names were, Mr. *Blindman*, Mr. *No-good*, Mr. *Malice*, Mr. *Love-lust*, Mr. *Live-loose*, Mr. *Heady*, Mr. *High-mind*, Mr. *Enmity*, Mr. *Liar*, Mr. *Cruelty*, Mr. *Hate-light*, and Mr. *Implacable*, who every one gave in his private Verdict against him among themselves, and afterwards unanimously concluded to bring him in guilty before the Judge.

** The Jury and their names.*

And first among themselves, Mr. *Blindman*, the Foreman, said, *I see clearly that this man is an Heretick.* Then said Mr. *No-good*, *away with such a fellow from the Earth.* *Ay*, said Mr. *Malice*,

Every ones private Verdict.

for I hate the very looks of him. Then said Mr. *Love-lust*, *I could never endure him. Nor I*, said Mr. *Live-loose*, *for he would always be condemning my way. Hang him, hang him*, said Mr. *Heady. A sorry Scrub* said Mr. *High-mind. My heart riseth against him*, said Mr. *Enmity*, *he is a Rogue*, said Mr. *Liar*, *Hanging is too good for him*, said Mr. *Cruelty*, *Let's dispatch him out of the way*, said Mr. *Hate-light*. Then said Mr. *Implacable*, *might I have all the world given me, I could not be reconciled to him, therefore let us forthwith bring him in guilty of death.* *And so they did, therefore he was presently condemned, to be had from the place where he was, to the place from whence he came, and there to be put to the most cruel death that could be invented.

** They conclude to bring him in guilty of death.*

They therefore brought him out, to do with him according to their Law; and first they scourged him, then they buffetted him, then they lanched his flesh with Knives; after that they stoned him with stones, then prickt him with their Swords; and last of all they burned him to ashes at the Stake. Thus came *Faithful* to his end, *Now I saw that there stood behind the multitude a Chariot and a couple of Horses, waiting for *Faithful*, who (so soon as his Adversaries had dispatched him) was taken up into it, and straightway was carried up through the Clouds, with sound of Trumpet, the nearest way to the Cœlestial Gate. But as for *Christian*, he had some respite, and was remanded back to Prison; so he there remained for a space: But he that over-rules all things, having the power of their rage in his own hand, so wrought it about, that *Christian* for that time escaped them and went his way.

The cruel death of Faithful.

** A Chariot and Horses wait to take away* Faithful.

Christian *still a Prisoner.*

And as he went he sang, saying,

**Well* Faithful, *thou hast faithfully profest*
Unto thy Lord; with whom thou shalt be blest;
When faithless *ones, with all their vain delight*
Are crying out under their Hellish plights;
Sing Faithful, *sing; and let thy name survive;*
For though they kill'd thee, thou art yet alive.

** The Song that* Christian *made of* Faithful *after his death.*

Now I saw in my Dream, that *Christian* went not forth alone, for there was one whose name was *Hopeful*, (being so made by the beholding of *Christian* and *Faithful* in their words and behaviour, in their sufferings at the *Fair*,) who joyned himself unto him, and entring into a brotherly Covenant, told him, that he would be his Companion. Thus one died to bear Testimony to the Truth, and another rises out of his Ashes to be a Companion with *Christian* in his Pilgrimage. This *Hopeful* also told *Christian*, that there were many more of the men in the *Fair* that would take their time, and follow after.

Christian *has another Companion.*

There are more of the men of the Fair *will follow.*

So I saw that quickly after they were got out of the *Fair*, they overtook one that was going before them, whose name was *By-ends*; So they said to him, what Countrey man, Sir? And how far go you this way? He told them, that he came from the Town of *Fair-speech*, and he was going to the Celestial City, (But told them not his name.)

They overtake By-ends.

*From *Fair-speech, said Christian? Is there any good that lives there?*

* Prov. 26. 25.

By-ends. Yes, said *By-ends*, I hope.

Chr. Pray Sir, what may I call you? said *Christian.*

By-ends. I am a stranger to you, and you to me; If you be going this way, I shall be glad of your Company: if not, I must be content.

By-ends *loth to tell his name.*

Chr. This Town of Fair-speech, *said* Christian *I have heard of, and, as I remember, they say it's a wealthy place.*

By-ends. Yes, I will assure you that it is, and I have very many rich kindred there.

Chr. Pray, who are your kindred there, if a man may be so bold?

By-ends. Almost the whole Town; And in particular my Lord *Turn-about*, my Lord *Time-server*, my Lord *Fair-speech*, (from whose Ancestors that Town first took its name:) Also Mr. *Smooth-Man*, Mr. *Facing both-ways*, Mr. *Any-thing*, and the Parson of our Parish, Mr. *Two-tongues*, was my Mothers own Brother by Fathers side: And to tell you the truth, I am become a Gentleman of good Quality, yet my Great Grandfather was but a Waterman, looking one way, and rowing another, and I got most of my Estate by the same occupation.

Chr. *Are you a married man?*

By-ends. Yes, and my Wife is a very virtuous Woman, the Daughter of a virtuous Woman; she was my Lady *Fainings* Daughter, therefore she came of a very honourable Family, and is arrived to such a pitch of Breeding, that she knows how to carry it to all, even to Prince and Peasant. 'Tis true, we somewhat differ in Religion from those of the stricter sort, yet but in two small points: First, we never strive against Wind and Tide. Secondly, we are always most zealous when Religion goes in his Silver Slippers; we love much to walk with him in the Street; if the Sun shines and the People applaud him.

The Wife and Kindred of By-ends.

Where By-ends *differs from others in Religion.*

Then *Christian* stept a little aside to his fellow *Hopeful*, saying, It runs in my mind that this is one *By-ends* of *Fair-speech*, and if it be he, we have as very a Knave in our company, as dwelleth in all these parts. Then said *Hopeful*, *Ask him; methinks he should not be ashamed of his name.* So *Christian* came up with him again and said, Sir you talk as if you knew something more than all the World doth, and if I take not my mark amiss, I deem I have half a guess of you; is not your name Mr. *By-ends* of *Fair-speech*?

By-ends. This is not my name, but indeed it is a Nick-name that is given me by some that cannot abide me, and I must be content to bear it as a reproach, as other good men have born theirs before me.

Chr. *But did you never give an occasion to men to call you by this name?*

By-ends. Never, never! The worst that ever I did to give them an occasion to give me this name, was, that I had always the luck to jump in my judgment with the present way of the times, whatever it was, and my chance was to get thereby, but if things are thus cast upon me, let me count them a blessing, but let not the malicious load me therefore with reproach.

How By-ends *got his name.*

Chr. *I thought indeed that you were the man that I heard*

of; *and to tell you what I think*, *I fear this name belongs to you more properly than you are willing we should think it doth.*

He desires to keep Company with Christian.

By-ends. Well, if you will thus imagine, I cannot help it. You shall find me a fair Company-keeper, if you will still admit me your Associate.

Chr. *If you will go with us*, *you must go against Wind and Tide*, *the which*, *I perceive*, *is against your opinion* : *You must also own Religion in his Rags*, *as well as when in his silver Slippers*, *and stand by him too*, *when bound in Irons*, *as well as when he walketh the Streets with applause.*

By-ends. You must not impose, nor Lord it over my Faith, leave me to my liberty, and let me go with you.

Chr. *Not a step further*, *unless you will do*, *in what I propound*, *as we.*

By-ends *and* Christian *part.*

Then said *By-ends*, I shall never desert my old principles, since they are harmless and profitable. If I may not go with you, I must do as I did before you overtook me, even go by my self, until some overtake me that will be glad of my company.

Now I saw in my Dream, that *Christian* and *Hopeful* forsook him and kept their distance before him, but one of them looking back saw three men following Mr. *By-ends*, and behold, as they came up with him he made them a very low *Congee*, and they also gave him a Complement. The mens names were Mr. *Hold-the-World*, Mr. *Money-love*, and Mr. *Save-all*; men that Mr. *By-ends* had formerly been acquainted with; for in their Minority they were School-fellows, and were taught by one Mr. *Gripe-man* a School-master in *Love-gain*, which is a Market-Town in the County of *Coveting* in the North. This School-master taught them the art of getting, either by violence, cozenage, flattery, lying, or by putting on a guise of Religion, and these four Gentlemen had attained much of the art of their Master, so that they could each of them have kept such a School themselves.

He has new Companions.

Well, when they had as I said, thus saluted each other, Mr. *Money-love* said to Mr. *By-ends*, who are they upon the Road before us? for *Christian* and *Hopeful* were yet within view.

By-ends. They are a couple of far Country men, that after their *mode* are going on Pilgrimage.

By-ends *Character of the* Pilgrims.

Money-love. Alas, why did they not stay, that we might have had their good company, for *they*, and *we*, and *you* Sir, I hope are all going on a Pilgrimage.

By-ends. We are so indeed, but the men before us are so rigid, and love so much their own notions, and do also lightly esteem the opinions of others; that let a man be never so godly, yet if he jumps not with them in all things, they thrust him quite out of their company.

Mr. *Save-all.* That's bad, but we read of some, *that are righteous overmuch*, and such mens rigidness prevails with them to judg and condemn all but themselves; but I pray what, and how many were the things wherein you differed?

By-ends. Why they, after their head-strong manner, conclude that it is duty to rush on their Journey *all* weathers, and I am for waiting for *Wind* and *Tide.* They are for hazarding all for God at a clap, and I am for taking all advantages to secure my Life and Estate. They are for holding *their notions* though all other men be against them, but I am for Religion in what, and so far as the times, and my safety will bear it. They are for Religion, when in rags and contempt, but I am for him when he walks in his golden Slippers in the Sun-shine, and with applause.

Mr. *Hold-the-World.* Ay, and hold you there still, good Mr. *By-ends*; for my part, I can count him but a Fool, that having the liberty to keep what he has, shall be so unwise to lose it. Let us be wise *as Serpents*, it's best to make Hay when the Sun shines; you see how the Bee lieth still all winter, and bestirs her only when she can have profit with pleasure. God sends sometimes Rain, and sometimes Sun-shine; if they be such fools to go through the first, yet let us be content to take fair weather along with us. For my part, I like that Religion best that will stand with the security of God's good Blessings unto us; for who can imagine, that is ruled by his reason, since God has bestowed upon us the good things of this life, but that he would have us keep them for his sake. *Abraham* and *Solomon* grew rich in Religion. And *Job* says, that a good man *shall lay up gold as dust.* But he must not be such as the men before us, if they be as you have described them.

Mr. *Save-all.* I think that we are all agreed in this matter, and therefore there needs no more words about it.

Mr. *Money-love.* No, there needs no more words about this matter indeed, for he that believes neither Scripture nor Reason (and you see we have both on our side) neither knows his own liberty, nor seeks his own safety.

Mr. *By-ends.* My Brethren, we are, as you see, going all on Pilgrimage, and for our better diversion from things that are bad, give me leave to propound unto you this question.

Suppose a Man, a Minister, or a Trades-man, &c. *should have an advantage lie before him to get the good blessings of this life; yet so as that he can by no means come by them except in appearance at least, he becomes extraordinary zealous in some points of Religion, that he meddled not with before, may he not use this means to attain his end, and yet be a right honest man?*

Mr. *Money-love.* I see the bottom of your question, and with these Gentlemens good leave, I will endeavour to shape you an answer. And first to speak to your question, as it concerns a *Minister* himself. *Suppose a Minister, a worthy man, possessed but of a very small Benefice, and has in his eye a greater, more fat and plump by far; he has also now an opportunity of getting of it; yet so as by being more studious, by preaching more frequently, and zealously, and because the temper of the people requires it, by altering of some of his principles, for my part, I see no reason but a man may do this (provided he has a call) Ay, and more a great deal besides, and yet be an honest man.* For why,

1. His desire of a greater Benefice is lawful (this cannot be contradicted) since 'tis set before him by Providence; so then he may get it if he can, *making no question for Conscience sake.*

2. Besides his desire after that Benefice, makes him more studious, a more zealous Preacher, *&c.* and so makes him a better man. Yea makes him better improve his parts, which is according to the mind of God.

3. Now as for his complying with the temper of his people, by deserting, to serve them, some of his Principles: This argueth 1. That he is of a self-denying temper. 2. Of a sweet and winning deportment. 3. And so more fit for the Ministerial Function.

4. I conclude then, that a Minister that changes a *Small*

for a *Great*, should not for so doing be judged as covetous, but rather since he is improved in his parts, and industry, thereby be counted as one that pursues his call, and the opportunity put into his hand to do good.

And now to the second part of the question, which concerns the *Tradesman* you mentioned: suppose such an one to have but a poor imploy in the world, but by becoming Religious he may mend his market, perhaps get a rich Wife, or more and far better customers to his shop. For my part, I see no reason, but that this may be lawfully done. For why.

1. To become religious is a vertue, by what means soever a man becomes so.

2. Nor is it unlawful to get a rich wife, or more custom to my Shop.

3. Besids the man that gets these by becoming religious, gets that which is good of them that are good, by becoming good himself; so then here is a good wife, and good customers, and good gain, and all these by becoming religious, which is good. Therefore to become religious to get all these, is a good and profitable design.

This answer, thus made by this Mr. *Money-love*, to Mr. *By-end*'s question was highly applauded by them all; wherefore they concluded upon the whole, that it was most wholsom and advantageous. And because, as they thought, no man was able to contradict it, and because *Christian* and *Hopeful* were yet within call, they joyntly agreed to assault them with the question as soon as they overtook them, and the rather, because they had opposed Mr. *By-ends* before. So they called after them and they stopt, and stood still till they came up to them, but they concluded as they went, that not Mr. *By-ends*, but old Mr. *Hold-the-World* should propound the question to them, because as they supposed their answer to him would be without the remainder of that heat that was kindled betwixt Mr. *By-ends* and them, at their parting a little before.

So they came up to each other, and after a short salutation, Mr. *Hold-the-world* propounded the question to *Christian* and his Fellow and bid them to answer it if they could.

Chr. Then said *Christian*, even a Babe in Religion may answer ten thousand such questions. For if it be unlawful to follow Christ for Loaves, as it is *John* 6. how much more is it abominable to make of him and Religion a stalking Horse to get and enjoy the World? Nor do we find any other than Heathens, Hypocrites, Devils, and Witches that are of this opinion.

1. *Heathens*, for when *Hamar* and *Sechem* had a mind to the daughter and Cattle of *Jacob*, and saw that there was no waies for them to come at them, but by becoming Circumcised, they say to their companions, *if every Male of us be circumcised, as they are circumcised, shall not their Cattle and their Substance, and every Beast of theirs be ours*? Their Daughters and their Cattle were that which they sought to obtain, and their Religion the stalking-horse they made use of to come at them. Read the whole story, *Gen.* 34. 20, 21, 22, 23.

2. The Hypocritical Pharisees were also of this Religion, long prayers were their pretence, but to get Widows Houses were their intent, and greater damnation was from God their Judgment, *Luk.* 20. 46, 47.

3. *Judas* the Devil was also of this Religion, he was religious for the Bag, that he might be possessed of what was therein; but he was lost, cast away, and the very son of Perdition.

4. *Simon* the Witch was of this Religion too, for he would have had the Holy Ghost that he might have got money therewith, and his sentence from *Peter*'s mouth was according, *Acts* 8. 19, 20, 21, 22.

5. Neither will it out of my mind, but that that man, that takes up Religion for the world, will throw away Religion for the world; for so surely as *Judas* designed the world in becoming Religious, so surely did he also sell religion and his Master for the same. To answer the question therefore affirmatively, as I perceive you have done, and to accept of as authentick, such answer, is both Heathenish, Hypocritical and Devilish, and your reward will be according to your works. Then they stood staring one upon another but had not wherewith to answer *Christian*. *Hopeful* also approved of the soundness of *Christians* answer, so there was a great silence among them. Mr. *By-ends* and his Company also staggered and kept behind, that *Christian* and *Hopeful* might out-go them. Then said *Christian* to his fellow, if these men cannot stand before the sentence of men, what will they do with the sentence of God?

and if they are mute when dealt with by vessels of clay, what will they do when they shall be rebuked by the flames of a devouring fire?

Then *Christian* and *Hopeful* out-went them again, and went till they came at a delicate Plain called *Ease*, where they went with much content; but that plain was but narrow, so they were quickly got over it. Now at the further side of that Plain was a little Hill called *Lucre*, and in that *Hill* a *Silver Mine*, which some of them that had formerly gone that way because of the rarity of it, had turned aside to see; but going too near the brim of the Pit, the ground being deceitful under them, broke, and they were slain; some also had been maimed there, and could not to their dying day be their own men again;

The Ease that Pilgrims have is but little in this life.

Lucre-*Hill a dangerous Hill.*

Then I saw in my Dream, that a little off the Road, over against the *Silver-Mine*, stood **Demas* (Gentleman like) to call Passengers to come and see, who said to *Christian* and his fellow; *Ho turn aside hither, and I will shew you a thing.

* Demas *at the Hill* Lucre.

* *He calls to* Christian *and* Hopeful *to come to him.*

Chr. *What thing so deserving as to turn us out of the way to see it.*

Dem. Here is a *Silver-mine*, and some digging in it for Treasure, if you will come, with a little pains you may richly provide for your selves.

Hope. Then said *Hopeful*, *let us go see.*

Chr. Not I, said *Christian*, I have heard of this place before now, and how many there have been slain; and besides, that Treasure is a snare to those that seek it; for it hindereth them in their Pilgrimage. Then *Christian* called to *Demas*, saying, *Is not the place dangerous? hath it not hindred many in their Pilgrimage.*

Hopeful *tempted to go, but* Christian *holds him back.*

Hos. 4. 18.

Dem. Not very dangerous, except to those that are careless; but withal he blushed as he spake.

Chr. Then said *Christian* to *Hopeful*, Let us not stir a step, but still keep on our way.

Hope. *I will warrant you, when* By-ends *comes up, if he hath the same invitation as we, he will turn in thither to see.*

Chr. No doubt thereof, for his Principles lead him that way, and a hundred to one but he dies there.

Dem. Then *Demas* called again, saying, but will you not come over and see?

Chr. Then *Christian* roundly answered, saying, *Demas*, thou art an Enemy to the right ways of the Lord of this way, and hast been already condemned for thine own turning aside, by one of his Majesties Judges; and why seekest thou to bring us into the like condemnation? Besides, if we at all turn aside, our Lord the King will certainly hear thereof, and will there put us to shame, where we would stand with boldness before him.

Christian *roundeth up* Demas.

2 Tim. 4. 10.

Demas cried again that he also was one of their fraternity; and that if they would tarry a little, he also himself would walk with them.

Chr. Then said *Christian*, what is thy name? is it not the same by the which I have called thee?

Dem. Yes, my name is *Demas*, I am the Son of *Abraham*.

Chr. I know you, *Gehazi* was your great Grandfather, and *Judas* your Father, and you have trod their steps; it is but a devilish prank that thou usest: Thy Father was hanged for a Traitor, and thou deservest no better reward. Assure thy self, that when we come to the King, we will do him word of this thy behaviour. Thus they went their way.

2 King. 5. 20. Matth. 26. 14, 15. ch. 27. 1, 2, 3, 5, 6.

By this time *By-ends* and his Companions were come again within sight, and they at the first beck went over to *Demas*. Now whether they fell into the Pit by looking over the brink thereof, or whether they went down to dig, or whether they were smothered in the bottom by the damps that commonly arise, of these things, I am not certain; but this I observed, that they never were seen again in the way.

By-ends *goes over to* Demas.

Then sang *Christian*,

> By-ends *and Silver* Demas *both agree,*
> *One calls, the other runs that he may be*
> *A sharer in his Lucre, so these do*
> *Take up in this world, and no further go.*

Now I saw, that just on the other side of this Plain, the Pilgrims came to a place where stood an old *Monument*, hard by the Highway side, at the sight of which they were both concerned, because of the strangeness of the form thereof; for it seemed to them as if it had been a *Woman* transformed into the shape of a Pillar: here therefore they stood looking, and looking upon it, but could not for a time tell what they should make thereof; at last *Hopeful* espied written above upon the head thereof, a writing in an unusual hand; but he being no Scholar called to *Christian* (for he was learned) to see if he could pick out the meaning: so he came, and after a little laying of Letters together, he found the same to be this, *Remember Lot's Wife*. So he read it to his fellow; after which they both concluded that that was the *Pillar of Salt into which *Lot*'s Wife was turned for her looking back with a *covetous heart*, when she was going from *Sodom* for safety. Which sudden and amazing sight gave them occasion of this discourse.

They see a strange Monument.

* Gen. 19. 26.

Chr. Ah my Brother, this is a seasonable sight, it came opportunely to us after the Invitation which *Demas* gave us to come over to view the Hill *Lucre*, and had we gone over as he desired us, and as thou wast inclined to do (my Brother) we had for ought I know been made like this Woman a spectacle for those that shall come after, to behold.

Hope. I am sorry that I was so foolish, and am made to wonder that I am not now as *Lot*'s Wife: for wherein was the difference' twixt her sin and mine? she only looked back, and I had a desire to go see; let Grace be adored and let me be ashamed, that ever such a thing should be in mine heart.

Chr. Let us take notice of what we see here for our help for time to come: This Woman escaped one Judgment; for she fell not by the destruction of *Sodom*, yet she was destroyed by another; as we see, she is turned into a Pillar of Salt.

Hope. True, and she may be to us both *Caution* and *Example*; *Caution*, that we should shun her sin, or a sign of what Judgment will overtake such as shall not be prevented by this caution: So *Korah*, *Dathan*, and *Abiram*, with the two hundred and fifty men, that perished in their sin, did also become *a Sign or Example to beware, but above all, I muse at one thing, to wit how *Demas* and his fellows can stand so confidently yonder to look for that treasure, which this Woman, but for looking behind her, after (for we read not that she stept one foot out of the way) was turned into a Pillar of Salt; specially since the Judgment which overtook her, did make her an Example, within sight of where they are: for they cannot chuse but see her, did they but lift up their eyes.

Numb. 26. 9, 10.

Chr. It is a thing to be wondred at, and it argueth that their hearts are grown desperate in that case, and I cannot tell who to compare them to so fitly, as to them that pick Pockets in the presence of the Judge, or that will cut purses under the Gallows. It is said of the men of *Sodom*, *that they were sinners* **exceedingly*, because they were sinners *before the Lord*; that is in his eye-sight, and notwithstanding the kindnesses that he had shewed them, for the Land of *Sodom* was now like the *Garden of *Eden heretofore.* This therefore provoked him the more to jealousie and made their plague as hot as the fire of the Lord out of Heaven could make it. And it is most rationally to be concluded, that such, even such as these are, they that shall sin in the sight, yea and that too in despight of such examples that are set continually before them to caution them to the contrary, must be partakers of severest Judgments.

* Gen. 13. 13.

* ver. 10.

Hope. Doubtless thou hast said the truth, but what a mercy is it, that neither thou, but especially I am not made my self this example. This ministreth occasion to us to thank God, to fear before him, and always to remember *Lot*'s Wife.

I saw then that they went on their way to a pleasant River; which *David the King* called the *River of God*; but *John*, *the River of the water of Life.* Now their way lay just upon the bank of the River; Here therefore *Christian* and his Companion walked with great delight; they drank also of the water of the River, which was pleasant and enlivening to their weary Spirits: Besides on the banks of this River, on either side, were *green Trees* for all manner of Fruit; and the Leaves they eat to prevent Surfeits, and other diseases that are incident

A River.
Psal. 65. 9.
Rev. 22.
Ezek. 47.

Trees by the River.

The fruit, and leaves of the Trees.

to those that heat their blood by Travels. On either side of the River was also a Meadow curiously beautified with Lillies; and it was green all the year long: In this Meadow they lay down and slept, for here they might *lie down safely*. When they awoke, they gathered again of the Fruit of the Trees, and drank again of the water of the River: and then lay down again to sleep. Thus they did several days and nights. Then they sang.

A Meadow in which they lie to sleep.

Psal. 22.

Isa. 14. 13.

Behold ye how those Crystal Streams do glide,
(To comfort Pilgrims) by the High-way side.
The Meadows green; besides their fragrant smell,
Yield dainties for them: and he that can tell
What pleasant Fruit, yea, Leaves, these Trees do yield,
Will soon sell all, that he may buy this Field.

So when they were disposed to go on (for they were not as yet at their Journeys end) they eat and drank, and departed.

Now I beheld in my Dream that they had not journeyed far, but the River and the way, (for a time) parted, at which they were not a little sorry, yet they durst not go out of the way: Now the way from the River was rough, and their feet tender by reason of their Travels; *So the Souls of the Pilgrims were much discouraged, because of the way*. Wherefore still as they went on, they wished for better way. Now a little before them, there was on the left hand of the Road a *Meadow*, and a Stile to go over into it, and that *Meadow* is called *By-path Meadow*. Then said *Christian* to his fellow, if this Meadow lieth along by our way-side, let's go over into it. Then he went to the Stile to see, and behold a Path lay along by the way on the other side of the fence. 'Tis according to my wish, said *Christian*, here is the easiest going; come good *Hopeful*, and let us go over.

Numb. 21. 4.

By-path Meadow.

One temptation does make way for another.

Hope. *But how if this Path should lead us out of the way?*

Chr. That's not like, said the other; look doth it not go along by the way side? so *Hopeful* being perswaded by his fellow, went after him over the Stile. When they were gone over, and were got into the Path they found it very easie for their feet;

Strong Christians may lead weak ones out of the way.

and withal, they looking before them, espied a man walking as they did, (and his name was *Vain-Confidence*) so they called after him, and asked him whither that way led? he said to the Celestial Gate. *Look said *Christian*, did not I tell you so? by this you may see we are right; so they followed, and he went before them. But behold the night came on, and it grew very dark; so that they that went behind, lost the sight of him that went before.

** See what it is too suddenly to fall in with strangers.*

He therefore that went before (*Vain-Confidence* by name) not seeing the way before him, fell into a deep Pit, which was on purpose there made by the Prince of those grounds to catch *vain-glorious* Fools withal, and was dashed in pieces with his fall.

Isa. 9. 16.

A pit to catch the vain-glorious in.

Now *Christian* and his fellow heard him fall. So they called to know the matter, but there was none to answer, only they heard a groaning, Then said *Hopeful*, where are we now? Then was his fellow silent, as mistrusting that he had led him out of the way. And now it began to rain and thunder, and lighten in a very dreadful manner, and the water rose amain.

Reasoning between Christian *and* Hopeful.

Then *Hopeful* groaned in himself, saying, *Oh that I had kept on my way!*

Chr. Who could have thought that this Path should have led us out of the way?

Hope. *I was afraid on't at the very first, and therefore gave you that gentle caution. I would have spoke plainer, but you are older than I.*

Chr. Good brother be not offended, *I am sorry I have brought thee out of the way, and that I have put thee into such eminent danger; pray my Brother forgive me, I did not do it of an evil intent.

Christian'*s repentance for leading of his Brother out of the way.*

Hope. *Be comforted my Brother, for I forgive thee; and believe too, that this shall be for our good.*

Chr. I am glad I have with me a merciful Brother: but we must not stand thus, let's try to go back again.

Hope. *But good Brother let me go before.*

Chr. No, if you please let me go first; that if there be any danger, I may be first therein, because by my means we are both gone out of the way.

Hope. *No said* Hopeful, *you shall not go first, for your mind being troubled may lead you out of the way again.* Then for their encouragement they heard the voice of one saying, *Let thine heart be towards the High-way, even the way that thou wentest, turn again.* But by this time the waters were greatly risen; by reason of which the way of going back was very dangerous. (Then I thought that it is easier going out of the way when we are in, than going in when we are out.) Yet they adventured to go back; but it was so dark, and the flood was so high, that in their going back they had like to have been drowned nine or ten times.

Jer. 31. 1.

They are in danger of drowning, as they go back.

Neither could they with all the skill they had get again to the Stile that night. Wherefore at last lighting under a little shelter, they sat down there till the day brake: But being weary, they fell asleep. Now there was not far from the place where they lay, a *Castle* called *Doubting-Castle*, the Owner whereof was *Giant Despair*, and it was in his grounds they were now sleeping; wherefore he getting up in the morning early, and walking up and down in his Fields, caught *Christian* and *Hopeful* asleep in his grounds. Then with a *grim* and *surly* voice he bid them awake, and asked them whence they were? and what they did in his grounds? They told him they were Pilgrims, and that they had lost their way. Then said the *Giant*, you have this night trespassed on me, by trampling in and lying on my Ground, and therefore you must go along with me. So they were forced to go, because he was stronger than they. They also had but little to say, for they knew themselves in a fault. The *Giant* therefore drove them before him, and put them into his Castle, into a very dark Dungeon, nasty and stinking to the Spirits of these two men: Here then they lay from *Wednesday* Morning till *Saturday* Night without one bit of bread, or drop of drink or light, or any to ask how they did: They were therefore here in evil case, and were far from friends and acquaintance. Now in this place *Christian* had double

They sleep in the grounds of Giant Despair.

He finds them in his ground and carries them to Doubting-Castle.

The grievousness of their Imprisonment.

Psal. 88. 16.

sorrow, because 'twas through his unadvised Counsel that they were brought into this distress.

Now *Giant Despair* had a Wife and her name was *Diffidence:* So when he was gone to bed, he told his Wife what he had done, to wit, that he had taken a couple of Prisoners, and cast them into his *Dungeon*, for trespassing on his Grounds. Then he asked her also what he had best to do further to them. So she asked what they were, whence they came, and whither they were bound? and he told her. Then she counselled him, that when he arose in the morning, he should beat them without mercy: So when he arose, he getteth him a grievous Crab-Tree Cudgel, and goes down into the *Dungeon* to them, and there first falls to rating of them as if they were dogs: although they gave him never a word of distaste; then he falls upon them, and beats them fearfully, in such sort that they were not able to help themselves, or to turn them upon the floor. This done he withdraws and leaves them, there to condole their misery, and to mourn under their distress: so all that day, they spent the time in nothing but sighs and bitter lamentations. The next night she talking with her Husband about them further, and understanding that they were yet alive, did advise him to counsel them to make away themselves: So when morning was come, he goes to them in a surly manner, as before, and perceiving them to be very sore with the stripes that he had given them the day before; he told them, that since they were never like to come out of that place, their only way would be, forthwith to make an end of themselves; either with Knife, Halter or Poison: For why, said he, should you chuse life, seeing it is attended with so much bitterness? But they desired him to let them go, with that he looked ugly upon them, and rushing to them, had doubtless made an end of them himself, but that he fell into one of his *fits; (for he sometimes in Sun-shiny weather fell into fits) and lost (for a time) the use of his hand: wherefore he withdrew and left them, (as before) to consider what to do. Then did the prisoners consult between themselves, whether 'twas best to take his counsel or no: and thus they began to discourse.

On Thursday *Giant* Despair *beats his Prisoners.*

* *On* Friday *Giant* Despair *counsels them to kill themselves.*

* *The Giant sometimes has fits.*

Chr. Brother, said *Christian*; *what shall we do? the life that we now live is miserable: for my part, I know not whether is best, to live thus, or die out of hand. **My Soul chuseth strangling rather than life*: and the Grave is more easie for me than this Dungeon: shall we be ruled by the Giant?

Christian *crushed.*

* Job 7. 15.

Hope. *Indeed our present condition is dreadful, and death would be far more welcome to me than* thus *for ever to abide: but yet let us consider, the Lord of the countrey to which we are going, hath said, Thou shalt do no Murther, no not to another mans person; much more then are we forbidden to take his counsel to kill our selves. Besides he that kills another, can but commit murder upon his body; but for one to kill himself, is to kill body and soul at once. And moreover, my Brother, thou talkest of ease in the Grave, but hast thou forgotten the Hell whither for certain the murderers go? for no murderer hath eternal life,* &c. *And let us consider again, that all the Law is not in the hand of* Giant Despair: *Others, so far as I can understand, have been taken by him, as well as we; and yet have escaped out of his hand: Who knows, but that God that made the World, may cause that* Giant Despair *may die; or that, at some time or other, he may forget to lock us in; or, but he may in a short time have another of his fits before us, and may lose the use of his limbs; and if ever that should come to pass again, for my part, I am resolved to pluck up the heart of a man, and to try my utmost to get from under his hand. I was a fool that I did not try to do it before, but however, my Brother, let's be patient, and endure a while; the time may come that may give us a happy release: but let us not be our own murderers. With these words,* Hopeful *at present did moderate the mind of his Brother; so they continuea together (in the dark) that day in their sad and doleful condition.*

* Hopeful *comforts him.*

Well towards Evening the Giant goes down into the Dungeon again, to see if his Prisoners had taken his counsel; but when he came there, he found them alive; and truly, *alive was all*: for now, what for want of Bread and Water, and by reason of the wounds they received when he beat them, they could do *little but breath*: But I say, he found them alive; at which he fell into a grievous rage, and told them, That seeing they had disobeyed his counsel, it should be worse with them than if they had never been born.

At this they trembled greatly, and I think that *Christian* fell into a Swound; but coming a little to himself again they renewed their discourse about the *Giant's* counsel; and whether yet they had best take it or no. *Now *Christian* again seemed to be for doing it, but *Hopeful* made his second reply as followeth.

* Christian *still dejected.*

Hope. **My Brother*, said he, *remembrest thou not how valiant thou hast been heretofore?* Apollion *could not crush thee, nor could all that thou didst hear or see, or feel in the Valley of the shadow of death; what hardship, terror and amazement hast thou already gone through, and art thou now nothing but fears? Thou seest that I am in the dungeon with thee, a far weaker man by nature, than thou art: Also this* Giant *has wounded me as well as thee; and hath also cut off the Bread and Water from my mouth; and with that I mourn without the light; But let's exercise a little more patience. Remember how thou plaidst the man at* Vanity Fair, *and wast neither afraid of the Chain or Cage; nor yet of bloody Death: Wherefore let us (at least to avoid the shame, that becomes not a Christian to be found in) bear up with patience as well as we can.*

* Hopeful *comforts him again by calling former things to remembrance.*

Now night being come again, and the *Giant* and his Wife being in Bed, she asked him concerning the Prisoners, and if they had taken his counsel: To which he replied, They are sturdy Rogues, they chuse rather to bear all hardship, than to make away themselves. Then said she, take them into the Castle-yard to morrow, and shew them the *Bones* and *Skulls* of those that thou hast already dispatched, and make them believe e're a week comes to an end, thou also wilt tear them in pieces as thou hast done their fellows before them.

So when the morning was come, the *Giant* goes to them again: and takes them into the Castle-yard, and shews them, as his Wife had bidden him. *These, said he, were Pilgrims, as you are, once, and they trespassed in my grounds, as you have done, and when I thought fit, I tore them in pieces; and so within ten days I will do you. Get you down into your den again: and with that he beat them all the way thither: they lay therefore all day on *Saturday* in a lamentable case, as before. Now when night was come, and

* *On* Saturday *the Giant threatned that shortly he would pull them in pieces.*

when Mrs. *Diffidence* and her husband, the *Giant*, were got to bed, they began to renew their discourse of their Prisoners; and withal the old *Giant* wondred that he could neither by his blows nor counsel, bring them to an end. And with that his wife replied, I fear said she, that they live in hopes that some will come to relieve them, or that they have pick-locks about them, by the means of which they hope to escape. And sayst thou so, my dear, said the *Giant*, I will therefore search them in the morning.

Well, on *Saturday* about midnight they began to *pray* and continued in prayer till almost break of day.

Now a little before it was day, good *Christian*, as one half amazed, brake out in this passionate speech, *What a fool (quoth he) am I, thus to lie in a stinking Dungeon when I may as well walk at liberty? I have a Key in my bosom, called Promise, that will, (I am perswaded) open any Lock in* Doubting-Castle. Then said *Hopeful*, That's good news; good Brother pluck it out of thy bosom and try. Then *Christian* pulled it out of his bosom and began to try at the Dungeon door, whose bolt (as he turned the Key) gave back, and the door flew open with ease, and *Christian* and *Hopeful* both came out. Then he went to the outward door, that leads into the *Castle-yard*, and with his Key opened that door also. After he went to the Iron-gate, for that must be opened too, but that Lock went *damnable* hard, yet the Key did open it: then they thrust open the gate to make their escape with speed; but that gate as it opened made such a cracking, that it waked *Giant Despair*, who hastily rising to pursue his Prisoners, felt his limbs to fail, for his fits took him again, so that he could by no means go after them. Then they went on, and came to the Kings High-way; and so were safe, because they were out of his Jurisdiction.

A Key in Christian's *bosom called* Promise, *opens any Lock in* Doubting-Castle.

Now when they were gone over the Stile, they began to contrive with themselves what they should do at that Stile, to prevent those that shall come after from falling into the hands of *Giant Despair*. So they consented to erect there a *Pillar, and to engrave upon the side thereof this Sentence, *over this Stile is the way to* Doubting-Castle, *which is kept by*

* *A Pillar erected by* Christian *and his fellow.*

Giant Despair, *who despiseth the King of the Celestial Country, and seeks to destroy the Holy Pilgrims.* Many therefore that followed after, read what was written, and escaped the danger. This done, they sang as follows.

Out of the way we went, and then we found
What 'twas to tread upon forbidden ground,
And let them that come after have a care
Lest they for trespassing, his Prisoners are,
Whose Castle's Doubting, *and whose name's* Despair.

They went then till they came to the delectable Mountains, which Mountains belong to the Lord of that Hill of which we have spoken before; so they went up to the Mountains to behold the Gardens and Orchards, the Vineyards and Fountains of Water; where also they drank and washed themselves, and did freely eat of the Vineyards. Now there was on the tops of these Mountaines, *Shepherds* feeding their flocks, and they stood by the High-way-side. The Pilgrims therefore went to them, and leaning upon their staves; (as is common with weary Pilgrims, when they stand to talk with any by the way,) they asked, * *Whose delectable Mountains are these; and whose be the sheep that feed upon them?*

The delectable Mountains.

They are refreshed in the Mountains.

** Talks with the Shepherds.*

Shep. These Mountains are *Immanuels Land*, and they are within sight of his City; and the Sheep also are his; and he laid down his life for them.

Chr. *Is this the way to the Celestial City?*

Shep. You are just in your way.

Chr. *How far is it thither?*

Shep. Too far for any, but those that shall get thither indeed.

Chr. *Is the way safe or dangerous?*

Shep. Safe for those for whom it is to be safe, *but Transgressors shall fall therein.*

Hos. 14. 9.

Chr. *Is there in this place any reliefe for Pilgrims, that are weary and faint in the way?*

Shep. The Lord of these Mountains hath given us a charge, *not to be forgetful to entertain strangers*; Therefore the good of the place is before you.

Heb. 13. 1, 2.

I also saw in my dream, that when the *Shepherds* perceived that they were way-faring-men, they also put questions to them (to which they made answer as in other places) as whence came you? and how got you into the way? And by what means have you so persevered therein? For but few of them that begin to come hither, do shew their faces on these Mountains. But when the Shepherds heard their answers, being pleased therewith, they looked very lovingly upon them, and said, * *Welcome to the delectable Mountains.*

** The Shepherds welcome them.*

The Names of the Shepherds.

The Shepherds, I say, whose names were *Knowledge*, *Experience*, *Watchful*, and *Sincere*, took them by the hand, and had them to their Tents, and made them partake of that which was ready at present. They said moreover, We would that you should stay here a while, to be acquainted with us, and yet more to solace your selves with the good of these delectable Mountains. They then told them, that they were content to stay; and so they went to their rest that night, because it was very late.

** They are sure wonders.*

The mountain of Error.

Then I saw in my Dream, that in the Morning, The Shepherds called up *Christian* and *Hopeful* to walk with them upon the Mountains: So they went forth with them, and walked a while, having a pleasant prospect on every side. Then said the Shepherds one to another, shall we shew these Pilgrims some *wonders? so when they had concluded to do it, they had them first to the top of an Hill called *Error*, which was very steep on the farthest side, and bid them look down to the bottom. So *Christian* and *Hopeful* looked down, and saw at the bottom several men, dashed all to pieces by a fall that they had from the top. Then said *Christian*, what meaneth this? The Shepherds answered, have you not heard of them that were made to err, by hearkning to **Hymeneus* and *Philetus*, as concerning the faith of the Resurrection of the body? They answered, yea. Then said the Shepherds, those that you see lie dashed in peices at the bottom of this Mountain, *are they*, and they have continued to this day unburied (as you see) for an Example to others to take heed how they clamber too high, or how they come too near the brink of this Mountain.

** 2 Tim. 2. 17, 18.*

* *Mount* Caution.

Then I saw that they had them to the top of another Mountain, and the name of that is **Caution*, and bid them look afar off: which when they did, they perceived, as they thought, several men walking up and down among the Tombs that were there. And they perceived that the men were blind because they stumbled sometimes upon the Tombs, and because they could not get out from among them. Then said *Christian*, *what means this?*

Prov. 21. 26.

The Shepherds then answer'd, did you not see a little below these Mountains, a *Stile* that lead into a Meadow, on the left hand of this way? They answered, Yes. Then said the Shepherds from that Stile there goes a path that leads directly to *Doubting-Castle*, which is kept by *Gyant-Despair*, and these men (pointing to them among the Tombs) came once on Pilgrimage, as you do now, even till they came to that same *Stile*. And because the right way was rough in that place, they chose to go out of it into that meadow, and there were taken by *Giant-Despair*, and cast into *Doubting-Castle*: where after they had a while been kept in the Dungeon, he at last did put out their eyes, and led them among those Tombs, where he has left them to wander to this very day: that the saying of the wise man might be fulfilled, *He that wandereth out of the way of understanding, shall remain in the Congregation of the dead.* Then *Christian* and *Hopeful* looked upon one another, with tears gushing out; but yet said nothing to the Shepherds.

A By-way to Hell.

Then I saw in my Dream, that the Shepherds had them to another place in a Bottom, where was a door in the side of a hill: and they opened the door, and bid them look in: They looked in therefore, and saw that within it was very dark and smoaky; they also thought, that they heard there a rumbling noise, as of fire, and a cry of some tormented, and that they smelt the scent of Brimstone. Then said *Christian*, *what means this?* The Shepherds told them, this is a By-way to Hell, a way that Hypocrites go in at; namely such as sell their Birth-right with *Esau*; such as sell their Master with *Judas*; such as blaspheme the Gospel, with *Alexander*; and that lye and dissemble, with *Ananias* and *Saphira* his Wife.

Hope. Then said *Hopeful* to the Shepherds, *I perceive that these had on them, even every one a shew of Pilgrimage, as we have now; had they not?*

Shep. Yea, and held it a long time too.

Hop. *How far might they go on in Pilgrimage in their day; since they notwithstanding were thus miserably cast away?*

Shep. Some further, and some not so far as these Mountains.

Then said the Pilgrims one to another, *we had need to cry to the strong for strength.*

Shep. Ay, and you will have need to use it when you have it too.

By this time the Pilgrims had a desire to go forwards, and the Shepherds a desire they should: so they walked together towards the end of the Mountains. Then said the Shepherds one to another: Let us here shew to the Pilgrims the Gates of the Celestial City, if they have skill to look through our *Perspective-Glass. The Pilgrims then lovingly accepted the motion: so they had them to the top of an high Hill, called **Clear*, and gave them their glass to look.

** The Shepherds Perspective-Glass.*

** The Hill* Clear.

Then they essayed to look, but the remembrance of that last thing that the Shepherds had shewed them, made their hands shake; by means of which impediment they could not look steddily through the glass, yet thought they saw something like the Gate, and also some of the Glory of the place. Then they went away and sang this Song.

The fruits of servile fear.

Thus by the Shepherds *Secrets are reveal'd.*
Which from all other men are kept conceal'd:
Come to the Shepherds *then, if you would see*
Things deep, things hid, and that mysterious be.

When they were about to depart, one of the Shepherds gave them a *Note of the Way.* Another of them *bid them *beware of the Flatterer.* The third *bid them take heed that they sleep not upon the Inchanted Ground.* And the fourth *bad them God speed.* So I awoke from my Dream.

** A two-fold Caution.*

And I slept, and dreamed again, and saw the same two Pilgrims going down the Mountains along the High-way, towards the City. Now a little below these Mountains on the left hand, lieth the Country of *Conceit*, from which Country there comes into the way, in which the Pilgrims walked, a little crooked Lane. Here therefore they met with a very brisk Lad, that came out of that Country; and his name was *Ignorance*. So *Christian* asked him, *from what Parts he came, and whither he was going?*

The Country of Conceit, *out of which came* Ignorance.

Ign. Sir, I was born in the Country that lieth off there, a little on the left hand; and am going to the Celestial City.

Christian *and* Ignorance *have some talk.*

Chr. *But how do you think to get in at the Gate, for you may find some difficulty there?*

Ign. As other good people doth, saith he.

Chr. *But what have you to shew at that Gate, that may cause that the Gate should be opened to you?*

Ign. I know my Lord's will, and have been a good Liver; I pay every man his own; I pray, fast, pay Tithes, and give Alms, and have left my Country for whither I am going.

The ground of Ignorance's *hope.*

Chr. *But thou camest not in at the Wicket-gate that is at the head of this way; Thou camest in hither through that same crooked Lane, and therefore I fear, however thou maist think of thy self, when the reckoning day shall come, thou wilt have laid to thy charge, that thou art a thief and a Robber, instead of getting admittance into the City.*

Ign. Gentlemen, ye be utter strangers to me, I know you not; be content to follow the Religion of your Country, and I will follow the Religion of mine. I hope all will be well. And as for the Gate that you talk of, all the world knows that that is a great way off of our Country. I cannot think that any man in all our parts doth so much as know the way to it; nor need they matter whether they do or no, since we have, as you see, a fine pleasant green Lane, that comes down from our Country the next way into the way.

He saith to every one that he is a fool.

When *Christian* saw that the man was wise in his own conceit, he said to *Hopeful*, whisperingly, *there is more hopes of a*

Fool than of him. And said moreover, *when he that is a Fool walketh by the way, his wisdom faileth him, and he saith to every one that he is a fool.* Prov. 26. 12. Eccles. 10. 3.

What, shall we talk farther with him, or out-go him at present, and so leave him to think of what he hath heard already; and then stop again for him afterwards, and see if by degrees we can do any good by him? *How to carry it to a Fool.*

Then said *Hopeful,*

Let Ignorance a little while now muse
On what is said, and let him not refuse
Good Counsel to embrace, lest he remain
Still ignorant of What's the chiefest gain.
God saith, these that no understanding have,
(Although he made them) them he will not save.

Hope. He further added, it is not good, I think, to say to him all at once; let us pass him by, if you will, and talk to him anon *even as he is able to bear it.*

So they both went on and *Ignorance* he came after. Now when they had passed him a little way they entred into a very dark Lane, where they met a man whom seven Devils had bound with seven strong Cords, and were carrying him back to the door that they saw on the side of the Hill: Now good *Christian* began to tremble, and so did *Hopeful* his Companion: Yet as the Devils led away the man, *Christian* looked to see if he knew him, and he thought it might be one *Turn-away* that dwelt in the Town of *Apostacy.* But he did not perfectly see his face; for he did hang his head like a Thief that is found. But being gone past, *Hopeful* looked after him, and espied on his back a paper with this Inscription, *Wanton Professor, and damnable Apostate.* Then said *Christian* to his Fellow, Now I call to remembrance that which was told me of a thing that happened to a good man hereabout. The name of the man was *Little faith,* but a good man, and he dwelt in the Town of *Sincere.* The thing was this; At the entring in of this passage, there comes down from

Mat. 12. 45. Prov. 5. 22.

The destruction of one Turn-away.

Christian *telleth his Companion a story of* Little-faith.

Broad-way-gate a Lane, called *Dead-man's Lane*; so called because of the Murders that are commonly done there. And this *Little-faith* going on Pilgrimage, as we do now, chanced to sit down there and slept. Now, there happened at that time to come down the *Lane* from *Broad-way-gate*, three sturdy Rogues; and their names were *Faint-heart*, *Mistrust*, and *Guilt*, (three Brothers) and they espying *Little-faith* where he was, came gallopping up with speed. Now the good man was just awaked from his sleep, and was getting up to go on his Journey. So they came up all to him, and with threatning language bid him stand. At this *Little-Faith* looked as white as a clout, and had neither power to fight or fly. Then said *Faint-heart* deliver thy purse; but he making no haste to do it, (for he was loth to lose his Money) *Mistrust* ran up to him, and thrusting his hand into his Pocket, pulled out thence a bag of Silver. Then he cry'd out Thieves, Thieves. With that *Guilt* with a great Club that was in his hand struck *Little-Faith* on the head, and with that blow fell'd him flat to the ground, where he lay bleeding as one that would bleed to death. All this while the Thieves stood by. But at last, they hearing that some were upon the Road, and fearing least it should be one *Great-Grace* that dwells in the City of *Good-confidence*, they betook themselves to their heels and left this good man to shift for himself, who getting up made shift to scramble on his way. This was the story.

Broad-way gate. Dead-man's Lane.

Little-Faith *robbed by* Faint-heart, Mistrust *&* Guilt.

They got away his Silver and knock'd him down.

Hope. *But did they take from him all that ever he had?*

Chr. No: The place where his Jewels were, they never ransack'd; so those he kept still. But as I was told, the good man was much afflicted for his Loss, for the Thieves got most of his spending money. That which they got not (as I said) were Jewels; also he had a little odd money left, but scarce enough to bring him to his Journies end; nay (if I was not mis-informed) he was forced to beg as he went, to keep himself alive, (for his Jewels he might not sell.) But beg, and

Little-Faith *lost not his best things.*

1 Pet. 4. 18.

Little-Faith *forced to beg to his Journies end.*

do what he could, *he went* (as we say) *with many a hungry belly*, the most part of the rest of the way.

Hope. *But is it not a wonder they got not from him his Certificate, by which he was to receive his admittance at the Celestial Gate?*

Chr. 'Tis a wonder, but they got not that; though they mist it not through any good cunning of his, for he being dismayed with their coming upon him, had neither power nor skill to hide any thing, so 'twas more by good providence, than by his endeavour that they mist of *that good thing.*

He kept not his best things by his own cunning.

2 Tim. 1. 14.

Hope. *But it must needs be a comfort to him that they got not his Jewels from him?*

Chr. It might have been great comfort to him, had he used it as he should: But they that told me the story, said that he made but little use of it all the rest of the way; and that because of the dismay that he had in the taking away his money: Indeed he forgot it a great part of the rest of his Journey; and besides, when at any time it came into his mind and he began to be comforted therewith; then would fresh thoughts of his Loss come again upon him, and those thoughts would swallow up all.

2 Pet. 1. 9.

Hope. *Alass, poor man! this could not but be a great grief unto him?*

He is pitied by both.

Chr. Grief! ay, a Grief indeed! would it not have been so to any of us, had we been used as he, to be robbed and wounded too, and that in a strange place, as he was? 'Tis a wonder he did not die with grief, poor heart? I was told that he scattered almost all the rest of the way with nothing but doleful and bitter Complaints. Telling also to all that overtook him, or that he overtook in the way as he went, where he was robbed, and how, who they were that did it, and what he lost; how he was wounded, and that he hardly escaped with life.

Hope. *But 'tis a wonder that his necessity did not put him upon* selling, *or* pawning *some of his Jewels, that he might have wherewith to relieve himself in his Journey.*

Chr. Thou talkest like one upon whose head is the *shell* to this very day: For what should he pawn them? or to whom should he sell them? In all that Country, where he was robbed, his Jewels were not accounted of; nor did he want that relief, which could from thence be administred to him. Besides, had his Jewels been missing at the Gate of the Celestial City, he had (and that he knew well enough) been excluded from an Inheritance there; and that would have been worse to him, than the appearance and villainy of ten thousand thieves.

Christian *snibbeth his fellow for unadvised speaking.*

Hope. *Why art thou so tart, my Brother?* Esau *sold his Birth-right, and that for a mess of Pottage; and that Birth-right was his greatest Jewel. And if he, why might not* Little-faith *do so too?*

Heb. 12. 16.

Chr. *Esau* did sell his Birth-right indeed, and so do many besides, and by so doing exclude themselves from the chief Blessing, as also that *Caitiff* did. But you must put a difference betwixt *Esau* and *Little-Faith*, and also betwixt their Estates. *Esau*'s Birth-right was Typical, but *Little Faith*'s Jewels were not so. *Esau*'s belly was his God, but *Little Faith*'s belly was not so. *Esau*'s want lay in his fleshly Appetite, *Little Faith*'s did not so. Besides *Esau* could see no further than to the fulfilling of his Lust; *for I am at the point to die*, said he, *and what good will this Birth-right do me?* But *Little-Faith*, though it was his lot to have but a *little faith*, was by his *little faith* kept from such extravagancies, and made to *see* and *prize* his Jewels more, than to sell them as *Esau* did his Birth-right. You read not any where that *Esau* had *Faith*, no not so much as a little: Therefore no marvel, if where the flesh only bears sway (as it will in that man where no Faith is to resist) if he sells his *Birth-right*, and his Soul and all, and that to the Devil of Hell; for it is with such, as it is with the Ass, *Who in her occasion cannot be turned away*. When their minds are set upon their Lust, they will have them whatever they cost. But *Little-Faith* was of another temper, his mind was on things Divine; his livelihood was upon things that were Spiritual and above: Therefore to what end should he that is of such a temper sell his Jewels (had there been any that would have bought them)

A Discourse about Esau *and* Little-Faith.

Esau *was ruled by his lusts.*

Gen. 25. 32.

Esau *never had Faith.*

Jer. 1. 24.

Little-faith *could not live upon* Esau's *Pottage.*

to fill his mind with empty things? Will a man give a penny to fill his belly with hay: or can you perswade the *Turtle Dove* to live upon Carrion like the *Crow*? Though *faithless* ones can for carnal lusts, pawn or morgage, or sell what they have, and themselves outright to boot; yet they that have *Faith*, *Saving-Faith*, though but a little of it, cannot do so. Here therefore, my Brother, is thy mistake.

A comparison between the Turtle-Dove *and the* Crow.

Hope. *I acknowledge it; but yet your severe reflection had almost made me angry.*

Chr. Why, I did but compare thee to some of the Birds that are of the brisker sort, who will run to and fro in untrodden Paths with the shell upon their heads: but pass by that, and consider the matter under debate, and all shall be well betwixt thee and me.

Hope. *But* Christian, *these three fellows, I am perswaded in my heart, are but a company of Cowards: would they have run else think you, as they did at the noise of one that was coming on the Road? Why did not* Little-faith *pluck up a greater heart? He might methinks have stood one brush with them, and have yielded when there had been no remedy?*

Hopeful *swaggers.*

Chr. That they are Cowards, many have said, but few have found it so in the time of Tryal. As for a great Heart, *Little-Faith* hath none; and I perceive by thee, my Brother, hadst thou been the man concerned, thou art but for a brush, and then to yield. And verily, since this is the height of thy stomach, now they are at a distance from us, should they appear to thee, as they did to him, they might put thee to second thoughts.

No great heart for God where there is but little-Faith.

We have more courage when out, than when we are in.

But consider again, they are but Journeymen Thieves, they serve under the King of the Bottomless-pit; who if need be, will come to their aid himself, and his voice is *as the roaring of a Lion.* I my self have been engaged as this *Little-Faith* was, and I found it a terrible thing. These three Villains set upon me, and I beginning like a *Christian* to resist, they gave but a call, and in came their Master: I would, as the saying is, have given my Life for a penny; but that, as God

Psal. 5. 8.

Christian *tells his own experience in this case.*

would have it, I was cloathed with Armour of Proof. Ay, and yet though I was so harnessed, I found it hard work to quit my self like a man; no man can tell what in that combat attends us, but he that hath been in the battle himself.

Hope. *Well, but they ran you see, when they did but suppose that one* Great-Grace *was in the way.*

Chr. True, they have often fled, both they and their Master, when *Great-Grace* hath appeared, and no marvel, for he is the *King's Champion*: But I tro, you will put some difference between *Little-Faith* and the *King's Champion*? all the King's Subjects are not his Champions, nor can they, when tryed, do such feats of War as he. Is it meet to think that a little Child should handle *Goliah* as *David* did? or that there should be the strength of an *Ox* in a *Wren*? Some are strong, some are weak; some have great Faith, some have little; this man was one of the weak, and therefore went to the walls.

The King's Champion.

Hope. *I would it had been* Great-Grace *for their sakes.*

Chr. If it had been he, he might have had his hands full, for I must tell you, that though *Great-Grace* is excellent good at his Weapon, and has, and can, so long as he keeps them at Swords-point, do well enough with them; yet if they get within him, even *Faint-heart*, *Mistrust*, or the other, it shall go hard but that they will throw up his heels. And when a man is down, you know what can he do?

Whoso looks well upon *Great-Grace*'s face, shall see those Scars and Cuts there that shall easily give demonstration of what I say. Yea, once I heard that he should say, (and that when he was in the Combat) *we despaired even of life*: How did these sturdy Rogues and their Fellows make *David* groan, mourn, and roar? Yea, *Heman* and *Hezekiah* too, though Champions in their days, were forced to bestir them, when by these assaulted; and yet, notwithstanding, they had their Coats soundly brushed by them. *Peter* upon a time would go try what he could do; but though some do say of him that he is the Prince of the Apostles, they handled him so, that they made him at last afraid of a sorry Girl.

Besides, their King is at their whistle, he is never out of hearing; and if at any time they be put to the worst, he if possible comes in to help them: And of him it is said, *The*

Sword of him that layeth at him cannot hold; the Spear, the Dart, nor the Habergeon; he esteemeth Iron as Straw, and Brass as rotten Wood. The Arrow cannot make him fly, sling-stones are turned with him into stubble; Darts are counted as stubble, he laugheth at the shaking of a Spear. What can a man do in this case? 'Tis true, if a man could at every turn have *Job*'s Horse, and had skill and courage to ride him, he might do notable things. *For his Neck is cloathed with Thunder; he will not be afraid as the Grashopper; the Glory of his Nostrils is terrible; he paweth in the Valley, rejoyceth in his Strength, and goeth out to meet the Armed Men. He mocketh at fear and is not affrighted, neither turneth back from the Sword. The Quiver ratleth against him, the glittering Spear and the Shield. He swallows the ground with fierceness and rage, neither believes he that it is the sound of the trumpet. He says, among the Trumpets, Ha, ha, and he smelleth the Battle afar off, the Thundring of the Captains, and the shoutings.*

Job 41. 26. Leviathan's *sturdiness.*

Job 39. 19. *The excellent Metal that is in* Job'*s Horse.*

But for such Footmen as thee and I are, let us never desire to meet with an Enemy, nor vaunt as if we could do better, when we hear of others that they have been foiled, nor be tickled at the thoughts of our own manhood; for such commonly come by the worst when tried. Witness *Peter*, of whom I made mention before: He would swagger ay he would: He would, as his vain mind prompted him to say, do better, and stand more for his Master than all men: But who so foiled and run down by those Villains as he?

When therefore we hear that such Robberies are done on the King's High-way, two things become us to do First, to go out harnessed, and to be sure *to take a shield with us*: For it was for want of that, that he that laid so lustily at *Leviathan* could not make him yield. For indeed, if that be wanting, he fears us not at all. Therefore he that had skill hath said, *Above all take this Shield of Faith, wherewith ye shall be able to quench all the fiery darts of the wicked.*

Ephes. 6.

'Tis good also that we desire of the King a Convoy, yea that he will go with us himself. This made *David* rejoyce, when in the Valley of the shadow of death; and *Moses* was rather for dying where

'Tis good to have a Convoy.

Exod. 32. 15.

he stood, than to go one step without his God. O my Brother, if he will but go along with us, what need we be afraid of ten thousands that shall set themselves against us; but without him, *the proud helpers fall under the slain.*

Psal. 3. 5, 6, 7, 8.
Psal. 27. 1, 2.
Isa. 10. 4.

I for my part have been in the fray before now, and though (through the goodness of him that is best) I am as you see alive: yet I cannot boast of any Manhood, glad shall I be, if I meet with no more such brunts: though I fear we are not got beyond all danger. However, since the Lion and the Bear hath not as yet devoured me, I hope God will also deliver us from the next uncircumcised *Philistines.* Then Sang *Christian*,

Poor Little-Faith! *hast been among the Thieves?*
Wast robb'd? remember this who so believes,
And get more Faith; then shall you Victors be
Over ten thousand, else scarce over three.

Away and away.

So they went on, and *Ignorance* followed. They went then till they came at a place, where they saw a way put it self into *their way*, and seemed withal to lie as streight as the way which they should go; and here they knew not which of the two to take, for both seemed streight before them, therefore here they stood still to consider. And as they were thinking about the way, behold, a man of black flesh but covered with a very light Robe, came to them and asked them why they stood there? They answered, they were going to the Celestial City, but knew not which of these ways to take. Follow me, said the man, it is thither that I am going. So they followed him in the way that but now came into the road, which by degrees turned and turned them so from the City that they desired to go to, that in little time their faces were turned away from it; yet they followed him. But by and by, before they were aware he led them within the compass of a Net, in which they were both so intangled, that they knew not what to do; and with that *the white robe fell off the black man's back*: then they saw where they were.

The Flatterer finds them.

Christian *and his fellow deluded.*

They are taken in a Net.

Wherefore there they lay crying some time, for they could not get themselves out.

Chr. Then said *Christian* to his fellow, Now do I see my self in an error. Did not the Shepherds bid us beware of the Flatterers? As is the saying of the wise man, so we have found it this day: *A man that flattereth his Neighbour, spreadeth a Net for his Foot.*

They bewail their condition.

Prov. 29. 6.

Hope. They also gave us a note of directions about the Way, for our more sure finding thereof: but therein we have also forgotten to read, and have not kept our selves from the Paths of the Destroyer. Here *David* was wiser than we; for saith he, *Concerning the Works of men, by the word of thy Lips, I have kept me from the paths of the Destroyer.* Thus they lay bewailing themselves in the Net. At last they espied a shining one coming toward them, with a Whip of small cord in his hand. When he was come to the place where they were, he asked them whence they came, and what they did there; they told him, that they were poor Pilgrims, going to *Sion*, but were led out of their way by a black man, cloathed in white; who bid us, said they, follow him, for he was going thither too. Then said he with the Whip, it is a *Flatterer*, a false Apostle, that hath transformed himself into an Angel of Light. So he rent the Net, and let the men out. Then said he to them follow me, that I may set you in your way again; so he led them back to the way, which they had left to follow the *Flatterer*. Then he asked them, saying, Where did you lie the last night? They said, with the Shepherds upon the delectable Mountain. He asked them then if they had not of those Shepherds, *a note of direction for the way*? They answered, Yes. But, did you, said he, when you were at a stand, pluck out and read your Note? They answered, No. He asked them, Why? They said, They forgot. He asked moreover if the Shepherds did not bid them beware of the *Flatterer*? They answered, Yes. But we did not imagine, said they, *that this fine-spoken man had been he.*

Psal. 17. 4.

A shining one comes to them with a Whip in his Hand.

Pro. 29. 4.
Dan. 11. 32.
2 Cor. 11. 13, 14.

They are examined, and convicted of forgetfulness.

Deceivers fine-spoken.

Rom. 16. 18.

Then I saw in my Dream, that he commanded them to *lie down*; which when they did he chastised them sore, to teach them the good way wherein they should walk; and as he chastised them, he said, *As many as I love, I rebuke and chasten; be zealous therefore, and repent.* This done, he bids them go on their way, and take good heed to the other Directions of the Shepherds. So they thanked him for all his kindness, and went softly along the right way, Singing,

Deut. 25. 2. 2 Chron. 6. 26, 27.

Rev. 3. 19.

They are whipt and sent on their way.

Come hither you that walk along the way;
See how the Pilgrims fare that go astray.
They catched are in an intangling Net,
'Cause they good Counsel highly did forget.
'Tis true they rescu'd were, but yet you see
They're scourg'd to boot: Let this your caution be.

Now after a while they perceived afar off, one coming softly and alone all along the High way to meet them. Then said *Christian* to his fellow, Yonder is a man with his back towards *Sion*, and he is coming to meet us.

Hope. I see him, let us take heed to our selves now, lest he should prove a *Flatterer* also. So he drew nearer and nearer, and at last came up unto them. His name was *Atheist*, and he asked them whither they were going.

The Atheist *meets them.*

Chr. *We are going to the Mount* Sion.

Then *Atheist* fell into a very great laughter.

He laughs at them.

Chr. *What's the meaning of your laughter?*

Atheist. I laugh to see what ignorant persons you are to take upon you so tedious a Journey; and yet are like to have nothing but your Travel for your Pains.

They reason together.

Chr. *Why man? Do you think we shall not be received?*

Atheist. Received! There is no such place as you dream of in all this World.

Chr. *But there is in the World to come.*

Atheist. When I was at home in mine own Country, I heard as you now affirm, and from that hearing went out to see, and have been seeking this City twenty years, but find no more of it than I did the first day I set out.

Jer. 22. 13. Eccl. 10. 15.

Chr. *We have both heard, and believe that there is such a place to be found.*

Atheist. Had not I when at home believed, I had not come thus far to seek; but finding none, (and yet I should, had there been such a place to be found, for I have gone to seek it further than you) I am going back again and will seek to refresh my self with the things that I then cast away for hopes of that which I now see is not.

The Atheist *takes up his content in this World.*

Chr. Then said *Christian* to *Hopeful*, his Companion, *Is it true which this man has said?*

Christian *provoketh his Brother.*

Hope. Take heed, he is one of the *Flatterers*; remember what it has cost us once already for our hearkning to such kind of Fellows. What! no Mount *Sion*? did we not see from the delectable Mountains, the Gate of the City? Also are we not now to walk by Faith? *Let us go on, said *Hopeful* lest the man with the Whip overtake us again.

Hopeful'*s gracious answer.*

2 Cor. 5. 7.

** A remembrance of former chastisements is an help against present temptations.*

You should have taught me that Lesson, which I will round you in the ears withal: *Cease my Son to hear the Instructions that causeth to err from the Words of Knowledge*: I say, my Brother, cease to hear him, and let us believe to the saving of the Soul.

Prov. 19. 27.
Heb. 10. 39.

Chr. *My Brother, I did not put the question to thee, for that I doubted of the Truth of our Belief my self, but to prove thee, and to fetch from thee a fruit of the honesty of thy heart. As for this man, I know that he is blinded by the God of this World: Let thee and I go on, knowing that we have belief of the Truth, and no lye is of the Truth.*

A fruit of an honest heart.

1 Joh. 2. 11.

Hope. Now do I rejoyce in hope of the glory of God: So they turned away from the man; and he laughing at them, went his way.

They are come to the enchanted ground.

I saw then in my Dream that they went till they came into a certain Country, whose Air, naturally tended to make one drowsie, if he came a stranger into it. And here *Hopeful* began to be very dull, and heavy of Sleep; wherefore he

Hopeful *begins to be drowsie.*

said unto *Christian*, I now begin to grow so drowsie that I can scarcely hold up mine eyes: let us lie down here, and take one nap.

Chr. *By no means* (said the other) *lest sleeping we never awake more.*

Christian *keeps him awake.*

Hope. Why my Brother? Sleep is sweet to the labouring man; we may be refreshed if we take a nap.

Chr. *Do you not remember, that one of the Shepherds bid us beware of the enchanted ground? He meant by that, that we should beware of sleeping; wherefore let us not sleep as do others, but let us watch and be sober.*

1 Thes. 5. 6.

Hope. I acknowledge my self in a fault, and had I been here alone, I had by sleeping run the danger of death. I see it is true that the wise man saith, *Two are better than one.* Hitherto hath thy Company been my mercy; *and thou shalt have a good reward for thy labour.*

He is thankful.

Eccles. 9. 8.

To prevent drowziness, they fall to good discourse. Good discourse prevents drowziness.

Chr. *Now then*, said *Christian*, *to prevent drowsiness in this place, let us fall into good discourse.*

Hope. With all my heart said the other.

Chr. *Where shall we begin?*

Hope. Where God began with us, but do you begin if you please.

Chr. *I will Sing you first this Song.*

☞

The Dreamers Note.

When Saints do sleepy grow, let them come hither,
And hear how these two Pilgrims talk together.
Yea, let them learn of them in any wise,
Thus to keep ope' their drowsie slumbring eyes.
Saints Fellowship, if it be manag'd well,
Keeps them awake and that in spight of Hell.

Chr. Then *Christian* began and said, *I will ask you a question, How came you to think at first of doing what you do now?*

They begin at the beginning of their conversion.

Hope. Do you mean, How came I at first to look after the good of my Soul?

Chr. *Yes, that is my meaning.*

Hope. I continued a great while in the delight of those

things which were seen and sold at our *Fair*; things, which I believe now, would have (had I continued in them still) drowned me in perdition and destruction.

Chr. *What things are they?*

Hope. All the Treasures and Riches of the World. Also I delighted much in Rioting, Revelling, Drinking, Swearing, Lying, Uncleanness, Sabbath-breaking, and what not, that tended to destroy the Soul. But I found at last, by hearing and considering of things that are Divine, which indeed I heard of you, as also of beloved *Faithful*, that was put to death for his Faith and Good-living in *Vanity-Fair*, *That the end of these things is death.* And that for these things sake, the wrath of God cometh upon the Children of Disobedience.

Rom. 6. 21, 22, 23. Ephes. 5. 6.

Chr. *And did you presently fall under the power of this Conviction?*

Hope. No: I was not willing presently to know the evil of sin, nor the Damnation that follows upon the commission of it; but endeavoured, when my Mind at first began to be shaken with the Word, to shut mine eyes against the light thereof.

Hopeful *at first shut his eyes against the light.*

Chr. *But what was the cause of your carrying of it thus to the first workings of Gods blessed Spirit upon you?*

Hope. The Causes were, 1. I was ignorant that this was the Work of God upon me, I never thought that by awakenings for sin, God at first begins the Conversion of a sinner. 2. Sin was yet very sweet to my flesh, and I was loath to leave it. 3. I could not tell how to part with mine old Companions, their presence and actions were so desirable unto me. 4. The hours in which Convictions were upon me, were such troublesome, and such heart-affrighting hours, that I could not bear, no not so much as the remembrance of them upon my heart.

Reasons of the resisting of light.

Chr. *Then as it seems, sometimes you got rid of your trouble.*

Hope. Yes verily, but it would come into my mind again; and then I should be as bad, nay worse than I was before.

Chr. *Why, what was it that brought your sins to mind again?*

Hope. Many things; as,

1. *If I did but meet a good man in the Street; or,

** When he had lost his sense of sin, what brought it again.*

2. If I have heard any read in the Bible; or,
3. If mine head did begin to ake; or,
4. If I were told that some of my Neighbours were sick; or,
5. If I heard the Bell toll for some that were dead; or,
6. If I thought of dying my self; or,
7. If I heard that sudden death hapned to others.
8. But especially, when I thought of my self, that I must quickly come to Judgment.

Chr. *And could you at any time with ease get off the guilt of sin, when by any of these ways it came upon you?*

Hope. No, not I, for then they got faster hold of my Conscience. And then, if I did but think of going back to sin (though my mind was turned against it) it would be double torment to me.

Chr. *And how did you do then?*

Hope. I thought I must endeavour to mend my life; or else, thought I, I am sure to be damned.

When he could no longer shake off his guilt by sinful courses, then he endeavours to mend.

Chr. *And did you endeavour to amend?*

Hope. Yes, and fled from not only my sins, but sinful company too, and betook me to religious Duties, as Praying, Reading, Weeping for sin, speaking Truth to my Neighbours, *&c.* These things did I, with many other too much here to relate.

Chr. *And did you think your self well then?*

Then he thought himself well.

Hope. Yes, for a while, but at the last my trouble came tumbling upon me again, and that over the neck of all my Reformation.

Chr. *How came that about, since you were now reformed?*

Reformation at last could not help, and why.

Isa. 64. 6.
Gal. 2. 6.
Luke 17. 10.

Hope. There were several things brought it upon me; especially such sayings as these; *All our Righteousnesses are as filthy rags. By the works of the Law no man shall be justified. When you have done all things, say, We are unprofitable*; with many more such like. From whence I began to reason with my self thus: If *All* my righteousnesses are filthy rags; if by the deeds of the Law, no man can be justified; and if when we have done *All* we are yet unprofitable: Then 'tis but a folly to think of Heaven by the Law. I further thought thus; *If a man runs 100 *l.* into the Shopkeeper's debt, and after that shall pay for all that he shall fetch; yet if this old debt stand still in the Book uncrossed, for that the Shopkeeper may sue him, and cast him into Prison, till he shall pay the debt.

** His being a debtor by the Law troubled him.*

Chr. *Well, and how did you apply this to your self?*

Hope. Why, I thought thus with my self; I have by my sins run a great way into God's Book, and that my now reforming will not pay off that score; therefore I should sink still under all my present amendments: But how shall I be freed from that damnation that I brought my self in danger of by my former transgressions?

Chr. *A very good Application: but pray go on.*

Hope. Another thing that hath troubled me, even since my late amendments, is, that If I look narrowly into the best of what I do now, I still see sin, new sin mixing it self with the best of that I do. So that now I am forced to conclude, that notwithstanding my former fond conceits of my self and Duties, I have committed sin enough in one Duty to send me to hell, though my former Life had been faultless.

His espying bad things in his best duties troubled him.

Chr. *And what did you do then?*

Hope. Do! I could not tell what to do, till I brake my mind to *Faithful*; for he and I were well acquainted. And he told me, that unless I could obtain the Righteousness of a man that never had sinned, neither mine own, nor all the Righteousness of the World could save me.

This made him break his mind to faithful *who told him the way to be saved.*

Chr. *And did you think he spake true?*

Hope. Had he told me so when I was pleased and satisfied with mine own amendment, I had called him Fool for his pains; but now since I see mine own infirmity, and the sin that cleaves to my best performance I have been forced to be of his Opinion.

Chr. *But did you think when at first he suggested it to you, that there was such a man to be found, of whom it might justly be said, That he never committed Sin?*

Hope. I must confess the words at first sounded strangely; but after a little more talk and company with him, I had full conviction about it.

At which he started at present.

Chr. *And did you ask him what man this was, and how you must be justified by him?*

Heb. 10.
Rom. 4.
Col. 1.
2 Pet. 1.

Hope. Yes, and he told me it was the Lord Jesus, that dwelleth on the right hand of the Most high: *And thus, said he, you must be justified by him, even by trusting to what he hath done by himself, in the days of his Flesh, and suffered when he did hang on the Tree. I asked him further, how that mans Righteousness could be of that Efficacy, to justifie another before God? And he told me, he was the mighty God, and did what he did; and died the Death also, not for himself but for me: to whom his doings, and the worthiness of them should be imputed if I believed on him.

** A more particular discovery of the way to be sav'd.*

Chr. *And what did you do then?*

Hope. I made my Objections against my believing; for that I thought he was not willing to save me.

He doubts of acceptation.

Chr. *And what said* Faithful *to you then?*

Hope. He bid me go to him and see: Then I said it was Presumption. He said, No; for I was invited to come. ||Then he gave me a Book of *Jesus* his inditing, to incourage me the more freely to come. And he said concerning that Book, that every jot and tittle thereof stood firmer than Heaven and Earth. Then I asked him, what I must do when I came? And he told me, I must intreat upon my knees, with all my heart and Soul, the Father to reveal him to me. Then I asked him further, how I must make my Supplication to him? And he said, Go, and thou shalt find him upon a Mercy-Seat, where he sits all the Year long, to give Pardon and Forgiveness to them that come. I told him, that I knew not what to say when I came: *And he bid me say to this effect, *God be merciful to me a sinner, and*

Mat. 11. 28.
|| *He is better instructed.*

Mat. 24. 35.
Psa. 95. 6.
Dan. 7. 10.
Jer. 29. 12, 13.
Exo. 25. 22.
Lev. 16. 2.
Num. 7. 8.
Heb. 4. 6.

** He is bid to pray.*

make me to know and believe in Jesus Christ: For I see, that if his Righteousness had not been, or I have not Faith in that Righteousness, I am utterly cast away: Lord, I have heard that thou art a merciful God, and hast ordained that thy Son Jesus Christ should be the Saviour of the World. And moreover that thou art willing to bestow him upon such a poor sinner as I am, (and I am a sinner indeed) Lord, take therefore this opportunity, and magnifie thy Grace in the Salvation of my Soul, through thy Son Jesus Christ, Amen.

Chr. *And did you do as you were bidden?*

Hope. Yes, over, and over, and over.

He prays.

Chr. *And did the Father reveal the Son to you?*

Hope. Not at the first, nor second, nor third, nor fourth, nor fifth; no nor at the sixth time neither.

Chr. *What did you do then?*

Hope. What! why I could not tell what to do.

Chr. *Had you not thoughts of leaving off Praying?*

|| He thought to leave off praying.

Hope. ||Yes, and 100 times twice told.

Chr. *And what was the reason you did not?*

Hope. *I believed that that was true which had been told me; to wit, That without the Righteousness of this Christ all the World could not save me: and therefore thought I with my self, if I leave off, I die; and I can but die at the Throne of Grace. And withal this came into my mind, *If it tarry, wait for it, because it will surely come, and will not tarry.* So I continued praying until the Father shewed me his Son.

** He durst not leave off praying and why?*

Hab. 2. 3.

Chr. *And how was he revealed unto you?*

Hope. I did not see him with my Bodily eyes, but with the eyes of my understanding; and thus it was. One day I was very sad, I think sadder than at any one time of my life; and this sadness was through a fresh sight of the greatness and vileness of my Sins: And as I was then looking for nothing but *hell*, and the everlasting damnation of my Soul, suddenly, as I thought, I saw the Lord Jesus look down from Heaven upon me, and saying, *Believe on the Lord Jesus Christ, and thou shalt be saved.*

Eph. 1. 18, 19.

Christ is revealed to him and how.

But I Replied; Lord I am a great, a very great sinner:
Acts 16. And he answered, *My Grace is sufficient for thee.*
30, 31. Then I said, But Lord, what is believing? And
then I saw from that saying. [*He that cometh to*
Joh. 6. 35. *me shall never hunger, and he that believeth on me, shall never thirst.*] that believing and coming was all one; and that he that came, that is, ran out in his heart and affections after Salvation by Christ, he indeed believed in Christ. Then the water stood in mine eyes, and I asked further, But Lord, may such a great sinner as I am, be indeed accepted of thee,
Joh. 6. 16. and be saved by thee? and I heard him say, *And*
him that cometh to me, I will in no wise cast out. Then I said, But how, Lord, must I consider of thee in my coming to thee, that my Faith may be placed aright upon thee?
Then he said, *Christ Jesus came into the World to*
1 Tim. 1. 15. *save sinners. He is the end of the Law for*
Rom. 10. 4. *righteousness to every one that believes. He died for*
chap. 4. *our sins, and rose again for our justification: he*
Heb. 7. 24, *loved us and washed us from our sins in his own*
25. *Blood.* He *is Mediator* betwixt God and us, he *ever liveth to make Intercession for us.* From all which I gathered, that I must look for Righteousness in his person, and for satisfaction for my sins by his Blood; that what he did in obedience to his Fathers Law, and in submitting to the penalty thereof; was not for himself, but for him that will accept it for his Salvation, and be thankful. And now was my heart full of joy, mine eyes full of tears, and mine affections running over with love to the name, People, and Ways of Jesus Christ.

Chr. *This was a Revelation of Christ to your Soul indeed: but tell me particularly what effect this had upon your spirit.*

Hope. It made me see that all the world, notwithstanding all the Righteousness thereof, is in a state of condemnation. It made me see that God the Father, though he be just, can justly justifie the coming sinner: It made me greatly ashamed of the vileness of my former life, and confounded me with the sense of mine own ignorance; for there never came thought into my heart before now, that shewed me so the beauty of Jesus Christ. It made me love a holy life, and long to do something for the Honour and Glory of the Lord Jesus. Yea,

I thought, that had I now 1000 gallons of blood in my body, I could spill it all for the sake of the Lord Jesus.

I saw then in my Dream, that *Hopeful* looked back, and saw *Ignorance*, whom they had left behind, coming after: *Look*, said he to *Christian*, *how far yonder youngster loitereth behind.*

Chr. Ay, ay, I see him; he careth not for our Company.

Hope. *But I tro it would not have hurt him*; *had he kept pace with us hitherto.*

* *Young* Ignorance *comes up again.*

Chr. That's true, but I warrant you, he thinketh otherwise.

Their Talk.

Hope. *That I think he doth*, *but however let us tarry for him.* So they did.

Then *Christian* said to him, *Come away Man*, *why do you stay so behind?*

Ign. I take my pleasure in walking alone, even more a great deal than in company, unless I like it the better.

Then said *Christian* to *Hopeful*, (but softly) *Did I not tell you he cared not for our company? But however*, said he, *come up*, *and let us talk away the time in this solitary place.* Then directing his speech to *Ignorance* he said, *Come*, *how do you? how stands it between God and your Soul now?*

Ignor. *I hope well, for I am always full of good motions, that come into my mind, to comfort me as I walk.

* Ignorance*'s hope, and the ground of it.*

Chr. *What good motions? pray tell us.*

Ignor. Why, I think of God and Heaven.

Chr. *So do the Devils and damned Souls.*

Prov. 28. 29.

Ign. But I think of them, and desire them.

Chr. *So do many that are never like to come there.* The Soul of the sluggard desires and hath nothing.

Ignor. But I think of them, and leave all for them.

Chr. *That I doubt*, *for leaving of* all *is an hard matter*; *yea*, *a harder matter than many are aware of. But why*, *or by what*, *art thou perswaded that thou hast left all for God and Heaven?*

Ignor. My heart tells me so.

Chr. *The wise man says*, He that trusts his own heart is a fool.

Prov. 28. 29.

Ignor. That is spoken of an evil heart, but mine is a good one.

Chr. *But how dost thou prove that?*

Ignor. It comforts me in hopes of Heaven.

Chr. *That may be through its deceitfulness; for a mans heart may minister comfort to him in the hopes of that thing, for which he yet has no ground to hope.*

Ign. But my heart and life agree together, and therefore my hope is well grounded.

Chr. *Who told thee that thy heart and life agree together?*

Ignor. My heart tells me so.

Chr. *Ask my fellow if I be a Thief:* Thy *heart tell thee so; Except the Word of God beareth witness in this matter, other testimony is of no value.*

Ign. But is it not a good heart that has good thoughts? And is not that a good life, that is according to Gods commandments?

Chr. *Yes, that is a good heart that hath good thoughts, and that is a good life that is according to Gods Commandments: But it is one thing indeed to have these, and another thing, only to think so.*

Ign. Pray, what count you good thoughts and a life according to Gods commandments?

Chr. *There are good thoughts of divers kinds, some respecting our selves, some God, some Christ, and some other things.*

Ign. What be good thoughts respecting our selves?

Chr. *Such as agree with the Word of God.*

Ignor. When do our thoughts of our selves agree with the Word of God?

What are good thoughts?

Chr. *When we pass the same Judgment upon our selves which the Word passes. To explain my self; The Word of God saith of persons in a natural condition,* There is none righteous, there is none that doth good, *It saith also,* That every imagination of the heart of a man is only evil, and that continually. *And again,* The imagination of mans heart is evil from his Youth. *Now then, when we think thus of our selves, having sense thereof, then are our thoughts good ones, because according to the Word of God.*

Rom. 3.
Gen. 6. 2.

Ignor. *I will never believe that my heart is thus bad.*

Chr. Therefore thou never hadst one good thought concerning thy self in thy life. But let me go on: As the word passeth a Judgment upon our hearts, so it passeth a Judgment upon our ways, and when our thoughts of our hearts and ways agree with the Judgment which the word giveth of both, then are both good, because agreeing thereto.

Ign. *Make out your meaning.*

Chr. Why, the word of God saith, That mans ways are crooked ways, not good, but perverse; It saith they are naturally out of the good way, that they have not known it. Now when a man thus thinketh of his ways, I say, when he doth sensibly and with heart-humiliation thus think, then hath he good thoughts of his own ways, because his thoughts now agree with the judgment of the word of God.

Psal. 125. 5. Prov. 2. 15. Rom. 3.

Ign. *What are good thoughts concerning God?*

Chr. Even (as I have said concerning our selves) when our thoughts of God do agree with what the word saith of him. And that is, when we think of his Being and Attributes as the word hath taught: of which I cannot now discourse at large. But to speak of him in reference to us, then we have right thoughts of God, when we think that he knows us better than we know our selves, and can see sin in us, when and where we can see none in our selves; when we think he knows our inmost thoughts, and that our heart, with all its depths, is always open unto his eyes: Also when we think that all our righteousness stinks in his nostrils, and that therefore he cannot abide to see us stand before him in any confidence, even in all our best performances.

Ign. *Do you think that I am such a fool, as to think God can see no farther than I? or that I would come to God i' th' best of my performances?*

Chr. Why how dost thou think in this matter?

Ign. *Why, to be short, I think I must believe in Christ for Justification.*

Chr. How! Think thou must believe in Christ, when thou seest not thy need of him! Thou neither seest thy original nor actual Infirmities, but hast such an Opinion of thy self, and of what thou doest, as plainly renders thee to be one that did never see a necessity of Christs personal Righteousness to justifie thee before God. How then doest thou say, I believe in Christ?

Ign. *I believe well enough for all that.*

Chr. How dost thou believe?

Ign. *I believe that Christ died for sinners, and that I shall be justified before God from the Curse, through his gracious acceptance of my obedience to his Law. Or thus, Christ makes my Duties that are Religious, acceptable to his Father by virtue of his Merits, and so shall I be justified.*

Chr. Let us give an answer to this confession of thy *Faith*, 1. Thou believest with a fantastical faith, for this faith is no where described in the Word. 2. Thou believest with a false Faith, because it taketh Justification from the personal Righteousness of Christ, and applies it to thy own. 3. This faith maketh not Christ a Justifier of thy person, but of thy actions; and of thy person for thy actions sake, which is false. 4. Therefore this faith is deceitful, even such as will leave thee under wrath, in the day of God Almighty. For true Justifying faith puts the soul (as sensible of its lost condition by the Law) upon flying for refuge unto Christs Righteousness: (which Righteousness of his is not an act of grace, by which he maketh for Justification, *thy* obedience accepted of God; but *his* personal obedience to the Law in doing and suffering for us, what that required at our hands.) This righteousness, I say, true faith accepteth; under the skirt of which the soul being shrouded, and by it, presented as spotless before God, it is accepted, and acquit from condemnation.

The faith of Ignorance.

Ign. What! would you have us trust to what Christ in his own person has done without us? This conceit would loosen the reins of our lust, and tolerate us to live as we list. For what matter how we live if we may be justified by Christs personal righteousness from all, when we believe it?

Chr. Ignorance is thy name, and as thy name is, so art thou; even this thy answer demonstrateth what I say. *Ignorant* thou art of what Justifying righteousness is, and, as *ignorant* how to secure thy Soul through the faith of it from the heavy wrath of God. Yea, thou also art *ignorant* of the true effects of saving faith in this righteousness of Christ, which is to bow and win over the heart to God in Christ, to love his Name, his Word, Ways and People, and not as thou *ignorantly* imaginest.

Hope. Ask him if ever he had Christ revealed to him from heaven?

Ign. *What? you are a man for Revelations! I believe that what both you, and all the rest of you say about that matter, is but the fruit of distracted brains.*

Ignorance *jangles with them.*

Hope. Why man! Christ is so hid in God from the natural apprehensions of the flesh, that he cannot by any man be savingly known, unless God the Father reveals him to them.

Ign. *That is your Faith, but not mine; yet mine, I doubt not, is as good as yours: though I have not in my head so many whimsies as you.*

He speaks reproachfully of what he knows not.

Chr. Give me leave to put in a word: You ought not so slightly to speak of this matter: For this I will boldly affirm (even as my good companion hath done) that no man can know Jesus Christ but by the revelation of the Father; yea, and faith too, by which the soul layeth hold upon Christ (if it be right) must be wrought by the exceeding greatness of his Mighty Power; the working of which Faith, I perceive, poor *Ignorance*, thou art ignorant of. Be awakened then, see thine own wretchedness, and fly to the Lord Jesus; and by his righteousness, which is the righteousness of God, (for he himself is God) thou shalt be delivered from condemnation.

Mat. 11. 28. 1 Cor. 11. 3. Eph. 1. 18, 19.

Ignor. You go so fast, I cannot keep pace with you: do you go on before, I must stay a while behind.

The Talk broke up.

Then they said;

Well, Ignorance, *wilt thou yet foolish be,*
To slight good Counsel, ten times given thee?
And if thou yet refuse it, thou shalt know
E're long the evil of thy doing so.
Remember, Man, in time, stoop, do not fear,
Good counsel taken well, saves: therefore hear:
But if thou yet shalt slight it, thou wilt be
The loser (Ignorance) *I'll warrant thee.*

Then *Christian* addressed thus himself to his fellow.

Chr. Well, come my good *Hopeful*, I perceive that thou and I must walk by our selves again.

So I saw in my Dream, that they went on a pace before,

and *Ignorance* he came hobling after. Then said *Christian* to his Companion, *It pities me much for this poor Man: it will certainly go ill with him at last.*

Hope. Alas, there are abundance in our Town in this condition; whole Families, yea, whole Streets, (and that of Pilgrims too;) and if there be so many in our parts, how many think you must there be in the place where he was born?

Chr. *Indeed the word saith,* He hath blinded their eyes, lest they should see, *&c.*

But now we are by our selves, what do you think of such Men? have they at no time, think you, convictions of sin, and so consequently fear that their state is dangerous?

Hope. Nay, do you answer that question your self, for you are the elder man.

Chr. *Then I say, sometimes (as I think) they may, but they being naturally ignorant, understand not that such convictions tend to their good; and therefore they do desperately seek to stifle them, and presumptuously continue to flatter themselves in the way of their own hearts.*

Hope. I do believe, as you say, that fear tends much to mens good, and to make them right, at their beginning to go on Pilgrimage.

The good use of fear.

Chr. *Without all doubt it doth, if it be right; For so says the Word,* The fear of the Lord is the beginning of Wisdom.

Job 28. 29. Psal. 111. 10. Prov. 17. ch. 9, 10.

Hope. How will you describe right fear?

Chr. *True or right fear is discovered by three things.*

Right Fears.

1. By its rise. It is caused by saving convictions for sin.

2. It driveth the Soul to lay fast hold of Christ for Salvation.

3. It begetteth and continueth in the Soul a great Reverence of God, his Word, and Ways, keeping it tender, and making it afraid to turn from them, to the right hand, or to the left, to any thing that may dishonour God, break its Peace, grieve the Spirit or cause the enemy to speak reproachfully.

Hope. Well said, I believe you have said the truth. Are we now almost got past the Inchanted Ground?

Chr. *Why art thou weary of this discourse?*

Hope. No verily, but that I would know where we are.

Chr. *We have not now above two Miles further to go thereon. But let us return to our matter.* **Now the ignorant know not that such convictions that tend to put them in fear, are for their good, and therefore they seek to stifle them.*

Why ignorant Persons stifle convictions.

* *In general.*

Hope. How do they seek to stifle them?

Chr. *1. They think that those fears are wrought by the Devil (though indeed they are wrought of God) and thinking so, they resist them, as things that directly tend to their Overthrow. 2. They also think that these fears tend to the spoiling of their Faith, when, (alas for them, poor men that they are they have none at all) and therefore they harden their hearts against them. 3. They presume they ought not to fear, and therefore, in despite of them, wax presumptuously confident. 4. They see that those fears tend to take away from them their pitiful old self-holiness, and therefore they resist them with all their might.

* 2. *Particular.*

Hope. I know something of this my self; for before I knew my self it was so with me.

Chr. *Well, we will leave at this time our Neighbour* Ignorance *by himself, and fall upon another profitable question.*

Hope. With all my heart, but you shall still begin.

Chr. *Well then, Did you not know about ten years ago, one* Temporary *in your parts, who was a forward man in Religion then?*

Talk about one Temporary.

Hope. Know him! yes, he dwelt in *Graceless*, a Town about two miles off of *Honesty*, and he dwelt next door to one *Turnback*.

Where he dwelt.

Chr. *Right, he dwelt under the same roof with him, Well, that man was much awakened once*. I believe that then he had some sight of his sins, and of the wages that were due thereto.*

* *He was towardly once.*

Hope. I am of your mind; for (my house not being above three miles from him) he would oft times come to me, and that with many tears. Truly I pitied the man, and was not altogether without hope of him, but one may see, it is not every one that cries, *Lord, Lord*.

Chr. *He told me once, That he was resolved to go on*

Pilgrimage, as we go now ; but all of a sudden he grew acquainted with one Saveself, *and then he became a stranger to me.*

Hope. Now since we are talking about him, let us a little enquire into the reason of the sudden back-sliding of him and such others.

Chr. *It may be very profitable, but do you begin.*

Hope. Well then, there are in my Judgment four reasons for it.

Reasons why towardly ones go back.

1. Though the Consciences of such men are awakened, yet their minds are not changed : therefore when the power of guilt weareth away, that which provoketh them to be religious ceaseth : Wherefore they naturally return to their own course again ; even as we see the Dog that is sick of what he hath eaten, so long as his Sickness prevails, he vomits and casts up all : not that he doth this of a free mind (if we may say a Dog has a mind) but because it troubleth his stomach ; but now when his sickness is over and so his stomach eased, his desires being not at all alienated from his vomit, he turns him about, and licks up all. And so it is true which is written, *The Dog is turned to his own vomit again.* Thus, I say, being hot for Heaven, by virtue only of the sense and fear of the torments of Hell, as their sense of Hell and the fears of damnation chills and cools, so their desires for Heaven ; and Salvation cool also. So then it comes to pass, that when their guilt and fear is gone, their desires for Heaven and Salvation cool also. So then it comes to pass, that when their guilt and fear is gone, their desires for Heaven and Happines die, and they return to their course again.

2 Pet. 2. 22.

2. Another reason is, they have slavish fears that do overmaster them ; I speak now of the fears that they have of men : *For the fear of men bringeth a snare.* So then, though they seem to be hot for heaven, so long as the flames of Hell are about their ears, yet when that terror is a little over, they betake themselves to second thoughts, namely, this 'tis good to be wise, and not to run (for they know not what) the hazzard of losing all ; or at least, of bringing themselves into unavoidable and unnecessary troubles, and so they fall in with the World again.

Prov. 29. 25.

3. The shame that attends Religion, lies also as a block

in their way; they are proud and haughty, and Religion in their eye is low and contemptible: Therefore when they have lost their sense of Hell, and Wrath to come, they return again to their former course.

4. *Guilt*, and to meditate terror, are grievous to them; they like not to see their misery before they come into it: Though perhaps the sight of it first, if they loved that sight might make them fly whither the righteous fly and are safe; but because they do, as I hinted before, even shun the thoughts of guilt and terror: Therefore when once they are rid of their awakenings about the terrors and wrath of God, they harden their hearts gladly, and chuse such ways, as will harden them more and more.

Chr. *You are pretty near the business, for the bottom of all is, for want of a change in their mind and will. And therefore they are but like the Felon that standeth before the Judge, he quakes and trembles, and seems to repent most heartily but the bottom of all is, the fear of the Halter, not that he hath any detestation of the offences, as is evident, because, let but this man have his liberty and he will be a Thief, and so a Rogue still, whereas, if his mind was changed, he would be otherwise.*

Hope. Now I have shewed you the reasons of their going back, do you shew me the manner thereof.

Chr. *So I will willingly.*

How the Apostate goes back.

1. They drew off their thoughts all that they may, from the remembrance of God, Death and Judgment to come.

2. Then they cast off by degrees private Duties, as Closet-prayer, curbing their lusts, Watching, sorrow for Sin, and the like.

3. Then they shun the company of lively and warm Christians.

4. After that they grow cold to publick Duty, as Hearing, Reading, Godly conference, and the like.

5. Then they begin to pick holes, as we say, in the coats of some of the Godly, and that develishly, that they may have a seeming colour to throw Religion (for the sake of some infirmity they have spied in them) behind their backs.

6. Then they begin to adhere to, and associate themselves with carnal, loose and wanton men.

7. Then they give way to carnal, and wanton discourses in secret; and glad are they if they can see such things in any that are counted honest, that they may the more boldly do it through their example.

8. After this, they begin to play with little sins openly.

9. And then being hardened, they shew themselves as they are. Thus being lanched again into the gulf of misery, unless a miracle of Grace prevent it, they everlastingly perish in their own deceivings.

Now I saw in my Dream, that by this time the Pilgrims were got over the Inchanted ground, and entering Isa. 62. 4. Cant. 2. 10, 11, 12. into the Country of *Beulah* whose Air was very sweet and pleasant, the way lying directly through it, they solaced themselves there for a season. Yea here they heard continually the singing of Birds, and saw every day the flowers appear in the Earth; and heard the voice of the Turtle in the Land. In this Country the Sun shineth night and day; wherefore this was beyond the Valley of the *shadow of Death*, and also out of the reach of *Giant Despair*, neither could they from this place so much as see *Doubting-Castle*. Here they were within sight of the City they were going to; also here met them some of the Inhabitants thereof. *Angels.* For in this Land the shining Ones commonly walked, because it was upon the borders of Heaven. In this Land also the Contract between the Bride and the Bridegroom was renewed: yea, here, Isa. 62. 5. ver. 8. *as the Bridegroom rejoiceth over the Bride, so did their God rejoice over them.* Here they had no want of Corn and Wine; for in this place they met abundance of what they had sought for in all their Pilgrimages. Here they heard Ver. 11. voices from out of the City, loud voices, saying, *Say ye to the Daughter of* Zion, *Behold thy Salvation cometh, behold his reward is with him.* Here all the Inhabitants Ver. 12. of the Country called them *the Holy People, the Redeemed of the Lord*; *sought out*, &c.

Now as they walked in this Land, they had more rejoicing than in parts more remote from the Kingdom, to which they were bound; and drawing near to the City, they had yet a more perfect view thereof; it was builded of Pearls and precious Stones; also the streets thereof were paved with Gold;

so that by reason of the natural glory of the City, and the reflection of the Sun-beams upon it, *Christian*, with desire fell sick, *Hopeful* also had a fit or two of the same Disease: Wherefore here they lay by it a while, crying out because of their pangs; *If you see my Beloved, tell him that I am sick of love.*

But being a little strengthned, and better able to bear their sickness, they walked on their way; and came yet nearer and nearer, where were Orchards, Vineyards and Gardens, and their Gates opened into the Highway. Now as they came up to these places, behold the Gardner stood in the way; to whom the Pilgrims said, whose goodly Vineyards and Gardens are these? He answered, They are the Kings, and are planted here for his own delights, and also for the solace of Pilgrims; So the Gardner had them into the Vineyards, and bid them refresh themselves with the dainties; he also shewed them there the Kings Walks and the Arbours where he delighted to be: And here they tarried and slept.

Deut. 23. 24.

Now I beheld in my Dream, that they talked more in their sleep at this time, than ever they did in all their Journey; and being in a muse thereabout, the Gardner said even to me, wherefore musest thou at the matter? It is the nature of the fruit of the Grapes of these Vineyards to go down so sweetly, as to cause the lips of them that are asleep to speak.

So I saw that when they awoke, they addressed themselves to go up to the City. But as I said, the reflections of the Sun upon the City (for the City was pure Gold) was so extreamly glorious, that they could not, as yet with open face behold it, but through an *Instrument* made for that purpose. So I saw, that as they went on, there met them two men, in Raiment that shone like Gold, also their faces shone as the light.

Rev. 21. 28.
1 Cor. 3. 18.

These Men asked the Pilgrims whence they came? and they told them. They also asked them, where they had lodged, what difficulties, and dangers, what comforts, and pleasures they had met in the way? and they told them. Then said the men that met them, You have but two difficulties more, to meet with, and then you are in the City.

Christian then and his Companion asked the men to go along with them, so they told them they would, but said they, you must obtain it by your own Faith. So I saw in my Dream that they went on together till they came in sight of the Gate.

Now I further saw, that betwixt them and the Gate was a River, but there was no Bridge to go over; the River was very deep: at the sight therefore of this River, the Pilgrims were much stunned, but the men that went with them, said, you must go through, or you cannot come at the Gate.

Death.

The Pilgrims then began to enquire if there was no other way to the Gate; to which they answered, Yes, but there hath not any save two, to wit, *Enoch* and *Elijah*, been permitted to tread that path, since the foundation of the World, nor shall, until the last Trumpet shall sound. The Pilgrims then, especially *Christian*, began to despond in his mind, and looked this way and that, but no way could be found by them, by which they might escape the River. Then they asked the men if the waters were all of a depth? they said no; yet they could not help them in that case; for, said they, *You shall find it deeper, or shallower, as you Believe in the King of the place.*

Death is not welcome to Nature, though by it we pass out of this World into Glory.

1 Cor. 15. 51, 52.

Angels help us not comfortably through Death.

They then addressed themselves to the Water, and entering, *Christian* began to sink, and crying out to his good friend *Hopeful*, he said, I sink in deep waters, the Billows go over my head, all his Waves go over me, *Selah.*

Then said the other, be of good chear my Brother, I feel the bottom, and it is good. Then said *Christian*, Ah my friend, the sorrows of Death hath compassed me about, I shall not see the Land that flows with Milk and Honey. And with that a great darkness and horror fell upon *Christian*, so that he could not see before him. Also here he in great measure lost his senses, so that he could neither remember nor orderly talk of any of those sweet refreshments that he had met with in the way of his Pilgrimage. But all the words that he spake still tended to discover that he had horror of mind, and heart-fears that he should die in that River, and never obtain entrance in at the Gate. Here also, as they that stood by perceived, he was much

Christian's conflict at the hour of Death.

in the troublesome thoughts of the sins that he had committed, both since and before he began to be a Pilgrim. 'Twas also observ'd, that he was troubled with apparitions of Hobgoblins and evil Spirits; for ever and anon he would intimate so much by words. *Hopeful* therefore here had much ado to keep his Brother's Head above water, yea sometimes he would be quite gone down, and then, 'ere a while would rise up again half dead. *Hopeful* also would endeavour to comfort him, saying Brother, I see the Gate and Men standing by to receive us, but *Christian* would answer, 'Tis you, 'tis you they wait for; You have been *Hopeful* ever since I knew you; and so have you, said he to *Christian.* Ah Brother, said he, surely, If I was right, he would now arise to help me, but for my sins he hath brought me into the Snare, and hath left me. Then said *Hopeful*, My Brother, you have quite forgot the Text, where it is said of the wicked, *There is no band in their death, but their strength is firm, they are not troubled as other men, neither are they plagued like other men.* These troubles and distresses that you go through in these Waters, are no sign that God hath forsaken you, but are sent to try you, whether you will call to mind that which heretofore you have received of his goodness, and live upon him in your distresses.

Then I saw in my Dream that *Christian* was in a muse a while, to whom also *Hopeful* added this word, *Be of good cheer, Jesus Christ maketh thee whole.* And with that *Christian* brake out with a loud voice, Oh I see him again! and he tells me, *When thou passest through the waters, I will be with thee, and through the Rivers they shall not overflow thee.* Then they both took courage, and the Enemy was after that as still as a stone, until they were gone over. *Christian* therefore presently found ground to stand upon, and so it followed, that the rest of the River was but shallow; Thus they got over. Now upon the bank of the River on the other side, they saw the two shining men again, who there waited for them. Wherefore being come out of the River, they saluted them saying, *We are Ministring Spirits, sent forth to Minister for those that shall be heirs of Salvation.* Thus they went along towards the

Christian delivered from his tears in Death.

Isa. 40. 2.

The Angels do wait for them so soon as they are passed out of this world. They have put off mortality.

Gate, now you must note that the City stood upon a mighty hill, but the Pilgrims went up that hill with ease, because they had these two men to lead them up by the arms; also they had left their *mortal* Garments behind them in the River: for though they went in with them, they came out without them. They therefore went up here with much agility and speed, though the foundation upon which the City was framed, was higher than the clouds. They therefore went up through the Region of the Air, sweetly talking as they went, being comforted, because they safely got over the River, and had such glorious Companions to attend them.

The talk that they had with the shining Ones was about the glory of the place, who told them, that the beauty and glory of it was inexpressible. There, said they,
Heb. 12. 22, 23, 24. is the Mount *Sion*, the heavenly *Jerusalem*, the
Rev. 2. 7. innumerable company of *Angels*, and the Spirits
Rev. 3. 4. of Just men made perfect. You are going now, said they, to the Paradise of God, wherein you shall see the Tree of Life, and eat of the never fading fruits thereof. And when you come there, you shall have white Robes given you, and your walk and talk shall be every day with the King, even all the days of eternity.
Rev. 22. 7. There you shall not see again, such things as you saw when you were in the lower Region upon the earth, to wit, sorrow, sickness, affliction, and death; *for*
Isa. 57. 1, 2. Isa. 65. 14. *the former things are passed away*. You are going now to *Abraham*, to *Isaac* and *Jacob*, and to the Prophets; men that God hath taken away from the evil to come, and that are now resting upon their Beds, each one walking in his Righteousness. The men then asked, what must we do in the holy place. To whom it was answered, you must there receive the comforts of all your toil, and have joy for all your sorrow; you must reap what
Gal. 6. 7. you have sown, even the fruit of all your Prayers and Tears, and Sufferings for the King by the way. In that
Joh. 3. 2. place you must wear Crowns of Gold, and enjoy the perpetual sight and visions of the *Holy One*, *for there you shall see him as he is*. There also you shall serve him continually with praise, with shouting and thanksgiving, whom you desired to serve in the World, though with much

difficulty, because of the infirmity of your flesh. There your eyes shall be delighted with seeing, and your ears with hearing the pleasant voice of the mighty One. There you shall enjoy your friends again; that are gone thither before you; and there you shall with joy receive, even every one that follows into the Holy place after you. There also you shall be cloathed with Glory and Majesty, and put into an equipage fit to ride out with the King of Glory. When he shall come with sound of Trumpet in the Clouds, as upon the Wings of the Wind, you shall come with him, and when he shall sit upon the Throne of Judgment, you shall sit by him; yea, and when he shall pass Sentence upon all the workers of iniquity, let them be Angels or men, you also shall have a voice in that Judgment, because they were his and your enemies. Also when he shall again return to the City, you shall go too, with sound of Trumpet, and be ever with him.

1 Thes. 4. 13, 14, 15, 16. Jud. 14. Dan. 7. 9, 10. 1 Cor. 6. 2, 3.

Now while they were thus drawing towards the Gate, behold a company of the Heavenly Host came out to meet them: To whom it was said, by the other two shining Ones; These are the men that have loved our Lord, when they were in the World: and that have left all for his holy Name, and he hath sent us to fetch them, and we have brought them thus far on their desired Journey, that they may go in and look their Redeemer in the face with Joy. Then the Heavenly Host gave a great shout, saying, *Blessed are they that are called to the Marriage Supper of the Lamb.* There came out also at this time to meet them, several of the Kings Trumpeters, cloathed in white and shining Raiment, who with melodious noises, and loud, made even the Heavens to echo with their sound. These Trumpeters saluted *Christian* and his Fellow with ten thousand welcomes from the World: and this they did with shouting and sound of Trumpet.

Rev. 19.

This done, they compassed them round on every side: Some went before, some behind, and some on the right hand, some on the left (as it were to guard them through the upper Regions) continually sounding as they went, with melodious noise, in notes on high; so that the very sight was to them that could behold it, as if Heaven it self was come down to meet them. Thus therefore they walked on together, and as they walked, ever and anon these Trumpeters even with joyful sound, would by mixing their Musick, with looks and gestures, still signifie to *Christian* and his Brother, how welcome they were into their company, and with what gladness they came to meet them: and now were these two men, as it were in Heaven, before they came at it; being swallowed up with the sight of Angels, and with hearing of their melodious notes. Here also they had the City it self in view, and they thought they heard all the Bells therein to ring, to welcome them thereto: but above all, the warm and joyful thoughts that they had about their own dwelling there, with such company, and that for ever and ever; Oh! by what tongue or pen can their glorious joy be expressed: Thus they came up to the Gate.

Now when they were come up to the Gate, there were written over it in Letters of Gold, *Blessed are they that do his Commandments, that they may have right to the Tree of Life; and may enter in through the Gates into the City.*

Rev. 22. 14.

Then I saw in my Dream, that the shining men bid them call at the Gate; the which when they did, some from above looked over the Gate, to wit, *Enoch*, *Moses* and *Elijah*, &c. to whom it was said, These Pilgrims are come from the City of *Destruction*, for the love that they bare to the King of this place: and then the Pilgrims gave in unto them each man his Certificate, which they had received in the beginning; those therefore were carried in to the King, who when he had read them, said, where are the men? to whom it was answered, they are standing without the Gate. The King then commanded to open the Gate, *That the righteous Nation*, said he, *that keepeth Truth, may enter in.*

Isa. 26. 2.

Now I saw in my Dream, that these two men went in at the Gate; and lo, as they entered, they were transfigured, and they had Raiment put on that shone like Gold. There was also that met them with harps and crowns, and gave them to them; the harps to praise withal, and the Crowns in token of honour: Then I heard in my Dream, that all the Bells in the City rang again for joy; and that it was said unto them, *Enter ye into the joy of our Lord.* I also heard the men themselves, that they sang with a loud voice, saying, *Blessing, Honour, Glory and Power, be to him that sitteth upon the Throne, and to the Lamb for ever and ever.*

Rev. 5. 13, 14.

Now just as the Gates were opened to let in the men, I look'd in after them; and behold, the City shone like the Sun, the Streets also were paved with Gold, and in them walked many men with crowns on their heads, Palms in their hands and golden harps to sing praises withal.

There were also of them that had wings, and they answered one another without intermission, saying *holy*, *holy*, *holy is the Lord.* And after that, they shut up the Gates, which when I had seen I wished myself among them.

Now while I was gazing upon all these things, I turned my head to look back and saw *Ignorance* come up to the River-side: but he soon got over, and that without half that difficulty which the other two men met with. For it happened, that there was then in that place one *Vain-hope*, a Ferry-man, that with his *Boat* helped him over; so he, as the other, I saw did ascend the hill to come up to the Gate, only he came alone; neither did any man meet him with the least encouragement. When he was come up to the Gate, he looked up to the Writing that was above, and then began to knock, supposing that entrance should have been quickly administred to him: But he was asked by the men that looked over the top of the Gate, whence come you? and what would you have? He answered, I have eat and drank in the presence of the King, and he has taught in our Streets. Then they asked him for his certificate, that they might go in and shew it to the King; so he fumbled in his bosom for one, and found none: Then said they, have you none? But the man answered never a word. So they told the King, but he would not come down to see him, but commanded the two shining Ones that conducted *Christian* and *Hopeful* to the City, to go out, and take *Ignorance*, and bind him hand and foot, and have him away. Then they took him up and carried him through the Air, to the door that I saw in the side of the hill, and put him in there. Then I saw that there was a way to hell, even from the Gates of Heaven, as well as from the City of Destruction. So I awoke, and beheld it was a Dream.

Ignorance comes up to the River.

Vain hope does ferry him over.

The Conclusion.

NOw Reader I have told my Dream to thee;
See if thou canst interpret it to me.
Or to thy self, or Neighbours, but take heed
Of Mis-enterpreting: for that, instead,
Of doing good, will but thy self abuse.
By Mis-interpreting, evil ensues.
Take heed also, that thou be not extream,
In playing with the out-side of my dream:
Nor let my figure, or similitude,
Put thee into a laughter, or a feud,
Leave this for Boys and Fools, *but as for thee,*
Do thou the substance of my matter see.
Put by the curtains; look within my Veil;
Turn up my Metaphors, and do not fail;
There, if thou seekest them such things to find,
As will be helpful to an honest mind.
What of my Dross *thou findest there, be bold*
To throw away, but yet preserve the Gold,
What if my Gold be wrapped up in Ore?
None throws away the Apple for the Core.
But If thou shalt cast all away as Vain,
I know not but 'twill make me dream again.

THE END.

THE
Pilgrim's Progress.
FROM
THIS WORLD
TO
That which is to come:
The Second Part.
Delivered under the Similitude of a
DREAM.

Wherein is set forth

The manner of the setting out of *Christian*'s Wife and Children, their Dangerous JOURNEY,

AND

Safe Arrival at the Desired Countrey.

By *JOHN BUNYAN*.

I have used Similitudes, Hos. 12. 10.

Licensed and Entred according to Order.

London, Printed for *Nath. Ponder* at the *Peacock* in the *Poultry*, near the Church, 1687.

THE

Authors Way of Sending forth HIS Second Part OF THE PILGRIM.

GO, *now my little Book, to every place,*
Where my first Pilgrim *has but shewn his Face,*
Call at their door: If any say, who's there?
Then answer thou, Christiana is here.
If they bid thee come in, *then enter thou*
With all thy boys. And then, as thou know'st how,
Tell who they are, also from whence they came,
Perhaps they'l know them, by their looks, or name:
But if they should not, ask them yet again
If formerly they did not Entertain
One Christian *a Pilgrim; If they say*
They did: And was delighted in his way:
Then let them know that those related were
Unto him: Yea, his Wife and Children are.
Tell them that they have left their House and Home,
Are turned Pilgrims, seek a World to come:
That they have *met with hardships in the way,*
That they do *meet with troubles night and day;*
That they have trod on Serpents, fought with Devils,

Have also overcome a many evils.
Yea tell them also of the next, who have
Of love to Pilgrimage *been stout and brave*
Defenders of that way, and how they still
Refuse this World, to do their Fathers will.
Go, tell them also of those dainty things,
That Pilgrimage *unto the* Pilgrim *brings,*
Let them acquainted be, too, how they are
Beloved of their King, under his care;
What goodly Mansions *for them he provides,*
Tho they meet with rough Winds, and swelling Tides.
How brave a calm they will enjoy at last,
Who to *their Lord, and* by *his ways hold fast.*
Perhaps with heart and hand they will imbrace
Thee, as they did my firstling, and will Grace
Thee, and thy fellows with such chear and fair,
As shew will, they of Pilgrims *lovers are.*

1 *Object.*

But how if they will not believe of me
That I am truly thine, 'cause some there be
That Counterfeit the Pilgrim, and his name,
Seek by disguise to seem the very same.
And by that means have wrought themselves into
The Hands and Houses of I know not who.

Answer.

'Tis true, some have of late, to Counterfeit
My *Pilgrim, to their own, my Title set;*
Yea others, half my Name and Title too;
Have stitched to their Book, to make them do;
But yet they by their Features *do declare*
Themselves not mine to be, whose ere they are.
If such thou meetst with, then thine only way
Before them all, is, to say out thy say,
In thine own native Language, which no man
Now useth, nor with ease dissemble can.
If after all, they still of you shall doubt,
Thinking that you like Gipsies *go about,*

In naughty-wise the Countrey to defile,
Or that you seek good People to beguile
With things unwarrantable: Send for me
And I will Testifie, you Pilgrims *be;*
Yea, I will Testifie that only you
My Pilgrims *are; And that alone will do.*

2 *Object.*

But yet, perhaps, I may enquire for him,
Of those that wish him Damned life and limb,
What shall I do, when I at such a door,
For *Pilgrims* ask, and they shall rage the more?

Answer.

Fright not thy self my Book, for such Bugbears
Are nothing else but ground for groundless fears,
My Pilgrims *Book has travel'd Sea and Land,*
Yet could I never come to understand,
That it was slighted, or turn'd out of Door
By any Kingdom, were they Rich or Poor.
In France *and* Flanders *where men kill each other*
My Pilgrim *is esteem'd a Friend, a Brother.*
In Holland *too, 'tis said, as I am told,*
My Pilgrim *is with some, worth more than Gold.*
Highlanders, *and* Wild-Irish *can agree,*
My Pilgrim *should familiar with them be.*
'Tis in New-England *under such advance,*
Receives there so much loving Countenance,
As to be Trim'd, new Cloth'd & deckt with Gems,
That it might shew its Features, and its Limbs,
Yet more; so comely doth my Pilgrim *walk,*
That of him thousands daily Sing and talk.
If you draw nearer home, it will appear
My Pilgrim *knows no ground of shame, or fear;*
City, and Countrey will him Entertain,
With welcome Pilgrim. *Yea, they can't refrain*
From smiling, if my Pilgrim *be but by,*
Or shews his head in any Company.

Brave Gallants do my Pilgrim *hug and love,*
Esteem it much, yea value it above
Things of a greater bulk, yea, with delight,
Say my Larks leg *is better then a* Kite.
Young Ladys, and young Gentle-women too,
Do no small kindness to my Pilgrim *shew;*
Their Cabinets, their Bosoms, and their Hearts
My Pilgrim *has, 'cause he to them imparts*
His pretty riddles in such wholsome strains
As yields them profit double to their pains
Of reading. Yea, I think I may be bold
To say some prize him far above their Gold.
The very Children that do walk the street,
If they do but my holy Pilgrim *meet,*
Salute him will, will wish him well and say,
He is the only Stripling *of the Day.*
They that have never seen him, yet admire
What they have heard of him, and much desire
To have his Company, and hear him tell
Those Pilgrim *storyes which he knows so well.*
Yea, some who did not love him at the first,
But call'd him Fool, *and* Noddy, *say they must*
Now they have seen & heard *him, him commend,*
And to those whom they love, they do him send.
Wherefore my Second Part, *thou needst not be*
Afraid to shew thy Head: None can hurt thee,
That wish but well to him, that went before,
'Cause thou com'st after with a Second store,
Of things as good, as rich, as profitable,
For Young, for Old, for Stag'ring and for stable.

3 *Object.*

But some there be that say he laughs too loud;
And some do say his Head is in a Cloud.
Some say, his Words and Storys are so dark,
They know not how, by them, to find his mark.

Answer.

One may (I think) say both his laughs & cryes,
May well be guest at by his watry Eyes.
Some things are of that Nature as to make
Ones fancie Checkle while his Heart doth ake,
When Jacob *saw his* Rachel *with the Sheep,*
He did at the same time both kiss and weep.
Whereas some say a Cloud is in his Head,
That doth but shew how Wisdom's covered
With its own mantles: And to stir the mind
To a search after what it fain would find,
Things that seem to be hid in words obscure,
Do but the Godly mind the more allure;
To study what those Sayings should contain,
That speak to us in such a Cloudy strain.
I also know, a dark Similitude
Will on the Fancie more it self intrude,
And will stick faster in the Heart and Head,
Than things from Similies not borrowed.
Wherefore, my Book, let no discouragement
Hinder thy travels. Behold, thou art sent
To Friends, not foes: to Friends that will give place
To thee, thy Pilgrims, *and thy words imbrace.*
Besides, what my first Pilgrim *left conceal'd,*
Thou my brave Second Pilgrim *hast reveal'd,*
What Christian *left lock't up and went his way;*
Sweet Christiana *opens with her Key.*

4 *Object.*

But some love not the method of your first,
Romance they count it, throw't away as dust,
If I should meet with such, what should I say?
Must I slight them as they slight me, or nay?

Answer.

My Christiana, *if with such thou meet,*
By all means in all Loving-wise, them greet;
Render them not reviling for revile:
But if they frown, I prethee on them smile,
Perhaps 'tis Nature, or some ill report
Has made them thus *despise, or* thus *retort.*
Some love no Cheese, some love no Fish, & some
Love not their Friends, nor their own House or home;
Some start at Pigg, slight Chicken, love not Fowl,
More than they love a Cuckow or an Owl,
Leave such, my Christiana, *to their choice,*
And seek those, who to find thee will rejoyce;
By no means strive, but in humble wise,
Present thee to them in thy Pilgrims *guise.*
Go then, my little Book and shew to all
That entertain, and bid thee welcome shall,
What thou shalt keep close, shut up from the rest,
And wish what thou shalt shew them may be blest
To them for good, may make them chuse to be
Pilgrims, better by far, then thee or me.
Go then, I say, tell all men who thou art,
Say, I am Christiana, *and my part*
Is now with my four Sons, to tell you what
It is for men to take a Pilgrims *lot;*
Go also tell them who, *and what they be,*
That now do go on Pilgrimage *with thee;*
Say, here's my neighbour Mercy, *she is one,*
That has long-time with me a Pilgrim *gone;*
Come see her in her Virgin *Face, and learn*
Twixt Idle ones, and Pilgrims *to discern.*
Yea let young Damsels learn of her to prize,
The World which is to come, in any wise;
When little Tripping *Maidens follow God,*
And leave old doting Sinners to his Rod;
'Tis like those Days wherein the young ones cry'd
Hosannah *to whom old ones did deride.*

Next tell them of old Honest, *who you found*
With his white hairs treading the Pilgrims ground;
Yea, tell them how plain hearted this *man was,*
How after his good Lord he bare his Cross:
Perhaps with some gray Head this may prevail,
With Christ to fall in Love, and Sin bewail.
Tell them also how Master Fearing *went*
On Pilgrimage, and how the time he spent
In Solitariness, with Fears and Cries,
And how at last, he won the Joyful Prize.
He was *a good man, though much down in Spirit,*
He is *a good Man, and doth Life inherit.*
Tell them of Master Feeblemind *also,*
Who, not before, but still behind would go;
Show them also how he had like been slain,
And how one Great-Heart *did his life regain:*
This man was true of Heart, tho weak in grace,
One might true Godliness read in his Face.
Then tell them of Master Ready-to-halt,
A Man with Crutches, but much without fault:
Tell them how Master Feeblemind, *and he*
Did love, and in Opinions *much agree.*
And let all know, tho weakness was their chance,
Yet sometimes one could Sing *the other* Dance.
Forget not Master Valiant-for-the-Truth,
That Man of courage, tho a very Youth.
Tell every one his Spirit was so stout,
No Man could ever make him face about,
And how Great-Heart, *and he could not forbear*
But put down Doubting Castle, slay Despair.
Overlook not Master Despondency.
Nor Much-a-fraid, *his Daughter, tho they lye*
Under such Mantles as may make them look
(With some) as if their God had them forsook.
They softly went, but sure, and at the end,
Found that the Lord of Pilgrims *was their Friend.*
When thou hast told the World of all these things,
Then turn about, my book, and touch these strings,
Which, if but *touched will such Musick make,*
They'l make a Cripple dance, a Gyant quake.

Those Riddles that lie couch't within thy breast,
Freely propound, expound: and for the rest
Of thy mysterious lines, let them remain,
For those whose nimble Fancies shall them gain.
Now may this little Book a blessing be,
To those that love this little Book and me,
And may its buyer have no cause to say,
His Money is but lost or thrown away,
Yea may this Second Pilgrim *yield that Fruit,*
As may with each good Pilgrims *fancie sute,*
And may it perswade some that go astray,
To turn their Foot and Heart to the right way.

Is the Hearty Prayer

of the Author

JOHN BUNYAN.

THE

Pilgrims Progress

In the Similitude of a

DREAM.

The Second Part.

COurteous Companions, sometime since, to tell you my Dream that I had of *Christian* the Pilgrim, and of his dangerous Journey toward the Celestial Countrey was pleasant to me, and profitable to you. I told you then also what I saw concerning his *Wife* and *Children*, and how unwilling they were to go with him on Pilgrimage: Insomuch that he was forced to go on his Progress without them, for he durst not run the danger of that destruction which he feared would come by staying with them in the City of Destruction: Wherefore, as I then shewed you, he left them and departed.

Now it hath so happened, thorough the Multiplicity of Business, that I have been much hindred, and kept back from my wonted Travels into those Parts whence he went, and so could not till now obtain an opportunity to make farther enquiry after whom he left behind, that I might give you an account of them. But having had some concerns that way of late, I went down again thitherward. Now, having taken up my Lodgings in a Wood about a mile off the Place, as I slept, I dreamed again.

And as I was in my Dream, behold, an aged Gentleman came by where I lay; and because he was to go some part of the way that I was travelling, me thought I got up and went with him. So as we walked, and as Travellers usually do, I was as if we fell into discourse, and our talk happened to be about *Christian* and his Travels: For thus I began with the Old-man.

Sir, said I, *what Town is that there below, that lieth on the left hand of our way?*

Then said Mr. *Sagasity*, for that was his name, it is the City of *Destruction*, a populous place, but possessed with a very ill conditioned, and idle sort of People.

I thought that was that City, quoth I, *I went once my self through that Town, and therefore know that this report you give of it is true.*

Sag. Too true, I wish I could speak truth in speaking better of them that dwell therein.

Well, Sir, quoth I, *Then I perceive you to be a well meaning man: and so one that takes pleasure to hear and tell of that which is good; pray did you never hear what happened to a man sometime ago in this Town (whose name was* Christian) *that went on Pilgrimage up toward the higher Regions?*

Sag. Hear of him! Aye, and I also heard of the Molestations, Troubles, Wars, Captivities, Cries, Groans, Frights and Fears that he met with, and had in his Journey, besides, I must tell you, all our Countrey rings of him, there are but few Houses that have heard of him and his doings, but have sought after and got the *Records* of his Pilgrimage; yea, I think I may say, that that his hazzardous Journey has got a many well-wishers to his wayes: For though when he was here, he was *Fool* in every mans mouth, yet now he is gone, he is highly commended of all. For 'tis said he lives bravely where he is: Yea, many of them that are resolved never to run his hazzards, yet have their mouths water at his gains.

Christians *are well spoken of when gone, tho' called Fools while they are here.*

They may, quoth I, *well think, if they think any thing that is true, that he liveth well where he is, for he now lives at, and in the Fountain of Life, and has what he has without Labour and Sorrow, for there is no grief mixed therewith.*

Sag. Talk! The People talk strangely about him: Some say that he *now walks in White*, that he has a Chain of Gold about his Neck, that he has a Crown of Gold, beset with Pearls upon his Head: Others say, that the shining ones that sometimes shewed themselves to him in his Journey, are become his Companions, and that he is as familiar with them in the place where he is, as here one Neighbour is with another. Besides, 'tis confidently affirmed concerning him, that the King of the place where he is, has bestowed upon him already, a very rich and pleasant Dwelling at Court, and that he every day eateth and drinketh, and walketh, and talketh with him, and receiveth of the smiles and favours of him that is Judge of all there. Moreover, it is expected of some that his Prince, the Lord of that Country, will shortly come into *these* parts, and will know the reason, if they can give any, why his Neighbours set so little by him, and had him so much in derision when they perceived that he would be a Pilgrim. *For they say, that now he is so in the Affections of his Prince, and that his *Sovereign* is so much concerned with the *Indignities* that were cast upon *Christian* when he became a Pilgrim, that he will look upon all as if done unto himself; and no marvel, for 'twas for the love that he had to his Prince, that he ventured as he did.

Revel. 3. 4. Chap. 6. 11. Zech. 3. 7. Luke 14. 15. Jude 14, 15.

* Christians *King will take* Christians *part.*

Luke 10. 16.

I dare say, quoth I, *I am glad on't, I am glad for the poor mans sake, for that now he has rest from his Labour, and for that he now reapeth the benefit of his Tears with Joy; and for that he is got beyond the Gun-shot of his Enemies, and is out of the reach of them that hate him. I also am glad for that a Rumour of these things is noised abroad in this Country; Who can tell but that it may work some good effect on some that are left behind? But, pray Sir, while it is fresh in my mind, do you hear any thing of his Wife and Children? Poor hearts, I wonder in my mind what they do.*

Revel. 14. 13. Psal. 126. 5, 6.

** Good Tidings of* Christians *Wife and Children.*

Sag. Who! *Christiana*, and her Sons! *They are like to do as well as did *Christian* himself, for though they all *plaid the Fool* at the first, and would by no means be perswaded by either the Tears or Intreaties of *Christian*, yet second thoughts have wrought wonderfully with them, so they have packt up and are also gone after him.

Better, and better, quoth I, *But What! Wife and Children and all?*

Sag. 'Tis true, I can give you an account of the matter, for I was upon the spot at the instant, and was throughly acquainted with the whole affair.

Then, said I, *a man it seems may report it for a truth?*

Sag. You need not fear to affirm it, I mean that they are all gon on Pilgrimage, both the good Woman and her four Boys. And being we are, as I perceive, going some considerable way together, I will give you an account of the whole of the matter.

This *Christiana* (for that was her name from the day that she with her Children betook themselves to a *Pilgrims* Life,) after her Husband was gone *over the River*, and she could hear of him no more, her thoughts began to work in her mind; First, for that she had lost her Husband, and for that the loving bond of that Relation was utterly broken betwixt them. For you know, said he to me, nature can do no less but entertain the living with many a heavy Cogitation in the remembrance of the loss of loving Relations. This therefore of her Husband did cost her many a Tear. But this was not all, for *Christiana* did also begin to consider with her self, whether her unbecoming behaviour towards her Husband was not one cause that she saw him no more, and that in such sort he was taken away from her. And upon this, came into her mind by *swarms*, all her unkind, unnatural, and ungodly Carriages to her dear Friend: Which also clogged her Conscience, and did load her with guilt. She was moreover much broken with recalling to remembrance the restless Groans, brinish Tears and self-bemoanings of her Husband, and how she did harden her heart against all his entreaties, and loving perswasions (of her and her Sons) to go with him, yea, there was not any thing that *Christian* either said to her, or did before her, all the while that his burden did hang on his back, but it returned upon her like

1 part pag. 275.

Mark this, you that are Churles to your godly Relations.

a flash of lightning, and rent the Caul of her Heart in sunder. Specially that bitter out-cry of his, *What shall I do to be saved*, did ring in her ears most dolefully.

1 *part, page* 143.

Then said she to her Children, Sons, we are all undone. I have sinned away your Father, and he is gone; he would have had us with him; but I would not go my self; I also have hindred you of Life. With that the Boys fell all into Tears, and cryed out to go after their Father. Oh! Said *Christiana*, that it had been but our lot to go with him, then had it fared well with us beyond what 'tis like to do now. For tho' I formerly foolishly imagin'd concerning the Troubles of your Father, that they proceeded of a foolish fancy that he had, or for that he was over-run with Melancholy Humours; yet now 'twill not out of my mind, but that they sprang from another cause, to wit, for that the Light of Light was given him, by the help of which, as I perceive, he has escaped the Snares of Death. Then they all wept again, and cryed out: Oh, Wo, worth the day.

James 1. 23, 24, 25.

The next night *Christiana* had a Dream, and behold she saw as if a broad Parchment was opened before her, in which were recorded the sum of her ways, and the times, as she thought, look'd *very black upon her*. Then she cryed out aloud in her sleep, Lord have mercy upon me a Sinner, and the little Children heard her.

Christiana'*s Dream.*

Luke 18. 13.

After this she thought she saw two very ill favoured ones standing by her Bed-side, and saying, **What shall we do with this Woman? For she cryes out for Mercy waking and sleeping: If she be suffered to go on as she begins, we shall lose her as we have lost her Husband.* Wherefore we must by one way or other, seek to take her off from the thoughts of what shall be hereafter: else all the World cannot help it, but she will become a Pilgrim.

* *Mark this, this is the quintescence of Hell.*

Now she awoke in a great Sweat, also a trembling was upon her, but after a while she fell to sleeping again. *And then she thought she saw *Christian* her Husband in a place of Bliss among many *Immortals*, with an *Harp* in his Hand, standing and

* *Help against Discouragement.*

playing upon it before one that sate on a Throne with a Rainbow about his Head. She saw also as if he bowed his Head with his Face to the Pav'd-work that was under the Princes Feet, saying, *I heartily thank my Lord and King, for bringing of me into this Place.* Then shouted a Company of them that stood round about, and harped with their Harps: but no man living could tell what they said, but *Christian* and his Companions.

Next Morning when she was up, had prayed to God, and talked with her Children a while, one knocked hard at the door; to whom she spake out saying, *If thou comest in Gods Name, come in.* So he said *Amen*, and opened the Door, and saluted her with *Peace be to this House.* *The which when he had done, he said, *Christiana*, knowest thou wherefore I am come? Then she blush'd and trembled, also her Heart began to wax warm with desires to know whence he came, and what was his Errand to her. So he said unto her; my name is *Secret*, I dwell with those that are high. It is talked of where I dwell, as if thou hadst a desire to go thither; also there is a report that thou art aware of the evil thou hast formerly done to thy Husband in hardening of thy Heart against his way, and in keeping of these thy Babes in their Ignorance. *Christiana*, the merciful one has sent me to tell thee that he is a God ready to forgive, and that he taketh delight to multiply to pardon offences. He also would have thee know that he inviteth thee to come into his Presence, to his Table, and that he will feed thee with the Fat of his House, and with the Heritage of *Jacob* thy Father.

** Convictions seconded with fresh Tidings of Gods readiness to Pardon.*

There is *Christian* thy Husband, *that was*, with Legions more his Companions, ever beholding that face that doth minister Life to beholders: and they will all be glad when they shall hear the sound of thy feet step over thy Fathers Threshold.

Christiana at this was greatly abashed in her self, and bowing her head to the ground, this *Visitor* proceeded and said, *Christiana*! Here is also a Letter for thee which I have brought from thy Husbands King. So she took it and opened it, but it smelt after the manner of the best Perfume, also it was Written in Letters of Gold.

Song 1. 3.

The Contents of the Letter was, *That the King would have her do as did* Christian *her Husband*; *For that was the way to come to his* City, *and to dwell in his Presence with Joy, for ever.* At this the good Woman was quite overcome: So she cried out to her *Visitor*, *Sir, will you carry me and my children with you, that we also may go and Worship this King?*

Christiana *quite overcome.*

Then said the Visitor, *Christiana! The bitter is before the sweet:* Thou must through Troubles, as did he that went before thee, enter this Celestial City. Wherefore I advise thee, to do as did *Christian* thy Husband: go to the *Wicket Gate* yonder, over the Plain, for that stands in the head of the way up which thou must go, and I wish thee all good speed. Also I advise that thou put this Letter in thy Bosome. That thou read therein to thy self and to thy Children, until you have got it by root-of-Heart. For it is one of the Songs that thou must Sing while thou art in this House of thy Pilgrimage. Also this thou must deliver in at the *further* Gate.

Further Instruction to Christiana.

Psal. 119. 54.

Now I saw in my Dream that this Old Gentleman, as he told me this Story, did himself seem to be greatly affected therewith. He moreover proceeded and said, So *Christiana* called her Sons together, and began thus to Address her self unto them. *My Sons, I have, as you may perceive, been of late under much exercise in my Soul about the Death of your Father; not for that I doubt at all of his Happiness: For I am satisfied now that he is well. I have also been much affected with the thoughts of mine own State and yours, which I verily believe is by nature miserable: My Carriages also to your Father in his distress, is a great load to my Conscience. For I hardened both mine own heart and yours against him, and refused to go with him on Pilgrimage.

* Christiana *prays well for her Journey.*

The thoughts of these things would now kill me out-right; but that for a Dream which I had last night, and but that for the incouragement that this Stranger has given me this Morning. Come, my Children, let us pack up, and be gon to the Gate that leads to the Celestial Countrey, that we may see your

Father, and be with him and his Companions in Peace according to the Laws of that Land.

Then did her Children burst out into Tears for Joy that the Heart of their Mother was so inclined: So their *Visitor* bid them farewel: and they began to prepare to set out for their Journey.

But while they were thus about to be gon, two of the Women that were *Christiana's* Neighbours, came up to her House and knocked at her Door. To whom she said as before. *If you come in Gods Name, come in.* *At this the Women were stun'd, for this kind of Language they used not to hear, or to perceive to drop from the Lips of *Christiana*. Yet they came in; but behold they found the good Woman a preparing to be gon from her House.

* Christiana's *new Language stunds her old Neighbours.*

So they began and said, *Neighbour, pray what is your meaning by this?*

Christiana answered and said to the eldest of them, whose name was Mrs. *Timorous*, I am preparing for a Journey (This *Timorous* was Daughter to him that met *Christian* upon the Hill *Difficulty*; and would a had him gone back for fear of the Lyons.)

1 *Part, pag.* 172.

Timorous. For what Journey I pray you?

Chris. *Even to go after my good Husband*, and with that she fell a weeping.

Timo. I hope not so, good Neighbour, pray, for your poor Childrens sakes, do not so unwomanly cast away your self.

Chris. *Nay, my Children shall go with me; not one of them is willing to stay behind.*

Timo. I wonder in my very Heart, what, or who, has brought you into this mind.

Timorous *comes to visit* Christiana, *with* Mercy, *one of her Neighbours.*

Chris. Oh, Neighbour, knew you but as much as I do, I doubt not but that you would go with me.

Timo. *Prithee what new knowledge hast thou got that so worketh off thy mind from thy Friends, and that tempteth thee to go no body knows where?*

Chris. Then *Christiana* reply'd, I have been sorely afflicted since my Husband's departure from me; but specially since he went *over the River.* But that

Death.

which troubleth me most, is, my churlish Carriages to him when he was under his distress. Besides, I am *now*, as he was *then*; nothing will serve me but going on Pilgrimage. I was a dreamed last night, that I saw him. O that my Soul was with him. He dwelleth in the presence of the King of the Country, he sits and eats with him at his Table, he is become a Companion of *Immortals*, and has a House now given him to dwell in, to which, the best Palaces on Earth, if compared, seems to me to be but as a Dunghil. The Prince of the Place has also sent for me, with promise of entertainment if I shall come to him; his messenger was here even now, and has brought me a Letter, which Invites me to come. And with that she pluck'd out her Letter, and read it, and said to them, what now will you say to this?

2 Cor. 5. 1, 2, 3, 4.

Timo. *Oh the madness that has possessed thee and thy Husband, to run your selves upon such difficulties! You have heard, I am sure, what your Husband did meet with, even in a manner at the first step, that he took on his way, as our Neighbour* Obstinate *yet can testifie; for he went along with him, yea and* Plyable *too, until they, like* wise men, *were afraid to go any further. We also heard over and above, how he met with the Lyons, Apollion, the shadow of death, and many other things: Nor is the danger he met with at* Vanity *fair to be forgotten by thee. For if he, tho' a man, was so hard put to it, what canst thou being but a poor Woman do? Consider also that these four sweet Babes are thy Children, thy Flesh and thy Bones. Wherefore, though thou shouldest be so rash as to cast away thy self: Yet for the sake of the Fruit of thy Body, keep thou at home.*

1 *Part, pages* 144—148.

The reasonings of the flesh.

But *Christiana* said unto her, tempt me not, my Neighbour: I have now a price put into mine hand to get gain, and I should be a Fool of the greatest size, if I should have no heart to strike in with the opportunity. And for that you tell me of all these Troubles that I am like to meet with in the way, *they are so far off from being to me a discouragement, that they shew I am in the right. *The bitter must come before the sweet*, and that also will make the sweet the sweeter. Wherefore,

* *A pertinent reply to fleshly reasonings.*

since you came not to my House, *in Gods name*, as I said, I pray you to be gon, and do not disquiet me further.

Then *Timorous* also revil'd her, and said to her Fellow, come Neighbour *Mercy*, lets leave her in her own hands, since she scorns our Counsel and Company. But *Mercy* was at a stand, and could not so readily comply with her Neighbour: and that for a two-fold reason. First, her Bowels yearned over *Christiana*: so she said within her self, If my Neighbour will needs be gon, I will go a little way with her, and help her. Secondly, her Bowels yearned over her own Soul, (for what *Christiana* had said, had taken some hold upon her mind.) Wherefore she said within her self again, I will yet have more talk with this *Christiana*, and if I find Truth and Life in what she shall say, my self with my Heart shall also go with her. Wherefore *Mercy* began thus to reply to her Neighbour *Timorous*.

Mercies *Bowels yearn over* Christiana.

Mercy. Neighbour, *I did indeed come with you, to see* Christiana *this Morning, and since she is, as you see, a taking of her last farewel of her Country, I think to walk this Sun-shine Morning, a little way with her to help her on the way.* But she told her not of her second Reason, but kept that to her self.

Timorous *forsakes her; but* Mercy *cleaves to her.*

Timo. Well, I see you have a mind to go a fooling too; but take heed in time, and be wise: while we are out of danger we are out; but when we are in, we are in. So Mrs. *Timorous* returned to her House, and *Christiana* betook her self to her Journey. But when *Timorous* was got home to her House, she sends for some of her Neighbours, to wit, Mrs. *Bats-eyes*, Mrs. *Inconsiderate*, Mrs. *Light-mind*, and Mrs. *Know-nothing*. So when they were come to her House, she falls to telling of the story of *Christiana*, and of her intended Journey. And thus she began her Tale.

Timorous *acquaints her Friends what the good* Christiana *intends to do.*

Timo. Neighbours, having had little to do this Morning, I went to give *Christiana* a Visit, and when I came at the Door, I knocked, as you know 'tis our Custom: And she answered, *If you come in God's Name, come in*. So in I went, thinking all was well: But when I came in, I found her preparing her self to depart the Town, she and also her

Children. So I asked her what was her meaning by that? and she told me in short, That she was now of a mind to go on Pilgrimage, as did her Husband. She told me also of a Dream that she had, and how the King of the Country where her Husband was, had sent her an inviting Letter to come thither.

Then said Mrs. Know-nothing. *And what! do you think she will go?*

Mrs. Know-nothing.

Timo. Aye, go she will, whatever come on't; and methinks I know it by this; for that which was my great Argument to perswade her to stay at home, (to wit, the Troubles she was like to meet with in the way) is one great Argument with her to put her forward on her Journey. For she told me in so many Words, *The bitter goes before the sweet.* Yea, and for as much as it so doth, it makes the sweet the sweeter.

Mrs. Bats-eyes.

Mrs. *Bats-eyes.* Oh this blind and foolish Woman, said she, Will she not take warning by her Husband's Afflictions? For my part, I see if he was here again he would rest him content in a whole Skin, and never run so many hazards for nothing.

Mrs. Inconsiderate.

Mrs. *Inconsiderate* also replied, saying, away with such Fantastical Fools from the Town; a good Riddance, for my part I say, of her. Should she stay where she dwels, and retain this her mind, who could live quietly by her? for she will either be dumpish or unneighbourly, or talk of such matters as no wise Body can abide: Wherefore, for my part, I shall never be sorry for her Departure; let her go, and let better come in her room: 'twas never a good World since these whimsical Fools dwelt in it.

Mrs. Light-mind.

Madam Wanton, *she that had like to a bin too hard for* Faithful *in time past.*

Then Mrs. *Light-mind* added as followeth. Come, put this kind of Talk away. I was Yesterday at Madam *Wantons*, where we were as merry as the Maids. For who do you think should be there, but I, and Mrs. *Love-the-flesh*, and three or four more, with Mr. *Lechery*, Mrs. *Filth*, and some others. So there we had Musick and Dancing, and what else was meet to fill up the pleasure. And I dare say my Lady her self is an admirably well-bred Gentlewoman, and Mr. *Lechery* is as pretty a Fellow.

By this time *Christiana* was got on her way, and *Mercy* went along with her. So as they went, her Children being there also, *Christiana* began to discourse. And, *Mercy*, said *Christiana*, I take this as an unexpected favour, that thou shouldest set foot out of Doors with me to accompany me a little in my way.

1 part, pag. 146.

Discourse betwixt Mercy *and good* Christiana.

Mercy. *Then said young* Mercy (*for she was but young,*) *If I thought it would be to purpose to go with you, I would never go near the Town any more.*

Chris. Well *Mercy*, said *Christiana*, cast in thy Lot with me. I well know what will be the end of our Pilgrimage, my Husband is where he would not but be, for all the Gold in the *Spanish* Mines. Nor shalt thou be rejected, tho thou goest but upon *my Invitation.* The King, who hath sent for me and my Children, is one that delighteth in *Mercy*. Besides, if thou wilt, I will hire thee, and thou shalt go along with me as my servant. Yet we will have all things in common betwixt thee and me, only go along with me.

Mercy *inclines to go.*

Christiana *would have her Neighbour with her.*

Mercy. *But how shall I be ascertained that I also shall be entertained? Had I this hope from one that can tell, I would make no stick at all, but would go, being helped by him that can help, tho' the way was never so tedious.*

Mercy *doubts of acceptance.*

Christiana. Well, loving *Mercy*, I will tell thee what thou shalt do, go with me to the *Wicket Gate*, and there I will further enquire for thee, and if there thou shalt not meet with encouragement, I will be content that thou shalt return to thy place. I also will pay thee for thy Kindness which thou shewest to me and my Children, in thy accompanying of us in our way as thou doest.

Christiana *allures her to the Gate which is Christ, and promiseth there to enquire for her.*

Mercy. *Then will I go thither, and will take what shall follow, and the Lord grant that my Lot may there fall even as the King of Heaven shall have his heart upon me.*

Mercy *prays.*

Christiana then was glad at her heart, not only that she

had a Companion, but also for that she had prevailed with this poor Maid to fall in love with her own Salvation. So they went on together, and *Mercy* began to weep. Then said *Christiana*, wherefore weepeth my Sister so?

Christiana *glad of* Mercy's *company.*

Mer. *Alas! said she, who can but lament that shall but rightly consider what a State and Condition my poor Relations are in, that yet remain in our sinful Town: and that which makes my Grief the more heavy, is, because they have no Instructor, nor any to tell them what is to come.*

Mercy *grieves for her carnal Relations.*

Chris. Bowels becometh Pilgrims. And thou dost for thy Friends, as my good *Christian* did for me when he left me; he mourned for that I would not heed nor regard him, but his Lord and ours did gather up his Tears and put them into his Bottle, and now both I, and thou, and these my sweet Babes, are reaping the Fruit and Benefit of them. I hope, *Mercy*, these Tears of thine will not be lost, for the Truth hath said, *That they that sow in Tears shall reap in Joy, in singing. And he that goeth forth and weepeth, bearing precious Seed, shall doubtless come again with rejoycing, bringing his Sheaves with him.*

Christian's *Prayers were answered for his Relations after he was dead.*

Psal. 126. 5, 6.

Then said *Mercy*,

Let the most blessed be my Guide,
If't be his blessed Will,
Unto *his Gate*, into *his Fold*,
Up *to his Holy Hill.*

And let him never suffer me
To swarve, or turn aside
From his Free Grace, and holy ways,
Whatere shall me betide.

And let him gather them of mine,
That I have left behind.
Lord make them pray they may be thine,
With all their Heart and Mind.

Now my old Friend proceeded, and said, But when *Christiana* came up to the Slow of *Despond*, she began to be at a stand; for, said she, This is the place in which my dear Husband had like to a been smothered with Mud. She perceived also, that notwithstanding the Command of the King to make this place for Pilgrims good; yet it was rather worse than formerly. So I asked if that was true? Yes, said the Old Gentleman, too true. For that many there be that pretend to be the Kings Labourers; and that say they are for mending the Kings High-ways, that bring *Dirt* and *Dung* instead of Stones, and so marr, instead of mending. Here *Christiana* therefore, with her Boys, did make a stand: but said *Mercy*, *come let us venture, only let us be wary. Then they looked well to the *Steps*, and make a shift to get staggeringly over.

1 *Part, pages* 147—149.

Their own carnal Conclusions, instead of the word of life.

* Mercy *the boldest at the Slow of* Despond.

Yet *Christiana* had like to a been in, and that not once nor twice. Now they had no sooner got over, but they thought they heard words that said unto them, *Blessed is she that believeth, for there shall be a performance of the things that have been told her from the Lord.*

Luke 1. 45.

Then they went on again; and said *Mercy* to *Christiana*, Had I as good ground to hope for a loving Reception at the *Wicket-Gate*, as you, I think no Slow of *Despond* would discourage me.

Well, said the other, you know *your sore*, and I know *mine*; and, good friend, we shall all have enough evil before we come at our Journeys end.

For can it be imagined, that the people that design to attain such excellent Glories *as we do*, and that are so envied that Happiness *as we are*; but that we shall meet with what Fears and Scares, with what Troubles and Afflictions they can possibly assault us with, that hate us?

And now Mr. *Sagacity* left me to Dream out my Dream by my self. Wherefore me-thought I saw *Christiana*, and *Mercy* and the *Boys* go all of them up to the Gate. To which when they were come, they betook themselves to a short debate about *how* they must manage their calling

Prayer should be made with Consideration, and Fear: As well as in Faith and Hope.

at the Gate, and what should be said to him that did open to them. So it was concluded, since *Christiana* was the eldest, that she should knock for entrance, and that she should speak to him that did open, for the rest. So *Christiana* began to knock, and as her poor Husband did, she *knocked* and *knocked* again. But instead of any that answered, they all thought that they heard, as if a Dog came barking upon them. A Dog, and a great one too, and this made the Woman and Children afraid. Nor durst they for a while dare to knock any more, for fear the *Mastiff* should fly upon them. *Now therefore they were greatly tumbled up and down in their minds, and knew not what to do. Knock they durst not, for fear of the Dog: go back they durst not, for fear that the Keeper of that Gate should espy them, as they so went, and should be offended with them. At last they thought of knocking again, and knocked more vehemently then they did at the first. Then said the Keeper of the Gate, who is there? So the *Dog* left off to bark, and he opened unto them.

1 *part, pag.* 156.

The Dog, the Devil, an Enemy to Prayer.

* Christiana *and her companions perplexed about Prayer.*

Then *Christiana* made low obeysance, and said, Let not our Lord be offended with his Handmaidens, for that we have knocked at his Princely Gate. Then said the Keeper, Whence come ye, and what is that you would have?

Christiana answered, We are come from whence *Christian* did come, and upon the same *Errand* as he; to wit, to be, if it shall please you, graciously admitted by this Gate, into the way that leads to the Celestial City. And I answer, my Lord, in the next place, that I am *Christiana*, once the Wife of *Christian*, that now is gotten above.

With that the Keeper of the Gate did marvel, saying, *What is she become now a Pilgrim, that but a while ago abhorred that Life?* Then she bowed her Head, and said, yes; and so are these my sweet Babes also.

Then he took her by the hand, and led her in, and said also, *Suffer the little Children to come unto me*, and with that he shut up the Gate. This done, he called to a Trumpeter that was above over the Gate, to entertain *Christiana* with shouting and sound of

How Christiana *is entertained at the Gate.*

Trumpet for joy. So he obeyed and sounded, and filled the Air with his melodious Notes.

Now all this while, poor *Mercy* did stand without, trembling and crying for fear that she was rejected. But when *Christiana* had gotten admittance for her self and her Boys; then she began to make Intercession for *Mercy*.

Chris. *And she said, my Lord, I have a Companion of mine that stands yet without, that is come hither upon the same account as my self.* †*One that is much dejected in her mind, for that she comes, as she thinks, without sending for, whereas I was sent to, by my Husband's King, to come.*

† Christiana's *Prayer for her friend* Mercy.

Now *Mercy* began to be very impatient, for each *minute* was as long to her as an Hour, wherefore she prevented *Christiana* from a fuller interceding for her, by knocking at the Gate her self. And she knocked then so loud, that she made *Christiana* to start. Then said the Keeper of the Gate, Who is there? And said *Christiana*, It is my Friend.

The Delays make the hungring Soul the ferventer.

So he opened the Gate, and looked out; *but *Mercy* was fallen down without in a Swoon, for she fainted, and was afraid that no Gate should be opened to her.

* Mercy *faints.*

Then he took her by the hand, and said, *Damsel*, I bid thee arise.

O Sir, said she, I am faint, there is scarce Life left in me. But he answered, That one once said, *When my Soul fainted within me, I remembred the Lord, and my prayer came in unto thee, into thy Holy Temple.* Fear not, but stand upon thy Feet, and tell me wherefore thou art come.

Jonah 2. 7.

Mer. I am come, for *that*, unto which I was never invited, as my Friend *Christiana* was. **Hers* was from the King, and *mine* was but from *her*: Wherefore I fear I presume.

* *The cause of her fainting.*

Did she desire thee to come with her to this Place?

Mer. Yes, And as my Lord sees, I am come. And if there is any Grace and forgiveness of Sins to spare, I beseech that I thy poor Handmaid may be partaker thereof.

Then he took her again by the Hand, and led her gently

in, and said: *I pray for all them that believe on me, by what means soever they come unto me. Then said he to those that stood by: Fetch something, and give it *Mercy* to smell on, thereby to stay her fainting. So they fetcht her a *Bundle* of *Myrrh*, and a while after she was revived.

* *mark this.*

And now was *Christiana*, and her Boys, and *Mercy*, received of the Lord at the head of the way, and spoke kindly unto by him.

Then said they yet further unto him, We are sorry for our Sins, and beg of our Lord his Pardon, and further information what we must do.

I grant Pardon, said he, by word, and deed; by word in the promise of forgiveness: by deed in the way I obtained it. Take the first from my Lips with a kiss, and the other, as it shall be revealed.

Song 1. 2.
John 20. 20.

Now I saw in my Dream that he spake many good words unto them, whereby they were greatly gladded. He also had them up to the top of the Gate and shewed them by what *deed* they were saved, and told them withall that that sight they would have again as they went along in the way, to their comfort.

Christ Crucified seen afar off.

So he left them a while in a Summer-Parler below, where they entered into talk by themselves. And thus *Christiana* began, *O Lord! How glad am I, that we are got in hither!*

* *Talk between the Christians.*

Mer. *So you well may; but I, of all have cause to leap for joy.*

Chris. *I thought, one time, as I stood at the Gate (because I had knocked and none did answer) that all our Labour had been lost: Specially when that ugly Curr made such a heavy barking at us.*

Mer. But my worst Fear was after I saw that you was taken into his favour, and that I was left behind: Now thought I, 'tis fulfiled which is Written. *Two Women shall be Grinding together; the one shall be taken, and the other left.* I had much ado to forbear crying out, Undone, undone.

Mat. 24. 41.

And afraid I was to knock any more; but when I looked

up, to what was Written over the Gate, I took Courage. I also thought that I must either knock again or dye. So I knocked; but I cannot tell how, for my spirit now *struggled* betwixt life and death.

1 Part, page 157.

Chris. *Can you not tell how you knocked? I am sure your knocks were so earnest, that the very sound of them made me start, I thought I never heard such knocking in all my Life. I thought you would a come in by violent hand, or a took the Kingdom by storm.*

Christiana *thinks her Companion prays better then she.*

Mat. 11. 12.

Mer. Alas, to be in my Case, who that so was, could but a done so? You saw that the Door was shut upon me, and that there was a most cruel *Dog* thereabout. Who, I say, that was so faint hearted as I, that would not a knocked with all their might? But pray, what said my Lord unto my rudeness, was he not angry with me?

Chris. **When he heard your lumbring noise, he gave a wonderful Innocent smile. I believe what you did pleas'd him well enough, For he shewed no sign to the contrary. But I marvel in my heart why he keeps such a Dog; had I known that afore, I fear I should not have had heart enough to a ventured my self in this manner. But now we are in, we are in, and I am glad with all my heart.*

* Christ pleased with loud and restless praises.

Mer. I will ask if you please next time he comes down, why he keeps such a filthy Cur in his Yard. I hope he will not take it amiss.

**Ay do, said the Children, and perswade him to hang him, for we are afraid that he will bite us when we go hence.*

** The Children are afraid of the dog.*

So at last he came down to them again, and *Mercy* fell to the Ground on her Face before him and worshipped, and said, Let my Lord accept of the Sacrifice of praise which I now offer unto him, with the calves of my Lips.

So he said to her, peace be to thee, stand up.

Jer. 12. 1, 2.

But she continued upon her Face and said, *Righteous art thou O Lord when I plead with thee, yet let me talk with thee of thy Judgments:* †*Wherefore dost thou keep so cruell a Dog in thy Yard, at the sight of*

† Mercy *expostulates about the dog.*

which, such Women and Children as we, are ready to fly from the Gate for fear?

He answered, and said; *That Dog* has another *Owner, he also is kept close in another man's ground; only my Pilgrims hear his barking. He belongs to the Castle which you see there at a distance: but can come up to the Walls of this Place. He has frighted many an honest Pilgrim from worse to better, by the great voice of his roaring. Indeed he that owneth him, doth not keep him of any good will to me or mine; but with intent to keep the Pilgrims from coming to me, and that they may be afraid to knock at this Gate for entrance. Sometimes also he has broken out and has *worried* some that I love; but I take all at present patiently, I also give my Pilgrims timely help: So they are not delivered up to his power to do to them what his Dogish nature would prompt him to. *But what! My purchased one, I tro, hadst thou known never so much before hand, thou wouldst not a bin afraid of a *Dog*.

* *Devill.*

1 *Part page* 157.

* *A Check to the carnal fear of the Pilgrims.*

The Beggers that go from Door to Door, will, rather then they will lose a supposed Alms, run the hazzard of the bauling, barking, and biting too of a Dog: and shall a Dog, a Dog in another Mans Yard: a Dog, whose barking I turn to the Profit of Pilgrims, keep any from coming to me? I deliver them from the *Lions*, their Darling from the power of the Dog.

Mer. Then said *Mercy*, **I confess my Ignorance: I spake what I understood not: I acknowledge that thou doest all things well.*

* Christians *when wise enough acquiesce in the wisdom of their Lord.*

Chris. Then *Christiana* began to talk of their Journey, and to enquire after the way. So he fed them, and washed their feet, and set them in the way of his Steps, according as he had dealt with her Husband before.

1 *Part, page* 159.

So I saw in my Dream, that they walkt on in their way, and had the weather very comfortable to them.

Then *Christiana* began to sing, saying,

Bless't be the Day that I began
A Pilgrim for to be;

And blessed also be that man
That thereto moved me.

'Tis true, 'twas long ere I began
To seek to live for ever:
But now I run fast as I can,
'Tis better late *then* never. Mat. 20. 6.

Our Tears *to joy, our fears to Faith*
Are turned, as we see:
Thus our beginning, (as one saith,)
Shews what our end will be.

Now there was, on the other side of the Wall that fenced in the way up which *Christiana* and her Companions was to go a *Garden; and that Garden belonged to him whose was that *Barking Dog*, of whom mention was made before. And some of the Fruit-Trees that grew in that Garden shot their Branches over the Wall, and being mellow, they that found them did gather them up and oft eat of them to their hurt. So *Christiana's* Boys, as Boys are apt to do, being pleas'd with the Trees, and with the Fruit that did hang thereon, did *Pluck* them, and began to eat. Their mother did also chide them for so doing; but still the Boys went on.

** The devils garden.*

The Children eat of the Enemies Fruit.

Well, said she, my Sons, you Transgress, for that Fruit is none of ours: but she did not know that they did belong to the Enemy; Ile warrant you if she had, she would a been ready to die for fear. But that passed, and they went on their way. Now by that they were gon about two Bows-shot from the place that led them into the way: they espyed two very *ill-favoured ones* coming down apace to meet them. With that *Christiana*, and *Mercie* her Friend, covered themselves with their Vails, and so kept on their Journey: The Children also went on before, so at last they met together. Then they that came down to meet them, came just up to the Women, as if they would imbrace them; but *Christiana* said, Stand back, or go peaceably by as you should. Yet these two, as men that are deaf, regarded not *Christiana's*

Two ill favoured ones.

They assault Christiana.

words; but began to lay hands upon them; at that *Christiana* waxing very wroth, spurned at them with her feet, *Mercie* also, as well as she could, did what she could to shift them. *Christiana* again said to them, Stand back and be gon, for we have no Money to lose, being Pilgrims as ye see, and such too as live upon the Charity of our Friends.

The pilgrims struggle with them.

Ill-fa. Then said one of the two of the Men, we make no assault upon you for Money; but are come out to tell you, that if you will but grant one small request which we shall ask, we will make Women of you for ever.

Christ. Now *Christiana*, imagining what they should mean, made answer again, *We will neither hear nor regard, nor yield to what you shall ask. We are in haste, cannot stay, our Business is a Business of Life and Death.* So again she and her Companions made a fresh assay to go past them. But they letted them in their way.

Ill-fa. And they said, we intend no hurt to your lives, 'tis an other thing we would have.

Christ. Ay, quoth *Christiana*, you would have us Body and Soul, for I know 'tis for that you are come; but we will die rather upon the spot, then suffer our selves to be brought into such Snares as shall hazzard our well being hereafter. And with that they both *Shrieked* out, and cryed Murder, Murder: and so put themselves under those Laws that are provided for the Protection of Women. But the men still made their approach upon them, with design to prevail against them: They therefore cryed out again.

She cryes out.

Deut. 22. 23, 26. 27.

*Now they being, as I said, not far from the Gate in at which they came, their voice was heard from where they was thither: Wherefore some of the House came out, and knowing that it was *Christiana*'s Tongue: they made haste to her relief. But by that they was got within sight of them, the Women was in a very great scuffle, the Children also stood crying by. Then did he that came in for their relief, call out to the Ruffins saying, What is that thing that you do? Would you make my Lords People to transgress? He also attempted to take them;

* *'Tis good to cry out when we are assaulted.*

The Reliever *comes.*

but they did make their escape over the Wall into the Garden of the Man, to whom the great Dog belonged, so the Dog became their Protector. This *Reliever* then came up to the Women, and asked them how they did. So they answered, we thank thy Prince, pretty well, only we have been somewhat affrighted, we thank thee also for that thou camest in to our help, for otherwise we had been overcome.

The Ill-ones *fly to the devill for relief.*

Reliever. So after a few more words, this *Reliever* said as followeth: *I marvelled much when you was entertained at the Gate above, being ye knew that ye were but weak Women, that you petitioned not the Lord there for a Conductor: Then might you have avoided these Troubles, and Dangers: For he would have granted you one.*

The Reliever *talks to the Women.*

Christ. *Alas said *Christiana*, we were so taken with our present blessing, that Dangers to come were forgotten by us; beside, who could have thought that so near the Kings Palace there should have lurked such naughty ones: indeed it had been well for us had we asked our Lord for one; but since our Lord knew 'twould be for our profit, I wonder he sent not one along with us.

* *mark this.*

Relie. *It is not always necessary to grant things not asked for, lest by so doing they become of little esteem; but when the want of a thing is felt, it then comes, under, in the Eyes of him that feels it, that estimate, that properly is its due, and so consequently will be thereafter used. Had my Lord granted you a Conductor, you would not neither, so have bewailed that oversight of yours in not asking for one, as now you have occasion to do. So all things work for good, and tend to make you more wary.*

We lose for want of asking for.

Christ. Shall we go back again to my Lord, and confess our folly, and ask one?

Relie. *Your Confession of your folly, I will present him with: To go back again, you need not. For in all places where you shall come, you will find no want at all, for in every of my Lord's Lodgings, which he has prepared for the reception of his Pilgrims, there is sufficient to furnish them against all attempts whatsoever. But, as I said, he will be enquired of by them to do it for them:*

and 'tis a poor thing that is not worth asking for. When he had thus said, he went back to his place, and the Pilgrims went on their way.

Ezek. 36. 37.

Mer. Then said *Mercy*, what a sudden blank is here? I made account we had now been past all danger, and that we should never see sorrow more.

The mistake of Mercy.

Christ. Thy *Innocency*, my Sister, said *Christiana* to *Mercy*, may excuse thee much; but as for me, my fault is so much the greater, for that I saw this danger before I came out of the Doors, and yet did not provide for it where provision might a been had. I am therefore much to be blamed.

Christiana'*s Guilt.*

Mer. *Then said* Mercy, *how knew you this before you came from home? pray open to me this Riddle.*

Christ. Why, I will tell you. Before I set Foot out of Doors, one Night, as I lay in my Bed, I had a Dream about this. For methought I saw two men, as like these as ever the World they could look, stand at my *Beds-feet*, plotting how they might prevent my Salvation. I will tell you their very words. They said, ('twas when I was in my Troubles,) *What shall we do with this Woman? for she cries out waking and sleeping for forgiveness, If she be suffered to go on as she begins, we shall lose her as we have lost her Husband.* This you know might a made me take heed, and have provided when Provision might a been had.

Christiana'*s Dream repeated.*

Mer. Well, said *Mercy*, *as by this neglect, we have an occasion ministred unto us to behold our own imperfections: So our Lord has taken occasion thereby, to make manifest the Riches of his Grace. For he, as we see, has followed us with un-asked kindness, and has delivered us from their hands that were stronger then we, of his meer good pleasure.*

Mercy *makes good use of their neglect of duty.*

Thus now when they had talked away a little more time, they drew nigh to an House which stood in the way, which House was built for the relief of Pilgrims: As you will find more fully related in the first part of these Records of the *Pilgrims Progress*. So they drew on towards the House (the House of the Inter-

1 *Part page* 159.

preter) and when they came to the Door, they heard a great talk in the House, they then gave ear, and heard, as they thought, *Christiana* mentioned by name. For you must know that there went along, even before her, a talk of her and her Childrens going on Pilgrimage. And this thing was the more pleasing to them, because they had heard that she was *Christian*'s Wife; that Woman who was sometime ago so unwilling to hear of going on Pilgrimage. Thus therefore they stood still and heard the good people within commending her, who they little thought stood at the Door. †At last *Christiana* knocked as she had done at the Gate before. Now when she had knocked, there came to the Door a young Damsel named *Innocent*, and opened the Door and looked, and behold two Women was there.

Talk in the Interpreter's house about Christiana's *going on pilgrimage.*

† She knocks at the Door.

The door is opened to them by Innocent.

Damsel. *Then said the Damsel to them, With whom would you speak in this Place?*

Christ. Christiana answered, we understand that this is a Priviledged place for those that are become Pilgrims, and we now at this Door are such: Wherefore we pray that we may be partakers of that for which we at this time are come; for the day, as thou seest, is very far spent, and we are loth to night to go any further.

Damsel. Pray what may I call your name, that I may tell it to my Lord within?

Christ. My name is *Christiana*, I was the Wife of that Pilgrim that some years ago did Travel this way, and these be his four Children. This Maiden is also my Companion, and is going on Pilgrimage too.

Innocent. Then ran *Innocent* in (for that was her name) and said to those within, Can you think who is at the Door? There is *Christiana* and her Children, and her Companion, all waiting for entertainment here. *Then they leaped for Joy, and went and told their Master. So he came to the Door, and looking upon her, he said, *Art thou that* Christiana, *whom* Christian, *the Good-man, left behind him, when he betook himself to a Pilgrims Life?*

** Joy in the house of the Interpreter that* Christiana *is turned Pilgrim.*

Christ. I am that Woman that was so hard-hearted as to

slight my Husbands Troubles, and that left him to go on in his Journey alone, and these are his four Children; but now I also am come, for I am convinced that no way is right but this.

Inter. *Then is fulfilled that which also is written of the Man that said to his Son, go work to day in my Vineyard, and he said to his Father, I will not; but afterwards repented and went.*

Mat. 21. 29.

Christ. Then said *Christiana*, So be it, *Amen*, God make it a true saying upon me, and grant that I may be found at the last, of him in peace without spot and blameless.

Inter. *But why standest thou thus at the Door, come in thou Daughter of* Abraham, *we was talking of thee but now: For tidings have come to us before, how thou art become a Pilgrim. Come Children, come in; come Maiden, come in; so he had them all into the House.*

So when they were within, they were bidden sit down and rest them, the which when they had done, those that attended upon the Pilgrims in the House, came into the Room to see them. And one smiled, and another smiled, and they all smiled for Joy that *Christiana* was become a Pilgrim. They also looked upon the Boys, they stroaked them over the Faces with the Hand, in token of their kind reception of them: they also carried it lovingly to *Mercy*, and bid them all welcome into their Masters House.

Old Saints glad to see the young ones walk in Gods ways.

After a while, because Supper was not ready, * the *Interpreter* took them into his *Significant* Rooms, and shewed them what *Christian*, *Christiana*'s Husband had seen sometime before. Here therefore they saw the *Man* in the *Cage*, the man and his Dream, the man that cut his way thorough his Enemies, and the Picture of the biggest of them all: together with the rest of those things that were then so profitable to *Christian*.

** The Significant Rooms.*

This done, and after these things had been somewhat digested by *Christiana*, and her Company: the *Interpreter* takes them apart again, and has them first into a Room, *where was a man that could look no way but downwards, with a Muck-rake in his hand. There stood also one over his head with a Celestial Crown in his Hand, and proffered to give him that Crown for his*

The man with the Muck-rake expounded.

Muck-rake; but the man did neither look up, nor regard; but raked to himself the Straws, the small Sticks, and Dust of the Floor.

Then said *Christiana*, *I perswade my self that I know somewhat the meaning of this: For this is a Figure of a man of this World: Is it not, good Sir?*

Inter. Thou hast said the right, said he, and his *Muck-rake* doth show his Carnal mind. And whereas thou seest him rather give heed to rake up Straws and Sticks, and the Dust of the Floor, then to what he says that calls to him from above with the Celestial Crown in his Hand; it is to show, That Heaven is but as a Fable to some, and that things here are counted the only things substantial. Now whereas it was also shewed thee, that the man could look no way but downwards: It is to let thee know that earthly things when they are with Power upon Mens minds, quite carry their hearts away from God.

Chris. *Then said* Christiana, *O! deliver me from this Muck-rake.*

Inter. That Prayer said the *Interpreter*, has lain by till 'tis almost rusty: *Give me not Riches*, is scarce the Prayer of one of ten thousand. Straws, and Sticks, and Dust, with most, are the great things now looked after.

* Christiana's *prayer against the* Muck-rake.

Pro. 30. 8.

With that *Mercy*, and *Christiana* wept, and said, It is alas! too true.

When the *Interpreter* had shewed them this, he has them into the very best Room in the house, (a very brave Room it was) so he bid them look round about, and see if they could find any thing profitable there. Then they looked round and round: For there was nothing there to be seen but a very great *Spider* on the Wall: and that they overlook't.

Mer. *Then said* Mercy, *Sir, I see nothing; but* Christiana *held her peace.*

Inter. But said the *Interpreter*, look again: she therefore lookt again and said, Here is not any thing, but an *ugly Spider*, who hangs by her Hands upon the Wall. Then said he, Is there but one *Spider* in all this spacious Room? Then the water stood in *Christiana*'s Eyes, for she was a Woman quick of apprehension: and she said, Yes Lord,

Of the Spider.

there is more here then one. Yea, and *Spiders* whose Venom is far more destructive than that which is in her. The *Interpreter* then looked pleasantly upon her, and said, Thou hast said the Truth. This made *Mercy* blush, and the Boys to cover their Faces. For they all began now to understand the Riddle.

Talk about the Spider.

Then said the *Interpreter* again, *The Spider taketh hold with her hands, as you see, and is in Kings Pallaces.* And wherefore is this recorded; but to show you, that how full of the Venome of Sin soever you be, yet you may by the hand of Faith lay hold of, and dwell in the best Room that belongs to the Kings House above?

Pro. 30. 28.

The Interpretation.

Chris. I thought, said *Christiana*, of something of this; but I could not imagin it all. I thought that we were like *Spiders*, and that we looked like ugly Creatures, in what fine Room soever we were: But that by this *Spider*, this venomous and ill favoured Creature, we were to learn *how to act Faith*, that came not into my mind. And yet she has taken hold with her hands as I see and dwells in the best Room in the House. God has made nothing in vain.

Then they seemed all to be glad; but the water stood in their Eyes: Yet they looked one upon another, and also bowed before the *Interpreter*.

He had them then into another Room where was a *Hen* and *Chickens*, and bid them observe a while. So one of the Chickens went to the Trough to drink, and every time she drank she lift up her head and her eyes towards Heaven. See, said he, what this little Chick doth, and learn of her to acknowledge whence your Mercies come, by receiving them with looking up. Yet again, said he, observe and look: So they gave heed, and perceived that the Hen did walk in a fourfold Method towards her Chickens. 1. She had a *common call*, and that she hath all day long. 2. She had a *special call*, and that she had but sometimes. 3. She had a *brooding note*. And 4. she had an *out-cry*.

Of the Hen and Chickens.

Now, said he, compare this *Hen* to your King, and these Chickens to his Obedient ones. For answerable to her, himself has his Methods, which he walketh

Mat. 23. 37.

in towards his People. By his common call, *he gives nothing*, by his special call, he always *has something to give*, he has also a brooding voice, *for them that are under his Wing*. And he has an out-cry, to give *the Alarm when he seeth the Enemy come*. I chose, my Darlings, to lead you into the Room where such things are, because you are Women, and they are easie for you.

Chris. And Sir, said *Christiana*, pray let us see some more: So he had them into the Slaughter-house, where was a *Butcher* a killing of a Sheep: And behold the Sheep was quiet, and took her Death patiently. Then said the *Interpreter*: You must learn of this Sheep, to suffer: And to put up wrongs without murmurings and complaints. Behold how quietly she takes her Death, and without objecting she suffereth her Skin to be pulled over her Ears. Your King doth call you his Sheep.

Of the Butcher and the Sheep.

After this, he led them into his Garden, where was great variety of Flowers: and he said, do you see all these? So *Christiana* said, yes. Then said he again, Behold the Flowers are divers in *Stature*, in *Quality*, and *Colour*, and *Smell*, and *Virtue*, and some are better then some: Also where the Gardiner has set them, there they stand, and quarrel not one with another.

Of the Garden.

Again he had them into his Field, which he had sowed with Wheat and Corn: but when they beheld, the tops of all was cut off, only the Straw remained. He said again, this Ground was Dunged, and Plowed, and Sowed; but what shall we do with the Crop? Then said *Christiana*, burn some and make muck of the rest. Then said the *Interpreter* again, Fruit you see is that thing you look for, and for want of that you condemn it to the Fire, and to be trodden under foot of men: Beware that in this you condemn not your selves.

Of the Field.

Then, as they were coming in from abroad, they espied a little *Robbin* with a great *Spider* in his mouth. So the *Interpreter* said, look here. So they looked, and *Mercy* wondred; but *Christiana* said, what a disparagement is it to such a little pretty Bird as the *Robbin-red-breast* is, he being also a Bird above many, that loveth to maintain a kind of Sociableness with men? I had thought

Of the Robbin *and the* Spider.

they had lived upon crums of Bread, or upon other such harmless matter. I like him worse then I did.

The *Interpreter* then replied, This *Robbin* is an Emblem very apt to set forth some Professors by; for to sight they are as this *Robbin*, pretty of Note, Colour and Carriages, they seem also to have a very great Love for Professors that are sincere; and above all other to desire to sociate with, and to be in their Company, as if they could live upon the good Mans Crums. They pretend also that therefore it is, that they frequent the House of the Godly, and the appointments of the Lord: but when they are by themselves, *as the Robbin*, they can catch and gobble up *Spiders*, they can change their Diet, drink *Iniquity*, and swallow down *Sin* like Water.

Pray, and you will get at that which yet lies unrevealed.

So when they were come again into the House, because Supper as yet was not ready, *Christiana* again desired that the *Interpreter* would either *show* or *tell* of some other things that are Profitable.

Then the *Interpreter* began and said, *The fatter the Sow is, the more she desires the Mire; the fatter the Ox is, the more gamesomly he goes to the Slaughter; and the more healthy the lusty man is, the more prone he is unto Evil.*

There is a desire in Women, to go neat and fine, and it is a comely thing to be adorned with that, that in Gods sight is of great price.

'Tis easier watching a night or two, then to sit up a whole year together: So 'tis easier for one to begin to profess well, then to hold out as he should to the end.

Every Ship-Master, when in a Storm, will willingly cast that over Board that is of the smallest value in the Vessel; but who will throw the best out first? none but he that feareth not God.

One leak will sink a Ship, and one Sin will destroy a Sinner.

He that forgets his Friend, is ungrateful unto him; but he that forgets his Saviour is unmerciful to himself.

He that lives in Sin, and looks for Happiness hereafter, is like him that soweth Cockle, and thinks to fill his Barn with Wheat, or Barley.

If a man would live well, let him fetch his last day to him, and make it always his company-Keeper.

Whispering and change of thoughts, proves that Sin is in the World.

If the world which God sets light by, is counted a thing of that worth with men: what is Heaven that God commendeth?

If the Life that is attended with so many troubles, is so loth to be let go by us, What is the Life above?

Every Body will cry up the Goodness of Men; but who is there that is, as he should, affected with the Goodness of God?

We seldom sit down to Meat but we eat, and leave. So there is in Jesus Christ more Merit and Righteousness then the whole World has need of.

When the *Interpreter* had done, he takes them out into his Garden again, and had them to a Tree whose *inside* was all rotten, and gone, and yet it grew and had Leaves. Then said *Mercy*, what means this? This Tree, said he, whose *out-side* is fair, and whose *inside* is rotten; is it to which many may be compared that are in the Garden of God: Who with their mouths speak high in behalf of God, but indeed will do nothing for him: Whose Leaves are fair; but their heart Good for nothing, but to be *Tinder* for the Devils *Tinder-box*.

Of the Tree that is rotten at heart.

Now Supper was ready, the Table spread, and all things set on Board; so they sate down and did eat when one had given thanks. And the *Interpreter* did usually entertain those that lodged with him with Musick at Meals, so the Ministrels played. There was also one that did Sing. And a very fine voice he had.

They are at Supper.

His Song was this.

The Lord is only my support,
And he that doth me feed:
How can I then want any thing
Whereof I stand in need?

When the Song and Musick was ended, the *Interpreter* asked *Christiana, what it was that at first did move her thus to betake her self to a Pilgrims Life?*

Christiana answered: *First*, the loss of my Husband came into my mind, at which I was heartily grieved: but all that was but natural Affection. Then after that, came the Troubles, and Pilgrimage of my Husband into my mind, and also how like a Churle I had carried it to him as to that. So

Talk at Supper.

A Repetition of Christiana's *Experience.*

guilt took hold of my mind, and would have drawn me into the *Pond*; but that opportunely I had a Dream of the well-being of my Husband, and a Letter sent me by the King of that Country where my Husband dwells, to come to him. The Dream and the Letter together so wrought upon my mind, that they forced me to this way.

Inter. *But met you with no opposition afore you set out of Doors?*

Chris. Yes, a Neighbour of mine, one Mrs. *Timerous.* (She was a kin to him that would have perswaded my Husband to go back for fear of the Lions.) She all-to-be-fooled me; for, as she called it, my intended desperate adventure; she also urged what she could, to dishearten me to it, the hardships and Troubles that my Husband met with in the way; but all this I got over pretty well. But a Dream that I had, of two ill-lookt ones, that I thought did Plot how to make me miscarry in my Journey, that hath troubled me much: Yea, it still runs in my mind, and makes me afraid of every one that I meet, lest they should meet me to do me a mischief, and to turn me out of the way. Yea, I may tell my Lord, tho' I would not have every body know it, that between this and the Gate by which we got into the way, we were both so sorely assaulted, that we were made to cry out Murder, and the two that made this assault upon us, were like the two that I saw in my Dream.

A question put to Mercy.

Then said the *Interpreter*, Thy beginning is good, thy latter end shall greatly increase. So he addressed himself to *Mercy*: and said unto her, *And what moved thee to come hither Sweet-heart?*

Mercy. Then *Mercy* blushed and trembled, and for a while continued silent.

Interpreter. *Then said he, be not afraid, only believe, and speak thy mind.*

Mercys *answer.*

Mer. So she began and said, Truly Sir, my want of Experience, is that that makes me covet to be in silence, and that also that fills me with fears of coming short at last. I cannot tell of Visions, and Dreams as my friend *Christiana* can; nor know I what it is to mourn for my refusing of the Counsel of those that were good Relations.

Interpreter. *What was it then, dear heart, that hath prevailed with thee to do as thou hast done?*

Mer. Why, when our friend here, was packing up to be gone from our Town, I and another went accidentally to see her. So we knocked at the Door and went in. When we were within, and seeing what she was doing, we asked what was her meaning. She said, she was sent for to go to her Husband, and then she up and told us, how she had seen him in a Dream, dwelling in a curious place among *Immortals* wearing a Crown, playing upon a Harp, eating and drinking at his Princes Table, and singing Praises to him for bringing him thither, *&c.* Now methought, while she was telling these things unto us, my heart burned within me. And I said in my Heart, if this be true, I will leave my Father and my Mother, and the Land of my Nativity, and will, if I may, go along with *Christiana.*

So I asked her further of the truth of these things, and if she would let me go with her: For I saw now that there was no dwelling, but with the danger of ruin, any longer in our Town. But yet I came away with a heavy heart, not for that I was unwilling to come away; but for that so many of my Relations were left behind. And I am come with all the desire of my heart, and will go if I may with *Christiana* unto her Husband and his King.

Inter. Thy setting out is good, for thou hast given credit to the truth, Thou art a *Ruth*, who did for the love that she bore to *Naomi*, and to the Lord her God, leave Father and Mother, and the land of her Nativity to come out, and go with a People that she knew not heretofore. *The Lord recompence thy work, and full reward be given thee of the Lord God of* Israel, *under whose Wings thou art come to trust.*

Ruth 2. 11, 12.

Now Supper was ended, and Preparations was made for Bed, the Women were laid singly alone, and the Boys by themselves. Now when *Mercy* was in Bed, she could not sleep for joy, for that now her doubts of missing at last, were removed further from her than ever they were before. So she lay blessing and Praising God who had had such favour for her.

They address themselves for bed.

Mercy's *good nights rest.*

In the Morning they arose with the *Sun*, and prepared themselves for their departure: But the *Interpreter* would have them tarry a while, for, said he, you must orderly go from hence. Then said he to the Damsel that at first opened unto them, Take them and have them into the Garden, to the *Bath*, and there wash them, and make them clean from the soil which they have gathered by travelling. Then *Innocent* the Damsel took them and had them into the Garden, and brought them to the *Bath*, so she told them that there they must wash and be clean, for so her Master would have the Women to do that called at his House as they were going on *Pilgrimage*. They then went in and washed, yea they and the Boys and all, and they came out of that *Bath* not only sweet, and clean; but also much enlivened and strengthened in their Joynts: So when they came in, they looked fairer a deal, than when they went out to the washing.

The Bath Sanctification.

They wash in it.

When they were returned out of the Garden from the *Bath*, the *Interpreter* took them and looked upon them and said unto them, *fair as the Moon*. Then he called for the *Seal* wherewith they used to be *Sealed* that were washed in his *Bath*. So the *Seal* was brought, and he set his Mark upon them, that they might be known in the Places whither they were yet to go: Now the seal was the contents and sum of the Passover which the Children of *Israel* did eat when they came out from the Land of *Egypt*: and the mark was set betwixt their Eyes. This seal greatly added to their Beauty, for it was an Ornament to their Faces. It also added to their gravity, and made their Countenances more like them of Angels.

They are sealed.

Exo. 13. 8, 9, 10.

Then said the *Interpreter* again to the Damsel that waited upon these Women, Go into the Vestry and fetch out Garments for these People: So she went and fetched out white Rayment, and laid it down before him; so he commanded them to put it on. *It was fine Linnen, white and clean.* When the Women were thus adorned they seemed to be a Terror one to the other; For that they could not see that glory each one on her self, which they could see in each other. Now therefore they began to esteem each other better then themselves. For you are fairer then I am, said one, and you are

They are clothed.

True humility.

more comely then I am, said another. The Children also stood amazed to see into what fashion they were brought.

The *Interpreter* then called for a *Manservant* of his, one *Great-heart*, and bid him take *Sword*, and *Helmet* and *Shield*, and take these my Daughters, said he, and conduct them to the House called *Beautiful*, at which place they will rest next. So he took his Weapons, and went before them, and the *Interpreter* said, God speed. Those also that belonged to the Family sent them away with many a good wish. So they went on their way, and Sung.

This place has been our second Stage,
Here we have heard and seen
Those good things that from Age to Age,
To others hid have been.
The Dunghil-raker, Spider, Hen,
The Chicken too to me
Hath taught a Lesson, let me then
Conformed to it be.
The Butcher, Garden and the Field,
The Robbin *and his bait,*
Also the Rotten-tree doth yield
Me Argument of weight
To move me for to watch and pray,
To strive to be sincere,
To take my Cross up day by day,
And serve the Lord with fear.

Now I saw in my Dream that they went on, and *Great-heart* went before them, so they went and came to the place where *Christians* Burthen fell off his Back, and tumbled into a Sepulchre. Here then they made a pause, and here also they blessed God. Now said *Christiana*, it comes to my mind what was said to us at the Gate, to wit, that we should have Pardon, by *Word* and *Deed*; by word, that is, by the promise; by *Deed*, to wit, in the way it was obtained. What the promise is, of that I know something: But what is it to have Pardon by deed, or in the way that it was obtained, Mr. *Great-heart*, I suppose you know; wherefore if you please let us hear you discourse thereof.

1 *part pag.* 168.

Great-heart. Pardon by the deed done, is Pardon obtained by some one, for another that hath need thereof: Not by the Person pardoned, but in the way, *saith another*, in which I have obtained it. So then to speak to the question more large, The pardon that you and *Mercy* and these Boys have *attained*, was *obtained* by another, to wit, by him that let you in at the Gate: And he hath obtain'd it in this double way. He has performed Righteousness to cover you, and spilt blood to wash you in.

A comment upon what was said at the Gate, or a discourse of our being justified by Christ.

Chris. *But if he parts with his Righteousness to us: What will he have for himself?*

Great-heart. He has more Righteousness than you have need of, or than he needeth himself.

Chris. *Pray make that appear.*

Great-heart. With all my heart, but first I must premise that he of whom we are now about to speak, is one that has not his Fellow. He has two Natures in one Person, plain to be *distinguished*, *impossible* to be *divided.* Unto each of these Natures a Righteousness belongeth, and each Righteousness is essential to that Nature. So that one may as easily cause the Nature to be extinct, as to separate its Justice or Righteousness from it. Of *these* Righteousnesses therefore, we are not made partakers so, as that they, or any of them, should be put upon us that we might be made just, and live thereby. Besides these there is a Righteousness which this Person has, as these two Natures are joyned in one. And this is not the Righteousness of the *God-head*, as distinguished from the *Manhood*; nor the Righteousness of the *Manhood*, as distinguished from the *Godhead*; but a Righteousness which standeth in the Union of both Natures: and may properly be called, the Righteousness that is essential to his being prepared of God to the capacity of the Mediatory Office which he was to be intrusted with. If he parts with his first Righteousness, he parts with his *God-head*; if he parts with his second Righteousness, he parts with the purity of his *Manhood*; if he parts with this third, he parts with that perfection that capacitates him to the Office of Mediation. He has therefore another Righteousness which standeth in *performance*, or obedience to a revealed Will: And that is it that he puts upon Sinners, and that by which their

Sins are covered. Wherefore he saith, *as by one mans disobedience many were made Sinners : So by the obedience of one shall many be made Righteous.* Rom. 5. 19.

Chris. *But are the other Righteousnesses of no use to us?*

Great heart. Yes, for though they are essential to his Natures and Office, and so cannot be communicated unto another, yet it is by Virtue of them that the Righteousness that justifies, is for that purpose efficacious. The *Righteousness* of his *God-head* gives *Virtue* to his Obedience; the *Righteousness* of his *Man-hood* giveth capability to his obedience to justifie, and the Righteousness that standeth in the Union of these two Natures to his Office, giveth Authority to that Righteousness to do the work for which it is ordained.

So then, here is a Righteousness that Christ, as God, has no need of, for he is God without it: here is a Righteousness that Christ, as Man, has no need of to make him so, for he is perfect Man without it. Again, here is a Righteousness that Christ as God man has no need of, for he is perfectly so without it. Here then is a Righteousness that Christ, as God, as Man, as God-man has no need of, with Reference to himself, and therefore he can spare it, a justifying Righteousness, that he for himself wanteth not, and therefore he giveth it away. Hence 'tis called the *gift of Righteousness*. This Righteousness, since Christ Jesus the Lord, has made himself under the Law, *must* be given away: For the Law doth not only bind him that is under it, *to do justly*; but to use Charity: Wherefore he *must*, he *ought* by the Law, if he hath two Coats, to give one to him that has none. Now our Lord hath indeed *two Coats*, one for himself, and one to spare: Wherefore he freely bestows one upon those that have none. And thus *Christiana*, and *Mercy*, and the rest of you that are here, doth your Pardon come by *deed*, or by the work of another man? Your Lord Christ is he that has worked, and given away what he wrought for to the next poor Beggar he meets. Rom. 5. 17.

But again, in order to Pardon by *deed*, there must something be paid to God as a price, as well as something prepared to cover us withal. Sin has delivered us up to the just Curse of a Righteous Law: Now from this Curse we must be justified by way of Redemption, a price being paid for the harms we have done, and this is by the Blood of your Lord: Who came and stood in your place, and stead, and died your Death for your Transgressions. Thus has he ransomed you from your Transgressions by Blood, and covered your polluted and deformed Souls with Righteousness: For the sake of which, God passeth by you, and will not hurt you, when he comes to Judge the World.

Ro. 4. 24.

Gala. 3. 13.

Chris. *This is brave. Now I see that there was something to be learnt by our being pardoned by* word *and* deed. *Good* Mercy, *let us labour to keep this in mind, and my Children do you remember it also. But, Sir, was not this it that made my good* Christians *Burden fall from off his Shoulder, and that made him give three leaps for Joy?*

Christiana *affected with this way of Redemption.*

Great-heart. *Yes, 'twas the belief of this, that cut those Strings that could not be cut by other means, and 'twas to give him a proof of the Virtue of this, that he was suffered to carry his Burden to the Cross.

* *How the Strings that bound Christians burden to him were cut.*

Chris. *I thought so, for tho' my heart was lightful and joyous before, yet it is ten times more lightsome and joyous now. And I am perswaded by what I have felt, tho' I have felt but little as yet, that if the most burdened Man in the World was here, and did see and believe, as I now do, 'twould make his heart the more merry and blithe.*

Great-heart. There is not only comfort, and the ease of a Burden brought to us, by the sight and Consideration of these; but an indeared Affection begot in us by it: For who can, if he doth but once think that Pardon comes, not only by promise, but thus; but be affected with the way and means of his Redemption, and so with the man that hath wrought it for him?

How affection to Christ is begot in the Soul.

Chris. *True, methinks it makes my Heart bleed to think that he should bleed for me. Oh! thou loving one, Oh! thou Blessed one. Thou deservest to have me, thou hast bought me: Thou deservest to have me all, thou hast paid for me ten thousand times more than I am worth. No marvel that this made the Water stand*

1 *Part pag.* 168.

Cause of admiration.

in my Husbands Eyes, and that it made him trudg so nimbly on. I am perswaded he wished me with him; but vile wretch, that I was, I let him come all alone. O Mercy, *that thy Father and Mother were here, yea, and Mrs.* Timorous *also. Nay I wish now with all my Heart, that here was Madam* Wanton *too. Surely, surely, their Hearts would be affected, nor could the fear of the one, nor the powerful Lusts of the other, prevail with them to go home again, and to refuse to become good Pilgrims.*

Great-heart. You speak now in the warmth of your Affections, will it, think you, be always thus with you? Besides, this is not communicated to every one, nor to every one that did see your Jesus bleed. There was that stood by, and that saw the Blood run from his Heart to the Ground, and yet was so far off this, that instead of lamenting, they laughed at him, and instead of becoming his Disciples, did harden their Hearts against him. So that all that you have my Daughters, you have by a peculiar impression made by a Divine contemplating upon what I have spoken to you. Remember that 'twas told you, that the *Hen* by her common call, gives no meat to her *Chickens.* This you have therefore by a special Grace.

To be affected with Christ and with what he has don is a thing special.

Now I saw still in my Dream, that they went on until they were come to the place that *Simple*, and *Sloth* and *Presumption* lay and slept in, when *Christian* went by on Pilgrimage. And behold they were hanged up in Irons a little way off on the other-side.

Simple *and* Sloth *and* Presumption *hanged, and why.*

Mercy. *Then said* Mercy *to him that was their Guide, and Conductor, What are those three men? and for what are they hanged there?*

Great-heart. These three men, were Men of very bad Qualities, they had no mind to be Pilgrims themselves, and whosoever they could they hindred; they were for *Sloth* and *Folly* themselves, and whoever they could perswade with, they made so too, and withal taught them to presume that they should do well at last. They were asleep when *Christian* went by, and now you go by they are hanged.

Mercy. *But could they perswade any to be of their Opinion?*

Great-heart. Yes, they turned several out of the way.

There was *Slow-pace* that they perswaded to do as they. They also prevailed with one *Short-wind*, with one *No-heart*, with one *Linger-after-lust*, and with one *Sleepy-head*, and with a young Woman her name was *Dull*, to turn out of the way and become as they. Besides, they brought up an ill report of your Lord, perswading others that he was a task-Master. They also brought up an evil report of the good Land, saying, 'twas not half so good as some pretend it was: They also began to vilifie his Servants, and to count the very best of them meddlesome, troublesome busie-Bodies: Further, they would call the Bread of God, *Husks*; the *Comforts* of his Children, *Fancies*, the Travel and Labour of Pilgrims, things to no purpose.

Their Crimes.

Who they prevailed upon to turn out of the way.

Chris. *Nay, said* Christiana, *if they were such, they shall never be bewailed by me, they have but what they deserve, and I think it is well that they hang so near the High-way that others may see and take warning. But had it not been well if their Crimes had been ingraven in some Plate of Iron or Brass, and left here, even where they did their Mischiefs, for a caution to other bad Men?*

Great-heart. So it is, as you well may perceive if you will go a little to the Wall.

Mercy. *No no, let them hang and their Names Rot, and their Crimes live for ever against them; I think it a high favour that they were hanged afore we came hither, who knows else what they might a done to such poor Women as we are?* Then she turned it into a Song, saying,

Now then, you three, hang there and be a Sign
To all that shall against the Truth combine:
And let him that comes after, fear this end,
If unto Pilgrims he is not a Friend.
And thou my Soul of all such men beware,
That unto Holiness Opposers are.

Thus they went on till they came at the foot of the Hill *Difficulty*. Where again their good Friend, Mr. *Great-heart*, took an occasion to tell them of what happened there when *Christian* himself went by. So he had them first to the Spring.

1 *Part pag.* 171.

Ezek. 34. 18.

Lo, saith he, *This is the Spring that* Christian *drank of*, before he went up this Hill, and then 'twas clear and good; but now 'tis Dirty with the feet of some that are not desirous that Pilgrims here should quench their Thirst: Thereat *Mercy* said, *And why so envious tro?* But said their Guide, It will do, if taken up, and put into a Vessel that is sweet and good; for then the Dirt will sink to the bottom, and the Water come out by it self more clear. Thus therefore *Christiana* and her Companions were compelled to do. They took it up, and put it into an Earthen-pot and so let it stand till the Dirt was gone to the bottom, and then they drank thereof.

'Tis difficult getting of good Doctrine in erroneous Times.

Next he shewed them the two *by-ways* that were at the foot of the Hill, where *Formality* and *Hypocrisy* lost themselves. And, said he, these are dangerous Paths: Two were here cast away when *Christian* came by. *And although, as you see, these ways are since stopt up with *Chains*, *Posts* and a *Ditch*: Yet there are that will chuse to adventure here, rather than take the pains to go up this Hill.

** By paths tho barred up will not keep all from going in them.*

1 Part pag. 172.

Christiana. *The way of Transgressors is hard. 'Tis a wonder that they can get into those ways, without danger of breaking their Necks.*

Pro. 13. 15.

Great-heart. They will venture, yea, if at any time any of the Kings Servants doth happen to see them, and doth call unto them, and tell them that *they* are in the wrong ways, and do bid them beware the danger. Then they will railingly return them answer and say, *As for the Word that thou hast spoken unto us in the name of the King, we will not hearken unto thee*; *but we will certainly do whatsoever thing goeth out of our own Mouths*, &c. Nay if you look a little farther, you shall see that these ways, are made cautionary enough, not only by these *Posts* and *Ditch* and *Chain*; but also by being hedged up. Yet they will chuse to go there.

Jer. 44. 16, 17.

Christiana. **They are Idle, they love not to take Pains, up-hill-way is unpleasant to them. So it is fulfilled unto them as it is written, The way of the slothful man is a Hedge of Thorns. Yea,*

** The reason why some do chuse to go in by-waies.*

Pro. 15. 19.

they will rather chuse to walk upon a Snare, then to go up this Hill, and the rest of this way to the City.

The Hill puts the Pilgrims to it.

Then they set forward and began to go up the Hill, and up the Hill they went; but before they got to the top, *Christiana* began to *Pant*, and said, I dare say this is a breathing Hill, no marvel if they that love their ease more than their Souls, chuse to themselves a smoother way. Then said *Mercy*, I must sit down, also the least of the Children began to cry. Come, come, said *Great-heart*, sit not down here, for a little above is the Princes *Arbour*. Then took he the little Boy by the Hand, and led him up thereto.

They sit in the Arbour.

1 Part pag. 172, 173.

Mat. 11. 28.

When they were come to the *Arbour* they were very willing to sit down, for they were all in a pelting heat. Then said *Mercy*, *How sweet is rest to them that Labour*! And how good is the Prince of Pilgrims, to provide such resting places for them! Of *this Arbour* I have heard much; but I never saw it before. But here let us beware of sleeping: For as I have heard, for that it cost poor *Christian* dear.

The little Boys answer to the guide, and also to Mercy.

Then said Mr. *Great-heart* to the little ones, Come my pretty *Boys*, how do you do? what think you now of going on Pilgrimage? Sir, said the least, I was almost beat out of heart; but I thank you for lending me a hand at my need. And I remember now what my Mother has told me, namely, That the way to Heaven is as up a Ladder, and the way to Hell is as down a Hill. But I had rather go up the Ladder to Life, then down the Hill to Death.

Which is hardest up Hill or down Hill.

Then said *Mercy*, But the Proverb is, *To go down the Hill is easie*: But *James* said (for that was his Name) The day is coming when in my Opinion, *going down Hill will be the hardest of all.* 'Tis a good Boy, said his Master, thou hast given her a right answer. Then *Mercy* smiled, but the little Boy did blush.

They refresh themselves.

Chris. Come, said *Christiana*, will you eat a bit, a little to sweeten your Mouths, while you sit here to rest your Legs? For I have here a piece of Pomgranate which Mr. *Interpreter* put in my Hand, just when I came out of his Doors; he gave me also a piece of an Honey-comb, and a little Bottle of Spirits. I thought he gave you something, said *Mercy*, because he called you a to-side. Yes, so he did, said the other, But *Mercy*, It shall still be as I said it should, when at first we came from home: Thou shalt be a sharer in all the good that I have, because thou so willingly didst become my Companion. Then she gave to them, and they did eat, both *Mercy*, and the Boys. And said *Christiana* to Mr. *Great-heart*, Sir will you do as we? But he answered, You are going on Pilgrimage, and presently I shall return; much good may what you have, do to you. At home I eat the same every day. Now when they had eaten and drank, and had chatted a little longer, their guide said to them, The day wears away, if you think good, let us prepare to be going. So they got up to go, and the little Boys went before; but *Christiana* forgat to take her Bottle of Spirits with her, so she sent her little Boy back to fetch it. Then said *Mercy*, I think this is a *losing* Place. Here *Christian* lost his *Role*, and here *Christiana* left her Bottle behind her: Sir what is the cause of this? so their guide made answer and said, The cause is *sleep*, or *forgetfulness*; some *sleep*, when they should keep *awake*; and some *forget*, when they should *remember*; and this is the very cause, why often at the resting places, some Pilgrims in some things come off losers. Pilgrims should watch and remember what they have already received under their greatest enjoyments: But for want of doing so, oft times their rejoycing ends in Tears, and their Sun-shine in a Cloud: Witness the story of *Christian* at this place.

Christiana *forgets her Bottle of Spirits.*

Mark this.

1 *part page* 173.

When they were come to the place where *Mistrust* and *Timorous* met *Christian* to perswade him to go back for fear of the Lions, they perceived as it were a Stage, and before it towards the Road, a broad plate with a Copy of Verses written thereon, and underneath, the reason of the raising up of that Stage in that place, rendred. The Verses were these.

Let him that sees this Stage take heed,
Unto his Heart and Tongue:
Lest if he do not, here he speed
As some have long agone.

The words underneath the Verses were. *This Stage was built to punish such upon, who through* Timorousness, *or* Mistrust, *shall be afraid to go further on Pilgrimage. Also on this Stage both* Mistrust, *and* Timorous *were burned thorough the Tongue with an hot Iron, for endeavouring to hinder* Christian *in his Journey.*

Then said *Mercy.* This is much like to the saying of the beloved, *What shall be given unto thee? or what shall be done unto thee thou false Tongue? sharp Arrows of the mighty, with Coals of* Juniper.

Psal. 120. 3, 4.

So they went on till they came within sight of the Lions. Now Mr. *Great-heart* was a strong man, so he was not afraid of a Lion. But yet when they were come up to the place where the Lions were, the Boys that went before, were now glad to cringe behind, for they were afraid of the Lions, so they stept back and went behind. At this their guide smiled, and said, How now my Boys, do you love to go before when no danger doth approach, and love to come behind so soon as the Lions appear?

1 *Part pag.* 175.

An Emblem of those that go on bravely, when there is no danger; but shrink when troubles come.

Now as they went up, Mr. *Great-heart* drew his Sword with intent to make a way for the Pilgrims in spite of the Lions. Then there appeared one, that it seems, had taken upon him to back the Lions. And he said to the Pilgrims guide, What is the cause of your coming hither? Now the name of that man was *Grim* or *Bloody man*, because of his slaying of Pilgrims, and he was of the race of the *Gyants*.

Of Grim *the* Giant, *and of his backing the Lions.*

Great-heart. Then said the *Pilgrims* guide, these Women and Children, are going on Pilgrimage, and this is the way they must go, and go it they shall in spite of thee and the Lions.

Grim. This is not their way, neither shall they go therein. I am come forth to with stand them, and to that end will back the Lions.

Now to say truth, by reason of the fierceness of the Lions, and of the *Grim*-Carriage of him that did back them, this way had of late lain much un-occupied, and was almost all grown over with Grass.

Christiana. Then said *Christiana*, Tho' the High-ways have been unoccupied heretofore, and tho' the Travellers have been made in time past, to walk thorough by-Paths, it must not be so now I am risen, *Now I am Risen a Mother in* Israel.

Judg. 5, 6, 7.

Grim. Then he swore *by the Lions*, but it should; and therefore bid them turn aside, for they should not have passage there.

Great-heart. But their guide made first his Approach unto *Grim*, and laid so heavily at him with his Sword, that he forced him to a retreat.

Grim. Then said he (that attempted to back the Lions) will you slay me upon mine own Ground?

Great-heart. 'Tis the Kings High-way that we are in, and in his way it is that thou hast placed thy Lions; but these Women and these Children, tho' weak, shall hold on their way in spite of thy Lions. And with that he gave him again a down-right blow, and brought him upon his Knees. With this blow he also broke his Helmet, and with the next he cut off an Arm. Then did the *Giant Roar* so hideously, that his Voice frighted the Women, and yet they were glad to see him lie sprawling upon the Ground. Now the Lions were chained, and so of themselves could do nothing. Wherefore when old *Grim* that intended to back them was dead, Mr. *Great-heart* said to the Pilgrims, Come now and follow me, and no hurt shall happen to you from the Lions. They therefore went on; but the Women trembled as they passed by them, the Boys also look't as if they would die; but they all got by without further hurt.

A fight betwixt Grim *and* Great-heart.

The Victory.

They pass by the Lyons.

Now then they were within sight of the *Porters* Lodge, and they soon came up unto it; but they made the more haste after this to go thither, because 'tis dangerous travelling there in the Night. So when they were come to the Gate, the guide knocked, and the Porter cried, *who is there*; but as soon as the Guide had said *it is I*, he knew his Voice and came down. (For the Guide had oft before that, come thither as a Conductor of Pilgrims) when he was come down, he opened the Gate, and seeing the Guide standing just before it (for he saw not the Women, for they were behind him) he said unto him, How now Mr. *Great-heart*, what is your business here so late to

They come to the Porters Lodge.

Night? I have brought, said he, some Pilgrims hither, where by my Lords Commandment they must Lodge. I had been here some time ago, had I not been opposed by the Giant that did use to back the Lyons. But I after a long and tedious combate with him, have cut him off, and have brought the Pilgrims hither in safety.

Great-heart *attempts to go back.*

Porter. *Will you not go in, and stay till Morning?*

Great-heart. No, I will return to my Lord to night.

Christiana. Oh Sir, I know not how to be willing you should leave us in our Pilgrimage, you have been so faithful, and so loving to us, you have fought so stoutly for us, you have been so hearty in counselling of us, that I shall never forget your favour towards us.

The Pilgrims implore his company still.

Mercy. Then said *Mercy*, O that we might have thy Company to our Journeys end! How can such poor Women as we, hold out in a way so full of Troubles as this way is, without a Friend, and Defender?

James. Then said *James*, the youngest of the Boys, Pray Sir be perswaded to go with us and help us, because we are so weak, and the way so dangerous as it is.

Great-heart. I am at my Lords Commandment. If he shall allot me to be your Guide quite thorough, I will willingly wait upon you; but here you failed at first; for when he bid me come thus far with you, then you should have begged me of him to have gon quite thorough with you, and he would have granted your request. However, at present I must withdraw, and so good *Christiana*, *Mercy*, and my brave Children, Adieu.

Help lost for want of asking for.

Then the Porter, Mr. *Watchful*, asked *Christiana* of her Country, and of her Kindred, and she said, *I came from the City of* Destruction, *I am a Widdow Woman, and my Husband is dead, his name was* Christian *the Pilgrim.* How, said the Porter, was he your Husband? Yes, said she, and these are his Children: and this, pointing to *Mercy*, is one of my Towns-Women. Then the Porter rang his Bell, as at such times he is wont and

1 *Part pag.* 175.

Christiana *makes her self known to the Porter, he tells it to a damsel.*

there came to the Door one of the Damsels, whose Name was *Humble-mind*. And to her the Porter said, Go tell it within that *Christiana* the Wife of *Christian* and her Children are come hither on Pilgrimage. She went in therefore and told it. But Oh what a Noise for gladness was there within, when the Damsel did but drop that word out of her Mouth!

Joy at the noise of the Pilgrims coming.

So they came with haste to the Porter, for *Christiana* stood still at the Door; then some of the most grave, said unto her, *Come in* Christiana, *come in thou Wife of that Good Man*, *come in thou Blessed Woman*, *come in with all that are with thee.* So she went in, and they followed her that were her Children, and her Companions. Now when they were gone in, they were had into a very large Room, where they were bidden to sit down: So they sat down, and the chief of the House was called to see, and welcome the Guests. Then they came in, and understanding who they were, did Salute each one with a kiss, and said, Welcome ye Vessels of the Grace of God, welcome to us your Friends.

Christians *love is kindled at the sight of one another.*

Now because it was somewhat late, and because the Pilgrims were weary with their Journey, and also made faint with the sight of the Fight, and of the terrible Lyons: Therefore they desired as soon as might be, to prepare to go to Rest. Nay, said those of the Family, refresh your selves first with a Morsel of Meat. For they had prepared for them a Lamb, with the accustomed Sauce belonging thereto. For the Porter had heard before of their coming, and had told it to them within. So when they had Supped, and ended their Prayer with a Psalm, they desired they might go to rest. But let us, said *Christiana*, if we may be so bold as to chuse, be in that Chamber that was my Husbands, when he was here. So they had them up thither, and they lay all in a Room. When they were at Rest, *Christiana* and *Mercy* entred into discourse about things that were convenient.

Exo. 12. 38.

Joh. 1. 29.

1 *Part pag.* 181.

Chris. *Little did I think once, that when my Husband went on Pilgrimage I should ever a followed.*

Mercy. And you as little thought of lying in his Bed, and in his Chamber to Rest, as you do now.

Christs Bosome is for all Pilgrims.

Chris. *And much less did I ever think of seeing his Face with Comfort, and of Worshipping the Lord the King, with him, and yet now I believe I shall.*

Mercy. Hark, don't you hear a Noise?

Christiana. Yes, 'tis as I believe a Noise of Musick, for Joy that we are here.

Musick.

Mer. Wonderful! Musick in the House, Musick in the Heart, and Musick also in Heaven, for joy that we are here.

Thus they talked a while, and then betook themselves to sleep; so in the morning, when they were awake, *Christiana* said to *Mercy*.

Mercy *did laugh in her sleep.*

Chris. *What was the matter that you did laugh in your sleep to Night? I suppose you was in a Dream?*

Mercy. So I was, and a sweet Dream it was; but are you sure I laughed?

Christiana. *Yes, you laughed heartily*; *But prethee* Mercy *tell me thy Dream?*

Mercy. I was a Dreamed that I sat all alone in a Solitary place, and was bemoaning of the hardness of my Heart. Now I had not sat there long, but methought many were gathered about me to see me, and to hear what it was that I said. So they hearkened, and I went on bemoaning the hardness of my Heart. At this, some of them laughed at me, some called me Fool, and some began to thrust me about. With that, methought I looked up, and saw one coming with Wings towards me. So he came directly to me, and said *Mercy*, what aileth thee? Now when he had heard me make my complaint; he said, *Peace be to thee*! he also wiped mine Eyes with his Hankerchief, and *clad* me in *Silver* and *Gold*; he put a Chain about my Neck, and Ear-rings in mine Ears, and a beautiful Crown upon my Head. Then he took me by the Hand, and said *Mercy*, come after me. So he went up, and I followed, till we came at a Golden Gate. Then he knocked, and when

Mercy's *Dream.*

What her dream was.

Ezek. 16. 8, 9, 10, 11.

they within had opened, the man went in and I followed him up to a Throne, upon which one sat, and he said to me, *welcome Daughter*. The place looked bright, and twinkling like the Stars, or rather like the *Sun*, and I thought that I saw your Husband there, so I awoke from my Dream. But did I laugh?

Christiana. *Laugh! Ay, and well you might to see your self so well. For you must give me leave to tell you, that I believe it was a good Dream, and that as you have begun to find the first part true, so you shall find the second at last.* God speaks once, yea twice, yet man perceiveth it not, in a Dream, in a Vision of the Night, when deep sleep falleth upon men, in slumbring upon the Bed. *We need not, when a-Bed, lie awake to talk with God; he can visit us while we sleep, and cause us then to hear his Voice. Our Heart oft times wakes when we sleep, and God can speak to that, either by Words, by Proverbs, by Signs and Similitudes, as well as if one was awake.*

Job 33. 14, 15.

Mercy. Well I am glad of my Dream, for I hope ere long to see it fulfilled, to the making of me laugh again.

Christiana. *I think it is now time to rise, and to know what we must do?*

Mercy *glad of her dream.*

Mercy. Pray, if they invite us to stay a while, let us willingly accept of the proffer. I am the willinger to stay awhile here, to grow better acquainted with these Maids; methinks *Prudence*, *Piety* and *Charity*, have very comly and sober Countenances.

Chris. *We shall see what they will do.* So when they were up and ready, they came down. And they asked one another of their rest, and if it was Comfortable, or not?

Mer. *Very good, said* Mercy. *It was one of the best Nights Lodging that ever I had in my Life.*

Then said *Prudence*, and *Piety*, If you will be perswaded to stay here a while, you shall have what the House will afford.

They stay here some time.

Charity. *Ay, and that with a very good will said* Charity. So they consented, and stayed there about a Month or above: And became very Profitable one to another. And because *Prudence* would see how *Christiana* had brought up her Children, she asked leave of her to Catechise them:

Prudence *desires to catechise* Christianas *Children.*

So she gave her free consent. Then she began at the youngest whose Name was *James*.

Pru. *And she said, Come* James, *canst thou tell who made thee?*

James *Catechised.*

Jam. God the Father, God the Son, and God the Holy Ghost.

Pru. *Good Boy. And canst thou tell who saves thee?*

Jam. God the Father, God the Son, and God the Holy Ghost.

Pru. *Good Boy still. But how doth God the Father save thee?*

Jam. By his Grace.

Pru. *How doth God the Son save thee?*

Jam. By his Righteousness, Death, and Blood, and Life.

Pru. *And how doth God the Holy Ghost save thee?*

Jam. By his *Illumination*, by his *Renovation*, and by his *Preservation.*

Then said *Prudence* to *Christiana*, You are to be commended for thus bringing up your Children. I suppose I need not ask the rest these Questions, since the youngest of them can answer them so well. I will therefore now apply my self to the Youngest next.

Prudence. Then she said, Come *Joseph*, (for his Name was *Joseph*) will you let me Catechise you?

Joseph *catechised.*

Joseph. with all my Heart.

Pru. *What is Man?*

Joseph. A Reasonable Creature, so made by God, as my Brother said.

Pru. *What is supposed by this Word, saved?*

Joseph. That man by Sin has brought himself into a State of Captivity and Misery.

Pru. *What is supposed by his being saved by the Trinity?*

Joseph. That Sin is so great and mighty a Tyrant, that none can pull us out of its clutches but God, and that God is so good and loving to man, as to pull him indeed out of this Miserable State.

Pru. *What is Gods design in saving of poor Men?*

Joseph. The glorifying of his Name, of his Grace, and Justice, *&c.* And the everlasting Happiness of his Creature.

Pru. *Who are they that must be saved?*

Joseph. Those that accept of his Salvation.

Good Boy *Joseph*, thy Mother has taught thee well, and thou hast hearkened to what she has said unto thee.

Then said *Prudence* to *Samuel*, who was the eldest but one.

Prudence. Come *Samuel*, are you willing that I should Catechise you also?

Samuel *Catechised.*

Sam. Yes, forsooth, if you please.

Pru. *What is Heaven?*

Sam. A palace, and State most blessed, because God dwelleth there.

Pru. *What is Hell?*

Sam. A Place and State most woful, because it is the dwelling place of Sin, the Devil, and Death.

Prudence. *Why wouldest thou go to Heaven?*

Sam. That I may see God, and serve him without weariness; that I may see Christ, and love him everlastingly; that I may have that fulness of the Holy Spirit in me, that I can by no means here enjoy.

Pru. *A very good Boy also, and one that has learned well.*

Then she addressed her self to the eldest, whose Name was *Matthew*, and she said to him, Come *Matthew*, shall I also Catechise you?

Matthew *Catechised.*

Mat. *With a very good will.*

Pru. *I ask then, if there was ever any thing that had a being, antecedent to, or before God?*

Mat. No, for God is Eternal, nor is there any thing excepting himself, that had a being until the beginning of the first day. *For in six days the Lord made Heaven and Earth, the Sea and all that in them is.*

Pru. *What do you think of the Bible?*

Mat. It is the Holy Word of God.

Pru. *Is there nothing Written therein, but what you understand?*

Mat. Yes, a great deal.

Pru. *What do you do when you meet with such places therein, that you do not understand?*

Mat. I think God is wiser then I. I pray also that he will please to let me know all therein that he knows will be for my good.

Pru. *How believe you as touching the Resurrection of the Dead?*

Mat. I believe they shall rise, the same that was buried: The same in *Nature*, tho' not in Corruption. And I believe this upon a double account. First, because God has promised it. Secondly, because he is able to perform it.

Prudences *conclusion upon the Catechising of the Boys.*

Then said *Prudence* to the Boys, You must still hearken to your Mother, for she can learn you more. You must also diligently give ear to what good talk you shall hear from others, for for your sakes do they speak good things. Observe also and that with carefulness, what the Heavens and the Earth do teach you; but especially be much in the Meditation of that Book that was the cause of your Fathers becoming a Pilgrim. I for my part, my Children, will teach you what I can while you are here, and shall be glad if you will ask me Questions that tend to Godly edifying.

Mercy *has a sweet heart.*

Now by that these Pilgrims had been at this place a week, *Mercy* had a Visitor that pretended some good Will unto her, and his name was Mr. *Brisk*; A man of some breeding, and that pretended to Religion; but a man that stuck very close to the World. So he came once or twice, or more to *Mercy*, and offered love unto her. Now *Mercy* was of a fair Countenance, and therefore the more alluring.

Mercies *temper.*

Her mind also was, to be always busying of her self in doing, for when she had nothing to do for her self, she would be making of Hose and Garments for others, and would bestow them upon them that had need. And Mr. *Brisk* not knowing where or how she disposed of what she made, seemed to be greatly taken, for that he found her never Idle. I will warrant her a good Huswife, quoth he to himself.

* *Mercy enquires of the Maids concerning Mr.* Brisk.

**Mercy* then revealed the business to the maidens that were of the House, and enquired of them concerning him: for they did know him better then she. So they told her that he was a very busie Young Man, and one that pretended to Religion; but was as they feared, a stranger to the Power of that which was good.

Nay then, said Mercy, *I will look no more on him, for I purpose never to have a clog to my Soul.*

Prudence then replied, That there needed no great matter of discouragement to be given to him, her continuing so as she had begun to do for the Poor, would quickly cool his Courage.

So the next time he comes, he finds her at her old work, a making of things for the Poor. Then said he, What always at it? Yes, said she, either for my self, or for others. And what canst thou *earn* a day, quoth he? I do these things, said she, *That I may be Rich in good Works, laying up in store a good Foundation against the time to come, that I may lay hold on Eternal Life:* Why prethee what dost thou with them? said he; Cloath the naked, said she. With that his Countenance fell. So he forbore to come at her again. And when he was asked the reason why, he said, *That* Mercy *was a pretty Lass; but troubled with ill Conditions.*

Talk betwixt Mercy *and Mr.* Brisk.

1 Tim. 6. 17, 18, 19.

He forsakes her, and why.

When he had left her, *Prudence* said, Did I not tell thee that Mr. *Brisk* would soon forsake thee? yea, he will raise up an ill report of thee: For notwithstanding his pretence to Religion, and his seeming love to *Mercy*: Yet *Mercy* and he are of tempers so different, that I believe they will never come together.

Mercy *in the practice of* Mercy *rejected; While* Mercy *in the Name of* Mercy *is liked.*

Mercy. *I might a had Husbands afore now, tho' I spake not of it to any; but they were such as did not like my Conditions, though never did any of them find fault with my Person: So they and I could not agree.*

Prudence. Mercy in our days is little set by, any further then as to its Name: the Practice, which is set forth by thy Conditions, there are but few that can abide.

Mercy. *Well, said* Mercy, *if no body will have me, I will dye a Maid, or my Conditions shall be to me as a Husband. For I cannot change my Nature, and to have one that lies cross to me in this, that I purpose never to admit of, as long as I live. I had a Sister named* Bountiful *that was married to one of these Churles; but he and she could never agree; but because my Sister was resolved to do as she had began, that is, to show Kindness to the Poor, therefore her Husband*

Mercy'*s resolution.*

How Mercy'*s Sister was served by her Husband.*

first cried her down at the Cross and then turned her out of his Doors.

Pru. And yet he was a Professor, I warrant you?

Mer. *Yes, such a one as he was, and of such as he, the World is now full; but I am for none of them all.*

* Matthew *falls sick.*

Gripes of Conscience.

* *The Physicians Judgment.*

*Now *Matthew* the eldest Son of *Christiana* fell Sick, and his Sickness was sore upon him, for he was much pained in his Bowels, so that he was with it, at times, pulled as 'twere both ends together. There dwelt also not far from thence, one Mr. *Skill*, an Ancient, & well approved Physician. So *Christiana* desired it, and they sent for him, and he came. When he was entred the Room, and had a little observed the Boy, he concluded that he was sick of the Gripes. Then he said to his Mother, *What Diet has* Matthew *of late fed upon?* Diet said *Christiana*, nothing but that which is wholsom. *The Physician answered, *This Boy has been tampering with something which lies in his Maw undigested, and that will not away without means.* And I tell you he must be purged or else he will dye.

Samuel *puts his Mother in mind of the fruit his Brother did eat.*

Samuel. *Then said *Samuel, Mother, Mother, what was that which my Brother did gather up and eat, so soon as we were come from the Gate, that is at the head of this way? You know that there was an Orchard on the left hand, on the otherside of the Wall, and some of the Trees hung over the Wall, and my Brother did pluck and did eat.*

Christiana. True my Child, said *Christiana*, he did take thereof and did eat; naughty Boy as he was, I did chide him, and yet he would eat thereof.

Skill. *I knew he had eaten something that was not wholsome Food. And that Food, to wit, that Fruit is even the most hurtful of all. It is the Fruit of* Belzebubs *Orchard. I do marvel that none did warn you of it; many have died thereof.*

Christiana. Then *Christiana* began to cry, and she said, O naughty Boy, and O careless Mother, what shall I do for my Son?

Skill. *Come, do not be too much Dejected; the Boy may do well again; but he must purge and Vomit.*

Christiana. Pray Sir try the utmost of your Skill with him whatever it costs.

Skill. *Nay, I hope I shall be reasonable*: So he made him a Purge; but it was too weak. 'Twas said, it was made of the Blood of a Goat, the Ashes of a Heifer, and with some of the Juice of Hyssop, *&c.* *When Mr. *Skill* had seen that that Purge was too weak, he made him one to the purpose. 'Twas made *ex Carne & Sanguine Christi.* (You know Physicians give strange Medicines to their Patients) and it was made up into Pills with a Promise or two, and a proportionable quantity of Salt. Now he was to take them three at a time fasting in half a quarter of a Pint of the Tears of Repentance. When this potion was prepared, and brought to the Boy; *he was loth to take it, tho' torn with the Gripes, as if he should be pulled in pieces. *Come, come, said the Physician, you must take it.* It goes against my Stomach, said the Boy. *I must have you take it, said his Mother.* I shall Vomit it up again, said the Boy. Pray Sir, said *Christiana* to Mr. *Skill*, how does it taste? It has no ill taste, said the Doctor, and with that she touched one of the pills with the tip of her Tongue. Oh *Matthew*, said she, this potion is sweeter then Honey. If thou lovest thy Mother, if thou lovest thy Brothers, if thou lovest *Mercy*, if thou lovest thy Life, take it. So with much ado, after a short Prayer for the blessing of God upon it, he took it; and it wrought kindly with him. It caused him to purge, it caused him to sleep, and rest quietly, it put him into a fine heat and breathing sweat, and did quite rid him of his Gripes.

Heb. 10. 1, 2, 3, 4.

* *Potion prepared.*

John 6. 54, 55, 56, 57.

Mark 9. 49. *The Latine I borrow.*

Heb. 9. 14.

* *The boy loth to take the Physick.*

Zech. 12. 10.

The Mother tasts it, and perswades him.

So in little time he got up, and walked about with a Staff, and would go from Room to Room, and talk with *Prudence*, *Piety*, and *Charity* of his Distemper, and how he was healed.

So when the Boy was healed, *Christiana* asked Mr. *Skill*, saying, Sir, what will content you for your pains and care to and of my Child? And he said, you must pay the *Master of the*

A word of God in the hand of his Faith.

Heb. 13. 11, 12, 13, 14. 15.

Colledge of Physicians, according to rules made, in that case, and provided.

Chris. *But Sir, said she, what is this Pill good for else?*

Skill. It is an universal Pill, 'tis good against all the Diseases that Pilgrims are incident to, and when it is well prepared it will keep good, *time* out of *mind.*

This Pill an Universal Remedy.

Christiana. Pray Sir, make me up twelve Boxes of them: For if I can get these, I will never take other Physick.

Skill. These *Pills* are good to prevent Diseases, as well as to *cure* when one is Sick. Yea, I dare say it, and stand to it, that if a man will but use this Physick as he should, *it will make him live for ever.* But, good *Christiana*, thou must give these Pills, *no other way*; *but as I have prescribed: For if you do, they will do no good. So he gave unto *Christiana* Physick for her self, and her Boys, and for *Mercy*: and bid *Matthew* take heed how he eat any more *Green Plums*, and kist them and went his way.

Joh. 6. 50.

* *In a Glass of the Tears of Repentance.*

It was told you before, That *Prudence* bid the Boys, that if at any time they would, they should ask her some Questions, that might be profitable, and she would say something to them.

Mat. Then *Matthew* who had been sick, asked her, *Why for the most part Physick should be bitter to our Palats?*

Of Physick.

Pru. To shew how unwelcome the word of God and the Effects thereof are to a Carnal Heart.

Of the Effects of Physick.

Matthew. *Why does Physick, if it does good, Purge, and cause that we Vomit?*

Prudence. To shew that the Word when it works effectually, cleanseth the Heart and Mind. For look what the one doth to the Body, the other doth to the Soul.

Matthew. *What should we learn by seeing the Flame of our Fire go upwards? and by seeing the Beams, and sweet Influences of the Sun strike downwards?*

Of Fire and of the Sun.

Prudence. By the going up of the Fire, we are taught to ascend to Heaven, by fervent and hot desires. And by the Sun his sending his Heat, Beams, and sweet Influences downwards; we are taught, that the Saviour of the

World; tho' high, reaches down with his Grace and Love to us below.

Matthew. *Where have the Clouds their Water?* *Of the Clouds.*

Pru. Out of the Sea.

Matthew. *What may we learn from that?*

Pru. That Ministers should fetch their Doctrine from God.

Mat. *Why do they empty themselves upon the Earth?*

Pru. To shew that Ministers should give out what they know of God to the World.

Mat. *Why is the Rainbow caused by the Sun?*

Prudence. To shew that the Covenant of Gods Grace is confirmed to us in Christ. *Of the Rainbow.*

Mat. *Why do the Springs come from the Sea to us, thorough the Earth?*

Prudence. To shew that the Grace of God comes to us thorough the Body of Christ.

Mat. *Why do some of the Springs rise out of the tops of high Hills?* *Of the Springs.*

Prudence. To shew that the Spirit of Grace shall spring up in *some* that are Great and Mighty, as well as in *many* that are Poor and low.

Mat. *Why doth the Fire fasten upon the Candle-wick?* *Of the Candle.*

Pru. To shew that unless Grace doth kindle upon the Heart, there will be no true Light of Life in us.

Matthew. *Why is the Wick and Tallow and all, spent to maintain the light of the Candle?*

Prudence. To shew that Body and Soul and all, should be at the Service of, and spend themselves to maintain in good Condition that Grace of God that is in us.

Mat. *Why doth the Pelican pierce her own Brest with her Bill?* *Of the Pelican.*

Pru. To nourish her Young ones with her Blood, and thereby to shew that Christ the blessed, so loveth his Young, his People, as to save them from Death by his Blood.

Mat. *What may one learn by hearing the Cock to Crow.* *Of the Cock.*

Prudence. Learn to remember *Peter*'s Sin, and *Peter's* Repentance. The Cocks crowing, shews also that day is coming on, let then the crowing of the Cock put thee in mind of that last and terrible Day of Judgment.

Now about this time their month was out, wherefore they signified to those of the House that 'twas convenient for them to up and be going. Then said *Joseph* to his Mother, It is convenient that you forget not to send to the House of Mr. *Interpreter*, to pray him to grant that Mr. *Great-heart* should be sent unto us, that he may be our Conductor the rest of our way. Good *Boy*, said she, I had almost forgot. So she drew up a Petition, and prayed Mr. *Watchful* the Porter to send it by some fit man to her good Friend Mr. *Interpreter*; who when it was come, and he had seen the contents of the Petition, said to the Messenger, Go tell them that I will send him.

The weak may sometimes call the strong to Prayers.

When the Family where *Christiana* was, saw that they had a purpose to go forward, they called the whole House together to give thanks to their King, for sending of them such profitable Guests as these. Which done, they said to *Christiana*, And shall we not shew thee something, according as our Custom is to do to Pilgrims, on which thou mayest meditate when thou art upon the way? So they took *Christiana*, her Children and *Mercy* into the Closet, and shewed them one of the *Apples* that *Eve* did eat of, and that she also did give to her Husband, and that for the eating of which they both were turned out of Paradice, and asked her what she thought that was? Then *Christiana* said, '*Tis Food, or Poyson*, I know not which; so they opened the matter to her, and she held up her hands and wondered.

They provide to be gone on their way.

Eves *Apple.*

A sight of Sin is amazing.

Gen. 3. 6.
Ro. 7. 24.

Then they had her to a place, and shewed her *Jacob*'s *Ladder*. Now at that time there were some Angels ascending upon it. So *Christiana* looked and looked, to see the Angels go up, and so did the rest of the Company. Then they were going into another place to shew them something else: But *James* said to his Mother, pray bid them stay here a little longer, for this is a curious sight. So they turned again, and stood feeding their Eyes with this *so pleasant a prospect*. After this they had them into a place where did

Jacob's *Ladder.*

A sight of Christ is taking.

hang up a *Golden Anchor*, so they bid *Christiana* take it down; for, said they, you shall have it with you, for 'tis of absolute necessity that you should, that you may lay hold of that within the vail, and stand stedfast, in case you should meet with turbulent weather: So they were glad thereof. Then they took them, and had them to the mount upon which *Abraham* our Father, had offered up *Isaac* his Son, and shewed them the *Altar*, the *Wood*, the *Fire*, and the *Knife*, for they remain to be seen to this very Day. When they had seen it, they held up their hands and blest themselves, and said, Oh! What a man, for love to his Master and for denial to himself, was *Abraham*! After they had shewed them all these things, *Prudence* took them into the Dining-Room, where stood a pair of Excellent Virginals, so she played upon them, and turned what she had shewed them into this excellent Song, saying;

Gen. 28. 12.

Golden Anchor.

Joh. 1. 51.

Heb. 6. 19, 12.

Gen. 20.

Of Abraham *offering up* Isaac.

Prudences *Virginals.*

> Eve's *Apple we have shewed you,*
> *Of that be you aware:*
> *You have seen* Jacobs *Ladder too,*
> *Upon which Angels are.*
>
> *An Anchor you received have;*
> *But let not these suffice,*
> *Until with* Abra'm *you have gave,*
> *Your best, a Sacrifice.*

Now about this time one knocked at the Door, So the Porter opened, and behold Mr. *Great-heart* was there; but when he was come in, what Joy was there! For it came now fresh again into their minds, how but a while ago he had slain old *Grim Bloody-man*, the Giant, and had delivered them from the Lions.

Mr. Great-heart *come again.*

Then said Mr. *Great-heart* to *Christiana*, and to *Mercy*, My Lord has sent each of you a Bottle of Wine, and also some parched Corn, together with a couple of Pomgranates. He has also sent the Boys some Figs, and Raisins to refresh you in your way.

He brings a token from his Lord with him.

Then they addressed themselves to their Journey, and *Prudence*, and *Piety* went along with them. When they came at the Gate, *Christiana* asked the Porter, if any of late went by. He said, No, only one some time since: who also told me that of late there had been a great Robbery committed on the Kings High-way, as you go: But he saith, the Thieves are taken, and will shortly be Tryed for their Lives. Then *Christiana*, and *Mercy*, was afraid; but *Matthew* said, Mother fear nothing, as long as Mr. *Great-heart* is to go with us, and to be our Conductor.

Robbery.

Then said *Christiana* to the Porter, Sir, I am much obliged to you for all the Kindnesses that you have shewed me since I came hither, and also for that you have been so loving and kind to my Children. I know not how to gratifie your Kindness: Wherefore pray as a token of my respects to you, accept of this small mite: So she put a Gold Angel in his Hand, and he made her a low obeisance, and said, Let thy Garments be always White, and let thy Head want no Ointment. Let *Mercy* live and not die, and let not her Works be few. And to the Boys he said, Do you fly Youthful lusts, and follow after Godliness with them that are Grave, and Wise, so shall you put Gladness into your Mothers Heart, and obtain Praise of all that are sober minded. So they thanked the Porter and departed.

Christiana *takes her leave of the Porter.*

The Porters blessing.

Now I saw in my Dream, that they went forward until they were come to the Brow of the Hill, where *Piety* bethinking her self cryed out, *Alas*! I have forgot what I intended to bestow upon *Christiana*, and her Companions. I will go back and fetch it. So she ran, and fetched it. While she was gone, *Christiana* thought she heard in a Grove a little way off, on the Right-hand, a most curious melodious Note, with Words much like these,

Through all my Life thy favour is
So frankly shew'd to me,
That in thy House for evermore
My dwelling place shall be.

And listning still she thought she heard another answer it, saying,

For why, the Lord our God is good,
His Mercy is for ever sure:
His truth at all times firmly stood:
And shall from Age to Age endure.

So *Christiana* asked *Prudence*, what 'twas that made those curious Notes? They are, said she, our Countrey Birds: They sing these Notes but seldom, except it be at the Spring, when the Flowers appear, and the Sun shines warm, and then you may hear them all day long. I often, said she, go out to hear them, we also oft times keep them tame in our House. They are very fine Company for us when we are *Melancholy*, also they make the Woods and Groves, and Solitary places, places desirous to be in.

Song 2. 11, 12.

By this time *Piety* was come again, So she said to *Christiana*, Look here, I have brought thee a *Scheme* of all those things that thou hast seen at our House: Upon which thou mayest look when thou findest thy self forgetful, and call those things again to remembrance for thy Edification, and comfort.

Piety *bestoweth somthing on them at parting.*

Now they began to go down the Hill into the Valley of *Humiliation*. It was a steep Hill, & the way was slippery; but they were very careful, so they got down pretty well. When they were down in the Valley, *Piety* said to *Christiana*. This is the place where *Christian* your Husband met with the foul Fiend *Apollion*, and where they had that dreadful fight that they had. I know you cannot but have heard thereof. But be of good Courage, as long as you have here Mr. *Great-heart* to be your Guide and Conductor, we hope you will fare the better. So when these two had committed the Pilgrims unto the Conduct of their Guide, he went forward, and they went after.

1 *part pag.* 172.

Great-heart. Then said Mr. *Great-heart*, We need not be so afraid of this Valley: For here is nothing to hurt us, unless we procure it to our selves. 'Tis true, *Christian* did here meet with *Apollion*, with whom he also had a sore Combate; but that *frey*, was the fruit of those slips that he got in his going down the Hill. For they that get *slips there*, must look for *Combats here*. And hence it is that this Valley

Mr. Great-heart *at the Valley of Humiliation.*

1 *partpag.* 172.

has got so hard a name. For the common people when they hear that some frightful thing has befallen such an one in such a place, are of an Opinion that that place is haunted with some foul Fiend, or evil Spirit; when alas it is for the fruit of their doing, that such things do befal them there.

The reason why Christian *was so beset here.*

This Valley of *Humiliation* is of it self as fruitful a place, as any the Crow flies over; and I am perswaded if we could hit upon it, we might find somewhere here about something that might give us an Account why *Christian* was so hardly beset in this place.

A Pillar with an Inscription on it.

Then *James* said to his Mother, Lo, yonder stands a Pillar, and it looks as if something was Written thereon: let us go and see what it is. So they went, and found there Written, *Let* Christian'*s slips before he came hither, and the Battels that he met with in this place, be a warning to those that come after.* Lo, said their Guide, did not I tell you, that there was something here abouts that would give Intimation of the reason why *Christian* was so hard beset in this place? Then turning himself to *Christiana*, he said: No disparagement to *Christian* more than to many others whose Hap and Lot his was. For 'tis easier going *up*, then *down this* Hill; and that can be said but of few Hills in all these parts of the World. But we will leave the good Man, he is at rest, he also had a brave Victory over his Enemy; let him grant that dwelleth above, that we fare no worse when we come to be tryed than he.

This Valley a brave place.

But we will come again to this Valley of *Humiliation.* It is the best, and most fruitful piece of Ground in all those parts. It is fat Ground, and as you see, consisteth much in Meddows: and if a man was to come here in the Summer-time, as we do now, if he knew not any thing before thereof, and if he also delighted himself in the sight of his Eyes, he might see that that would be delightful to him. Behold, how green this Valley is, also how beautified *with Lillies.* I have also known many labouring Men that have got good Estates in this Valley of *Humiliation.* (For God resisteth the Proud; but gives *more, more* Grace to the Humble;) for indeed it is a very

Song, 2. 1.
Jam. 4. 6.
1 Pet. 5. 5.
Men thrive in the Valley of Humiliation.

fruitful Soil, and doth bring forth by handfuls. Some also have wished that the next way to their Fathers House were here, that they might be troubled no more with either Hills or Mountains to go over; but the way is the way, and there's an end.

Now as they were going along and talking, they espied a Boy feeding his Fathers Sheep. The Boy was in very mean Cloaths, but of a very fresh and well-favoured Countenance, and as he sate by himself he Sung. Hark, said Mr. *Great-heart*, to what the Shepherds Boy saith. So they hearkned, and he said,

He that is down, needs fear no fall,
He that is low, no Pride:
He that is humble, ever shall Philip. 4.
Have God to be his Guide. 12, 13.

I am content with what I have,
Little be it, or much:
And, Lord, Contentment still I crave,
Because thou savest such.

Fulness to such a burden is Heb. 13. 5.
That go on Pilgrimage:
Here little, and hereafter Bliss,
Is best from Age to Age.

Then said their *Guide*, Do you hear him? I will dare to say, that this Boy lives a merrier Life, and wears more of that Herb called *Hearts-ease* in his Bosom, than he that is clad in Silk and Velvet; but we will proceed in our Discourse.

In this Valley our Lord formerly had his *Countrey-House*, he loved much to be here; He loved also to walk these Medows, for he found the Air was pleasant: Besides here a man shall be free from the Noise, and from the hurryings of this Life; all States are full of Noise and Confusion, only the Valley of *Humiliation* is that empty and Solitary Place. Here a man shall not be so let and hindred in his Contemplation, as in other places he is apt to be. This is a Valley that no body walks in, but those that love a Pilgrims Life. And though *Christian* had the hard hap to meet here with *Apollion*, and to enter with him a brisk encounter: Yet I

Christian, when in the Flesh, had his Countrey-House in the Valley of Humiliation.

must tell you, that in former times men have met with Angels here, have found Pearls here, and have in this place found the words of Life.

Hos. 12. 4, 5.

Did I say, our Lord had here in former Days his Countrey-house, and that he loved here to walk? I will add, in this Place, and to the People that live and trace these Grounds, he has left a yearly revenue to be faithfully payed them at certain Seasons, for their maintenance by the way, and for their further incouragement to go on in their Pilgrimage.

Mat. 11. 29.

Samuel. Now as they went on, *Samuel* said to Mr. *Great-heart: Sir, I perceive that in this Valley, my Father and* Apollyon *had their Battel; but whereabout was the Fight, for I perceive this Valley is large?*

Great-heart. Your Father had that Battel with *Apollyon* at a place yonder, before us, in a narrow Passage just beyond *Forgetful-Green*: And indeed that place is the most dangerous place in all these Parts. For if at any time the Pilgrims meet with any brunt, it is when they forget what Favours they have received, and how unworthy they are of them: This is the Place also where others have been hard put to it: But more of the place when we are come to it; for I perswade my self, that to this day there remains either some sign of the Battel, or some Monument to testifie that such a Battle there was fought.

Forgetful-Green.

Mercy. Then said *Mercy*, I think I am as well in this Valley, as I have been any where else in all our Journey: The place methinks suits with my Spirit. I love to be in such places where there is no ratling with Coaches, nor rumbling with Wheels: Methinks here one may without much molestation be thinking what he is, whence he came, what he has done, and to what the King has called him: Here one may think, and break at Heart, and melt in ones Spirit, until ones Eyes become like the *Fish Pools of Heshbon.* They that go rightly thorough this Valley of *Bacha* make it a Well, the Rain that God sends down from Heaven upon them that are here also *filleth the Pools.* This Valley is that from whence also the King will give to his their Vineyards, and they that go

Humility a sweet Grace.

Song. 7. 4.

Psal. 84. 5, 6, 7.

Hos. 2. 15.

through it, shall sing, (as *Christian* did, for all he met with *Apollyon.*)

Great-heart. 'Tis true, said their Guide, I have gone thorough this Valley many a time, and never was better than when here.

An Experiment of it.

I have also been a Conduct to several Pilgrims, and they have confessed the same; *To this man will I look, saith the King, even to him that is Poor, and of a contrite Spirit, and that trembles at my Word.*

Now they were come to the place where the afore mentioned Battel was fought. Then said the Guide to *Christiana*, her Children, and *Mercy:* This is the place, on this Ground *Christian* stood, and up there came *Apollyon* against him: And look, did not I tell you, here is some of your Husbands Blood upon these Stones to this day: Behold also how here and there are yct to be seen upon the place, some of the Shivers of *Apollyon*'s Broken *Darts*: See also how they did beat the Ground with their Feet as they fought, to make good their Places against each other, how also with their by-blows, they did split the very stones in pieces. Verily *Christian* did here play the Man, and shewed himself as stout, as could, had he been here, even *Hercules* himself. When *Apollyon* was beat, he made his retreat to the next Valley, that is called *The Valley of the shadow of Death*, unto which we shall come anon.

The place where Christian *and the* Fiend *did fight, some signs of the Battel remains.*

Lo yonder also stands a Monument, on which is Engraven this Battle, and *Christian*'s Victory to his Fame throughout all Ages: So because it stood just on the way-side before them, they stept to it and read the Writing, which word for word was this;

A Monument of the Battel.

Hard by, here was a Battle fought,
Most strange, and yet most true.
Christian *and* Apollyon *sought*
Each other to subdue.

The Man so bravely play'd the Man,
He made the Fiend *to fly:*
Of which a Monument I stand,
The same to testifie.

A Monument of Christians *Victory.*

When they had passed by this place, they came upon the Borders of the shadow of Death, and this Valley was longer than the other, a place also most strangely haunted with evil things, as many are able to testifie: But these Women and Children went the better thorough it, because they had day-light, and because Mr. *Great-heart* was their Conductor.

1 Part pag. 189.

When they were entred upon this Valley, they thought that they heard a groaning as of dead men; a very great groaning. They thought also they did hear Words of Lamentation spoken, as of some in extream Torment. These things made the Boys to quake, the Women also looked pale and wan; but their Guide bid them be of Good Comfort.

Groanings heard.

So they went on a little further, and they thought that they felt the Ground begin to shake under them, as if some hollow place was there; they heard also a kind of a hissing as of Serpents, but nothing as yet appeared. Then said the Boys, Are we not yet at the end of this doleful place? But the Guide also bid them be of good Courage, and look well to their Feet, lest haply, said he, you be taken in some Snare.

The Ground shakes.

Now *James* began to be Sick; but I think the cause thereof was Fear, so his Mother gave him some of that Glass of Spirits that she had given her at the *Interpreters* House, and three of the Pills that Mr. *Skill* had prepared, and the Boy began to revive. Thus they went on till they came to about the middle of the Valley, and then *Christiana* said, Methinks I see something yonder upon the Road before us, a thing of a shape such as I have not seen. Then said *Joseph*, Mother, what is it? An ugly thing, Child; an ugly thing, said she. But Mother, what is it like, said he? 'Tis like I cannot tell what, said she. And now it was but a little way off: Then said she, it is nigh.

James *sick with fear.*

The Fiend *appears.*

The Pilgrims are afraid.

Well, well, said Mr. *Great-heart*, let them that are most afraid keep close to me: So the *Fiend* came on, and the Conductor met it; but when it was just come to him, it vanished to all their sights.

Great-heart *incourages them.*

Then remembered they what had been said sometime agoe; *Resist the Devil, and he will fly from you.*

They went therefore on, as being a little refreshed; but they had not gone far, before *Mercy* looking behind her, saw as she thought, something most like a Lyon, and it came a great padding pace after; and it had a hollow Voice of Roaring, and at every Roar that it gave, it made all the Valley Eccho, and their Hearts to ake, save the Heart of him that was their Guide. So it came up, and Mr. *Great-heart* went behind, and put the Pilgrims all before him. The Lion also came on apace, and Mr. *Great-heart* addressed himself to give him Battel: But when he saw that it was determined that resistance should be made, he also drew back and came no further.

A Lion.

1 Pet. 5. 8, 9.

Then they went on again, and their Conductor did go before them, till they came at a place where was cast up a pit, the whole breadth of the way, and before they could be prepared to go over that, a great mist and a darkness fell upon them, so that they could not see: Then said the Pilgrims, Alas! now what shall we do? But their Guide made answer; Fear not, stand still and see what an end will he put to this also; so they stayed there because their Path was marr'd. They then also thought that they did hear more apparently the noise and rushing of the Enemies, the fire also and the smoke of the Pit was much easier to be discerned. Then said *Christiana* to *Mercy*, Now I see what my poor Husband went through: I have heard much of this place, but I never was here afore now; poor man, he went here all alone in the night; he had night almost quite through the way, also these Fiends were busie about him, as if they would have torn him in pieces. Many have spoke of it, but none can tell what the Valley of the shadow of death should mean, until they come in it themselves; *The heart knows its own bitterness, and a stranger intermedleth not with its Joy:* To be here is a fearful thing.

A pit and darkness.

Christiana *now knows what her Husband felt.*

Greath. This is like doing business in great Waters, or like going down into the deep; this is like being in the heart of the Sea, and like going down to the Bottoms of the Mountains: Now it seems as if

Great-heart*'s Reply.*

the Earth with its bars were about us for ever. *But let them that walk in darkness and have no light, trust in the name of the Lord, and stay upon their God.* For my part, as I have told you already, I have gone often through this Valley, and have been much harder put to it than now I am, and yet you see I am alive. I would not boast, for that I am not mine own Saviour. But I trust we shall have a good deliverance. Come let us pray for light to him that can lighten our darkness, and that can rebuke, not only these, but all the Satans in Hell.

They pray.

So they cryed and prayed, and God sent light and deliverance, for there was now no lett in their way, no not there, where but now they were stopt with a pit.

Mercy *to* Christiana.

Yet they were not got through the Valley; so they went on still, and behold great stinks and loathsome smells, to the great annoyance of them. Then said *Mercy* to *Christiana*, there is not such pleasant being here as at the *Gate*, or at the Interpreters, or at the House where we lay last.

One of the Boys Reply.

O but, said one of the Boys, *it is not so bad to go through here, as it is to* abide *here always, and for ought I know, one reason why we must go this way to the house prepared for us, is, that our home might be made the sweeter to us.*

Well said, *Samuel*, quoth the *Guide*, thou hast now spoke like a man. Why, if ever I get out here again, said the *Boy*, I think I shall prize light and good way better than ever I did in all my life. Then said the *Guide*, we shall be out by and by.

So on they went, and *Joseph* said, *Cannot we see to the end of this Valley as yet?* Then said the *Guide*, Look to your feet, for you shall presently be among the Snares. So they looked to their feet and went on; but they were troubled much with the Snares. Now when they were come among the Snares, they espyed a Man cast into the Ditch on the left hand, with his flesh all rent and torn. Then said the *Guide*, that is one *Heedless*, that was a going this way; he has lain there a great while. There was one *Takeheed* with him, when he was taken and slain, but *he* escaped their hands. You cannot imagine how many are killed hereabout, and yet men are so foolishly venturous, as to set out lightly on Pilgrimage, and to come

Heedless *is slain, and* Takeheed *preserved.*

without a *Guide*. Poor *Christian*, it was a wonder that he here escaped, but he was beloved of his God, also he had a good heart of his own, or else he could never a done it. Now they drew towards the end of the way, and just there where *Christian* had seen the Cave when he went by, out thence came forth *Maul* a Gyant. This *Maul* did use to spoil young Pilgrims with Sophistry, and he called *Great-heart* by his name, and said unto him, how many times have you been forbidden to do these things? Then said Mr. *Great-heart*, what things? What things, quoth the Gyant, you know what things; but I will put an end to your trade. But pray, said Mr. *Great-heart*, before we fall to it, let us understand wherefore we must fight; (now the Women and Children stood trembling, and knew not what to do) quoth the Gyant, You rob the Countrey, and rob it with the worst of Thefts. These are but Generals, said Mr. *Great-heart*, come to particulars, man.

1 *Part* pag. 193.

Maul *a Gyant.*

He quarrels with Great-heart.

Then said the *Gyant*, thou practisest the craft of a *Kidnapper*, thou gatherest up Women and Children, and carriest them into a strange Countrey, to the weakning of my Masters Kingdom. But now *Great-heart* replied, I am a Servant of the God of Heaven, my business is to perswade sinners to Repentance, I am commanded to do my endeavour to turn Men, Women and Children, from darkness to light, and from the power of Satan to God, and if this be indeed the ground of thy quarrel, let us fall to it as soon as thou wilt.

God's Ministers counted as Kidnappers.

The Gyant *and Mr.* Great-heart *must fight.*

Then the *Giant* came up, and Mr. *Great-heart* went to meet him, and as he went, he drew his sword, but the *Giant* had a *Club*: So without more ado they fell to it, and at the first blow the *Giant* stroke Mr. *Great-heart* down upon one of his knees; with that the Women and Children cried: So Mr. *Great-heart* recovering himself, laid about him in full lusty manner, and gave the *Giant* a wound in his arm; thus he fought for the space of an hour, to that height of heat, that the breath came out of the *Giants* nostrils, as the heat doth out of a boiling Caldron.

Weak folks Prayers do sometimes help strong folks Cries.

Then they sat down to rest them, but Mr. *Great-heart*

betook him to prayer; also the Women and Children did nothing but sigh and cry all the time that the Battle did last.

When they had rested them, and taken breath, they both fell to it again, and Mr. *Great-heart* with a full blow fetch't the *Giant* down to the ground. Nay hold, and let me recover, quoth he. So Mr. *Great-heart* fairly let him get up: So to it they went again: And the *Giant* mist but little of all to breaking Mr. *Great-heart*'s Skull with his Club.

The Gyant *struck down.*

Mr. *Great-heart* seeing that, runs to him in the full heat of his Spirit, and pierced him under the fifth rib; with that the *Giant* began to faint, and could hold up his Club no longer. Then Mr. *Great-heart* seconded his blow, and smit the head of the *Giant* from his shoulders. Then the Women and Children rejoyced, and Mr. *Great-heart* also praised God, for the deliverance he had wrought.

He is slain, and his head disposed of.

When this was done, they amongst them erected a Pillar, and fastned the *Gyant's* head thereon, and wrote underneath in letters that Passengers might read,

He that did wear this head, was one
That Pilgrims did misuse;
He stopt their way, he spared none,
But did them all abuse;
Until that I, Great heart, *arose,*
The Pilgrims Guide *to be;*
Until that I did him oppose,
That was their Enemy.

Now I saw, that they went to the Ascent that was a little way off cast up to be a Prospect for Pilgrims. (That was the place from whence *Christian* had the first sight of *Faithful* his Brother.) Wherefore here they sat down, and rested, they also here did eat and drink, and make merry; for that they had gotten deliverance from this so dangerous an Enemy. As they sat thus and did eat, *Christiana* asked the *Guide*, *if he had caught no hurt in the battle.* Then said Mr. *Great-heart*, *No*, save a little on my flesh; yet that also shall be so far from being to my determent,

1 *Part pag.* 193.

that it is at present a proof of my love to my Master and you, and shall be a means by Grace to increase my reward at last.

2 Cor. 4.

Discourse of the fights.

But was you not afraid, good Sir, when you see him come with his Club?

It is my duty, said he, to distrust mine own ability, that I may have reliance on him that is stronger than all. *But what did you think when he fetched you down to the ground at the first blow?* Why I thought, quoth he, that so my master himself was served, and yet he it was that conquered at the last.

Matt. *When you all have thought what you please, I think God has been wonderful good unto us, both in bringing us out of this Valley, and in delivering us out of the hand of this Enemy; for my part I see no reason why we should distrust our God any more, since he has* now, *and in* such *a place as this, given us such testimony of his love as this.*

Mat. *here admires* Goodness.

Then they got up and went forward, now a little before them stood an Oak, and under it when they came to it, they found an old *Pilgrim* fast asleep, they knew that he was a *Pilgrim* by his *Cloaths*, and his *Staff*, and his *Girdle*.

Old Honest *asleep under an Oak.*

So the *Guide* Mr. *Great-heart* awaked him, and the old Gentleman, as he lift up his eyes cried out; What's the matter? who are you? and what is your business here?

Great. Come man be not so hot, here is none but Friends; yet the old man gets up and stands upon his guard, and will know of them what they were. Then said the *Guide*, My name is *Great-heart*, I am the guide of these Pilgrims which are going to the Celestial Countrey.

Honest. Then said Mr. *Honest*, I cry you mercy; I feared that you had been of the Company of those that some time ago did rob *Little-faith* of his money; but now I look better about me, I perceive you are honester People.

One Saint sometimes takes another for his Enemy.

Talk between Great-heart *and he.*

Greath. *Why what would, or could you a-done, to a helped your self, if we indeed had been of that Company?*

Hon. Done! Why I would have fought as long as breath had been in me; and had I so done, I am sure you could never have given me the worst on't, for a *Christian* can never be overcome, unless he shall yield of himself.

Greath. *Well said*, Father Honest, *quoth the Guide*, *for by this I know that thou art a Cock of the right kind*, *for thou hast said the Truth*.

Hon. And by this also I know that thou knowest what true Pilgrimage is; for all others do think that we are the soonest overcome of any.

Greath. *Well*, *now we are so happily met*, *pray let me crave your Name*, *and the name of the Place you came from?*

Whence Mr. Honest *came.*

Hon. My Name I cannot, but I came from the Town of *Stupidity*; It lieth about four Degrees beyond the City of *Destruction*.

Greath. Oh! *Are you that Country-man then? I deem I have half a guess of you*, *your Name is old* Honesty, *is it not?* So the old Gentleman blushed, and said, Not Honesty in the *Abstract*, but *Honest* is my Name, and I wish that my *Nature* shall agree to what I am called.

Hon. But Sir, said the old Gentleman, how could you guess that I am such a Man, since I came from such a place?

Stupified ones are worse then those meerly Carnal.

Greath. *I had heard of you before*, *by my Master*, *for he knows all things that are done on the Earth: But I have often wondred that any should come from your place; for your Town is worse than is the City of* Destruction *it self*.

Hon. Yes, we lie more off from the Sun, and so are more Cold and Sensless; but was a Man in a Mountain of Ice, yet if the Sun of Righteousness will arise upon him, his frozen Heart shall feel a Thaw; and thus it hath been with me.

Greath. I believe it, Father *Honest*, I believe it, for I know the thing is true.

Then the old Gentleman saluted all the Pilgrims with a holy Kiss of Charity, and asked them of their Names, and how they had fared since they set out on their Pilgrimage.

Old Honest *and* Christiana *talk.*

Christ. Then said *Christiana*, My name I suppose you have heard of, good *Christian* was my Husband, and these four were his Children. But can you think how the old Gentleman was taken, when she told him who she was! He skip'd, he smiled, and blessed them with a thousand good Wishes, saying,

Hon. *I have heard much of your Husband, and of his Travels and Wars which he underwent in his days. Be it spoken to your Comfort, the Name of your Husband rings all over these parts of the World; His Faith, his Courage, his Enduring, and his Sincerity under all, has made his name Famous.* Then he turned him to the Boys, and asked them of their names, which they told him: And then said he unto them, *Matthew*, be thou like *Matthew* the Publican, not in Vice, but Virtue. *Samuel*, said he, be thou like *Samuel* the Prophet, a Man of Faith and Prayer. *Joseph*, said he, be thou like *Joseph* in *Potiphar*'s House, Chast, and one that flies from Temptation. And, *James*, be thou like *James* the *Just*, and like *James* the brother of our Lord.

He also talks with the Boys. Old Mr. Honest'*s Blessing on them.*

Mat. 10. 3. Psal. 99. 6. Gen. 39. Acts.

Then they told him of *Mercy*, and how she had left her Town and her Kindred to come along with *Christiana*, and with her Sons. At that the old Honest man said, *Mercy*, is thy Name? by *Mercy* shalt thou be sustained, and carried thorough all those Difficulties that shall assault thee in thy way; till thou shalt come thither where thou shalt look the Fountain of Mercy in the Face with Comfort.

He blesseth Mercy.

All this while the Guide Mr. *Great-heart*, was very much pleased, and smiled upon his Companion.

Now as they walked along together, the Guide asked the old Gentleman, *if he did not know one Mr.* Fearing, *that came on Pilgrimage out of his Parts?*

Talk of one Mr. Fearing.

Hon. Yes, very well, said he; he was a Man that had the Root of the Matter in him, but he was one of the most troublesome Pilgrims that ever I met with in all my days.

Greath. *I perceive you knew him, for you have given a very right Character of him.*

Hon. Knew him! I was a great Companion of his, I was with him most an end; when he first began to think of what would come upon us hereafter, I was with him.

Greath. *I was his Guide from my Master's House, to the Gates of the Celestial City.*

Hon. Then you knew him to be a troublesom one?

Greath. *I did so, but I could very well bear it: for Men of my Calling are often times intrusted with the Conduct of such as he was.*

Hon. Well then, pray let us hear a little of him, and how he managed himself under your Conduct.

Greath. Why he was always afraid that he should come short of whither he had a desire to go. Every thing frightned him that he heard any body speak of, that had but the least appearance of Opposition in it. I heard that he lay roaring at the *Slough* of *Despond*, for about a Month together, nor durst he, for all he saw several go over before him, venture, tho they, many of them, offered to lend him their Hand. *He would not go back again neither.* The Celestial City, he said he should die if he came not to it, and yet was dejected at every Difficulty, and stumbled at every Straw that any body cast in his way. Well, after he had layn at the *Slough of Despond* a great while, as I have told you; one sun-shine Morning, I do not know how, he ventured, and so got over. But when he was over, he would scarce believe it. He had, I think, a *Slough of Despond* in his Mind, a *Slough* that he carried every where with him, or else he could never have been as he was. So he came up to the Gate, you know what I mean, that stands at the head of this way, and there also he stood a good while before he would adventure to knock. When the Gate was opened he would give back, and give place to others, and say that he was not worthy. For, for all he gat before some to the Gate, yet many of them went in before him. There the poor man would stand shaking and shrinking; I dare say it would have pitied ones heart to have seen him: *Nor would he go back again.* At last he took the Hammer that hanged on the Gate in his hand, and gave a small Rapp or two; then one opened to him, but he shrunk back as before. He that opened, stept out after him, and said, Thou trembling one, what wantest thou? with that he fell down to the Ground. He that spoke to him wondered to see him so faint. So he said to him, *Peace*

Mr. Fearing's *troublesom Pilgrimage.*

His behaviour at the Slough of Despond.

His behaviour at the Gate.

be to thee; up, for I have set open the Door to thee; come in, for thou art blest. With that he gat up, and went in trembling, and when he was in, he was ashamed to show his Face. Well, after he had been entertained there a while, as you know how the manner is, he was bid go on his way, and also told the way he should take. So he came till he came to our House, but as he behaved himself at the Gate, so he did at my master the *Interpreters* Door. He lay thereabout in the Cold a good while, before he would adventure to call; *Yet he would not go back*. And the Nights were long and cold then. Nay he had a Note of *Necessity* in his Bosom to my Master, to receive him, and grant him the Comfort of his House, and also to allow him a stout and valiant Conduct, because he was himself so *Chicken-hearted* a Man; and yet for all that he was afraid to call at the Door. So he lay up and down thereabouts, till, poor man, he was almost starved; yea so great was his Dejection, that tho he saw several others for knocking got in, yet he was afraid to venture. At last, I think I looked out of the Window, and perceiving a man to be up and down about the Door, I went out to him, and asked what he was; but poor man, the water stood in his Eyes. So I perceived what he wanted. I went therefore in, and told it in the House, and we shewed the thing to our Lord; So he sent me out again, to entreat him to come in, but I dare say I had hard work to do it. At last he came in, and I will say that for my Lord, he carried it wonderful lovingly to him. There were but a few good bits at the Table, but some of it was laid upon his Trencher. Then he presented the *Note*, and my Lord looked thereon and said, His desire should be granted. So when he had bin there a good while, he seemed to get some Heart, and to be a little more Comfortable. For my Master, you must know, is one of very tender Bowels, especially to them that are afraid, wherefore he carried it so towards him, as might tend most to his Incouragement. Well, when he had had a sight of the things of the place, and was ready to take his Journey to go to the City, my Lord, as he did to *Christian* before, gave him a Bottle of Spirits, and some comfortable things to eat. Thus we set forward, and

His behaviour at the Interpreters Door.

How he was entertained there.

He is a little encouraged at the Interpreters house.

I went before him; but the man was but of few Words, only he would sigh aloud.

When we were come to where the three Fellows were hanged, he said, that he doubted that that would be his end also. Only he seemed glad when he saw the *Cross* and the Sepulcher. There I confess he desired to stay a little, to look; and he seemed for a while after to be a little *Cheary*. When we came at the Hill *Difficulty*, he made no stick at that, nor did he much fear the Lyons. For you must know that his Trouble *was not about such things as those*, his Fear was about his Acceptance at last.

He was greatly afraid when he saw the Gibbit, Cheary when he saw the Cross.

I got him in at the House *Beautiful*, I think before he was willing; also when he was in, I brought him acquainted with the Damsels that were of the Place, but he was ashamed to make himself much for Company, he desired much to be alone, yet he always loved good talk, and often would get behind the *Skreen* to hear it; he also loved much to see *ancient* things, and to be *pondering* them in his Mind. He told me afterwards, that he loved to be in those two Houses from which he came last, to wit, at the Gate, and that of the *Interpreters*, but that he durst not be so bold to ask.

Dumpish at the house Beautiful.

When we went also from the House *Beautiful*, down the Hill, into the Valley of *Humiliation*, he went down *as well as ever I saw man in my Life*, for he cared not how mean he was, so he might be happy at last. Yea, I think there was a kind of a Sympathy betwixt that Valley and him: For I never saw him better in all his Pilgrimage, than when he was in that Valley.

He went down into, and was very Pleasant in the Valley of Humiliat.

Here he would lye down, embrace the Ground, and kiss the very Flowers that grew in this Valley. He would now be up every Morning by break of Day, tracing, and walking to and fro in this Valley.

Lam. 3. 27, 28, 29.

But when he was come to the entrance of the Valley of the Shadow of death, I thought I should have lost my Man; not for that he had any Inclination *to go back*, that he alwayes abhorred, but he was ready to dye for Fear. O, the *Hobgoblins*

Much perplexed in the Valley of the Shadow of Death.

will have me, the *Hobgoblins* will have me, cried he; and I could not beat him out on't. He made such a noyse, and such an outcry here, that, had they but heard him, 'twas enough to encourage them to come and fall upon us.

But this I took very great notice of, that this Valley was as quiet while he went thorow it, as ever I knew it before or since. I suppose, those Enemies here, had now a special Check from our Lord, and a Command not to meddle until Mr. *Fearing* was pass'd over it.

It would be too tedious to tell you of all; we will therefore only mention a Passage or two more. When he was come at *Vanity Fair*, I thought he would have fought with all the men in the Fair; I feared there we should both have been knock'd o'th' Head, so hot was he against their Fooleries; upon the inchanted Ground, he also was very wakeful. But when he was come at the *River* where was no Bridge, there again he was in a heavy Case; now, now he said he should be drowned for ever, and so never see that Face with Comfort, that he had come so many miles to behold.

His behaviour at Vanity-Fair.

And here also I took notice of what was very remarkable, the Water of *that River* was lower at *this* time, than ever I saw it in all my Life; so he went over at last, not much above *wet-shod*. When he was going up to the Gate, Mr. *Great-heart* began to take his Leave of him, and to wish him a good Reception above; So he said, *I shall, I shall.* Then parted we asunder, and I saw him no more.

His Boldness at last.

Honest. *Then it seems he was well at last.*

Greath. Yes, yes, I never had doubt about him, he was a man of a choice Spirit, only he was alwayes kept very low, and that made his Life so burthensome to himself, and so troublesome to others. He was above many, tender of Sin; he was so afraid of doing Injuries to others, that he often would deny himself of that which was lawful, because he would not offend.

Psal. 88. Rom. 14. 21. 1 Cor. 8. 13.

Hon. *But what should be the reason that such a good Man should be all his dayes so much in the dark?*

Greath. There are two sorts of Reasons for it; one is, The wise God will have it so. Some must *Pipe*, and some must *Weep*: Now Mr. *Fearing* was one that play'd upon *this Base*. He and his fellows sound the *Sackbut*, whose Notes are more doleful than the Notes of other Musick are: Tho indeed some say, the Base is the ground of Musick. And for my part, I care not at all for that Profession that begins not in heaviness of Mind. The first string that the Musician usually touches, *is the Base*, when he intends to put all in tune; God also plays upon this string first, when he sets the Soul in tune for himself. Only here was the imperfection of Mr. *Fearing*, he could play upon no other Musick but this, till towards his latter end.

Reason why good men are so in the dark.

Mat. 11. 16, 17, 18.

I make bold to talk thus Metaphorically, for the ripening of the Wits of young Readers, and because in the Book of the Revelations, the Saved are compared to a company of Musitians that play upon their *Trumpets* and Harps, and sing their Songs before the Throne.

Revel. 8. 2. *Chap* 14. 2, 3.

Hon. *He was a very zealous man, as one may see by what Relation you have given of him. Difficulties, Lyons, or Vanity-Fair, he feared not at all: 'Twas only Sin, Death and Hell, that was to him a Terror*; because he had some Doubts about his Interest in that Celestial Countrey.

Greath. You say right: *Those* were the things that were his Troublers, and they, as you have well observed, arose from the weakness of his Mind thereabout, not from weakness of Spirit as to the practical part of a Pilgrims Life. I dare believe, that as the Proverb is, he could have bit a Firebrand, had it stood in his way: But the things with which he was oppressed, no man ever yet could shake off with ease.

A Close about him.

Christiana. *Then said* Christiana, *This Relation of Mr.* Fearing *has done me good. I thought no body had been like me, but I see there was some Semblance 'twixt this good man and I, only we differed in two things. His Troubles were so great they brake out, but mine I kept within. His also lay so hard upon him, they made him that he could not knock at the Houses provided for Entertainment; but my Trouble was always such, as made me knock the louder.*

Christiana'*s Sentence.*

Mer. If I might also speak my Heart, I must say that something of him has also dwelt in me.

Mercy'*s Sentence.*

For I have ever been more afraid of the Lake and the loss of a place in *Paradise*, then I have been of the loss of other things. Oh, thought I, may I have the Happiness to have a Habitation *there*, 'tis enough, though I part with all the World to win it.

Matt. *Then said* Matthew, *Fear was one thing that made me think that I was far from having that within me that accompanies Salvation, but if it was so with such a good man as he, why may it not also go well with me?*

Matthew's *Sentence.*

Jam. No fears, no Grace, said *James*. Though there is not alwayes Grace where there is the fear of Hell; yet to be sure there is no Grace where there is no fear of God.

James's *Sentence.*

Greath. *Well said* James, *thou hast hit the Mark, for the fear of God is the beginning of Wisdom; and to be sure they that want the* beginning, *have neither* middle *nor* end. *But we will here conclude our Discourse of Mr.* Fearing, *after we have sent after him this Farewel.*

Well, Master Fearing, *thou didst fear*
Thy God: And wast afraid
Of doing any thing, while here,
That would have thee betray'd.
And didst thou fear the Lake and Pit?
Would others did so too:
For, as for them that want thy Wit,
They do themselves undo.

Their Farewell about him.

Now I saw, that they still went on in their Talk. For after Mr. *Great-heart* had made an end with Mr. *Fearing*, Mr. *Honest* began to tell them of another, but his Name was Mr. *Self-will*. He pretended himself to be a *Pilgrim*, said Mr. *Honest*; But I perswade my self, he never came in at the Gate that stands at the head of the way.

Of Mr. Self-will.

Greath. *Had you ever any talk with him about it?*

Hon. Yes, more than once or twice; but he would always be like himself, *self-willed*. He neither cared for man, nor Argument, nor yet Example; what his Mind prompted him to, that he would do, and nothing else could he be got to.

Old Honest *had talked with him.*

Greath. *Pray what Principles did he hold, for I suppose you can tell?*

Hon. He held that a man might follow the Vices as well as the Virtues of the Pilgrims, and that if he did both, he should be certainly saved.

Self-will's *Opinions.*

Greath. How! *If he had said, 'tis possible for the best to be guilty of the Vices, as well as to partake of the Virtues of Pilgrims, he could not much have been blamed: For indeed we are exempted from no Vice absolutely, but on condition that we Watch and Strive. But this I perceive is not the thing: But if I understand you right, your meaning is, that he was of that Opinion, that it was allowable so to be.*

Hon. Ai, ai, so I mean, and so he believed and practised.

Greath. *But what Ground had he for his so saying?*

Hon. Why, he said he had the Scripture for his Warrant.

Greath. *Prethee, Mr.* Honest, *present us with a few particulars.*

Hon. So I will. He said, to have to do with other mens Wives, had been practised by *David*, Gods Beloved, and therefore he could do it. He said, to have more Women than one, was a thing that *Solomon* practised, and therefore he could do it. He said, that *Sarah* and the godly Midwives of *Egypt* lyed, and so did saved *Rahab*, and therefore he could do it. He said, that the Disciples went at the bidding of their Master, and took away the Owners *Ass*, and therefore he could do so too. He said, that *Jacob* got the Inheritance of his Father in a way of Guile and Dissimulation, and therefore he could do so too.

Greath. *High base! indeed, and you are sure he was of this Opinion?*

Hon. I have heard him plead for it, bring Scripture for it, being Argument for it, *&c.*

Greath. *An Opinion that is not fit to be, with any Allowance in the World.*

Hon. You must understand me rightly: He did not say that any man might do this; but, that those that had the Virtues of those that did such things, might also do the same.

Greath. *But what more false than such a Conclusion? For this is as much as to say, that because good men heretofore have sinned of Infirmity, therefore he had allowance to do it of a presumptuous mind. Or if because a Child, by the blast of the Wind, or for that it stumbled at a stone, fell down and so defiled it self in Mire, therefore he might wilfully lye down and wallow like a Bore therein. Who could a thought that any one could so far a been blinded by the power of Lust? But what is written must be true: They stumble at the Word, being disobedient, whereunto also they were appointed.* 1 Pet. 2. 8.

His supposing that such may have the godly Mans Virtues, who addict themselves to their Vices, is also a Delusion as strong as the other. 'Tis just as if the Dog *should say, I have, or may have the* Qualities *of the* Child, *because I lick up its stinking Excrements. To eat up the Sin of Gods People, is no sign of one that is possessed with their Virtues. Nor can I believe that one that is of this Opinion, can at present have Faith or Love in him. But I know you have made strong Objections against him, prethee what can he say for himself?* Hos. 4. 8.

Hon. Why, he says, To do this by way of Opinion, seems abundance more honest, than to do it, and yet hold contrary to it in Opinion.

Greath. *A very wicked Answer, for thô to let loose the Bridle to Lusts, while our Opinions are against such things, is bad; yet to sin, and plead a Toleration so to do, is worse; the one stumbles Beholders accidentally, the other pleads them into the Snare.*

Hon. There are many of this mans mind, that have not this mans mouth, and *that* makes going on Pilgrimage of so little esteem as it is.

Greath. *You have said the Truth, and it is to be lamented: But he that feareth the King of Paradice, shall come out of them all.*

Christiana. There are strange Opinions in the World. I know one that said 'twas time enough to repent when they came to die.

Greath. *Such are not over Wise: That man would a been loath, might he have had a week to run twenty mile in for his Life, to have deferred that Journey to the last hour of that Week.*

Hon. You say right, and yet the generality of them that count themselves Pilgrims, do indeed do thus. I am, as you see, an old Man, and have been a Traveller in this Road many a day; and I have taken notice of many things.

I have seen some that have set out as if they would drive all the World afore them; who yet have in few dayes dyed as they in the Wilderness, and so never gat sight of the promised Land.

I have seen some that have promised nothing at first setting out to be Pilgrims, and that one would a thought could not have lived a day, that have yet proved very good Pilgrims.

I have seen some that have run hastily forward, that again have after a little time, run as fast just back again.

I have seen some who have spoke very well of a Pilgrims Life at first, that after a while have spoken as much against it.

I have heard some, when they first set out for Paradice, say positively, there is such a place, who when they have been almost there, have come back again, and said there is none.

I have heard some vaunt what they would do in case they should be opposed, that have even at a false Alarm fled Faith, the Pilgrims way, and all.

Now as they were thus in their way, there came one runing to meet them, and said, Gentlemen, and you of the weaker sort, if you love Life, shift for your selves, for the Robbers are before you.

Fresh News of trouble.

Greath. Then said Mr. *Greatheart*, They be the three that set upon *Littlefaith* heretofore. Well, said he, we are ready for them; so they went on their way: Now they looked at every Turning when they should a met with the Villains: But whether they heard of Mr. *Greatheart*, or whether they had some other Game, they came not up to the Pilgrims.

1 Part p. 246.

Greatheart's *Resolution.*

Chris. *Christiana* then wished for an Inn for her self and her Children, because they were weary. Then said Mr. *Honest*, There is one a little before us, where a very honourable Disciple, one *Gaius*, dwells. So they all concluded to turn in thither; and the rather, because the old Gentleman gave him so good a Report. So when they came to the Door, they went in, not knocking, for folks use not to knock at the Door of an Inn. Then they called for the Master of the House, and he came to them: *So they asked if they might lye there that Night?*

Christiana *wisheth for an Inn.*

Rom. 16. 23.

Gaius.

They enter into his House.

Gaius. Yes Gentlemen, if you be true Men, for my House is for none but Pilgrims. Then was *Christiana*, *Mercy*, and the *Boys*, the more

Gaius *Entertains them, and how.*

glad, for that the Inn-keeper was a lover of Pilgrims. So they called for Rooms; and he shewed them one for *Christiana*, and her Children, and *Mercy*, and another for Mr. *Great-heart* and the old Gentleman.

Greath. *Then said Mr.* Great-heart, *good* Gaius, *what hast thou for Supper? for these Pilgrims have come far to day, and are weary.*

Gaius. It is late, said *Gaius*; so we cannot conveniently go out to seek Food; but such as we have you shall be welcome to, if that will content.

Greath. *We will be content with what thou hast in the House, for as much as I have proved thee; thou art never destitute of that which is convenient.*

Then he went down, and spake to the Cook, whose Name was *Taste-that-which-is-good*, to get ready Supper for so many Pilgrims. This done, he comes up again, saying, come my good Friends, you are welcome to me, and I am glad that I have an House to entertain you; and while Supper is making ready, if you please, let us entertain one another with some good Discourse: So they all said, content.

Gaius *his Cook.*

Gaius. *Then said* Gaius, *Whose Wife is this aged Matron? and whose Daughter is this young Damsel?*

Talk between Gaius *and his Guests.*

Greath. The Woman is the Wife of one *Christian*, a Pilgrim of former times, and these are his four Children: The Maid is one of her Acquaintance, one that she hath perswaded to come with her on Pilgrimage. The Boys take all after their Father, and covet to tread in his Steps: Yea, if they do but see any place where the old Pilgrim hath lain, or any print of his Foot, it ministreth Joy to their Hearts, and they covet to lye, or tread in the same.

Mark this.

Gaius. Then said *Gaius*, is this *Christian*'s Wife, and are these *Christian*'s Children? I knew your Husband's Father, yea, also, his Fathers Father. Many have been good of this stock, their Ancestors dwelt first at *Antioch*. *Christian*'s Progenitors (I suppose you have heard your Husband talk of them) were very worthy men. They have above any that I know, shewed themselves men of great Virtue and Courage, for the Lord of

Act. 11. 26.

Of Christian'*s Ancestors.*

the Pilgrims, his ways, and them that loved him. I have heard of many of your Husbands Relations that have stood all Tryals for the sake of the Truth. *Stephen* that was one of the first of the Family from whence your Husband sprang, was knocked o'th' Head with Stones. *James*, another of this Generation, was slain with the edge of the Sword. To say nothing of *Paul* and *Peter*, men anciently of the Family from whence your Husband came: There was *Ignatius*, who was cast to the Lyons: *Romanus*, whose Flesh was cut by pieces from his Bones; and *Policarp*, that played the man in the Fire: There was he that was hanged up in a Basket in the Sun, for the Wasps to eat; and he who they put into a Sack, and cast him into the Sea to be drowned. 'Twould be impossible, utterly to count up all of that Family that have suffered Injuries and Death, for the love of a Pilgrims Life. Nor can I, but be glad, to see that thy Husband has left behind him four such Boys as these. I hope they will bear up their Fathers Name, and tread in their Fathers Steps, and come to their Fathers End.

Acts 7. 59, 60.
Cha. 12. 2.

Greath. *Indeed Sir, they are likely Lads, they seem to chuse heartily their Fathers Wayes.*

Gaius. That is it that I said, wherefore *Christians* Family is like still to spread abroad upon the face of the Ground, and yet to be numerous upon the Face of the Earth: Wherefore let *Christiana* look out some Damsels for her Sons, to whom they may be Betroathed, *&c.* that the Name of their Father, and the House of his Progenitors may never be forgotten in the World.

Advice to Christiana *about her Boys.*

Hon. *'Tis pity this Family should fall and be extinct.*

Gaius. Fall it cannot, but be diminished it may; but let *Christiana* take my Advice, and that's the way to uphold it.

And *Christiana*, said *This* Inn-keeper, I am glad to see thee and thy Friend *Mercy* together here, a lovely Couple. And may I advise, take *Mercy* into a nearer Relation to thee: If she will, let her be given to *Matthew* thy eldest Son: 'Tis the way to preserve you a posterity in the Earth. So this match was concluded, and in process of time they were married: But more of that hereafter.

Mercy *and* Matthew *Marry.*

Gaius also proceeded, and said, I will now speak on the behalf of Women, to take away their Reproach. For as Death and the Curse came into the World by a Woman, so also did Life and Health; *God sent forth his Son*, *made of a Woman*: Yea, to shew how much those that came after did abhor the Act of their Mother; this Sex, in the old Testament, coveted Children, if happily this or that Woman might be the Mother of the Saviour of the World. I will say again, that when the Saviour was come, Women rejoyced in him, before either Man or Angel. I read not that ever any man did give unto Christ so much as one *Groat*, but the Women followed him, and ministred to him of their Substance. 'Twas a Woman that washed his Feet with Tears, and a Woman that anointed his Body to the Burial: They were Women that wept when he was going to the Cross; and Women that followed him from the Cross, and that sat by his Sepulcher when he was buried: They were Women that was first with him at his Resurrection *Morn*, and Women that brought Tidings first to his Disciples that he was risen from the Dead: Women therefore are highly favoured, and shew by these things that they are sharers with us in the Grace of Life.

Gen. 3.
Gal. 4.

Why Women of old so much desired Children.

Luke 2.

Chap. 8. 2, 3.
Chap. 7. 37, 50.
Joh. 11. 2.
Chap. 12. 3.
Luk. 23. 27.
Matt. 27. 55, 56, 61.
Luke 24. 22, 23.

Now the Cook sent up to signifie that Supper was almost ready, and sent one to lay the Cloath, the Trenchers, and to set the Salt and Bread in order.

Supper ready.

Then said *Matthew*, *The sight of this Cloath*, *and of this Forerunner of the Supper*, *begetteth in me a greater Appetite to my Food than I had before.*

Gaius. So let all ministring Doctrines *to* thee in this Life, beget *in* thee a greater desire to sit at the Supper of the great King in his Kingdom; for all Preaching, Books, and Ordinances here, are but as the laying of the Trenchers, and as setting of Salt upon the Board, when compared with the Feast that our Lord will make for us when we come to his House.

What to be gathered from laying of the Board with the Cloath and Trenchers.

So Supper came up, and first a *Heave-shoulder*, and a *Wave-breast* was set on the Table before them: To shew that they must begin their *Meal* with Prayer and Praise to God. The *Heave-shoulder David* lifted his Heart up to God with, and with the *Wave-breast*, *where his heart lay*, with that he used to lean upon his Harp when he played. These two Dishes were very fresh and good, and they all eat heartily well thereof.

Levit. 7. 32, 33, 34. *Chap.* 10. 14, 15. Psal. 25. 1. Heb. 13. 15.

The next they brought up, was a Bottle of Wine, red as Blood. So *Gaius* said to them, Drink freely, this is the Juice of the true Vine, that makes glad the Heart of God and Man. So they drank and were merry.

Deut. 32. 14. Judg. 9. 13. Joh. 15. 1.

The next was a Dish of Milk well crumbed. But *Gaius* said, *Let the Boys have that*, *that they may grow thereby*.

1 Pet. 2. 1, 2.

A Dish of Milk.

Of Honey and Butter.

Then they brought up in course a Dish of *Butter* and *Honey*. Then said *Gaius*, Eat freely of *this*, for this is good to chear up, and strengthen your Judgments and Understandings: This was our Lords Dish when he was a Child; *Butter and Honey shall he eat*, *that he may know to refuse the Evil*, *and choose the Good*.

Isa. 7. 15.

Then they brought them up a Dish of Apples, and they were very good tasted Fruit. Then said *Matthew*, May we eat Apples, since they were such, by, and with which the Serpent beguiled our first Mother?

A Dish of Apples.

Then said *Gaius*,

> *Apples were they* with *which we were beguil'd*,
> *Yet* Sin, *not Apples hath our Souls defil'd.*
> *Apples forbid*, *if eat*, *corrupts the Blood:*
> *To eat such*, *when commanded*, *does us good.*
> *Drink of his Flagons then*, *thou Church*, *his Dove*,
> *And eat* his *Apples*, *who art sick of Love.*

Then said *Matthew*, *I made the Scruple*, *because I a while since was sick with eating of Fruit.*

Gaius. Forbidden Fruit will make you sick, but not what our Lord has tolerated.

While they were thus talking, they were presented with another Dish, and 'twas a dish of *Nuts*. Then said some at the Table, *Nuts* spoyl tender Teeth, especially the Teeth of Children: Which when *Gaius* heard, he said,

Song 6. 11. *A Dish of Nuts.*

> *Hard* Texts *are* Nuts (*I will not call them* Cheaters,)
> *Whose* Shells *do keep their* Kernels *from the* Eaters.
> *Ope then the Shells, and you shall have the Meat,*
> *They here are brought, for you to crack and Eat.*

Then were they very Merry, and sate at the Table a long time, talking of many things. Then said the old Gentleman, My good Landlord, while we are cracking your *Nuts*, if you please, do you open this Riddle.

A Riddle put forth by old Honest.

A man there was, thô some did count him mad,
The more he cast away, the more he had.

Then they all gave good heed, wondering what good *Gaius* would say, so he sat still a while, and then thus replyed:

He that bestows his Goods upon the Poor,
Shall have as much again, and ten times more.

Gaius *opens it.*

Then said *Joseph*, I dare say Sir, I did not think you could a found it out.

Oh! said *Gaius*, I have been trained up in this way a great while: Nothing teaches like Experience; I have learned of my Lord to be kind, and have found by experience that I have gained thereby: *There is that scattereth, yet increaseth, and there is that withholdeth more than is meet, but it tendeth to Poverty. There is that maketh himself Rich, yet hath nothing; there is that maketh himself poor, yet hath great Riches.*

Joseph *wonders.*

Prov. 11. 24. *Chap.* 13. 7.

Then *Samuel* whispered to *Christiana* his Mother, and said, Mother, this is a very good mans House, let us stay here a good while, and let my Brother *Matthew* be married here to *Mercy*, before we go any further.

The which *Gaius* the Host overhearing, said, *With a very good Will my Child.*

Matthew *and* Mercy *are Married.*

So they stayed there more than a Month, and *Mercy* was given to *Matthew* to Wife.

While they stayed here, *Mercy* as her Custom was, would be making Coats and Garments to give to the Poor, by which she brought up a very good Report upon the Pilgrims.

But to return again to our Story. After Supper, the *Lads* desired a Bed, for that they were weary with Travelling. Then *Gaius* called to shew them their Chamber, but said *Mercy*, I will have them to Bed. So she had them to Bed, and they slept well, but the rest sat up all Night: For *Gaius* and they were such suitable Company, that they could not tell how to part. Then after much talk of their Lord, themselves, and their Journey: Old Mr. *Honest*, he that put forth the Riddle to *Gaius*, began to *nod*. Then said *Great-heart*, What Sir, you begin to be drouzy, come rub up, now here's a *Riddle* for you. Then said Mr. *Honest*, let's hear it.

The Boys go to Bed, the rest sit up.

Old Honest *Nods.*

Then said Mr. *Great-heart*,

A Riddle.

He that will kill, must first be overcome:
Who live abroad would, first must die at home.

Hah, said Mr. *Honest*, it is a hard one, hard to expound, and harder to practise. But come Landlord, said he, I will, if you please, leave my part to you, do you expound it, and I will hear what you say.

No, said *Gaius*, 'twas put to you, and 'tis expected that you should answer it.

Then said the old Gentleman,

The Riddle opened.

He first by Grace must conquered be,
That Sin would mortifie.
And who, that lives, would convince me,
Unto himself must die.

It is right, said *Gaius*; good Doctrine, and Experience teaches this. For first, until Grace displays it self, and overcomes the Soul with its Glory, it is altogether without Heart to oppose Sin. Besides, if Sin is Satan's Cords, by which the Soul lies bound, how should it make Resistance, before it is loosed from that Infirmity?

Secondly, Nor will any that knows either Reason or Grace,

believe that such a man can be a living Monument of Grace, that is a Slave to his own Corruptions.

And now it comes in my mind, I will tell you a Story, worth the hearing. There were two Men that went on Pilgrimage, the one began when he was young, the other when he was old: The young man had strong Corruptions to grapple with, the old mans were decayed with the decays of Nature: The young man trod his steps as even as did the old one, and was every way as light as he; who now, or which of them had their Graces shining clearest, since both seemed to be alike?

A Question worth the minding.

Honest. *The young Mans doubtless. For that which heads it against the greatest Opposition, gives best demonstration that it is strongest; especially when it also holdeth pace with that that meets not with half so much; as to be sure old Age does not.*

A Comparison.

Besides, I have observed, that old men have blessed themselves with this mistake; Namely, taking the decayes of Nature for a gracious Conquest over Corruptions, and so have been apt to beguile themselves. Indeed old men that are gracious, are best able to give Advice to them that are young, because they have seen most of the emptiness of things. But yet, for an old and a young to set out both together, the young one has the advantage of the fairest discovery of a work of Grace within him, thô the old mans Corruptions are naturally the weakest.

A Mistake.

Thus they sat talking till break of Day. Now when the Family was up, *Christiana* bid her Son *James* that he should read a Chapter; so he read the 53[d] of *Isaiah*. When he had done, Mr. *Honest* asked why it was said, *That the Saviour is said to come out of a dry ground, and also that he had no Form nor Comeliness in him?*

Another Question.

Greath. Then said Mr. *Great-heart*, To the first I answer, Because, the Church of the Jews, of which Christ came, had then lost almost all the Sap and Spirit of Religion. To the Second I say, The Words are spoken in the Person of the Unbelievers, who because they want *that* Eye that can see into our Princes Heart, therefore they judge of him by the meanness of his Outside.

Just like those that know not that precious Stones are

covered over with a homely *Crust*; who when they have found one, because they know not what they have found, cast it again away as men do a common Stone.

Well, said *Gaius*, Now you are here, and since, as I know, Mr. *Great-heart* is good at his Weapons, if you please, after we have refreshed our selves, we will walk into the Fields, to see if we can do any good. About a mile from hence, there is one *Slaygood*, a *Gyant*, that doth much annoy the Kings High-way in these parts: And I know whereabout his Haunt is, he is Master of a number of Thieves; 'twould be well if we could clear these Parts of him.

Gyant Slaygood *assaulted and slain.*

So they consented and went, Mr. *Great-heart* with his *Sword*, *Helmet* and *Shield*; and the rest with Spears and Staves.

When they came to the place where he was, they found him with one *Feeble-mind* in his Hands, whom his Servants had brought unto him, having taken him in the Way; now the Gyant was rifling of him, with a purpose after that to pick his Bones; for he was of the nature of *Flesh-eaters*.

He is found with one Feeble-mind *in his hand.*

Well, so soon as he saw Mr. *Great-heart*, and his Friends, at the mouth of his Cave with their Weapons, he demanded what they wanted?

Greath. We want thee; for we are come to revenge the Quarrel of the many that thou hast slain of the Pilgrims, when thou hast dragged them out of the Kings High-way; wherefore come out of thy Cave. So he armed himself and came out, and to a Battle they went, and fought for above an Hour, and then stood still to take Wind.

Slaygood. *Then said the Gyant, Why are you here on my Ground?*

Greath. To revenge the Blood of Pilgrims, as I also told thee before; so they went to it again, and the Gyant made Mr. *Great-heart* give back, but he came up again, and in the greatness of his Mind, he let fly with such stoutness at the Gyants Head and Sides, that he made him let his Weapon fall out of his Hand: So he smote him, and slew him, and cut off his Head, and brought it away to the *Inn*. He also took *Feeble-mind* the Pilgrim, and brought him with him to his Lodgings. When they

Feeble-mind *rescued from the Gyant.*

were come home, they shewed his Head to the Family, and then set it up as they had done others before, for a Terror to those that should attempt to do as he, hereafter.

Then they asked Mr. *Feeblemind* how he fell into his hands?

Feeblem. Then said the poor man, I am a sickly man, as you see, and because *Death* did usually once a day *knock at my Door*, I thought I should never be well at home: So I betook my self to a Pilgrims life; and have travelled hither from the Town of *Uncertain*, where I and my Father were born. I am a man of no strength at all, of Body, nor yet of Mind, but would, if I could, thô I can but *craul*, spend my Life in the Pilgrims way. When I came at the Gate that is at the head of the Way, the Lord of that place did entertain me freely: Neither objected he against my weakly Looks, nor against my *feeble Mind*; but gave me such things that were necessary for my Journey, and bid me hope to the end. When I came to the House of the *Interpreter*, I received much Kindness there, and because the Hill *Difficulty* was judged too hard for me, I was carried up that by one of his Servants. Indeed I have found much Relief from Pilgrims, thô none was willing to go so softly as I am forced to do: Yet still as they came on, they bid me be of good Chear, and said that it was the will of their Lord, that Comfort should be given to the *feeble minded*, and so went on their *own* pace. When I was come up to *Assault-Lane*, then this *Gyant* met with me, and bid me prepare for an *Encounter*; but alas, feeble one that I was, I had more need of a *Cordial*: So he came up and took me, I conceited he should not kill me; also when he had got me into his Den, since I went not with him *willingly*, I believed I should come out alive again. For I have heard, that not any Pilgrim that is taken Captive by Violent Hands, if he keeps Heart-whole towards his Master, is by the Laws of Providence to die by the Hand of the Enemy. *Robbed*, I looked to be, and Robbed to be sure I am; but I am as you see escaped with Life, for the which I thank my King as Author, and you as the Means. Other Brunts I also look for, but this I have resolved on, to wit, to *run* when I can, to *go* when I cannot *run*, and to *creep* when I cannot *go*. As to the main, I thank him that loves me, I am fixed; my

How Feeble-mind *came to be a Pilgrim.*

1 Thess. 5. 14.

Mark this.

Mark this.

way is before me, my Mind is beyond the *River* that has no Bridge, thô I am as you see, but of a *feeble Mind.*

Hon. *Then said old Mr.* Honest, *Have not you some time ago, been acquainted with one Mr.* Fearing, *a* Pilgrim ?

Feeble. Acquainted with him ; Yes. He came from the Town of *Stupidity*, which lieth *four Degrees* to the Northward of the City of *Destruction*, and as many off, of where I was born ; Yet we were well acquainted, for indeed he was mine Uncle, my Fathers Brother; he and I have been much of a Temper, he was a little shorter than I, but yet we were much of a Complexion.

Mr. Fearing *Mr.* Feeble-mind'*s Uncle.*

Hon. *I perceive you know him, and I am apt to believe also that you were related one to another ; for you have his whitely Look, a Cast like his with your Eye, and your Speech is much alike.*

Feeble-mind *has some of Mr.* Fearing'*s Features.*

Feebl. Most have said so, that have known us both, and besides, what I have read in him, I have for the most part found in my self.

Gaius. *Come Sir, said good* Gaius, *be of good Chear, you are welcome to me, and to my House ; and what thou hast a mind to, call for freely ; and what thou would'st have my Servants do for thee, they will do it with a ready Mind.*

Gaius *Comforts him.*

Feebl. Then said Mr. *Feeble-mind*, This is unexpected Favour, and as the Sun shining out of a very dark Cloud : Did Gyant *Slay-good* intend me this Favour when he stop'd me, and resolved to let me go no further ? Did he intend that after he had rifled my Pockets, I should go to *Gaius mine Host?* Yet so it is.

Notice to be taken of Providence.

Now, just as Mr. *Feeble-mind*, and *Gaius* was thus in talk ; there comes one running, and called at the Door, and told, That about a Mile and an half off, there was one Mr. *Not-right* a Pilgrim, struck dead upon the place where he was, with a *Thunder bolt.*

Tidings how one Not-right *was slain with a Thunder-bolt, and Mr.* Feeble-mind'*s Comment upon it.*

Feebl. Alas ! said Mr. *Feeble-mind*, is he slain ? he overtook me some days before I came so far as hither, and would be my Company-keeper: He also was with me when *Slay-good* the Gyant took me, but he was nimble of his Heels, and escaped: But it seems, he escaped to die, and I was took to live.

What, one would think, doth seek to slay out-right,
Oft times, delivers from the saddest Plight.
That very Providence, *whose Face is* Death,
Doth oft-times, to the lowly, Life bequeath.
I taken was, he did escape and flee,
Hands Crost, gives Death to him, and Life to me.

Now about this time *Matthew* and *Mercy* were Married; also *Gaius* gave his Daughter *Phebe* to *James*, *Matthew*'s Brother, to Wife; after which time, they yet stayed above ten days at *Gaius*'s House, spending their time, and the Seasons, like as Pilgrims use to do.

When they were to depart, *Gaius* made them a Feast, and they did eat and drink, and were merry. Now the Hour was come that they must be gone, wherefore Mr. *Great-heart* called for a Reckoning. But *Gaius* told him, that at his House, it was not the Custom for *Pilgrims* to pay for their Entertainment. He boarded them by the year, but looked for his pay from the good *Samaritane*, who had promised him at his return, whatsoever Charge he was at with them, faithfully to repay him. Then said Mr. *Great-heart* to him,

The Pilgrims prepare to go forward.

Luke 10. 33, 34, 35.

How they greet one another at parting.

Greath. *Beloved, thou dost faithfully, whatsoever thou dost, to the Brethren and to Strangers, which have born Witness of thy Charity before the Church. Whom if thou (yet) bring forward on their Journey after a Godly sort, thou shalt do well.*

3 John 6.

Then *Gaius* took his leave of them all, and of his Children, and particularly of Mr. *Feeble-mind*. He also gave him something to drink by the way.

Gaius *his last kindness to* Feeble-mind.

Now Mr. *Feeblemind*, when they were going out of the Door, made as if he intended to linger. The which, when Mr. *Great-heart* espied, he said, come Mr. *Feeblemind*, pray do you go along with us, I will be your *Conductor*, and you shall fare as the rest.

Feebl. *Alas, I want a suitable Companion, you are all lusty and strong, but I, as you see, am weak; I chuse therefore rather to come behind, lest, by reason of my many Infirmities, I should be both a Burthen to my self, and to you. I am, as I said, a man of a weak and feeble Mind, and shall be offended and made weak at that which others can bear. I shall like no Laughing, I shall like no gay Attire, I shall like no unprofitable Questions. Nay, I am so weak a Man, as to be offended with that which others have a liberty to do. I do not yet know all the Truth; I am a very ignorant* Christian-man; *sometimes if I hear some rejoyce in the Lord, it troubles me because I cannot do so too. It is with me, as it is with a weak Man among the strong, or as with a sick Man among the healthy, or as a Lamp despised. (He that is ready to slip with his Feet, is as a Lamp despised, in the Thought of him that is at ease.)* So that I know not what to do.

Feeble-mind *for going behind.*

His Excuse for it.

Job 12. 5.

Greath. But Brother, said Mr. *Great-heart.* I have it in *Commission*, to comfort the *feeble-minded*, and to support the weak. You must needs go along with us; we will wait for you, we will lend you our help, we will deny our selves of some things, both *Opinionative* and *Practical*, for your sake; we will not enter into doubtful Disputations before you, we will be made all things to you, rather than you shall be left behind.

Great-heart's *Commission.*
1 Thes. 35. 14.
Rom. 14.
1 Cor. 8.
Chap. 9. 22.
A Christian Spirit.

Now, all this while they were at *Gaius*'s Door; and behold as they were thus in the heat of their Discourse, Mr. *Ready-to-hault* came by, with his *Crutches* in his hand, and he also was going on Pilgrimage.

Psa. 38. 17.
Promises.

Feebl. *Then said Mr.* Feeble-mind *to him, Man! how camest thou hither? I was but just now complaining that I had not a suitable Companion, but thou art according to my Wish. Welcome, welcome, good Mr.* Ready-to-hault, *I hope thee and I may be some help.*

Feeble-mind *glad to see* Ready-to-hault *come by.*

Ready-to. I shall be glad of thy Company, said the other; and good Mr. *Feeble-mind*, rather than we will part, since we are thus happily met, I will lend thee one of my Crutches.

Feebl. *Nay, said he, thô I thank thee for thy good Will, I am not inclined to hault before I am Lame. How be it, I think when occasion is, it may help me against a Dog.*

Ready-to. If either my *self*, or my *Crutches*, can do thee a pleasure, we are both at thy Command, good Mr. *Feeble-mind.*

Thus therefore they went on, Mr. *Great-heart* and Mr. *Honest* went before, *Christiana* and her Children went next, and Mr. *Feeble-mind* and Mr. *Ready-to-hault* came behind with his Crutches. Then said Mr. *Honest,*

Hon. *Pray Sir, now we are upon the Road, tell us some profitable things of some that have gone on Pilgrimage before us.* *New Talk.*

Greath. With a good Will. I suppose you have heard how *Christian* of old, did meet with *Apollyon* in the Valley of *Humiliation*, and also what hard work he had to go thorow the Valley of the Shadow of Death. Also I think you cannot but have heard how *Faithful* was put to it with *Madam Wanton*, with *Adam* the first, with one *Discontent*, and *Shame*; four as deceitful Villains, as a man can meet with upon the Road. 1 Part *from* pag. 195, to pag. 198.

Hon. *Yes, I have heard of all this; but indeed, good* Faithful *was hardest put to it with* Shame, *he was an unwearied one.*

Greath. Ai, for as the Pilgrim well said, He of all men had the wrong Name.

Hon. *But pray Sir, where was it that* Christian *and* Faithful *met* Talkative? *that same was also a notable one.*

Greath. He was a confident Fool, yet many follow his wayes.

Hon. *He had like to a beguiled* Faithful.

Greath. Ai, But *Christian* put him into a way quickly to find him out. Thus they went on till they came at the place where *Evangelist* met with *Christian* and *Faithful*, and Prophesied to them of what should befall them at *Vanity-Fair.* 1 Part pag. 203. pag. 212. pag. 216.

Greath. Then said their *Guide*, Hereabouts did *Christian* and *Faithful* meet with *Evangelist*, who Prophesied to them of what Troubles they should meet with at *Vanity-Fair*.

Hon. *Say you so! I dare say it was a hard Chapter that then he did read unto them.*

Greath. 'Twas so, but he gave them incouragement withall. But what do we talk of them, they were a couple of Lyon-like Men; they had set their Faces like Flint. Don't you remember how undaunted they were when they stood before the Judge?

1 Part pag. 219. *&c.*

Hon. *Well* Faithful *bravely suffered!*

Greath. So he did, and as brave things came on't: For *Hopeful* and some others, as the Story relates it, were Converted by his Death.

Hon. *Well, but pray go on; for you are well acquainted with things.*

Greath. Above all that *Christian* met with after he had passed thorow *Vanity-Fair*, one *By-ends* was the arch one.

1 Part pag. 229.

Hon. *By-ends; what was he?*

Greath. A very arch Fellow, a downright Hypocrite; one that would be Religious, which way ever the World went, but so cunning, that he would be sure neither to lose, nor suffer for it.

He had his *Mode* of Religion for every fresh occasion, and his Wife was as good at it as he. He would turn and change from Opinion to Opinion; yea, and plead for so doing too. But so far as I could learn, he came to an ill End with his *By-ends*, nor did I ever hear that any of his Children were ever of any Esteem with any that truly feared God.

Now by this time, they were come within sight of the Town of *Vanity*, where *Vanity Fair* is kept. So when they saw that they were so near the Town, they consulted with one another how they should pass thorow the Town, and some said one thing, and some another. At last Mr. *Greatheart* said, I have, as you may understand, often been a *Conductor* of Pilgrims thorow *this* Town; Now I am acquainted with one Mr. *Mnason*, a *Cyprusian* by Nation, an old Disciple, at whose House we may Lodge. If you think good, said he, we will turn in there.

They are come within sight of Vanity.

Psa. 21. 16.

They enter into one Mr. Mnasons *to Lodge.*

Content, said old *Honest*; Content, said *Christiana*; Content, said Mr. *Feeble-mind*; and so they said all. Now you must think it was *Even-tide*, by that they got to the outside of the Town, but Mr. *Great-heart* knew the way to the Old man's House. So thither they came; and he called at the Door, and the old Man within knew his Tongue so soon as ever he heard it; so he opened, and they all came in. Then said *Mnason* their Host, How far have ye come to day? So they said, From the House of *Gaius* our Friend. I promise you, said he, you have gone a good stitch, you may well be a-weary; sit down. So they sat down.

Greath. *Then said their Guide, Come what Chear Sirs, I dare say you are welcome to my Friend.*

Mna. I also, said Mr. *Mnason*, do bid you Welcome; and whatever you want, do but say, and we will do what we can to get it for you.

They are glad of entertainment.

Hon. *Our great Want, a while since, was Harbour, and good Company, and now I hope we have both.*

Mna. For Harbour, you see what it is, but for good Company, that will appear in the Tryal.

Greath. *Well, said Mr.* Great-heart, *will you have the Pilgrims up into their Lodging?*

Mna. I will, said Mr. *Mnason*. So he had them to their respective Places; and also shewed them a very fair Dining-Room, where they might be and sup together, untill time was come to go to Rest.

Now when they were set in their places, and were a little cheary after their Journey, Mr. *Honest* asked his Landlord if there were any store of good People in the Town?

Mna. We have a few, for indeed they are but a few, when compared with them on the other side.

Hon. *But how shall we do to see some of them? for the sight of good men to them that are going on Pilgrimage, is like to the appearing of the Moon and the Stars to them that are sailing upon the Seas.*

They desire to see some of the good People in the Town.

Mna. Then Mr. *Mnason* stamped with his Foot, and his Daughter *Grace* came up; so he said unto her, *Grace*, go you, tell my Friends, Mr. *Contrite*, Mr. *Holy-man*, Mr. *Love-saint*, Mr. *Dare-not-ly*, and Mr. *Penitent*; that I have a Friend or two at my House, that have a mind this Evening to see them.

Some sent for.

So *Grace* went to call them, and they came, and after Salutation made, they sat down together at the Table.

Then said Mr. *Mnason* their Landlord, My Neighbours, I have, as you see, a company of *Strangers* come to my House, they are *Pilgrims*: They come from afar, and are going to Mount *Sion*. But who, quoth he, do you think this is? pointing with his Finger to *Christiana*. It is *Christiana*, the Wife of *Christian*, that famous Pilgrim, who with *Faithful* his brother were so shamefully handled in our Town. At that they stood amazed, saying, We little thought to see *Christiana*, when *Grace* came to call us, wherefore this is a very comfortable Surprize. Then they asked her of her welfare, and if these young men were her Husbands Sons. And when she had told them they were; they said, The King whom you love, and serve, make you as your Father, and bring you where he is in Peace.

Some Talk betwixt Mr. Honest *and* Contrite.

Hon. Then Mr. *Honest* (*when they were all sat down*) *asked Mr.* Contrite *and the rest*, *in what posture their Town was at present?*

The Fruit of Watchfulness.

Cont. You may be sure we are full of Hurry, in Fair time. 'Tis hard keeping our Hearts and Spirits in any good Order, when we are in a cumbred condition. He that lives in such a place as this is, and that has to do with such as we have, has need of an Item to caution him to take heed, every moment of the Day.

Hon. *But how are your Neighbours for quietness?*

Persecution not so hot at Vanity Fair as formerly.

Cont. They are much more moderate now than formerly. You know how *Christian* and *Faithful* were used at our Town; but of late, I say, they have been far more moderate. I think the Blood of *Faithful* lieth with load upon them till now; for since they burned him, they have been ashamed to burn any more: In *those* days we were afraid to walk the Streets, but *now* we can shew our Heads. *Then* the Name of a Professor was odious, *now*, specially in some parts of our Town (for you know our Town is large) Religion is counted Honourable.

Then said Mr. Contrite *to them*, *Pray how fareth it with you in your Pilgrimage*, *how stands the Countrey affected towards you?*

Hon. It happens to us, as it happeneth to Way-faring men; sometimes our way is clean, sometimes foul; sometimes up hill, sometimes down hill; We are seldom at a Certainty. The Wind is not alwayes on our Backs, nor is every one a Friend that we meet with in the Way. We have met with some notable Rubs already; and what are yet behind we know not, but for the most part we find it true, that has been talked of of old, *A good Man must suffer Trouble.*

Contrit. *You talk of Rubs, what Rubs have you met withal?*

Hon. Nay, ask Mr. *Great-heart* our Guide, for he can give the best Account of that.

Greath. We have been beset three or four times already: First *Christiana* and her Children were beset with two Ruffians, that they feared would a took away their Lives; We was beset with Gyant *Bloody-man*, Gyant *Maul*, and Gyant *Slay-good*. Indeed we did rather beset the last, than were beset of him: And thus it was. After we had been some time at the House of *Gaius, mine Host, and of the whole Church*, we were minded upon a time to take our Weapons with us, and go see if we could light upon any of those that were Enemies to Pilgrims; (for we heard that there was a notable one thereabouts.) Now *Gaius* knew his *Haunt* better than I, because he dwelt thereabout, so we looked and looked, till at last we discerned the mouth of his Cave; then we were glad and pluck'd up our Spirits. So we approached up to his *Den*, and lo when we came there, he had dragged by meer force into his Net, this *poor man*, Mr. *Feeble-mind*, and was about to bring him to his End. But when he saw us, supposing as we thought, he had had another Prey, he left the poor man in his Hole, and came out. So we fell to it full sore, and he lustily laid about him; but in conclusion, he was brought down to the Ground, and his Head cut off, and set up by the Way-side for a Terror to such as should after practise such Ungodliness. That I tell you the Truth, here is the man himself to affirm it, who was as a Lamb taken out of the Mouth of the Lyon.

Feebl. *Then said Mr.* Feeble-mind, *I found this true to my Cost, and Comfort; to my Cost, when he threatned to pick my Bones every moment; and to my Comfort, when I saw Mr.* Great-heart *and his Friends with their Weapons approach so near for my* Deliverance.

Holym. Then said Mr. *Holy-man*, There are two things that they have need to be possessed with that go on Pilgrimage, *Courage* and an *unspotted Life*. If they have not *Courage*, they can never hold on their way; and if their Lives be *loose*, they will make the very Name of a *Pilgrim* stink.

Mr. Holy-man's *Speech.*

Loves. Then said Mr. *Love-saint*; I hope this Caution is not needful amongst you. But truly there are many that go upon the Road, that rather declare themselves Strangers to Pilgrimage, than Strangers and Pilgrims in the Earth.

Mr. Love-saint's *Speech.*

Darenot. *Then said Mr.* Dare-not-ly, *'Tis true; they neither have the Pilgrims* Weed, *nor the Pilgrims Courage; they go not uprightly, but all* awrie *with their Feet, one Shoo goes* inward, *another* outward, *and their Hosen out behind*; there a *Rag*, and there a *Rent*, to the Disparagement of their Lord.

Mr. Dare-not-ly *his Speech.*

Penit. These things, said Mr. *Penitent*, they ought to be troubled for, nor are the Pilgrims like to have that Grace put upon them and their Pilgrims Progress, as they desire, until the way is cleared of such Spots and Blemishes.

Mr. Penitent *his Speech.*

Thus they sat talking and spending the time, until Supper was set upon the Table. Unto which they went and refreshed their weary Bodies, so they went to Rest. Now they stayed in this Fair a great while, at the House of this Mr. *Mnason*, who in process of time gave his Daughter *Grace* unto *Samuel Christiana*'s Son, to Wife, and his Daughter *Martha* to *Joseph*.

The time, as I said, that they lay here, was long (for it was not now as in former times.) Wherefore the *Pilgrims* grew acquainted with many of the good people of the Town, and did them what service they could. *Mercy*, as she was wont, laboured much for the Poor, wherefore their Bellyes and Backs blessed her, and she was there an Ornament to her Profession. And to say the truth, for *Grace*, *Phebe*, and *Martha*, they were all of a very good Nature, and did much good in their place. They were also all of them very Fruitful, so that *Christian's* Name, as was said before, was like to live in the World.

While they lay here, there came a *Monster* out of the

Woods, and slew many of the People of the Town. It would also carry away their Children, and teach them to suck its Whelps. Now no man in the Town durst so much as Face this *Monster*; but all Men fled when they heard of the noise of his coming.

A Monster.

The *Monster* was like unto no one Beast upon the Earth. Its Body was like a Dragon, and it had seven Heads and ten Horns, *It made great havock of Children, and yet it was governed by a Woman.* This *Monster* propounded Conditions to men; and such men as loved their Lives more then their Souls, accepted of those Conditions. So they came under.

Rev. 17. 3.
His Shape.
His Nature.

Now this Mr. *Great-heart*, together with these that came to visit the Pilgrims at Mr. *Mnason*'s House, entred into a Covenant to go and ingage this Beast, if perhaps they might deliver the People of this Town, from the Paws and Mouth of this so devouring a Serpent.

Then did Mr. *Great-heart*, Mr. *Contrite*, Mr. *Holy-man*, Mr. *Dare-not-ly*, and Mr. *Penitent*, with their Weapons go forth to meet him. Now the *Monster* at first was very Rampant, and looked upon these Enemies with great Disdain, but they so be-labored him, being sturdy men at Arms, that they made him make a Retreat: so they came home to Mr. *Mnasons* House again.

How he is ingaged.

The *Monster*, you must know, had his certain Seasons to come out in, and to make his Attempts upon the Children of the People of the Town, also these Seasons did these valiant Worthies watch him in, and did still continually assault him; in so much, that in process of time, he became not only wounded, but lame; also he has not made that havock of the Towns-mens Children, as formerly he has done. And it is verily believed by some, that this Beast will die of his Wounds.

This therefore made Mr. *Great-heart* and his Fellows, of great Fame in this Town, so that many of the People that wanted their taste of things, yet had a Reverend Esteem and Respect for them. Upon this account therefore it was that these Pilgrims got not much hurt here. True, there were some of the baser sort that could see no more then a *Mole*, nor understand more than a Beast, these had no reverence for these men, nor took they notice of their Valour or Adventures.

Well, the time drew on that the Pilgrims must go on their way, wherefore they prepared for their Journey. They sent for their Friends, they conferred with them, they had some time set apart therein to commit each other to the Protection of their Prince. There was again, that brought them of such things as they had, that was fit for the weak, and the strong, for the Women, and the Men; and so *laded* them with such things as was necessary.

Act. 28. 10.

Then they set forwards on their way, and their Friends accompanying them so far as was convenient; they again committed each other to the Protection of their King, and parted.

They therefore that were of the Pilgrims Company went on, and Mr. *Great-heart* went before them; now the Women and Children being weakly, they were forced to go as they could bear, by this means Mr. *Ready-to-hault* and Mr. *Feeble-mind* had more to sympathize with their Condition.

When they were gone from the Towns-men, and when their Friends had bid them farewel, they quickly came to the place where *Faithful* was put to Death: There therefore they made a stand, and thanked him that had enabled him to bear his Cross so well, and the rather, because they now found that they had a benefit by such a manly Suffering as his was.

They went on therefore after this, a good way further, talking of *Christian* and *Faithful*, and how *Hopeful* joyned himself to *Christian* after that *Faithful* was dead.

1 Part p. 222.

Now they were come up with the *Hill Lucre*, where the *Silver-mine* was, which took *Demas* off from his Pilgrimage, and into which, as some think, *By-ends* fell and perished; wherefore they considered that. But when they were come to the old Monument that stood over against the *Hill Lucre*, to wit, to the Pillar of Salt that stood also within view of *Sodom*, and its stinking Lake; they marvelled, as did *Christian* before, that men of that Knowledge and ripeness of Wit as they was, should be so blinded as to turn aside here. Only they considered again, that Nature is not affected with the Harms that others have met with, specially if that thing upon which they look, has an attracting Virtue upon the foolish Eye.

I saw now that they went on till they came at the River that was on this side of the delectable Mountains.
To the River where the fine Trees grow on 1 Part pag. 232.
both sides, and whose Leaves, if taken inwardly, are good against Surfeits; where the Medows are green
all the year long, and where they might lie Psal. 23.
down safely.

By this River side in the Medow, there were Cotes and Folds for Sheep, an House built for the *nourishing* and bringing up of those Lambs, the Babes of those Women that go on Pilgrimage. Also there was here one that was
intrusted with them, who could have compassion, Heb. 5. 2. Isa. 40. 11.
and that could gather these Lambs with his Arm, and carry them in his Bosom, and that could gently lead those that were with young. Now to the Care of *this Man*, *Christiana* admonished her four Daughters to commit their little ones; that by these Waters they might be housed, harbored, succored and nourished, and that none
of them might *be lacking in time to come*. This Jer. 23. 4.
man, if any of them go astray, or be lost, he will Ezek. 34. 11, 12, 13, 14, 15, 16.
bring them again, he will also bind up that which was broken, and will strengthen them that are sick. Here they will never want Meat, and Drink and Cloathing, here they will be kept from Thieves and Robbers, for this man will dye before one of those committed to his Trust, shall be lost. Besides, here they shall be sure to have good *Nurture* and Admonition, and shall be taught
to walk in right Paths, and that you know is John 10. 16.
a Favour of no small account. Also here, as you see, are delicate *Waters*, pleasant *Medows*, dainty *Flowers*, variety of *Trees*, and such as bear *wholsom Fruit*. Fruit, not like that that *Matthew* eat of, that fell over the Wall out of *Belzebubs* Garden, but Fruit that procureth Health where there is none, and that continueth and increaseth it where it is.

So they were content to commit their little Ones to him; and that which was also an Incouragement to them so to do, was, for that all this was to be at the Charge of the King, and so was an Hospital to young Children, and *Orphans*.

They being come to By-path *Stile, have a mind to have a pluck with* Gyant Despair.

1 Part, pag. 233, 239.

Now they went on: And when they were come to *By-path* Medow, to the Stile over which *Christian* went with his Fellow *Hopeful*, when they were taken by Gyant *Despair*, and put into *Doubting* Castle: They sate down and consulted what was best to be done, to wit, now they were so strong, and had got such a man as Mr. *Great-heart* for their Conductor; whether they had not best to make an Attempt upon the Gyant, demolish his Castle, and if there were any Pilgrims in it, to set them at liberty before they went any further. So one said one thing, and another said the contrary. One questioned if it was lawful to go upon *Unconsecrated* Ground, another said they might, provided their end was good; but Mr. *Great-heart* said, Though that Assertion offered last, cannot be universally true, yet I have a Comandment to resist Sin, to overcome Evil, to fight the good Fight of Faith: And I pray, with whom should I fight this good Fight, if not with Gyant *Despair*? I will therefore attempt the taking away of his Life, and the demolishing of *Doubting* Castle. Then said he, who will go with me? Then said old *Honest*, I will, and so will we too, said *Christian*'s four Sons, *Matthew*, *Samuel*, *James* and *Joseph*, for they were young men and strong.

1 John 2. 13, 14.

So they left the Women in the Road, and with them Mr. *Feeble-mind*, and Mr. *Ready-to-hault*, with his Crutches, to be their *Guard*, until they came back, for in that place thô Gyant *Despair* dwelt so near, they keeping in the Road, *A little Child might lead them*.

Isa. 11. 6.

So Mr. *Great-heart*, old *Honest*, and the four young men, went to go up to *Doubting* Castle, to look for Gyant *Despair*: When they came at the Castle Gate, they knocked for Entrance with an unusual Noise. At that the old Gyant comes to the Gate, and *Diffidence* his Wife follows: Then said he, Who, and what is he, that is so hardy, as after this manner to molest the Gyant *Despair*? Mr. *Great-heart* replyed, It is I, *Great-heart*, one of the King of the Celestial Countreys Conductors of Pilgrims to their Place. And I demand of thee that thou open thy Gates for my Entrance, prepare thy self also to Fight, for I am come to take away thy Head, and to demolish *Doubting* Castle.

Now Gyant *Despair*, because he was a Gyant, thought no man could overcome him, and again, thought he, since heretofore I have made a Conquest of Angels, shall *Great-heart* make me afraid? So he harnessed himself and went out: He had a Cap of Steel upon his Head, a Brestplate of Fire girded to him, and he came out in Iron Shooes, with a great Club in his Hand: Then these six men made up to him, and beset him behind and before; also when *Diffidence*, the Gyantess, came up to help him, old Mr. *Honest* cut her down at one Blow. Then they fought for their Lives, and Gyant *Despair* was brought down to the Ground, *but was very loth to dye*: He strugled hard, and had, as they say, as many Lives as a Cat, but *Great-heart* was his death, for he left him not till he had severed his head from his shoulders.

Despair *has overcome Angels.*

Despair *is loth to die.*

Then they fell to demolishing *Doubting* Castle, and that you know might with ease be done, since Gyant *Despair* was dead. They were seven Days in destroying of that; and in it of Pilgrims, they found one Mr. *Dispondency*, almost starved to Death, and one *Much-afraid* his Daughter; these two they saved alive. But it would a made you a wondered to have seen the dead Bodies that lay here and there in the Castle Yard, and how full of dead mens Bones the Dungeon was.

Doubting-Castle *demolished.*

When Mr. *Great-heart* and his Companions had performed this Exploit, they took Mr. *Despondency*, and his Daughter *Much-afraid*, into their Protection, for they were honest People, thô they were Prisoners in *Doubting* Castle, to that Tyrant Gyant *Despair*. They therefore I say, took with them the Head of the Gyant (for his Body they had buried under a heap of Stones) and down to the Road and to their Companions they came, and shewed them what they had done. Now when *Feeble-mind*, and *Ready-to-hault* saw that it was the Head of Gyant *Despair* indeed, they were very jocond and merry. Now *Christiana*, if need was, could play upon the *Vial*, and her Daughter *Mercy* upon the *Lute*: So, since they were so merry disposed, she plaid them a Lesson, and *Ready-to-hault* would Dance. So he took *Dispondencie*'s Daughter, named *Much-afraid*, by the Hand, and to Dancing they went in the Road. True, he

They have Musick and Dancing for Joy.

could not Dance without one Crutch in his Hand, but I promise you, he footed it well; also the Girl was to be commended, for she answered the Musick handsomely.

As for Mr. *Despondency*, the Musick was not much to him, he was for feeding rather then Dancing, for that he was almost starved. So *Christiana* gave him some of her bottle of Spirits for present Relief, and then prepared him something to eat; and in little time the old Gentleman came to himself, and began to be finely revived.

Now I saw in my Dream, when all these things were finished, Mr. *Great-heart* took the Head of *Gyant Despair*, and set it upon a Pole by the High-way side, right over against the Pillar that *Christian* erected for a *Caution* to Pilgrims that came after, to take heed of entring into his Grounds.

Then he writ under it upon a *Marble* stone, these Verses following.

This is the Head *of* him, *whose* Name *only*,
In former times, *did* Pilgrims *terrifie*.
His Castle'*s down*, *and* Diffidence *his Wife*,
Brave Master Great-heart *has bereft of Life*.
Despondency, *his Daughter* Much-afraid,
Great-heart, *for them also the Man has play'd*.
Who hereof doubts, *if he'l but cast his Eye*,
Up hither, *may his Scruples satisfie*.
This Head, *also when doubting Cripples dance*,
Doth shew from Fears they have Deliverance.

A Monument of Deliverance.

When these men had thus bravely shewed themselves against *Doubting-Castle*, and had slain *Gyant-Despair*, they went forward, and went on till they came to the *Delectable* Mountains, where *Christian* and *Hopeful* refreshed themselves with the Varieties of the Place. They also acquainted themselves with the Shepherds there, who welcomed them as they had done *Christian* before, unto the delectable Mountains.

Now the Shepherds seeing so great a train follow Mr. *Great-heart* (for with him they were well acquainted;) they said unto him, Good Sir, you have got a goodly Company here; pray where did you find all these?

Then Mr. *Great-heart* replyed,

First here's Christiana *and her train,*
Her Sons, and her Sons Wives, who like the Wain
Keep by the Pole, and do by Compass steer,
From Sin to Grace, else they had not been here.
Next here's old Honest *come on Pilgrimage,*
Ready-to-halt *too, who I dare ingage,*
True hearted is, and so is Feeble-mind,
Who willing was, not to be left behind.
Despondency, *good-man, is coming after,*
And so also is Much-afraid, *his Daughter.*
May we have Entertainment here, or must
We further go? let's know whereon to trust.

The Guides Speech to the Shepherds.

Then said the Shepherds; This is a comfortable Company, you are welcome to us, for we have for the *Feeble*, as for the *Strong*; our Prince has an Eye to what is done to the least of these. Therefore Infirmity must not be a block to our Entertainment. So they had them to the Palace Door, and then said unto them, Come in Mr. *Feeble-mind*, come in Mr. *Ready-to-halt*, come in Mr. *Despondency*, and Mrs. *Much-afraid* his Daughter. *These* Mr. *Great-heart*, said the Shepherds to the Guide, we call in by Name, for that they are most subject to draw back; but as for you, and the rest that are *strong*, we leave you to your wonted Liberty. Then said Mr. *Great-heart*, This day I see that Grace doth shine in your Faces, and that you are my Lords Shepherds indeed; for that you have not *pushed* these Diseased neither with Side nor Shoulder, but have rather strewed their way into the Palace with Flowers, as you should.

Their Entertainment. Matt. 25. 40.

A Description of false Shepherds. Ezek. 34. 21.

So the Feeble and Weak went in, and Mr. *Great-heart*, and the rest did follow. When they were also set down, the Shepherds said to those of the weakest sort, What is it that you would have? For said they, all things must be managed here, to the supporting of the weak, as well as to the warning of the Unruly.

So they made them a Feast of things easie of Digestion, and that were pleasant to the Palate, and nourishing; the which when they had received, they went to their rest, each one respectively unto his proper place. When Morning was come, because the Mountains were high, and the day clear; and because it was the Custom of the Shepherds to shew to the Pilgrims, before their Departure, some Rarities; therefore after they were ready, and had refreshed themselves, the Shepherds took them out into the Fields, and shewed them first, what they had shewed to *Christian* before.

Mount-Marvel.

1 Part, pag. 246.

Then they had them to some new places. The first was to *Mount-Marvel*, where they looked, and behold a man at a Distance, *that tumbled the Hills about with Words.* Then they asked the Shepherds what that should mean? So they told him, that that man was the Son of one *Great-grace*, of whom you read in the first part of the Records of the *Pilgrims Progress.* And he is set there to teach Pilgrims how to believe down, or to tumble out of their wayes, what Difficulties they shall meet with, by Faith. Then said Mr. *Great-heart*, I know him, he is a man above many.

Mar. 11. 23, 24.

Mount-Innocent.

Then they had them to another place, called *Mount-Innocent.* And there they saw a man cloathed all in White; and two men, *Prejudice*, and *Ill-will*, continually casting Dirt upon him. Now behold the Dirt, whatsoever they cast at him, would in little time fall off again, and his Garment would look as clear as if no Dirt had been cast thereat.

Then said the Pilgrims what means this? The Shepherds answered, This man is named *Godly-man*, and this Garment is to shew the Innocency of his Life. Now those that throw Dirt at him, are such as hate his *Well-doing*, but as you see the Dirt will not stick upon his Cloaths, so it shall be with him that liveth truly Innocently in the World. Whoever they be that would make such men dirty, they labour all in vain; for God, by that a little time is spent will cause that their *Innocence* shall break forth as the Light, and their Righteousness as the Noon day.

Mount-Charity.

Then they took them, and had them to *Mount-Charity*, where they shewed them a man that had a bundle of Cloth lying before him, out of which he cut Coats and Garments, for the Poor that stood about him; yet his Bundle or Role of Cloth was never the less.

Then said they, what should this be? This is, said the Shepherds, to shew you, That he that has a Heart to give of his Labour to the Poor, shall never want wherewithal. He that watereth shall be watered himself. And the Cake that the Widdow gave to the Prophet, did not cause that she had ever the less in her Barrel.

They had them also to a place where they saw one *Fool*, and one *Want-wit*, washing of an *Ethiopian* with intention to make him white, but the more they washed him, the blacker he was. They then asked the Shepherds what that should mean. So they told them, saying, Thus shall it be with the vile Person; all means used to get such an one a good Name, shall in Conclusion tend but to make him more abominable. Thus it was with the *Pharisees*, and so shall it be with all Hypocrites.

The Work of one Fool, *and one Want-witt.*

Then said *Mercy* the Wife of *Matthew* to *Christiana* her Mother, Mother, I would, if it might be, see the Hole in the Hill; or that, commonly called the *By-way* to Hell. So her Mother brake her mind to the Shepherds. Then they went to the Door; it was in the side of an Hill, and they opened it, and bid *Mercy* hearken awhile. So she hearkened, and heard one saying, *Cursed be my Father for holding of my Feet back from the way of Peace and Life*; and another said, *O that I had been torn in pieces before I had, to save my Life, lost my Soul*; and another said, *If I were to live again, how would I deny my self rather then come to this Place.* Then there was as if the very Earth had groaned, and quaked under the Feet of this young Woman for fear; so she looked white, and came trembling away, saying, Blessed be he and she that is delivered from this Place.

1 Part, pag. 242.

Mercy *has a mind to see the hole in the Hill.*

Now when the Shepherds had shewed them all these things, then they had them back to the Palace, and entertained them with what the House would afford; But *Mercy* being a young, and breeding Woman, longed for something which she saw there, but was ashamed to ask. Her Mother-in-law then asked her what she ailed, for she looked as one not well. Then said *Mercy*,

Mercy *longeth, and for what.*

There is a Looking-glass hangs up in the Dining-room, off of which I cannot take my mind; if therefore I have it not, I think I shall Miscarry. Then said her Mother, I will mention thy Wants to the Shepherds, and they will not deny it thee. But she said, I am ashamed that these men should know that I longed. Nay my Daughter, said she, it is no Shame, but a Virtue, to long for such a thing as that; so *Mercy* said, Then Mother, if you please, ask the Shepherds if they are willing to sell it.

It was the Word of God.

Jam. 1. 23.

1 Cor. 13. 12.

2 Cor. 3. 18.

Now the Glass was one of a thousand. It would present a man, one way with his own Feature exactly, and turn it but another way, and it would shew one the very Face and Similitude of the Prince of Pilgrims himself. Yea I have talked with them that can tell, and they have said, that they have seen the very Crown of Thorns upon his Head, by looking in that Glass, they have therein also seen the holes in his Hands, in his Feet, and his Side. Yea such an excellency is there in that Glass, that it will shew him to one where they have a mind to see him; whether living or dead, whether in Earth or Heaven, whether in a State of Humiliation, or in his Exaltation, whether coming to Suffer, or coming to Reign.

1 Part, pag. 241.

Christiana therefore went to the Shepherds apart. (Now the Names of the Shepherds are *Knowledge*, *Experience*, *Watchful*, and *Sincere*,) and said unto them, There is one of my Daughters a breeding Woman, that, I think doth long for some thing that she hath seen in this House, and she thinks she shall miscarry if she should by you be denyed.

She doth not lose her Longing.

Experience. Call her, call her, She shall assuredly have what we can help her to. So they called her, and said to her, *Mercy*, what is that thing thou wouldest have? Then she blushed and said, The great Glass that hangs up in the Dining-room: So *Sincere* ran and fetched it, and with a joyful Consent it was given her. Then she bowed her Head, and gave Thanks, and said, By this I know that I have obtained Favour in your Eyes.

They also gave to the other young Women such things as

they desired, and to their Husbands great Commendations, for that they joyned with Mr. *Great-heart* to the slaying of *Gyant-Despair*, and the demolishing of *Doubting-Castle*.

About *Christiana*'s Neck, the Shepherds put a Bracelet, and so they did about the Necks of her four Daughters, also they put Ear-rings in their Ears, and Jewels on their Fore-heads.

How the Shepherds adorn the Pilgrims.

When they were minded to go hence, they let them go in Peace, but gave not to them those certain Cautions which before were given to *Christian* and his Companion. The Reason was, for that these had *Great-heart* to be their Guide, who was one that was well acquainted with things, and so could give them their Cautions more seasonably, to wit, even then when the Danger was nigh the approaching.

1 Part, pag. 243.

What Cautions *Christian* and his Companions had received of the Shepherds, they had also lost, by that the time was come that they had need to put them in practice. Wherefore here was the Advantage that this Company had over the other.

1 Part, pag. 253.

From hence they went on Singing, and they said,

Behold, how fitly *are the Stages set!*
For their Relief, that Pilgrims are become;
And how they us *receive without* one *let,*
That make the other *Life our* Mark *and Home.*
What Novelties *they have, to* us *they give,*
That we, thô *Pilgrims, joyful Lives may live.*
They do upon us too such things bestow,
That shew we Pilgrims are, where e're we go.

When they were gone from the Shepherds, they quickly came to the Place where *Christian* met with one *Turn-a-way*, that dwelt in the Town of *Apostacy*. Wherefore of him Mr. *Great-heart* their Guide did now put them in mind; saying, This is the place where *Christian* met with one *Turn-a-way*, who carried with him the Character of his Rebellion at his Back. And this I have to say concerning this man, He would hearken to no Counsel, but once a falling, perswasion could not stop him. When he came to

1 Part, pag. 245.

How one Turn-a-way *managed his Apostacy.*

the place where the Cross and the Sepulcher was, he did meet with one that did bid him *look there*, but he gnashed with his Teeth, and stamped, and said, he was resolved to go back to his own Town. Before he came to the Gate, he met with *Evangelist*, who offered to lay Hands on him, to turn him into the way again. But this *Turn-a-way resisted him*, and having done much *despite* unto him, he got away over the Wall, and so escaped his Hand.

Heb. 10. 26, 27, 28, 29.

Then they went on, and just at the place where *Little-faith* formerly was Robbed, there stood a man with his Sword drawn, and his Face all bloody. Then said Mr. *Great-heart*, What art thou? The man made Answer, saying, I am one whose Name is *Valiant-for-Truth*, I am a Pilgrim, and am going to the Celestial City. Now as I was in my way, there was three men did beset me, and propounded unto me these three things. 1. Whether I would become one of them? Or go back from whence I came? Or die upon the Place? To the first I answered, I had been a true Man a long Season, and therefore, it could not be expected that I now should cast in my Lot with Thieves. Then they demanded what I would say to the Second. So I told them that the Place from whence I came, had I not found Incommodity there, I had not forsaken it at all, but finding it altogether unsuitable to me, and very unprofitable for me, I forsook it for this Way. Then they asked me what I said to the third. And I told them, my Life cost more dear far, than that I should lightly give it away. Besides, you have nothing to do thus to put things to my Choice; wherefore at your Peril be it, if you meddle. Then these three, to wit, *Wild-head*, *Inconsiderate*, and *Pragmatick*, drew upon me, and I also drew upon them.

One Valiant-for-truth *beset with Thieves.*

Prov. 1. 10, 11, 12, 13, 14.

So we fell to it, one against three, for the space of above three Hours. They have left upon me, as you see, some of the Marks of their Valour, and have also carried away with them some of mine. They are but just now gone, I suppose they might, as the saying is, hear your Horse dash, and so they betook them to flight.

How he behaved himself, and put them to flight.

Greath. *But here was great Odds, three against one.*

Valiant. 'Tis true, but *little* and *more*, are nothing to him that has the Truth on his side. *Though an Host should encamp against me, said one, My Heart shall not fear. Thô War should rise against me, in this will I be Confident*, &c. Besides, said he, I have read in some Records, that one man has fought an Army; and how many did *Sampson* slay with the Jaw Bone of an Ass!

Psal. 27. 3.

Great-heart *wonders at his Valour.*

Greath. *Then said the Guide, Why did you not cry out, that some might a-came in for your Succour?*

Valiant. So I did, to my King, who I knew could hear, and afford invisible Help, and that was sufficient for me.

Has a mind to see his Sword, and spends his Judgment on it.

Greath. *Then said* Great-heart *to Mr.* Valiant-for-Truth, *Thou hast worthily behaved thy self; Let me see thy Sword; so he shewed it him.*

When he had taken it in his Hand, and looked thereon a while, he said, Ha! *It is a right* Jerusalem *Blade.*

Isa. 2. 3.

Valiant. It is so. Let a man have one of *these Blades*, with a Hand to wield it, and skill to use it, and he may venture upon an Angel with it. He need not fear its holding, if he can but tell how to lay on. Its Edges will never blunt. It will cut *Flesh*, and *Bones*, and *Soul*, and *Spirit*, and all.

Ephes. 6. 12, 13, 14, 15, 16, 17.

Heb. 4. 12.

Greath. *But you fought a great while, I wonder you was not weary?*

Valiant. I fought till my Sword did cleave to my Hand, and when they were joyned together, as if a Sword grew out of my Arm, and when the Blood run thorow my Fingers, then I fought with most Courage.

2 Sam. 23. 10.

The Word. The Faith. Blood.

Greath. *Thou hast done well, thou hast resisted unto Blood, striving against Sin. Thou shalt abide by us, come in, and go out with us; for we are thy Companions.*

Then they took him and washed his Wounds, and gave him of what they had, to refresh him, and so they went on together. Now as they went on, because Mr. *Great-heart* was delighted in him (for he loved one greatly that he found to be a man of his Hands) and because there was with his Company, them that was feeble and weak; Therefore he questioned with him about many things; as first, *What Countrey-man he was?*

What Countrey man Mr. Valiant *was.*

Valiant. I am of *Dark-land*, for there I was born, and there my Father and Mother are still.

Greath. *Dark-land*, said the Guide, *Doth not that ly upon the same Coast with the City of* Destruction.

Valiant. Yes it doth. Now that which caused me to come on Pilgrimage, was this: We had one Mr. *Tell-true* came into our parts, and he told it about, what *Christian* had done, that went from the City of *Destruction*. Namely, how he had forsaken his *Wife* and *Children*, and had betaken himself to a *Pilgrims* Life. It was also confidently reported how he had killed a *Serpent* that did come out to resist him in his Journey, and how he got thorow to whither he intended. It was also told what Welcome he had at all his Lords Lodgings; specially when he came to the Gates of the Celestial City. For there, said the man, He was received with sound of Trumpet, by a company of shining ones. He told it also, how all the Bells in the City did ring for Joy at his Reception, and what Golden Garments he was cloathed with; with many other things that now I shall forbear to relate. In a word, that man so told the Story of *Christian* and his Travels, that my Heart fell into a burning hast to be gone after him, nor could Father or Mother stay me, so I got from them, and am come thus far on my Way.

How Mr. Valiant *came to go on Pilgrimage.*

Greath. *You came in at the Gate, did you not?*

Valiant. Yes, yes. For the same man also told us, that all would be nothing if we did not begin to enter this way at the Gate.

He begins right.

Greath. *Look you, said the Guide to* Christiana, *The Pilgrimage of your Husband, and what he has gotten thereby, is spread abroad far and near.*

Christian'*s Name famous.*

Valiant. Why, is this *Christian*'s Wife.

Greath. *Yes, that it is, and these are also her four Sons.*

Valiant. What! and going on Pilgrimage too?

Greath. *Yes verily, they are following after.*

Valiant. It glads me at the Heart! Good man! How Joyful will he be, when he shall see them that would not go with him, yet to enter after him, in at the Gates into the City?

He is much rejoyced to see Christian's *Wife.*

Greath. *Without doubt it will be a Comfort to him; for next to the Joy of seeing himself there, it will be a Joy to meet there his Wife and his Children.*

Valiant. But now you are upon that, pray let me see your Opinion about it. Some make a question whether we shall know one another when we are there.

Whether we shall know one another when we come to Heaven.

Greath. *Do they think they shall know themselves then? Or that they shall rejoyce to see themselves in that Bliss? and if they think they shall know and do these; Why not know others, and rejoyce in their Welfare also?*

Again, Since Relations are our second self, thô that State will be dissolved there, yet why may it not be rationally concluded that we shall be more glad to see them there, than to see they are wanting?

Valiant. Well, I perceive whereabouts you are as to this. Have you any more things to ask me about my beginning to come on Pilgrimage.

Greath. *Yes, Was your Father and Mother willing that you should become a Pilgrim?*

Valiant. Oh, no. They used all means imaginable to perswade me to stay at Home.

Greath. *Why, what could they say against it?*

Valiant. They said it was an idle Life, and if I my self were not inclined to Sloath and Laziness, I would never countenance a Pilgrims Condition.

The great stumbling-Blocks that by his Friends were laid in his way.

Greath. *And what did they say else?*

Valiant. Why, They told me that it was a dangerous Way, yea the most dangerous Way in the World, said they, is that which the Pilgrims go.

Greath. *Did they shew wherein this Way is so dangerous?*

Valiant. Yes. And that in many Particulars.

Greath. *Name some of them.*

Valiant. They told me of the *Slough* of *Despond*, where *Christian* was well nigh Smothered. They told me that there were Archers standing ready in *Belzebub-Castle*, to shoot them that should knock at the *Wicket* Gate for Entrance. They told me also of the Wood, and dark Mountains, of the Hill *Difficulty*, of the Lyons, and also of the three Gyants, *Bloodyman*, *Maul*, and *Slay-good*. They said moreover, That there was a foul *Fiend* haunted the Valley of *Humiliation*, and that *Christian* was, by him, almost bereft of Life. Besides, said they, You must go over the *Valley of the Shadow of Death*, where the *Hobgoblins* are, where the Light is Darkness, where the Way is full of Snares, Pits, Traps and Ginns. They told me also of *Gyant Despair*, of *Doubting Castle*, and of the *Ruins* that the Pilgrims met with there. Further, They said, I must go over the enchanted Ground, which was dangerous. And that after all this I should find a River, over which I should find no Bridg, and that that River did lye betwixt me and the Celestial Countrey.

The first Stumbling-Block.

Greath. *And was this all?*

Valiant. No, They also told me that this way was full of *Deceivers*, and of Persons that laid await there, to turn good men out of the Path.

The Second.

Greath. *But how did they make that out?*

Valiant. They told me that Mr. *Worldly-wise-man* did there lye in wait to deceive. They also said that there was *Formality* and *Hypocrisie* continually on the Road. They said also that *By-ends*, *Talkative*, or *Demas*, would go near to gather me up; that the Flatterer would catch me in his Net, or that with greenheaded *Ignorance* I would presume to go on to the Gate, from whence he always was sent back to the Hole that was in the side of the Hill, and made to go the By-way to Hell.

The Third.

Greath. *I promise you, This was enough to discourage. But did they make an end here?*

Valiant. No, stay. They told me also of many that had tryed that way of old, and that had gone a great way therein, to see if they could find something of the Glory there, that so many had so much talked of from time to time; and how they came back again, and befooled themselves for setting a Foot out of Doors in that Path, to the

The Fourth.

Satisfaction of all the Countrey. And they named several that did so, as *Obstinate*, and *Plyable*, *Mistrust*, and *Timerous*, *Turn-a-way*, and old *Atheist*, with several more; who, they said, had, some of them, gone far to see if they could find, but not one of them found so much Advantage by going, as amounted *to the weight of a Feather.*

Greath. *Said they any thing more to discourage you?*

Valiant. Yes, They told me of one Mr. *Fearing*, who was a Pilgrim, and how *he* found this way so Solitary, that he never had comfortable Hour therein, also that Mr. *Despondency* had like to been starved therein; Yea, and also, which I had almost forgot, that *Christian* himself, about whom there has been such a Noise, after all his Ventures for a Celestial Crown, was certainly drowned in the black River, and never went foot further, however it was smothered up.

The Fifth.

Greath. *And did none of these things discourage you?*

Valiant. No. They seemed but as so many Nothings to me.

Greath. *How came that about?*

Valiant. Why, I still believed what Mr. *Tell-true* had said, and that carried me beyond them all.

How he got over these Stumbling-Blocks.

Greath. *Then this was your Victory, even your Faith?*

Valiant. It was so, I believed and therefore came out, got into the Way, fought all that set themselves against me, and by believing am come to this Place.

Who would true Valour see,
Let him come hither;
One here will Constant be,
Come Wind, come Weather.
There's no Discouragement,
Shall make him once Relent,
His first avow'd Intent,
To be a Pilgrim.

Who so beset him round,
With dismal Stories,
Do but themselves Confound;
His Strength the more is.

No Lyon *can him fright,*
He'l with a Gyant *Fight,*
But he will have a right,
To be a Pilgrim.

Hobgoblin, *nor foul* Fiend,
Can daunt *his Spirit :*
He knows, he at the end,
Shall Life Inherit.
Then Fancies fly away,
He'l fear not what men say,
He'l labour Night and Day,
To be a Pilgrim.

By this time they were got to the *enchanted Ground*, where the Air naturally tended to make one *Drowzy*. And that place was all grown over with Bryers and Thorns; excepting *here* and *there*, where was an *inchanted Arbor*, upon which, if a Man sits, or in which if a man sleeps, 'tis a question, say some, whether ever they shall rise or wake again in this World. Over this Forrest therefore they went, both one with an other, and Mr. *Great-heart* went before, for that he was the Guide, and Mr. *Valiant-for-truth*, he came behind, being there a Guard, for fear lest peradventure some *Fiend*, or *Dragon*, or *Gyant*, or *Thief*, should fall upon their Rere, and so do Mischief. They went on here each man with his Sword drawn in his Hand; for they knew it was a dangerous place. Also they cheared up one another as well as they could. *Feeble-mind*, Mr. *Great-heart* commanded should come up after him, and Mr. *Despondency* was under the Eye of Mr. *Valiant*.

1 Part, pag. 255.

Now they had not gone far, but a great Mist and a darkness fell upon them all; so that they could scarce, for a great while, see the one the other. Wherefore they were forced for some time, to feel for one another, by Words; for they walked not by Sight.

But any one must think, that here was but sorry going for the best of them all, but how much worse for the Women and Children, who both of *Feet* and *Heart* were but tender. Yet so it was, that, thorow the incouraging Words of he that led in the Front, and of him that brought them up behind, they made a pretty good shift to wagg along.

The Way also was here very wearysom, thorow Dirt and Slabbiness. Nor was there on *all* this Ground, so much as one *Inn*, or *Victualling-House*, therein to refresh the feebler sort. Here therefore was *grunting*, and *puffing*, and *sighing*: While one tumbleth over a Bush, another sticks fast in the Dirt, and the Children, some of them, lost their Shoos in the Mire. While one cries out, I am down, and another, Ho, Where are you? and a third, The Bushes have got such fast hold on me, I think I cannot get away from them.

Then they came at an *Arbor*, warm, and promising much refreshing to the Pilgrims; for it was finely wrought above-head, beautified with *Greens*, furnished with *Benches*, and *Settles*. It also had in it a soft Couch whereon the weary might lean. This, you must think, all things considered, was tempting; for the Pilgrims already began to be foyled with the badness of the way; but there was not one of them that made so much as a motion to stop there. Yea, for ought I could perceive, they continually gave so good heed to the Advice of their Guide, and he did so faithfully tell them of *Dangers*, and of the *Nature* of Dangers when they were at them, that usually when they were nearest to them, they did most pluck up their Spirits, and hearten one another to deny the Flesh. This *Arbor* was called *The sloathfuls Friend*, on purpose to allure, if it might be, some of the Pilgrims there, to take up their Rest when weary.

An Arbor *on the Inchanting Ground.*

The Name of the Arbor.

I saw then in my Dream, that they went on in this their *solitary* Ground, till they came to a place at which a man is apt to lose his Way. *Now*, thô when it was light, their Guide could well enough tell how to miss those ways that led wrong, yet in the dark he was put to a stand: But he had in his Pocket a Map of all ways leading to, or from the Celestial City; wherefore he strook a Light (for he never goes also without his Tinder-box) and takes a view of his Book or Map; which bids him be careful in that place to turn to the right-hand-way. And had he not here been careful to look in his Map, they had

The way difficult to find.

The Guide has a Map of all ways leading to or from the City.

all, in probability, been smothered in the Mud, for just a little before them, and that at the end of the cleanest Way too, was a Pit, none knows how deep, full of nothing but Mud; there made on purpose to destroy the Pilgrims in.

God's Book.

Then thought I with my self, who, that goeth on Pilgrimage, but would have one of these Maps about him, that he may look when he is at a *stand*, which is the way he must take?

An Arbor and two asleep therein.

They went on then in this *inchanted* Ground, till they came to where was another *Arbor*, and it was built by the High-way-side. And in that *Arbor* there lay two men whose Names were *Heedless* and *Too-bold*. These two went thus far on Pilgrimage, but here being wearied with their Journy, they sat down to rest themselves, and so fell fast asleep. When the Pilgrims saw them, they stood still and shook their Heads; for they knew that the Sleepers were in a pitiful Case. Then they consulted what to do; whether to go on and leave them in their Sleep, or to step to them and try to awake them. So they concluded to go to them and wake them; that is, if they could; but with this Caution, namely, to take heed that themselves did not sit down, nor imbrace the offered Benefit of that *Arbor*.

The Pilgrims try to wake them.

So they went in and spake to the men, and called each by his Name, (for the Guide, it seems, did know them) but there was no Voice nor Answer. Then the Guide did shake them, and do what he could to disturb them. Then said one of them, *I will pay you when I take my Money*; At which the Guide shook his Head. *I will fight so long as I can hold my Sword in my Hand*, said the other. At that, one of the Children laughed.

Their Endeavour is fruitless.

Prov. 23. 34, 35.

Then said *Christiana*, What is the meaning of this? The Guide said, *They talk in their Sleep.* If you strike them, beat them, or whatever else you do to them, they will answer you after this fashion; or as one of them said in old time, when the Waves of the Sea did beat upon him, and he slept as one upon the Mast of a Ship, *When I awake I will seek it again.* You know when men talk in their Sleeps, they say any thing; but their Words are not governed, either by Faith or Reason.

There is an *Incoherencie* in their Words *now*, as there was before betwixt their going on Pilgrimage, and sitting down here. This then is the Mischief on't, when *heedless* ones go on Pilgrimage, 'tis twenty to one, but they are served thus. For this *inchanted* Ground is one of the last Refuges that the Enemy to Pilgrims has; wherefore it is as you see, placed almost at the end of the Way, and so it standeth against us with the more advantage. For when, thinks the Enemy, will these Fools be so desirous to sit down, as when they are weary; and when so like to be weary, as when almost at their Journeys end? Therefore it is, I say, that the *inchanted* Ground is placed so nigh to the Land *Beulah*, and so neer the end of their Race. Wherefore let Pilgrims look to themselves, lest it happen to them as it has done to these, that, as you see, are fallen asleep, and none can wake them.

Then the Pilgrims desired with trembling to go forward, only they prayed their Guide to strike a Light, that they might go the rest of their way by the help of the light of a Lanthorn. So he strook a light, and they went by the help of that thorow the rest of this way, thô the Darkness was very great.

The light of the Word.

2 Pet. 1. 19.

But the Children began to be sorely weary, and they cryed out unto him that loveth Pilgrims, to make their way more Comfortable. So by that they had gone a little further, a Wind arose that drove away the Fog, so the Air became more clear.

The Children cry for weariness.

Yet they were not off (by much) of the *inchanted* Ground; only now they could see one another better, and the way wherein they should walk.

Now when they were almost at the end of this Ground, they perceived that a little before them, was a *solemn* Noise, as of one that was much concerned. So they went on and looked before them, and behold, they saw, as they thought, *a Man upon his Knees*, with Hands and Eyes lift up, and speaking, as they thought, earnestly to one that was above. They drew nigh, but could not tell what he said; so they went softly till he had done. When he had done, he got up and began to run towards the Celestial City. Then Mr. *Great-heart* called after him, saying, So-ho, Friend, let us have

Standfast *upon his Knees in the Inchanted Ground.*

your Company, if you go, as I suppose you do, to the Celestial City. So the man stopped, and they came up to him. But so soon as Mr. *Honest* saw him, he said, I know this man. Then said Mr. *Valiant-for-truth*, Prethee who is it? 'Tis one, said he, that comes from whereabouts I dwelt, his Name is *Stand-fast*, he is certainly a right good Pilgrim.

The Story of Standfast.

So they came up one to another, and presently *Stand-fast* said to old *Honest*, Ho, Father *Honest*, are you there? Ai, said he, that I am, as sure as you are there. Right glad am I, said Mr. *Stand-fast*, that I have found you on this Road. And as glad am I, said the other, that I espied you upon your Knees. Then Mr. *Standfast* blushed, and said, But why, did you see me? Yes, that I did, quoth the other, and with my Heart was glad at the Sight. Why, what did you think, said *Stand-fast*? Think, said old *Honest*, what should I think? I thought we had an honest Man upon the Road, and therefore should have his Company by and by. If you thought not amiss, how happy am I? But if I be not as I should, I alone must bear it. That is true, said the other; but your fear doth further confirm me that things are right betwixt the Prince of Pilgrims and your Soul. For he saith, *Blessed is the Man that feareth always.*

Talk betwixt him and Mr. Honest.

Valiant. Well, But Brother, I pray thee tell us what was it that was the cause of thy being upon thy Knees, even now? Was it for that some special Mercy laid Obligations upon thee, or how?

They found him at Prayer.

Stand. Why we are as you see, upon the *inchanted Ground*, and as I was coming along, I was musing with my self of what a dangerous Road, the Road in this place was, and how many that had come even thus far on Pilgrimage, had here been stopt, and been destroyed. I thought also of the manner of the Death with which this place destroyeth Men. Those that die here, die of no violent Distemper; the Death which such die, is not grievous to them. For he that goeth away in a *Sleep*, begins that Journey with Desire and Pleasure. Yea such acquiesce in the Will of that Disease.

What it was that fetched him upon his Knees.

Hon. *Then Mr.* Honest, *Interrupting of him, said, Did you see the two Men asleep in the Arbor?*

Stand. Ai, ai, I saw *Heedless*, and *Too-bold* there; and for ought I know, there they will lye till they Rot. But let me go on in my Tale: As I was thus Musing, as I said, there was one in very pleasant Attire, *but old*, that presented her self unto me, and offered me three things, to wit, her *Body*, her *Purse*, and her *Bed*. Now the Truth is, I was both a weary, and sleepy, I am also as poor as a *Howlet*, and that, perhaps, the *Witch* knew. Well, I repulsed her once and twice, but she put by my Repulses, and smiled. Then I began to be angry, but she mattered that nothing at all. Then she made Offers again, and said, If I would be ruled by her, she would make me great and happy. For, said she, I am the Mistriss of the World, and men are made happy by me. Then I asked her Name, and she told me it was *Madam Bubble*. This set me further from her; but she still followed me with Inticements. Then I betook me, as you see, to my Knees, and with Hands lift up, and cries, I pray'd to him that had said, he would help. So just as you came up, the Gentlewoman went her way. Then I continued to give thanks for this my great Deliverance; for I verily believe she intended no good, but rather sought to make stop of me in my Journey.

Prov. 10. 7.

Madam Buble, *or this vain World.*

Hon. *Without doubt her Designs were bad. But stay, now you talk of her, methinks I either have seen her, or have read some story of her.*

Standf. Perhaps you have done both.

Hon. *Madam Buble! Is she not a tall comely Dame, something of a Swarthy Complexion?*

Standf. Right, you hit it, she is just such an one.

Hon. *Doth she not speak very smoothly, and give you a Smile at the end of a Sentence?*

Standf. You fall right upon it again, for these are her very Actions.

Hon. *Doth she not wear a great Purse by her Side, and is not her Hand often in it fingering her Money, as if that was her Hearts delight?*

Standf. 'Tis just so. Had she stood by all this while, you could not more amply have set her forth before me, nor have better described her Features.

Hon. Then he that drew her Picture was a good *Limner*, and he that wrote of her, said true.

Greath. This Woman is a *Witch*, and it is by Virtue of her *Sorceries* that this Ground is *enchanted*; whoever doth lay their Head down in *her Lap*, had as good lay it down upon that Block over which the Ax doth hang; and whoever lay their Eyes upon her Beauty, are counted the Enemies of God. This is she that maintaineth in their Splendour, all those that are the Enemies of Pilgrims. Yea, This is she that has bought off many a man from a Pilgrims Life. She is a great *Gossiper*, she is always, both she and her Daughters, at one Pilgrim's Heels or other, now Commending, and then preferring the excellencies of this Life. She is a bold and impudent Slut; She will talk with any Man. She always laugheth Poor Pilgrims to scorn, but highly commends the Rich. If there be one cunning to get Mony in a Place, she will speak well of him, from House to House. She loveth Banqueting, and Feasting, mainly well; she is always at one full Table or another. She has given it out in some places, that she is a Goddess, and therefore some do Worship her. She has her times and open places of Cheating, and she will say and avow it, that none can shew a Good comparable to hers. She promiseth to dwell with Childrens Children, if they will but love and make much of her. She will cast out of her Purse, Gold like Dust, in some places, and to some Persons. She loves to be sought after, spoken well of, and to ly in the Bosoms of Men. She is never weary of commending of her Commodities, and she loves them most that think best of her. She will promise to some Crowns, and Kingdoms, if they will but take her Advice, yet many has she brought to the Halter, and ten thousand times more to Hell.

The World.

Jam. 4. 4.
1 John 2. 15.

Standf. *O! Said* Stand-fast, *What a Mercy is it that I did resist her*; *for whither might she a drawn me?*

Greath. Whither! Nay, none but God knows whither. But in general to be sure, she would a drawn thee *into many foolish and hurtful Lusts, which drown men in Destruction and Perdition.*

1 Tim. 6. 9.

'Twas she that set *Absalom* against his Father, and *Jeroboam* against his Master. 'Twas she that perswaded *Judas* to sell his Lord, and that prevailed with *Demas* to forsake the godly

Pilgrims Life; none can tell of the Mischief that she doth. She makes Variance betwixt Rulers and Subjects, betwixt Parents and Children, 'twixt Neighbour and Neighbour, 'twixt a Man and his Wife, 'twixt a Man and himself, 'twixt the Flesh and the Heart.

Wherefore good Master *Stand-fast*, be as your Name is, and when you have done all, *stand*.

At this Discourse there was among the Pilgrims a mixture of Joy and Trembling, but at length *they brake* out and Sang:

What Danger is the Pilgrim in,
How many are his Foes?
How many ways there are to Sin,
No living Mortal knows.
Some of the Ditch, shy are, yet can
Lie tumbling in the Mire:
Some thô they shun the Frying-pan,
Do leap into the Fire.

After this I beheld, until they were come into the Land of *Beulah*, where the Sun shineth Night and Day. Here, because they was weary, they betook themselves a while to Rest. And because this Country was common for Pilgrims, and because the Orchards and Vineyards that were here, belonged to the King of the Celestial Country; therefore they were licensed to make bold with any of his things.

1 Part, pag. 272, 273.

But a little while soon refreshed them here, for the Bells did so ring, and the Trumpets continually sound so Melodiously, that they could not sleep, and yet they received as much refreshing, as if they had slept their Sleep never so soundly. Here also all the noise of them that walked the Streets, was, *More Pilgrims are come to Town.* And another would answer, saying, And so many went over the Water, and were let in at the Golden Gates to Day. They would cry again, There is now a Legion of Shining ones, just come to Town; by which we know that there are more Pilgrims upon the Road, for here they come to wait for them and to comfort them after all their Sorrow. Then the Pilgrims got up and walked to and fro: But how were their Ears now filled with heavenly Noises, and their Eyes delighted with Celestial Visions? In this Land, they *heard* nothing, *saw* nothing, *felt* nothing, *smelt* nothing, *tasted* nothing, that was offensive to their Stomach or Mind; only when they tasted of the Water of the River, over which they were to go, they thought that tasted a little Bitterish to the Palate, but it proved sweeter when 'twas down.

Death bitter to the Flesh, but sweet to the Soul.

In this place there was a Record kept of the Names of them that had been Pilgrims of old, and a History of all the famous Acts that they had done. It was here also much discoursed how the *River* to some had had its *flowings*, and what *ebbings* it has had while others have gone over. It has been in a manner *dry* for some, while it has overflowed its Banks for others.

Death has its Ebbings and Flowings like the Tide.

In this place, the Children of the Town would go into the Kings Gardens and gather Nose-gaies for the Pilgrims, and bring them to them with much affection. Here also grew *Camphire*, with *Spicknard*, and *Saffron*, *Calamus*, and *Cinamon*, with all its Trees of *Frankincense*, *Myrrh*, and *Aloes*, with all *chief* Spices. With these the Pilgrims Chambers were perfumed, while they stayed here; and with these were their Bodies anointed to prepare them to go over the *River* when the time appointed was come.

Now, while they lay here, and waited for the good Hour; there was a Noyse in the Town, that there was a *Post* come from the Celestial City, with Matter of great Importance, to one *Christiana*, the Wife of *Christian* the Pilgrim. So Enquiry was made for her, and the House was found out where she was, so the Post presented her with a Letter; the Contents whereof was, *Hail, Good Woman, I bring thee Tidings that the Master calleth for thee, and expecteth that thou shouldest stand in his Presence, in Cloaths of Immortality, within this ten Days.*

A Messenger of Death sent to Christiana.

His Message.

When he had read this Letter to her, he gave her therewith a *sure* Token that he was a true Messenger, and was come to bid her make hast to be gone. The Token was, *An Arrow with a Point sharpened with Love, let easily into her Heart, which by degrees wrought so effectually with her, that at the time appointed she must be gone.*

How welcome is Death to them that have nothing to do but to dye.

When *Christiana* saw that her time was come, and that she was the first of this Company that was to go over: She called for Mr. *Great-heart* her Guide, and told him how Matters were. So he told her he was heartily glad of the News, and could a been glad had the Post came for him. Then she bid that he should give Advice, how all things should be prepared for her Journey.

Her Speech to her Guide.

So he told her, saying, Thus and thus it must be, and we that Survive will accompany you to the River-side.

Then she called for her Children, and gave them *her Blessing*; and told them that she yet read with Comfort the Mark that was set in their Foreheads, and was glad to see them with her there, and that they had kept their Garments so white. Lastly, She bequeathed to the Poor that little she had, and commanded her Sons and her Daughters to be ready against the Messenger should come for them.

To her Children.

When she had spoken these Words to her Guide and to her Children, she called for Mr. *Valiant-for-truth*, and said unto him, Sir, You have in all places shewed your self true-hearted, be Faithful unto Death, and my King will give you a Crown of Life. I would also intreat you to have an Eye to my Children, and if at any time you see them faint, speak comfortably to them. For my Daughters, my Sons Wives, they have been Faithful, and a fulfilling of the Promise upon them, will be their end. But she gave Mr. *Stand-fast* a Ring.

To Mr. Valiant.

To Mr. Stand-fast.

Then she called for old Mr. *Honest*, and said of him, Behold an Israelite indeed, in whom is no Guile. Then said *he*, I wish you a fair Day when you set out for Mount *Sion*, and shall be glad to see that you go over the River dry-shod. But she answered, Come *Wet*, come *Dry*, I long to be gone; for however the Weather is in my Journey, I shall have time enough when I come there to sit down and rest me, and dry me.

To old Honest.

Then came in that good Man Mr. *Ready-to-halt* to see her. So she said to him, Thy Travel hither has been with Difficulty, but that will make thy Rest the sweeter. But watch, and be ready,

To Mr. Ready-to-halt.

for at an Hour when you think not, the Messenger may come.

After him, came in Mr. *Dispondencie*, and his Daughter *Much-a-fraid*. To whom she said, You ought with Thankfulness for ever, to remember your Deliverance from the Hands of Gyant *Despair*, and out of *Doubting-Castle*. The effect of that Mercy is, that you are brought with Safety hither. Be ye watchful, and cast away Fear; be sober, and hope to the End.

To Dispondencie, *and his Daughter.*

Then she said to Mr. *Feeble-Mind*, Thou was delivered from the Mouth of Gyant *Slay-good*, that thou mightest live in the Light of the Living for ever, and see thy King with Comfort. Only I advise thee to repent thee of thy aptness to fear and doubt of his Goodness before he sends for thee, lest thou shouldest when he comes, be forced to stand before him for that Fault with Blushing.

To Feeble-mind.

Now the Day drew on that *Christiana* must be gone. So the Road was full of People to see her take her Journey. But behold all the Banks beyond the River were full of Horses and Chariots, which were come down from above to accompany her to the City-Gate. So she came forth and entered the *River* with a *Beck'n* of Fare well, to those that followed her to the River side. The last word she was heard to say here was, *I come Lord, to be with thee and bless thee.*

Her last Day, and manner of Departure.

So her Children and Friends returned to their Place, for that those that waited for *Christiana*, had carried her out of their Sight. So she went, and called, and entered in at the Gate with all the Ceremonies of Joy that her Husband *Christian* had done before her.

At her Departure her Children wept, but Mr. *Great-heart*, and Mr. *Valiant*, played upon the well tuned Cymbal and Harp for Joy. So all departed to their respective Places.

In process of time there came a *Post* to the Town again, and his Business was with Mr. *Ready-to-halt*. So he enquired him out, and said to him, I am come to thee in the Name of him whom thou hast Loved and Followed, tho' upon *Crutches*. And my Message is to tell thee, that he expects thee at his Table to Sup

Ready-to-halt *Summoned.*

with him in his Kingdom the next Day after *Easter*. Wherefore prepare thy self for this Journey.

Then he also gave him a Token that he was a true Messenger, saying, *I have broken thy golden Bowl,* and loosed *thy silver Cord.* Eccles. 12. 6.

After this Mr. *Ready-to-halt* called for his Fellow Pilgrims, and told them, saying, I am sent for, and God shall surely visit you also. So he desired Mr. *Valiant* to make his *Will*. And because he had nothing to bequeath to them that should Survive him, but his *Crutches*, and his good *Wishes*, therefore thus he said: *These Crutches, I bequeath to my Son that shall tread in my Steps; with an hundred warm Wishes that he may prove better then I have done.*

Promises. *His Will.*

Then he thanked Mr. *Great-heart*, for his Conduct, and Kindness, and so addressed himself to his Journey. When he came at the brink of the River, he said, Now I shall have no more need of these *Crutches*, since yonder are Chariots and Horses for me to ride on. The last Words he was heard to say, was, *Welcome Life*. So he went his Way.

His last words.

After this, Mr. *Feeble-mind* had Tidings brought him, that the Post sounded his Horn at his Chamber Door. Then he came in and told him, saying, I am come to tell thee that the Master has need of thee, and that in very little time thou must behold his Face in Brightness. And take this as a Token of the Truth of my Message. *Those that look out at the Windows shall be darkned.*

Feeble-mind *Summoned.*

Eccles. 12. 3.

Then Mr. *Feeble-mind* called for his Friends, and told them what Errand had been brought unto him, and what Token he had received of the truth of the Message. Then he said, Since I have nothing to bequeath to any, to what purpose should I make a Will? As for my *feeble Mind*, that I will leave behind me, for that I shall have no need of that in the place whither I go; nor is it worth bestowing upon the poorest Pilgrim: Wherefore when I am gone, I desire, that you Mr. *Valiant*, would bury it in a Dungil. This done, and the Day being come, in which he

He makes no Will.

was to depart; he entered the *River* as the rest. His last Words were, *Hold out Faith and Patience.* So he went over to the other Side.

His last words.

When Days, had many of them passed away: Mr. *Dispondency* was sent for. For a *Post* was come, and brought this Message to him: *Trembling Man, These are to summon thee to be ready with thy King, by the next Lords Day, to shout for Joy for thy Deliverance from all thy Doubtings.*

Mr. Dispondencie's *Summons.*

And said the Messenger, That my Message is true, take this for a Proof. So he gave him *The Grashopper to be a Burthen unto him.* Now Mr. *Dispondencie*'s Daughter, whose Name was *Much-a-fraid*, said, when she heard what was done, that she would go with her Father. Then Mr. *Dispondency* said to his Friends; My self and my Daughter, you know what we have been, and how troublesomly we have behaved our selves in every Company. My Will and my Daughters is, that our *Disponds*, and slavish Fears, be by no man ever received, from the day of our Departure, for ever; For I know that after my Death they will offer themselves to others. For, to be plain with you, they are *Ghosts*, the which we entertained when we first began to be Pilgrims, and could never shake them off after. And they will walk about and seek Entertainment of the Pilgrims, but for our Sakes, shut ye the Doors upon them.

Eccl. 12. 5.

His Daughter goes too.

His Will.

When the time was come for them to depart, they went to the Brink of the *River.* The last Words of Mr. *Dispondency*, were, *Farewel Night, welcome Day.* His Daughter went thorow the River singing, but none could understand what she said.

His last words.

Then it came to pass, a while after, that there was a *Post* in the Town that enquired for Mr. *Honest.* So he came to the House where he was, and delivered to his Hand these Lines: *Thou art Commanded to be ready against this Day seven Night, to present thy self before thy Lord, at his Fathers House.* And for a Token that my Message is true, *All thy Daughters of Musick shall be brought low.* Then Mr. *Honest* called

Mr. Honest *Summoned.*

Eccl. 12. 4.

for his Friends, and said unto them, I Die, but shall make no Will. As for my Honesty, it shall go with me; let him that comes after be told of this. When the Day that he was to be gone, was come, he addressed himself to go over the *River*. Now the *River* at that time overflowed the Banks in some places. But Mr. *Honest* in his Life time had spoken to one *Good-conscience* to meet him there, the which he also did, and lent him his Hand, and so helped him over. The last Words of Mr. *Honest* were, *Grace Reigns*. So he left the World.

He makes no Will.

Good-conscience *helps Mr.* Honest *over the River.*

After this it was noised abroad that Mr. *Valiant-for-truth* was taken with a Summons, by the same *Post* as the other; and had this for a Token that the Summons was true, *That his Pitcher was broken at the Fountain*. When he understood it, he called for his Friends, and told them of it. Then said he, I am going to my Fathers, and tho with great Difficulty I am got hither, yet now I do not repent me of all the Trouble I have been at to arrive where I am. *My Sword*, I give to him that shall succeed me in my Pilgrimage, and my *Courage* and *Skill*, to him that can get it. My *Marks* and *Scarrs* I carry with me, to be a witness for me, that I have fought his Battels, who now will be my Rewarder. When the Day that he must go hence, was come, many accompanied him to the River side, into which, as he went, he said, *Death, where is thy Sting?* And as he went down deeper, he said, *Grave where is thy Victory?* So he passed over, and the Trumpets sounded for him on the other side.

Mr. Valiant *Summoned.*

Eccl. 12. 6.

His Will.

His last words.

Then there came forth a Summons for Mr. *Stand-fast*, (This Mr. *Stand-fast*, was he that the rest of the Pilgrims found upon his Knees in the *inchanted* Ground.) For the *Post* brought it him open in his Hands. The Contents whereof were, *That he must prepare for a change of Life, for his Master was not willing that he should be so far from him any longer.* At this Mr. *Stand-fast* was put into a Muse; Nay, said the Messenger, you need not doubt of the truth of my Message; for here is

Mr. Stand-fast *is Summoned.*

a Token of the Truth thereof, *Thy Wheel is broken at the Cistern.* Then he called to him Mr. *Great-heart*, who was their Guide, and said unto him, Sir, Altho it was not my hap to be much in your good Company in the Days of my Pilgrimage, yet since the time I knew you, you have been profitable to me. When I came from home, I left behind me a Wife, and five small Children. Let me entreat you, at your Return (for I know that you will go, and return to your Masters House, in Hopes that you may yet be a Conductor to more of the Holy Pilgrims,) that you send to my Family, and let them be acquainted with all that hath, and shall happen unto me. Tell them moreover, of my happy Arrival to this Place, and of the present late blessed Condition that I am in. Tell them also of *Christian*, and of *Christiana* his Wife, and how *She* and her Children came after her Husband. Tell them also of what a happy End she made, and whither she is gone. I have little or nothing to send to my Family, except it be Prayers, and Tears for them; of which it will suffice, if thou acquaint them, if peradventure they may prevail. When Mr. *Stand-fast* had thus set things in order, and the time being come for him to hast him away; he also went down to the River. Now there was a great Calm at that time in the River, wherefore Mr. *Stand-fast*, when he was about half way in, he stood a while and talked to his Companions that had waited upon him thither. And he said:

Eccl. 12. 6.

He calls for Mr. Great-Heart.

His Speech to him.

His Errand to his Family.

This River has been a Terror to many, yea the thoughts of it also have often frighted me. But now methinks I stand easie, my Foot is fixed upon that, upon which the Feet of the Priests that bare the Ark of the Covenant stood while *Israel* went over this *Jordan*. The Waters indeed are to the Palate bitter, and to the Stomach cold; yet the thoughts of what I am going to, and of the Conduct that waits for me on the other side, doth lie as a glowing Coal at my Heart.

His last words.

Jos. 3. 17.

I see my self now at the *end* of my Journey, my *toilsome* Days are ended. I am going now to see *that* Head that was

Crowned with Thorns, and *that* Face that was spit upon for me.

I have formerly lived by Hear-say, and Faith, but now I go where I shall live by sight, and shall be with him, in whose Company I delight my self.

I have loved to hear my Lord spoken of, and wherever I have seen the print of his Shooe in the Earth, there I have coveted to set my Foot too.

His Name has been to me as a *Civit-Box*, yea sweeter then all Perfumes. His Voice to me has been most sweet, and his Countenance, I have more desired than they that have most desired the Light of the Sun. His Word I did use to gather for my Food, and for Antidotes against my Faintings. He has held me, and I have kept me from mine Iniquities: Yea, my Steps hath he strengthened in his Way.

Now while he was thus in Discourse his Countenance changed, his *strong men* bowed under him, and after he had said, *Take me*, *for I come unto thee*, he ceased to be seen of them.

But glorious it was, to see how the open Region was filled with Horses and Chariots, with Trumpeters and Pipers, with Singers, and Players on stringed Instruments, to welcome the Pilgrims as they went up and followed one another in at the beautiful Gate of the City.

As for *Christian*'s Children, the four Boys that *Christiana* brought with her with their Wives and Children, I did not stay where I was, till they were gone over. Also since I came away, I heard one say, that they were yet alive, and so would be for the Increase of the Church in that Place where they were for a time.

Shall it be my Lot to go that way again, I may give those that desire it, an Account of what I here am silent about; mean time I bid my Reader *Adieu*.

FINIS.

APPENDIX

GRACE ABOUNDING.

A = first edition of 1666.

B = sixth edition of 1688.

Preface, p. **6**, l. 9. A] God did not play in convincing of me; the Devil did not play in tempting of me.

p. **8**, l. 27. B] we. A] me. l. 30. A] thoughts of the day of Judgement, and that both night and day: and should tremble at the thoughts of the fearful. l. 33. A] bonds of eternal darkness, *and omits* unto the judgement of the great Day.

p. **9**, l. 30. A] Yet this. l. 36. as it made.

pp. **9**, **10**. B *adds* §§ 12, 13, 14 *from*] But God did not utterly...mine own salvation.

p. **10**, l. 25. B *adds*] house-hold-stuff.

p. **11**, l. 2. A] a spirit. l. 38. B *adds*] notwithstanding my Religion.

p. **12**, l. 12. B *adds*] that I might sin again without control!

p. **13**, l. 36. A] a whole Town.

p. **14**, l. 20. A] and Scriptures of that nature. l. 39. B *adds*] This I say, continued about a twelve-month or more.

pp. **14—16**. B *adds* §§ 32, 33, 34, 35, 36] But, I sáy,...more of my state by nature.

p. **16**, l. 35. A] as mistrusting my condition.

p. **17**, l. 23. B *adds*] By these things.

pp. **17—19**. B *adds* §§ 43, 44, 45] One thing I may not omit...The Bible was precious to me in those days.

p. **19**, l. 21. B *adds*] especially...Faith or no, *and omits* for I feared it shut me out of all the blessings that other good people had given them of God. l. 38. B *adds*] insomuch, *and omits* That I might in this deceive myself.

p. **20**, l. 1. B *adds*] And besides, I saw for certain, if I had it not, I was sure to perish for ever. l. 13. A] this delusion.

p. **21**, l. 11. A] But the passage.

p. **22**, l. 39. A] There lay all the question.

pp. **24**, **25**. B *adds* § 70 *and* § 71 *to* l. 20] But I was not...let a man be never so devout, Deut. 14.

APPENDIX

p. 25, l. 30. B *adds*] None but those who are effectually called inherit the Kingdom of Heaven.

p. 27, l. 4. A] that rate for wickedness. l. 9. my heart began to hanker. l. 13. to hinder her.

p. 28, l. 1. A] these Bars. l. 6. B *adds*] my hinder parts were inward.

pp. 28, 29. B *adds* §§ 84, 85, 86] But I observe...*A wounded Spirit who can bear.*

p. 30. B *adds* § 89] Yea I thought...as any of theirs. l. 35. thou art my Love twenty times.

p. 31, l. 7. B *adds*] yea, I was now so taken...to have understood me. l. 28. B *adds*] methought he called so loud...meant me.

p. 34, l. 9. A] now again I blessed the condition. l. 14. for sin. B *adds* § 106] And now my heart...get rid of these things, I could not.

p. 35, l. 5. A] I have thought I should see the Devil, nay thought. l. 34. Alas, poor fool.

p. 37, l. 34. A] unsound rests. l. 35. we are prone to take and make to our souls. He pressed us to take special heed.

pp. 39, 40. B *adds* § 125 *and part of* § 126] The errors that this people... comforted in the truth.

p. 40, l. 37. B *adds*] an evidence as I thought of my salvation.

p. 41. B *adds* §§ 130, 131, 132] But before I had got thus far...my love was tried to purpose.

p. 42, l. 30. B *adds*] and yet then I had almost none others, but such blasphemous ones.

p. 43, l. 13. B *adds*] with my hands or elbows; *also* § 139] At these seasons...the Law of God indeed.

p. 44, l. 2. B *adds*] Oh the diligence of Satan! Oh, the desperateness of Man's heart! *also* § 143] Now was I bound...in the sequel you will see. l. 34. A] hear and steal away.

p. 45. B *adds* § 146] But chiefly...*carefully with tears.*

p. 46, l. 1. B *adds*] And this stuck always with me...and to be saved from wrath to come. l. 3. I had sold my Saviour.

pp. 45, 46. B *adds* § 154] What thought I...*Oh! none knows the terrors of these days but my self.*

pp. 47, 48. B *adds* § 158] Now I saw...and for my eternal overthrow.

pp. 49, 50. B *adds* §§ 161, 162, 163, 164] I was often now ashamed... *carefully with tears.*

p. 50, l. 12. A] Then was I struck. B *adds* ll. 34 *to* 37] and this thought I...why not for me?

p. 51, l. 16. A *adds after* circumstances] but alas! 'twas all in vain. B *adds* §§ 170, 171, 172] I should think with myself...*you have sold your Saviour.*

In the first edition pages 45 *to* 48 *are wanting, including in this text from* p. 52, l. 10 God as from the face...*to* p. 58, l. 33 but I was gone and lost.

APPENDIX

p. 59. B *adds from* l. 1 *to* l. 20] The fitness of the word...Word and Prayer as any of they. l. 30. A *reads*] the sorrow of it. B *omits* it *and adds* despair...this word. l. 34. B *adds*] with strong cries. l. 37. B *adds*] as an echo, or sounding again. l. 40. B *adds*] and I believed it.

p. 61, l. 1. A] from being again afflicted. l. 15. as I have done.

p. 62, l. 21. B *adds*] helped by it. l. 27. B *adds*] therefore it was but in vain to pray. l. 29. A] Yet said I. l. 34. A *omits*] him. l. 38. A] as I lay on my knees. l. 39. B *adds*] that this was a prayer of faith.

p. 63, l. 4. A] condition, crying, Is his mercy clean gone? Is his mercy clean gone for ever? And I thought sometimes, even while I was groaning on these expressions they did seem to make a question whether it was or no; yet I greatly feared it was. B *omits this passage and adds* § 203] There was nothing ...nor clean gone for ever. l. 23. A] I remember. l. 28. within me. l. 30. such a great word.

p. 64, l. 2. A] comfort and threw down. l. 3. B *adds*] Then I thought...large enough. l. 5. such as I. l. 20. B *adds*] for as yet I... could not go.

p. 65. B *adds* § 211] These, as the Elders...Josh. 20. 3, 4.

p. 66, l. 24. A *gives references*] 2 Cor. 3. 8, 9, 10, 11; Mar. 9. 5, 6, 7; Joh. 6. 37.

p. 69, l. 8. A] tendence. B *adds* ll. 24 *to* 34] First I confessed...unsearchable Grace.

p. 72, l. 10. A *adds*] that as he sat. l. 12. because of this.

p. 73, l. 30. A *omits*] his.

p. 74, l. 29. A] she continued. l. 31. fell to sleeping.

p. 75, l. 17. A *omits*] that went before. B *adds* ll. 18 *to* 21] with unbelief ...tormented.

p. 77, l. 1. A] Satan. l. 29. yoak.

p. 79, l. 3. A *omits*] of my. l. 11. as if it had. l. 18. B *adds*] But oh what a turn it made upon me!

p. 80. B *adds* § 261] Again as I was...Work for God again. l. 28. A] senseless. l. 33. B *adds*] to me.

p. 81, l. 5. B adds] *Heb.* 12. 24. l. 34. my self.

p. 82, l. 1. B *adds*] also.

p. 83, l. 32. A *adds*] touched by the Word.

p. 84, l. 19. A] 2 Cor. 9. 2. l. 40. *omits*] I.

p. 85, l. 20. A *reads*] I have lain as long to.

p. 87, l. 5. A] an offence. l. 13. *omits*] the. l. 30. I have also. l. 34. catch. B *adds* ll. 15 *to* 23] Jam. 5. 20...to me; *also* § 289] I have also observed...but I forbear.

p. 88, l. 2. A *reads*] in the country. l. 16. *inserts after* thought of that] He that winneth souls is wise, Pro. 11. 20, and again. l. 32. speak the word. l. 38. *for* been] bin. l. 39. *reads*] to speak them with my mouth. l. 40. times.

p. 89, l. 4. A] bin *for* been. l. 10. scorching *for* searching. l. 30. infected *for* affected. B *adds* § 296] But, I thank...help also in this.

APPENDIX

pp. 90—94. B *adds* §§ 302—318] Thus therefore I came to perceive...give you a brief account.

p. 94, l. 15. A] and had Preached. l. 26. A] after some conference there with the Justices was sentenced to perpetual banishment. B *adds*] they taking my...did sentence me. l. 31. A *reads*] have lain now above five years and a quarter.

p. 96, l. 5. A *inserts after* the first was] How to be able to endure should my imprisonment be long and tedious ; the second was.

p. 97, l. 8. A *reads*] I thought this might go under.

p. 98, l. 7. A *reads*] before the Sons of Men; and of the glory.

p. 99, l. 5. A] scrabling *for* scambling.

p. 101, B *adds* § 2] Sometimes...been upon me.

p. 102, l. 17. A *reads for* pray unto] looks to.

THE PILGRIMS PROGRESS. PART I.

A=first edition. B=second edition. C=third edition.

[*The term "marginal notes" does not include Scripture references in the margin.*]

p. 138, l. 36. A *and* B] durst *for* dare.

p. 139, l. 7. A *and* B] doth *for* did. ll. 15 *and* 16 *transposed in all editions from* 1st *to* 7th.

p. 141, l. 3. A *and* B] loose *for* lose.

p. 142. Marginal note, *The Goal,* not inserted in A and B. l. 12 *to* l. 27 *inserted in* B] In this plight...saved first. l. 12. B] restrained *for* refrained. l. 17. 7th, 8th, *and* 9th] saith he. *Third marginal note first in* 9th.

p. 143. *First marginal note inserted in* 8th, *second in* 9th. l. 4. 7th] At these his revelations they were. l. 5. 1st *to* 8th] said he. l. 12. 7th] and he told.

p. 144. *First marginal note inserted in* B. l. 2. A] I am sure.

p. 145, l. 6. 7th] which you shall forsake. B] and hold it. l. 16. A] and fast there. l. 17. B] Read it so if you will in my Book. l. 34. Nay but do thou, *first in* 8th. B *third marginal note.*

p. 146. *Second marginal note first in* 7th, *fourth in* 9th. l. 21. B] the bag. l. 40. A] This is excellent.

p. 147, l. 16. A] drownded. Margin, *The Slough of Despond,* first in 8th.

p. 148. B *fifth marginal note.* l. 19. A] I was directed. l. 23. A] did not you. l. 27. A] Then, said he.

p. 149. A *first marginal note.* B *second.* l. 35. 7th] Tailes. *The whole of the passage relating the interview with Mr Worldly Wiseman and its consequences,* p. 149, l. 37, Now as Christian...counsel, p. 156, l. 32, *was first inserted in* B.

p. 150. C *third marginal note.*

p. 151. C *second and third marginal notes.*

APPENDIX

p. 152. C *first marginal note.* l. 28. C] he wot not.

p. 154. C *all three marginal notes.* l. 23. A] Mortality. l. 26. A] prevent.

p. 156. C *both marginal notes.* l. 32. B] So in process of time Christian got up to the gate.

p. 157. B *second and third marginal notes.* l. 27. A] hazzards.

p. 158, l. 3. A] *Slow of Dispond. From* l. 15. B] Truly said Christian... cast out, p. 159, l. 3.

p. 159, l. 3. A] Well good Christian. l. 38. Travailer.

p. 160, ll. 17, 18. A] lift up, in its hand, its lips.

p. 162, *first marginal note.* A] Will have all now. l. 2. A] the name.

p. 163, l. 33. B] ( ).

p. 164, l. 8. A] walked. l. 17. man. l. 18. a muse, *also marginal note.* l. 31. Of the three that walked. B] saying.

p. 165, l. 29. A] Nay, said Christian, pray Sir, do you. l. 40. A] fearful threatenings.

p. 166, l. 1. B] and fiery indignation. l. 32. 7th] rackt.

p. 167, l. 4. A] fiery Flame. l. 29. Conscience too within.

p. 169. C *fourth marginal note.* l. 24. A *inserts*] What is the answer else that I should give thee. l. 35. 9th] Whither do you go.

p. 170, l. 8. B] over it as. C] over the Wall. l. 38. A] This Hill.

p. 172. B *fourth marginal note.* l. 21. A] refreshment. l. 36. 8th] running amain. l. 37. B] and the name of the other Mistrust.

p. 173. B *third and fourth marginal notes.* l. 27. A] that his foolish fact. l. 32. from his weariness.

p. 174. B *marginal note.* l. 26. A] Ah thou sinful sleep. l. 37. A] the name whereof.

p. 176. B *marginal note.* l. 31. A] one or two of them. l. 33. B] and Charity.

p. 177, l. 28. A] Was that all that you saw. l. 35. A] I could have stayed.

p. 178, l. 2. A] a weary burden. B] a heavy. 8th] a very heavy. l. 13. A] other small matters. l. 16. Formalist. lions mouths. B] *first marginal note.*

p. 179. *The whole of the passage from* l. 30, Then said Charity...from their blood, p. 181, l. 6, *first inserted in* B.

p. 180, l. 36. A] myself of sins.

p. 181, l. 22. A] did it of pure love. l. 24. A] had seen and spoke.

p. 182, l. 12. A] by an eternal.

p. 183, l. 5. A] Moses rod. l. 19. ( ). l. 22. Haven. l. 28. *omits*] with. l. 32. A] from thence, said they.

p. 184, l. 3. B] said he. 8th *second marginal note.* 9th *third.* A *fourth*] at the approach. l. 36. A, *only*, *inserts marginal note*] Apollyon pretends to be merciful.

p. 185, l. 20. A] considerated.

APPENDIX

p. **186**, l. 14. A] out of our hands.

p. **187**, l. 10. A] strodled. l. 12. B] by my Infernal Den that.

p. **188**, l. 5. A] for a season. l. 10. groans brast. B *fourth marginal note.*

p. **190**, l. 8. A] he can find.

p. **191**, l. 18. A] could he have helped. l. 38. B] also.

p. **192**, l. 1. A] not out of desire. l. 6. lay betwixt. l. 20. C *adds*] ( ).

p. **195**, l. 4. A] stired. l. 25. percieve. l. 38. Know what.

p. **196**, l. 8. 7th] I went away. l. 18. A] and do dwell. l. 25. if he had any children. l. 27. lusts of the eyes. l. 28. them all.

p. **197**, l. 20. A] brest. l. 23. I know not to. l. 24. made a hand. l. 28. and his side. l. 37. did you not.

p. **198**, l. 29. A] most worth.

p. **199**, l. 3. A] make me the Ridicule. B] make the Ridicule. C] make him. l. 23. at the first. l. 34. 8th] indeed. l. 37. B] man.

p. **200**, l. 12. B] And when I had shaken him off then I began to sing. l. 32. 7th] have us to be valiant. A] for the Truth.

p. **201**, l. 11. A] a been. l. 12. the Sun rise. l. 23. that same. l. 24. 7th] That's well.

p. **202**, l. 4. A] What thing so pleasant. l. 19. may learn by talk. l. 28. C] a work's. 7th] the works. 9th] a work of grace in their souls.

p. **203**, l. 4. A] things forraign. l. 16. 7th] Yea better. l. 31. A] shews best. l. 39. C] hath on. 8th] hath in.

p. **204**, l. 15. A] bruit.

p. **206**, l. 2. A] As the Hare, retaineth. l. 31. A] let be this.

p. **207**. *First marginal note.* A] To cry out. l. 9. in the heart and house. l. 27. 7th] that do them. l. 28. in the knowledge of them. l. 31. 8th] of it.

p. **209**, l. 22. A] appeals.

p. **210**, l. 5. A] melancholly. l. 13. B] ( ). l. 21. A] so stink. B] to stink. C] to stink so. l. 25. A] do stumble the world. l. 29. B] Then did faithful say. l. 34. A] the Wain.

p. **211**. *The whole of the passage relating the interview with Evangelist,* l. 1, Now when they...faithful Creator, p. **213**, l. 2, *first appeared in* C. l. 24. 8th] have met.

p. **212**, l. 6. A] on heaven.

p. **213**, l. 1. 8th] in well doing. l. 30. A] that of all sorts. l. 31. B] that too. l. 33. A] the several Rows.

p. **214**, l. 6. A] thorow. l. 18. B] ( ).

p. **215**. B *first and second marginal notes.* l. 31. A] none occasion.

p. **216**, l. 21. A] themselves behaving themselves. l. 22. C] among themselves. l. 29. A] and a terror; lest any should further speak.

p. **217**. *The passage from* l. 6, Here therefore...disposed of, l. 16, *first in* B. l. 6. A] Here also. l. 8. A] was the more. l. 11. that even he. l. 31. A] the Party that were. l. 40. They was then.

p. **218**. C *first and second marginal notes.* l. 36. A] two wit.

p. **219**, l. 15. A] by which. l. 23. let us see. l. 24. 8th] vile Runagate. l. 36. A] to a divine Revelation. l. 38. A] will not profit. B] not be profit. 8th] not be profitable.

p. **220**, l. 2. A] for a being. l. 21. any God but his. l. 35. C] among themselves.

p. **221**. C *third and fifth marginal notes.* A *second marginal note.* A] still alive. 8th] still a Prisoner. l. 35. A] with him thou shalt be blest.

p. **222**, l. 7. A] Thus one died to make Testimony. l. 9. in his Pilgrimage, *added to* 8th. l. 21. A] Is there any that be good live there. B] any that be good that lives there. C] any good that lives there. ll. 24 *and* 28. C] said Christian. l. 29. I have heard of it. *The entire passage from* l. 35, By-ends. Almost the whole Town...Father's side : And, l. **40**, *first in* B. l. 40. C] the truth.

p. **223**, l. 1. C] I am become. l. 16. A] applaud it. l. 17. A] stept a little a to side. l. 26. A] That is not my name. l. 39. you was the man ; that I had heard of.

p. **224**. *The whole of the passage describing the interview between By-ends and his Company*, l. 21, Now I saw in my Dream...flames of a devouring fire, p. **229**, l. 3, *was first inserted in* C.

p. **225**, l. 20. A] are against them. l. 27. leaving the liberty. l. 30. Bestirs her then only. l. 39. C] But he must.

p. **227**, l. 26. A] joyfully agreed. l. 30. C] Mr.

p. **229**, l. 4. A] outwent him. l. 23. 9th] to see it. l. 25. A] paines. *Third and fourth marginal notes added in* C.

p. **230**, l. 18. A] is it not it by the which. l. 27. C] and his Companions. l. 35. B] Then sang Christian. l. 38. A] so these two.

p. **231**. *The whole of the passage about Lot's wife*, l. 1, Now I saw... lift up their Eyes, p. **232**, l. 9, *was first introduced in* B. *marginal note* C. l. 16. looking back. l. 24. A] been made ourselves; like this woman, *added in* 8th.

p. **232**, l. 1. A] example to others, *omitted after* 9th. l. 38. A] and the leaves of the Trees were good for medicine. with the Fruit of these Trees they were much delighted, *omitted after* A.

p. **233**, l. 9. B] Then they sang. l. 24. 8th] souls of the Pilgrims were. l. 33. A] lets us go over. l. 25. 7th] who would. l. 29. B] bolder than I.

p. **235**, l. 38. A] or any light.

p. **236**. l. 1. 8th] unadvised Counsel. *The passage about the Giant's Wife Diffidence*, l. 3, Now Giant Despair...in the morning, p. **239**, l. 9, *was first introduced in* B. l. 11. A] without any mercy. l. 33. B] of them and himself. l. 35. C] in sunshine weather. *Third marginal note in* C *to* 9th. in sunshiney weather *in* 9th.

p. **237**. C *both marginal notes.* l. 3. B] or to die. l. 22. B] in short time.

p. **238**. *Two first marginal notes inserted in* B.

p. **239**, l. 5. B] in hope. l. 24. A] The door. l. 28. 7th] a craking. l. 30. C] for his fits took him again. l. 32. B] Kings highway again. l. 39. 8th] this sentence.

APPENDIX

p. 240. *Between* ll. 7 *and* 8, *the following line*: Lest heedlessness makes them, as we, to fare, *was, apparently by accident, omitted from the* 10th *and* 11th. l. 38. A] is even before you. C *third marginal note.*

p. 241. C *three first marginal notes.* l. 15. A] to acquaint with us.

p. 242, l. 26. A] looked upon one another. l. 32. they heard there a lumbring noise. l. 35. told them saying. B *first marginal note.*

p. 243. *Third marginal note.* A] the fruit of slavish fear. l. 24. their hand shake. l. 28. C] Then they went away and sang. 8th] this song. B *fourth marginal note.*

p. 244. A] and I am going. l. 28. instead of admittance. l. 38. next way into it. 8th *third marginal note.*

p. 245, l. 16. B] He further added. A] to say all to Him at once. l. 23. were carrying of him. l. 24. in the side of the Hill.

p. 246, l. 11. B] all up. l. 28. A] to scrabble.

p. 247, l. 6. B *omits* No, *and inserts* 'Tis a wonder but. l. 18. A] in their taking away of his Money. l. 19. the rest of the journey. l. 25. would it not a been. l. 35. his necessities.

p. 249, l. 12. A] in troden paths. l. 20. a great heart.

p. 250, l. 33. A] that notwithstanding.

p. 251, l. 39. A] Valley of the Shaddows.

p. 252. 8th *second marginal note.* l. 12. C] Then sang Christian. l. 16. A] And gets more faith shall then a Victor be.

p. 253, l. 32. A] of them shepherds. l. 35. you was at a stand.

p. 254, l. 9. C] singing. l. 36. A] this twenty years.

p. 255. B *third marginal note.* l. 10. A] Hopeful his Fellow.

p. 256. C *fourth marginal note.* B *fifth.* l. 13. A] in fault. l. 26. 8th] I will sing you first this song.

p. 257. B *two marginal notes.* l. 2. A] Which as I believe now. l. 3. drownded.

p. 258. B *all four marginal notes.* l. 15. A] No, not latterly. B] No, not heartily. C] No, not I. l. 27. A] These things I did. l. 40. the like.

p. 259. B *all three marginal notes.* l. 7. A] yet his old debt stands still. l. 16. that I have brought.

p. 260. B *four first marginal notes.* l. 17. for me. l. 25. A] but he said.

p. 261. B *all the marginal notes.* l. 12. A] his son.

p. 263, l. 3. A] I saw then. l. 18. C] however, said he.

p. 264. B *marginal note.* l. 1. In the hopes.

p. 265, l. 25. A] even of all. B *marginal note.*

p. 267, l. 5. A] of all flesh. l. 36. B] Then Christian addressed thus himself to his fellow.

p. 269. B *first and fourth marginal notes.*

p. 270, l. 1. A] As we do now. l. 12. which provoked them.

p. 271, l. 18. A] not of any detestation.

p. 272, l. 29. A] they met with abundance.

p. 274, l. 2. A] came within sight. l. 7. were much stounded. l. 38. hearty fears.

p. 275, l. 9. A] standing by it. l. 23. was as in a muse. l. 37. being come up out of the river.

p. 276, l. 32. A] the comfort.

p. 277, l. 4. A] that are got thither. B *inserts the passage*, l. 28, There came out also...and thus they came up to the gate, p. 278, l. 13.

p. 278, l. 34. A] the harp to praise withall. l. 36. the city rang for joy. l. 37. the men themselves say.

p. 279. 8th *second marginal note.*

THE PILGRIMS PROGRESS. PART II.

A = first edition of 1684.

B = second edition of 1687.

p. 287, l. 13. A] in all humble wise.

p. 292. B *adds both marginal notes.*

p. 294. B *adds last marginal notes ; also the one on* p. 295.

p. 296. B *adds three marginal notes ; also first on* p. 297.

p. 298. B *adds both marginal notes.*

p. 301. B *adds third and sixth marginal notes.*

p. 302. B *adds all three marginal notes.*

p. 303, l. 4. A] like to have a been smuthered.

p. 304. B *adds second and third marginal notes.*

p. 305. B *adds first, third and fourth marginal notes.*

p. 306. B *adds first and third marginal notes.*

p. 307. B *adds second, third and fourth marginal notes ; and omits from* A] If the Soul at first did know all it should meet with in its Journey to Heaven it would hardly ever set out.

p. 308. B *adds all three marginal notes.* l. 21. A] did Plash them.

p. 309. B *first marginal note.*

p. 310. B *adds first and third marginal notes.*

p. 311. B *adds first and third marginal notes.*

p. 312. B *adds fourth marginal note.*

p. 313. B *adds all four marginal notes.*

p. 314. B *adds second marginal note.*

p. 315. B *adds second marginal note.*

p. 316. B *adds first and second marginal notes.*

p. 320. B *adds second marginal note.*

p. 321. B *adds the two marginal notes.*

p. 322. B *adds the second and third marginal notes.*

APPENDIX

p. 323, l. 3. B *adds*] one Great-heart.
p. 326. B *adds the three last marginal notes.*
p. 327. B *adds first marginal note.*
p. 328. B *adds second marginal note.*
p. 329. B *adds second and third marginal notes.*
p. 330. B *adds the fourth marginal note.*
p. 331. B *adds the first marginal note.*
p. 332, l. 27. B *inserts*] *Grim*, or.
p. 333. B *adds all four marginal notes.*
p. 334. B *adds first, second and fourth marginal notes.*
p. 335. B *adds first marginal note.*
p. 336. B *adds second and fourth marginal notes.*
p. 337. B *adds first and third marginal notes.*
p. 340. B *adds first, third and fourth marginal notes.*
p. 341. B *adds first, fourth and fifth marginal notes.*
p. 342. B *adds first, third and fourth marginal notes.*
p. 343. B *adds first, third, fourth and fifth marginal notes.*
p. 346. B *adds second, third and fourth marginal notes.*
p. 347. B *adds first, second, third and fifth marginal notes.*
p. 348. B *adds all three marginal notes.*
p. 349. B *adds both marginal notes.*
p. 350. B *adds first and second marginal notes.*
p. 353. B *adds third marginal note.*
p. 354. B *adds fifth and sixth marginal notes.*
p. 355. B *adds fourth marginal note.*
p. 356. B *adds second and third marginal notes.*
p. 357. B *adds second marginal note.*
p. 359. B *adds fifth marginal note.*
p. 360. B *adds third marginal note.*
p. 361. B *adds first and third marginal notes.*
p. 363. B *adds third marginal note.*
p. 364. B *adds third marginal note.*
p. 365. B *adds first and second marginal notes.*
p. 366. B *adds all four marginal notes.*
p. 367. B *adds all except fourth marginal note.*
p. 370. B *adds all five marginal notes.*
p. 371. B *adds all four marginal notes.*
p. 372. B *adds both marginal notes.*
p. 373. B *adds the second marginal note.*
p. 375. B *adds second, fourth and fifth marginal notes.*
p. 376. B *adds first and fourth marginal notes.*
p. 377. B *adds first, third and fourth marginal notes.*

APPENDIX

p. 378. B *adds second and third marginal notes.*
p. 379. B *adds second and third marginal notes.*
p. 380. B *adds first marginal note.*
p. 382. B *adds first, second, third, fourth and sixth marginal notes.*
p. 383. B *adds marginal note*] New Talk.
p. 386. B *adds second marginal note.*
p. 388, l. 38. A] They were all also.
p. 391, l. 29. A] good Nurtriture. l. 40. so was as an Hospital.
p. 397. B *adds second marginal note.*
p. 399. B *adds first marginal note.*
p. 400. B *adds both marginal notes.*
p. 401. B *adds first and second marginal notes.*
p. 402. B *adds first marginal note.*
p. 403. B *adds second marginal note.*
p. 409. B *adds third marginal note.*

CAMBRIDGE: PRINTED BY JOHN CLAY, M.A. AT THE UNIVERSITY PRESS.